From Submarines to Suburbs

From SUBMARINES to SUBURBS

Selling a Better America, 1939–1959

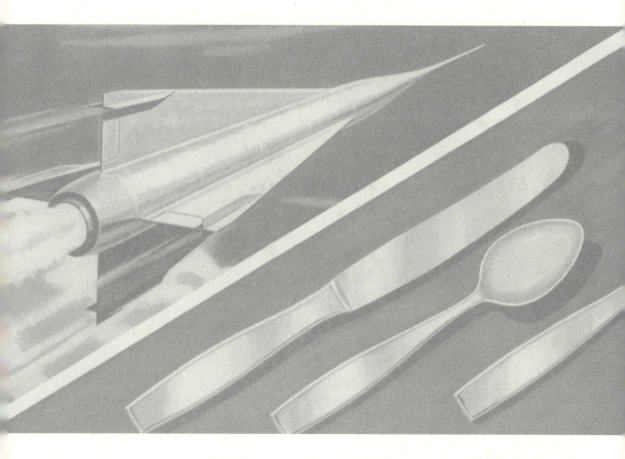

CYNTHIA LEE HENTHORN

Ohio University Press   *Athens*

Ohio University Press, Athens, Ohio 45701
www.ohio.edu/oupress
© 2006 by Ohio University Press

14 13 12 11 10 09 08 07 06   5 4 3 2 1

Library of Congress Cataloging-in-Publication Data

Henthorn, Cynthia Lee, 1963–
  From submarines to suburbs : selling a better America, 1939–1959 / Cynthia Lee Henthorn.
    p. cm.
  Includes bibliographical references and index.
  ISBN-13: 978-0-8214-1677-8 (cloth : alk. paper)
  ISBN-10: 0-8214-1677-4 (cloth : alk. paper)
  ISBN-13: 978-0-8214-1678-5 (pbk. : alk. paper)
  ISBN-10: 0-8214-1678-2 (pbk. : alk. paper)
  1. Marketing—United States—History—20th century. 2. Advertising—United States—History—20th century. 3. Consumer behavior—United States—History—20th century. 4. United States—Social conditions—20th century. I. Title.
  HF5415.1.H463 2006
  381.0973'09044—dc22

                                                                2006013468

This book is dedicated to the memory of my great-uncle,
Robert Lee Bivins, California, Private First Class, 349th Infantry,
88th Infantry Division, 12 June 1921–24 July 1944.

And to my parents, who were
instrumental in making this book a reality,
James Lee Henthorn and Carol Jean Henthorn.

CONTENTS

ILLUSTRATIONS

ACKNOWLEDGMENTS

This book would not have been completed without the indefatigable assistance I received from my family: my parents, James and Carol; my brothers Dennis, Thomas, and Andrew; and my remarkable Woody. I owe a deeply heartfelt thanks to each one for contributing their time, energy, efforts, talents, and resources to making this book become a reality. Each played an irreplaceable role in this book's development—all to its lasting benefit—and I could not have written and finished this work without them. My family was key to all phases of the project, from research assistance and photocopying, to permissions gathering, scanning, printing, editing, and preparing the manuscript and images for delivery. My dogs, Ginger and Pepper, were also instrumental as this project grew. Not only were they great writing companions, but they also turned me into a morning person, which expanded the hours of my days. Thank you to my niece, Shelby Sawyer, for wanting to read this book and to my aunt, Virginia Henthorn, who enthusiastically drove across the desert to see me present a paper based on this book in Las Vegas, Nevada.

I would especially like to thank the director of Ohio University Press, David Sanders, who contacted me about this book project in 2000 and who waited patiently for its completion. His belief in this work's merit was a tremendous inspiration to persevere. The Author's League Fund provided financial assistance for the manuscript's preparation, and I wish to thank this organization for their generous support. A travel-to-collections grant from the John W. Hartman Center for Sales, Advertising, and Marketing History at Duke University was essential to completing the research at the dissertation stage.

I would like to gratefully acknowledge those corporations who generously gave their permission to publish their advertisements and other materials from the World War II and early cold war era. I want to stress that this book is not intended as a criticism of these companies. It is an examination of historical promotional media within a specific cultural matrix, and it is the matrix that I critique here. My observations articulated in this book should in no manner whatsoever be assumed to be a reflection of those companies and their employees today. Many companies from the World War II era are no longer in business or have merged with other companies. We made every effort to track down the original copyright holders of the illustrated material herein and any lengthy extracts from quoted material beyond fair use.

Next, I am very grateful for the interest Dr. Arthur K. Peters took in the development of this study. Although he is no longer with us, his role as mentor and patron helped support this work many drafts ago when it was a Ph.D. dissertation. Dr. Rosemarie H. Bletter, of the Graduate Center of the City University of New York, was my Ph.D. dissertation advisor. I would like to thank her for believing in this project from the start, as did Dr. Pat Kirkham. Several friends played significant roles in this work's development over the years, and I am very grateful for their care and input. Dr. Mary Donahue read chapters, suggested books and articles, and was a great sounding board and inspiration for several ideas. Laurence Frommer, Dr. Hugo Azerad, Dr. Valerie Sessa, Dr. David Howard, Dr. Marie Mulvey-Roberts, and Dr. Susan Aberth offered essential advice and encouragement. Dr. David G. Wilkins kept his keen eyes open for obscure and out-of-print books. David A. Vis read chapters and offered invaluable suggestions from a journalist's standpoint. Faith S. Vis read chapters, found articles and books, and created an enriching atmosphere in which to write. Abigail Baxter, a stellar copyright expert, offered her time and energy to help finalize last-minute permissions issues. Heather King, an excellent editor and wordsmith, provided a thorough copyediting of the book. Lance Dellabovi and Robert Steigerwald found key articles just when I needed them. Donald Albrecht gave me access to his research for his exhibition at the National Building Museum (see the introduction), and I am especially grateful for his support and generosity. For their photographic expertise, I thank Mark Cotrupe and Dominic Suchyta. I also wish to thank colleagues who supplied copies of their unpublished manuscripts: Dr. Kerry Sopel, Dr. Susan Reid, and Dr. Daniel Opler.

I am exceptionally grateful to the several librarians and archivists I have encountered over the years who contributed their unique knowledge to helping me access elusive historical documents. I would especially like to acknowledge the assistance of Wayne Furman of the New York Public Library; Marjorie McNinch of the Hagley Museum and Library; Amy LaRue of the Susquehanna Public Library; Polly Dwyer of the Levittown Historical Society; Ann Glorioso of the Levittown Public Library; Thomas McNulty of Bobst Library, New York University; Kathy Thomas of Dow Chemical Corporation Post Street Archives; Ellen Gartrell, Elizabeth Dunn, and the staffs of the John W. Hartman Center and Libraries of Duke University; Pat Thomson, Fine Arts Librarian, Michigan State University; the staffs of Hoyt Public Library, Saginaw, Michigan, and the Brooklyn Public Library; and Caroline Davis and Diane Cooter of Special Collections at Syracuse University.

The excellent production, design, and marketing staff at Ohio University Press deserve more than the words of thanks I can write here for their invaluable expertise and gracious assistance: Beth Pratt, Jean Cunningham, Jeff Kallet, and Carolyn King. Special acknowledgment goes to Nancy Basmajian, managing editor, and Lori Rider, copyeditor, who polished the manuscript with their remarkable editorial precision.

This manuscript was shaped by the helpful insights of its reviewers, Dr. Christina Cogdell and Dr. Katherine Jellison, and I would like to thank them for their support and encouraging critiques.

I am especially grateful to my many bright and energetic students from City College, Hunter College, and New York City Tech of the City University of New York; the Fashion Institute of Technology; Pratt Institute; and Parsons School of Design who enthusiastically read assignments and listened to lectures based on portions of this book.

Though I could not have written this book without the assistance of those named herein, along with several other individuals who positively touched this work with their magic, any errors or omissions are my responsibility alone.

ABBREVIATIONS

AAA	Agricultural Adjustment Act
AC	Advertising Council
B2B	business-to-business
CED	Committee for Economic Development
CDI	Center for Defense Information
CIO	Congress of Industrial Organizations
DPC	Defense Plant Corporation
DoD	Department of Defense
FCDA	Federal Civil Defense Administration
FEPC	Fair Employment Practices Committee
FHA	Federal Housing Administration
FMCGs	fast-moving consumer goods
FSA	Farm Security Administration
GE	General Electric
GM	General Motors
GNP	gross national product
ICBM	intercontinental ballistic missile
L-O-F	Libbey-Owens-Ford
NAM	National Association of Manufacturers
NDAC	National Defense Advisory Commission
NGA	National Governors Association
NIIC	National Industrial Information Committee
NIRA	National Industrial Recovery Act
NRA	National Recovery Administration
NYWF	1939 New York World's Fair
OPA	Office of Price Administration
OPM	Office of Production Management
OWI	Office of War Information
PMF	privatized military firm
RA	Resettlement Administration
RFC	Reconstruction Finance Corporation
UAW	United Auto Workers
WAC	War Advertising Council
WFA	War Food Administration
WMC	War Manpower Commission
WPB	War Production Board

Introduction

Legacy of the Postwar Commercial Fallout

Soviet Premier Nikita Khrushchev: "In another seven years, we shall be on the same level as America. . . . In passing you by, we shall wave. We can stop and say: If you want capitalism you can live that way . . . we feel sorry for you."

Vice-President Richard M. Nixon: "You may be ahead of us . . . in the thrust of your rockets. . . . We may be ahead . . . in our color television."

Khrushchev: "No, we are up with you on this too."

Nixon (pointing to a panel-controlled washing machine): "In America, these are designed to make things easier for our women."

Khrushchev: "A capitalist attitude. . . . Newly built Russian houses have all this equipment right now. In America, if you don't have a dollar you have the right to [sleep] on the pavement."

Nixon (showing the Russian a model American house): "We hope to show our diversity and our right to choose. . . . Would it not be better to compete in the relative merits of washing machines than in the strength of rockets?"

Khrushchev: "Yes, that's the kind of competition we want. But your generals say: Let's compete in rockets."[1]

On the cold war's commercial front, a free enterprise outlook invaded the Eastern Bloc. Throughout the 1950s, overseas trade exhibits packaged democracy and capitalism as the best tools for accessing higher standards of living. Objects of persuasion—that is, privately owned suburban houses, chrome-bumper automobiles, streamlined kitchens, and electric appliances—were meant to engineer consumer envy among the beleaguered subjects of Communism. By displaying the material advantages of capitalism, U.S. business and government leaders implied what the Communists lacked, thus attempting to weaken the Red stronghold through the management of commercial and class symbols.[2]

The 1959 U.S. Exhibition held in Moscow stood out from other parades of cold war "symbol management."[3] What distinguished this trade exhibit from its contemporaries was a lively conversation between Vice President Richard M. Nixon and Soviet Premier Nikita Khrushchev. The usual tensions between the postwar superpowers erupted into a paradoxical competition in which household labor-saving aids were used as testaments of national strength and, implicitly, as justifications for military dominance. This time a cold war political confrontation entered the annals of history as the "kitchen debate."[4]

While touring a model house filled with every conceivable amenity, yet supposedly priced to fit the average American's wallet, Nixon and Khrushchev argued over whose economic philosophy offered a better standard of living, one that included emancipation from drudgery.[5] Although capitalists and Communists both pursued "liberty," the West's concept of emancipation derived from free market competition, limitless consumer choice, and an abundance of leisure time gained from using a variety of labor-saving conveniences. This concept was buttressed by the American ideal of individualism: pursuing a business or consumer initiative without government restrictions and without having to share the comforts or profits—a sacrosanct tradition lauded as the "American Way."[6] The Soviets' understanding of liberty, at the opposite end of the spectrum, was based on collectivism and was overseen by the heavy hand of government regulation.[7] Despite Khrushchev's protestations that Communist liberty was more highly evolved than capitalist liberty, Nixon claimed superiority over the Soviets, not by measuring weapon power but by extolling the hallmarks of American liberty: democratized comfort, convenience, and expanded leisure time.

The American free enterprise system had long been recognized as a catalyst for social mobility and democratizing technological progress. To "democratize" basically meant making a commodity, affectation, or experience "affordable for the masses." This assumption was based on the notion that goods produced en masse accorded more people easier access to amenities and symbols of class status because they were less expensive.[8] Following World War I, free enterprise in tandem with mass production and mechanization gained credit for gradually but steadily democratizing a middle-class standard of living, and as a result, mass-produced labor-saving designs and devices were seen as instrumental for increasing political, economic, and social liberty.[9] During the 1920s and 1930s, the material "proof" of democracy in action centered on the rational kitchen. According to this domestic paradigm, which intensified after World War II, modern technology and stream-lined design in the home exempted the American middle-class housewife from irrational drudgery, making housework more hygienic and efficient and virtually effortless. Identified more closely with the corporate elite than with the blue-collar labor force, she was elevated to the status of manager in household affairs. Overseeing electric servants, she found her chores reduced to the push of a button, which lent her housework a glamorous rather than an arduous aura. With "free" time on her hands instead of calluses, she was hailed as the apex of civilization.

At the 1959 U.S. exhibition in Moscow, comfort, convenience, and expanded leisure time were emphasized because such "liberties" stressed the disparities between Communism and the American Way. It was boldly argued that, at least in the standard of living race, the capitalists were way ahead. Echoing Nixon's inferences in the "kitchen debate," the American media covering the fair dramatized the Soviets' lower standards of living as an indirect way of applauding the precepts of capitalism. American reporters highlighted the contrast between the democratic and Communist systems by focusing on the peasantlike Soviet woman and her primitive surroundings: "[Moscow, a] city of many aspects—poorly dressed, tired-looking people . . . jerry-built apartment developments . . . boasts of Sputniks, but makes no attempt to conceal its reliance on the primitive abacus as a means of figuring. It is a city of women—hard-working women who show few of the physical charms of women in the West. Most Moscow women seem unconcerned about their looks."[10] Obviously, middle-class priorities on "keeping up appearances" were the first of many "freedoms" to go when the Communists took over.

Drudgery, brutish women, and poor-quality housing were signs of not only totalitarianism but also national and social inferiority. Measuring a country's evolutionary worth by comparing its women and standards of living helped reassert the moral authority of capitalism and, especially, middle-class propriety, which, to Americans, the Russians significantly lacked.[11] But certainly such assumptions did not spring forth overnight—nor could they be unique to this particular trade fair. What were the justifications for such attitudes, and what experiences helped shape them in the collective American conscious?

The 1959 U.S. Exhibition in Moscow was more than a trade fair; it also functioned as an illustrated narrative of progress, a story line indicative of a larger commercial and political agenda. Although displays of American consumer products were intended to spread the capitalist version of democracy, the fair's rhetoric of hygiene and efficiency congealed into another form of ideological attack on Communism. Judging the Soviets through a contemptuous middle-class, managerial lens may not have been a conscious objective of the American participants at the Moscow fair. Planned or not, the underlying message in the "kitchen debate" and in the promotion of consumer goods was that "nature" had accorded Americans not only the inborn abilities to innovate technologies for a superior standard of living, but also the managerial intelligence to profitably democratize these conveniences. The fair's more overt message suggested that abundance, cleanliness, and drudgery's absence were the automatic by-products of capitalism. The more covert, and condescending, message implied that a hygienic and efficient household (that was also affordable and effortless to run) reflected the intellectual, genetic, and moral strength of a nation. If the Russians lacked the comforts and conveniences of modern civilization, were they not more primitive than Americans? If they were backward and inferior, didn't such a disparity justify U.S. military dominance?[12] Nixon's conflation of cold war political rhetoric with a middle-class domestic paradigm was nothing out of the ordinary. By 1959, America's cold war defense ideology was intricately entwined with assumptions about the moral authority of hygiene and efficiency. Indeed, throughout the 1950s, attitudes such as those expressed in the "kitchen debate" were the norm.[13]

This cultural belief in the symbiosis between military standing and standards of living raises two questions this book will address: What *was* the ideological role of modern comforts and conveniences that made them symbolic markers of national military superiority, and how did such concepts evolve into a marketing strategy deployed during the early cold war years? *From Submarines to Suburbs* traces the path of this ideological development back to the iconic role ascribed to modern comforts and conveniences illustrated in American commercial propaganda of World War II. In wartime advertising and promotional literature, the cultural territories of military superiority and middle-class domesticity did not simply overlap but became intricately allied. This book explores how and why modern comforts and conveniences functioned as barometers of both domestic and military superiority during World War II and why this new archetype of progress became infused with corporate America's political marketing agenda.

From Submarines to Suburbs is a study of both the symbols identified with progress in World War II–era commercial propaganda *and* the management of those symbols. For this study, I have relied heavily on the pictorial displays—the visual idioms—illustrating narratives of progress created in the context of war. The narratives I trace are often a mix of factual information and advertising fiction, and no matter to what extent they may be true or pure hype, these story lines are heavy with symbolism concerning Western civilization, especially America, advancing along a presaged trajectory toward a technological and socially harmonious utopia. Visual idioms illuminate these narratives of progress and shed light on these stories' underlying symbolism. I am especially interested in those idioms derived from consumer merchandise (such as labor-saving devices) and architectural designs (houses and kitchen interiors) published in a commercial or marketing context. These visual idioms were part of an established lexicon of cultural symbols and possessed a recognizable iconic role in American society. Vance Packard in his 1957 critique of "the new world of symbol manipulation," *The Hidden Persuaders,* wrote that consumer goods are translated into "socially approved symbols" related to status seeking.[14] Our inquiry into wartime narratives of progress will thus involve an examination of the symbolic value attributed to the social appearances of progress; that is, we will be reading the surface meanings of housing styles, kitchen interiors, and labor-saving merchandise and how these signifiers functioned as critical ingredients for negating social stigma with an armature of hygiene and personal betterment.

A full study of the symbolic values within wartime narratives of progress involves exploring the rhetorical strategies used to structure arguments of persuasion. Due to the propagandizing function of all print media during World War II, articles and editorials published in business, industry, design, and advertising trade journals; women's magazines; general-circulation magazines and newspapers; as well as promotional literature published as books, booklets, or pamphlets possessed persuasive communication qualities and intentions similar to advertisements.[15] I have therefore chosen to regard such propagandizing material as part of the broad category of "persuasive media," and I will often generalize references to these commercial narratives of progress under the broad labels of "advertising" or "commercial propaganda."

There are two main themes found in World War II–era commercial propaganda—*mobilization* (preparing for or converting to war) and *reconversion* (postwar planning). This pool of persuasive media was created and disseminated by a variety of symbol managers in design, architecture, advertising, marketing, and public relations as well as by magazine and newspaper columnists writing for businesses or consumers. Shaping the war's commercial propaganda, then, was not the prerogative of a single profession or business group. Therefore, I chose to categorize these symbol managers as "commercial propagandists." Whenever the theme of commercial propaganda shifted to a focus on reconversion and the future, the reader will find that I labeled such wartime symbol managers as "forecasters," most of whom can also be considered "commercial propagandists." Apart from these variations, I found several journalists and columnists who did not quite seem to fit the commercial propagandist mold. Their intentions were to criticize the political, social, and economic status quo, rather than to promote a brand or corporate ideology. The arguments articulated by these authors, many of whom wrote for African American newspapers, definitely had a persuasive edge to them, but it may be that the term "symbol manager" would not be seen as an appropriate title in such cases. Certainly, these authors did not function as commercial propagandists, but their insights would have indeed influenced public perceptions about the war.

Many of the war's symbol managers were professional "consumer engineers." The term was first coined by the advertising executive and pioneer Earnest Elmo Calkins and popularized in 1932 by Roy Sheldon and designer Egmont Arens in their book *Consumer Engineering: A New Technique for Prosperity*. Consumer engineering encompassed a broad category of experts and, according to Sheldon and Arens, was an attempt to create a "science of finding customers," "making customers when the findings are slim," and taking over "the job to be done in converting those millions who have stood in the bread line into consumers with money to spend."[16] Indeed, members of both the advertising and design fields were considered "consumer engineers" with tools to rationalize the consumer through efficiently targeted psychological appeals.

Although consumer engineers played an important role in wartime propaganda, this study will focus on the visual and verbal *messages* released through print media venues and their persuasive content, more so than examining the historical unfolding of any particular profession's (or medium's) participation in the war. Advertising, marketing, and "consumer engineering" topics have attracted much scholarly attention in recent years. As a complement to these investigations, historians' focus on the dynamics of home front consumer issues has grown.[17] However, commercial imagery and content found in persuasive media (especially advertising) have remained largely on the periphery of these histories, and conspicuously absent is a thorough assessment of the variety of commercial icons illustrated in the print media of World War II.[18] The fact remains that a consumer culture existed and the influence of commercial media espousing a consumption ethic flourished in America during the war.[19] This book illuminates how a consumption ideology played a significant role in determining the content of American wartime propaganda.

What is interesting to note about World War II–era media is that the government propaganda machine and the corporate world were not sealed off from each other. Therefore, the distinctions between propaganda, war information, and advertising were completely obscured. In his 1948 book *Warlords of Washington,* Bruce Catton, who served in the Information Division of the Office for Emergency Management, confirms these fluid boundaries: "Democracy drew its war cries from the philosophy of the salesman. . . . When government wanted to explain to the people the need for this, that, or the other thing required by the exigencies of war . . . it simply turned the job over to the advertising profession."[20] And, indeed, it did. Through advertising imagery, advertising channels, and marketing techniques, corporate America helped the government shape wartime media policies, and it offered many of its publicity services for free. Much of the "free" war information in the United States was thus formatted and disseminated in the form of advertisements and marketing literature.

Advertising became the engine behind this particular business/government/war dynamic. But the advertising industry did not enter the war that way. Well before Pearl Harbor, advertising agencies, copywriters, and art staff feared that if they found no practical role for their industry in wartime, a war-minded New Deal administration might stifle their work for the duration.[21] Moreover, years of economic hardship had inspired liberal reformers to inveigh against the wastefulness and chicanery they saw as the by-products of a corrupt and selfish capitalism. Consumer engineers in the advertising profession bore a large share of these attacks.[22] As a result of this doghouse dilemma, many in business surmised that the ad industry might not survive into the postwar future if it could not justify advertising's purpose for the war effort. Because advertising was considered in business circles as a monument of American democracy, many businessmen believed the profession was well worth preserving. If the ad industry became a casualty of mobilization, so might the American Way and private enterprise:

> The burden of . . . the attack on wartime advertising seems to be based on the assumption that when there is little need to stimulate current consumption, there can be little need for advertising. . . . The really vital reason why every business should continue and if practicable increase its advertising during the war is to help preserve the framework of the American economy. That is what we are fighting for—at least what most of us are fighting for. But the collectivists have other war aims.[23]

Business Week's ominous reference to "the collectivists" represents a callous dig at liberal reformers and the New Deal administration. The remark reveals how wartime America inherited the political battles left over from the Depression. Fear of advertising censorship by a federal "collectivist" regime and its liberal supporters sparked the creation of the corporate-sponsored War Advertising Council (WAC). The WAC was designed to absorb the country's propaganda needs by cooperating with the government on behalf of the business community. One of the reasons the WAC was formed was to create a self-governing mechanism for wartime advertising to avoid strict limitations that might be imposed by the New Deal, especially if advertising had no officially defined wartime purpose. As a result of the business community's inherent profit motives, much of the "free" advertising the government received was very much self-serving on the part of manufacturers, who were anxious to hold on to their company's public recognition for the duration. The WAC thus felt the need to curb advertisers who were too eager to capitalize on the conflict. Using the established corporate advertising and marketing infrastructure, the WAC helped standardize "useful" and "sanitized" information about the war and how Americans at home could help win it. The WAC wrote advertising guidelines, instructing businessmen about the degree to which they could safely inform the public about war-related products they were manufacturing without leaking critical details. The WAC's publications explained how to properly convey concepts of patriotism and sacrifice to the American citizen, providing manufacturers, store owners, and other businessmen with ideas for war-related advertising that could be appropriately "tied in" to government-sponsored campaigns for rationing, recruitment, scrap salvage, Victory Gardens, and war bonds, among other similar concerns. Such guidelines also explained the amount a business could spend for war-related advertising and still deduct the expenditure from the federal taxes it owed, thus including a financial incentive for appropriately formed wartime advertising.[24] The Office of War Information (OWI), a *government* bureau in charge of disseminating war news, provided guidelines for media professionals, such as editors, journalists, scriptwriters, publishers, broadcasters, movie producers, and so on. These guidelines functioned much like the ones the WAC wrote for businessmen. Bearing in mind the constitutional right to free speech and freedom of the press, the OWI made strong suggestions to media professionals about the appropriate messages they could convey to a country involved in total war. Working with the WAC, however, the liberal OWI was eventually overrun by businessmen from advertising and public relations.[25] The disbandment of the OWI left the propaganda field wide open for disseminating postwar "information" tinged with a business, as opposed to a New Deal, agenda. Naturally, abuses abounded in this new relationship between government bureaucracy, advertising, and the business community. *From Submarines to Suburbs* argues that their "cooperation" was not about the war, but rather a thinly veiled competition over which entity would control and define the course of the postwar economy.

Why did such competition exist between the New Deal and business, especially big business, at the opening of the war? It is important to take a moment to explore this question in depth because the history of the New Deal/big business dynamic plays a key role in the contours of this study. Champions of laissez-faire economics during the 1930s felt threatened by the New Deal's legislative reforms giving government an unprecedented active role in administering certain aspects of the nation's economy.[26] Ironically, an examination of the bureaucratic mechanism of liberal reform as it emerged in the 1930s shows more of a correlation between the New Deal and the modern corporate system of managerial organization than we might expect, given the animosity between the business and political worlds at that time. As Alan Brinkley points out in his 1995 book *The End of Reform,* political thought of the post–World War I years adapted many of the methods, traits, and attitudes cultivated by giant aggregates of economic and mechanistic power with a penchant for systemization—that is, the modern techno-corporate order. A steadily rising pace of mass production and mass consumption after the turn of the century dominated and directed business dynamics, which were "scientifically" organized and deployed through massive bureaucratic channels. Corporate authority felt its way through the "mass" (whether in the factory or in the marketplace) by making a "scientific system" out of producing, managing, and selling.

Individual workers and consumers were dealt with in an assembly-line manner, and this method intensified after World War I. But the autocracy upholding the modern corporate-capitalist order grew dependent on these masses—massive amounts of cooperative labor and consumer spending. A dependence on unpredictable, irrational human behavior put the techno-corporate order in a vulnerable position, and so in its usual adaptive mode, it developed "scientific" systems of psychological persuasion to rationalize and standardize the masses of flawed humans, keeping them docile, but functional, in order to sustain corporate dictates and desires. The concept of studying consumers and developing ad campaigns according to "fixed principles" and "fundamental laws" was articulated by the advertising pioneer Claude C. Hopkins in his 1923 book *Scientific Advertising.*[27] These communication systems were influenced by a human-engineering mindset that believed that in order to make a mass of buyers (or workers) function more predictably and precisely like machines, they should be treated and engineered as such. Predicating action through the lens of an assembly-line mentality, corporate authority became more mechanistic itself in order to transform the unruly masses into a manageable machine.[28]

The idea that irrational flaws could be cured and perfected through industrial managerial methods of "scientific" aloofness and "engineered" efficiency seeped into political thought during the Progressive Era.[29] Although political "machines" had existed before, the new emphasis in Progressive political practice was to adapt and "retool" the (supposed) rationality of modern industry to effect social change. Society, once conceptualized as a machine with interchangeable, standardized parts, could be planned and fixed to run more efficiently. Such human-engineering reform practices thus challenged and reorganized (if they did not completely supplant) the power structures of the political machines from the past.[30] Not only did social reform techniques begin to mimic managerial methods and systems in the industrial sector, but government bureaucrats and social planners began to conceive of the individuals under their tutelage as a "mass"—especially as a mass of consumers.[31] Because government bureaucrats and social planners had begun to adopt the logic, language, and organization of modern business, Progressive social reform issues began to be perceived in terms of consumer orientations or resolutions. Labor unrest was a consumer issue; unemployment was a consumer issue; substandard housing was a consumer issue. This shift in perception also influenced the dynamic between reformers and the public. Just as business sought to rationalize the unpredictable and imprecise mass public mind through "scientifically" designed psychological persuasions, so too did politicians. Government and so-cial reform by public relations methods mediated the relationship between political advocates and their constituents.

The New Deal was an offspring of the human-engineering impulse that arose in the reform politics and the techno-corporate order of the Progressive Era as much as it was a reaction against the excesses of the 1920s free market. It is ironic that a universal complaint of business leaders during the 1930s was that the archi-tecture of government bureaucracy, as embodied by the New Deal, had grown too pervasive, too powerful, and too intrusive. Surely big business should have recognized (if not admired) its expansive corporate self in the flourishing mana-gerial hierarchy that systematically sought to reform the country's irrational flaws with an engineer's sense of order.

The New Deal's reform policies were influenced by the British economist John Maynard Keynes, who realized the intimate connection between govern-ment spending and the health of the private sector. Eschewing romantic ideals about the sanctity of a free market economy, Keynes advocated federal spending, even to the point of creating a deficit. He argued that this practice would actually stimulate growth in the private sector during periods of economic stagnation. Keynes's theory, unlike conventional economic thought, recognized that balanced government budgets did little to assist the economy, especially in times of crisis. Keynesianism, and other related forms of federal intervention in economic affairs, were sometimes referred to as "state capitalism." No matter the moniker, such concepts were not unanimously appreciated or accepted throughout the business community.[32]

The historical record shows that businessmen expressed a variety of responses to Keynesianism, revealing that corporate America was not monolithic in its out-look. A single, unanimous mindset did not characterize members of the New Deal administration and their liberal supporters either. Many New Dealers and liberals were anti–big business and used their party's power to rally against capitalism. But others, such as President Franklin Roosevelt, sought only to fine-tune the Ameri-can Way. Roosevelt himself was not interested in antagonizing the business com-munity or replacing America's free enterprise system. However, the increasing infiltration of government into everyday life (especially during the war) and the socialist-like proposals behind certain New Deal programs were hard for stalwart capitalists to swallow. Therefore, Roosevelt, the New Deal, and liberal reformers in general were perceived by many conservative business leaders as antithetical to the American Way.

Roosevelt's primary plan for pulling the country out of the Depression was to revive consumer spending and enhance the average American's purchasing power by "promoting work and security."[33] Part of the "security" Roosevelt envisioned involved rights to fair treatment on the job, including legislation that forbade child labor, imposed a minimum wage and maximum labor hours, and protected the right to organize unions.[34] The New Deal's intention was to create an industrial and business environment in which consumerism could prosper. But some of the means toward this end involved restrictions that many business leaders denounced as "un-American" because they perceived any economic controls from the public sector as a disregard for the "sacred" tenets of free enterprise.[35] Limits, such as those imposed by the New Deal's Agricultural Adjustment Act (AAA) and the National Industrial Recovery Act (NIRA), were received with bitterness. The AAA, for example, sought to regulate agricultural overproduction by demanding that certain crops be plowed under and livestock slaughtered. NIRA regulations, through the National Recovery Administration (NRA), aimed to jump-start production, competition, and thus consumption by establishing various codes to control prices, industrial output, and trading practices. Despite their goal of creating a fairer and healthier economy, New Deal reforms were blocked or counterattacked by conservative corporate organizations nearly every step of the way throughout the 1930s. When America entered World War II, both moderate and conservative business leaders were convinced that a wartime economy would strengthen the New Deal's regulatory powers. The emergency of the war years and the uncertainty of the postwar future helped unify business leaders from both ends of the spectrum, uniting them in opposition against the New Deal. Thus the war lent the New Deal's enemies reinforcements and bolstered conservatives' conviction to destroy it.

From Submarines to Suburbs uncovers an ideological debate that reveals big business's motives behind wartime narratives of progress, and explains how the rhetoric and symbols woven into advertising and promotional literature were shaped by business leaders' political and economic agenda. Wartime narratives of progress were invested with two basic scenarios: producing for war and preparing for peace. Narratives about producing for war were largely accolades about the mobilization process. Such propaganda was geared to shore up the public's confidence in industry's ability to fight a global war, despite the fact that its managers had not been able to avoid economic depression. Although many mobilization narratives were designed as "official" government information, their sponsorship was predicated on the fact that most manufacturers of durable products (and even nondurable, fast-moving consumer goods, such as Brillo cleansing pads) had virtually nothing to sell the wartime consumer as a result of industry's conversion to produce specifically for war. America's involvement in the war signaled the total subordination of the country's raw materials, distribution lines, and industrial infrastructure to the government's military needs. Furthermore, factories were converted to manufacturing matériel specific to the military, thus eliminating or severely restricting the mass production of most consumer goods. This meant that goods and services essential to the war effort—priorities—were removed from the civilian market or at least significantly reduced. Mobilization narratives conceptualized this transition process in advertising and war information literature, explaining how a given product or industry was harnessed for war and suggesting how consumer goods and war matériel were symbiotic parts of the same equation that would naturally add up to victory. Wartime narratives about mobilization harbored a potluck of social and political sentiments pointing to the American industrial success of the past and its potential for even better things in the future. *From Submarines to Suburbs* explores the prevailing symbols found in mobilization narratives and reveals the extent to which modern comforts and conveniences were credited with helping the Allies' efficient military buildup and ultimate victory.

The reversal of mobilization was reconversion, that is, postwar planning. However, reconversion messages were published in tandem with those related to the mobilization process. American business leaders began anticipating postwar prospects and plans well in advance of America's formal entry into the war. The months preceding America's declaration of war against Germany and Japan, roughly late 1939 to December 1941, were usually referred to as the "defense period." The years following Pearl Harbor and before the Japanese surrender in 1945 were considered the "war period."[36] Though mobilization narratives were more numerous than reconversion tales before 1943, both types can be found throughout the war years. It was as if the defense period prompted business leaders to start looking ahead.[37] Because both reconversion and mobilization narratives exist pretty much simultaneously from the defense period through the end of the war, this overlap encourages a thematic approach to studying wartime propaganda and makes following a chronological history a less enriching process of inquiry for this context.

Postwar planning narratives, found in advertisements and promotional literature, were *built* on mobilization messages. Such narratives about the future harbored the hidden agenda of strengthening consumer faith in corporate authority and the free enterprise system. *From Submarines to Suburbs* explores the ways in which wartime marketing strategies defined the postwar world by "positioning" the war in the public mind as a sanitary instrument for the betterment of America.[38] Wartime forecasters describing the "world of tomorrow" encouraged Americans to believe they were fighting for a utopian life generated by the war. The argument behind postwar planning narratives followed a logic cut from the ideological fabric of American Way dogma. If free enterprise, industry, and big business could win the war, then they could also democratize progress and build a successful bridge to higher standards of living. Clearly, visions of a utopian postwar world built on the progress of wartime industry were not only about selling Americans the business of victory, but also about enticing them with the consumer benefits of capitalism, as opposed to the state-controlled economic plans of the New Deal. Such a strategy would not only pay off in the postwar economy by demonstrating the patriotic "sacrifices" of manufacturers, but also serve a propagandistic purpose by reinstilling public confidence in the power of the American Way and its corporate/industrial infrastructure.

Historians' attention has focused on corporate America's wartime paternalism and its ulterior postwar intentions. Yet the emphasis has *not* been on the interplay between *advertising content* produced during the war and corporate calculations to undermine the New Deal.[39] As a case study of conservative wartime corporate motives and strategies, *From Submarines to Suburbs* looks to the wartime campaign directed by the National Association of Manufacturers (NAM), which encouraged its members to deploy advertising messages about postwar progress as weapons to (1) undermine the New Deal and (2) regain public trust in a capitalist economy run solely by the techno-corporate order. *From Submarines to Suburbs* reveals the correlation between reconversion narratives about the postwar future and the NAM's ulterior purpose. It also demonstrates how wartime advertising was structured to habituate consumers to the idea that victory *and* postwar prosperity were achieved by big business, not the federal government—especially the New Deal.

Two top members of the industrial design profession possessed a similar political and economic agenda. The inclusion of this consumer engineering profession in its synthesis of the New Deal/big business battle distinguishes *From Submarines to Suburbs* from other studies that touch on this topic. Designers, like their clients and the ad industry, often felt threatened by New Deal policies and wartime regulations. Some specifically sought to secure a sound footing for capitalism—and their own firms—in the postwar world. Toward this end, many designers wrote articles for the manufacturing trade, attempting to persuade potential clients that they needed to lay plans well before the war ended in order to secure a competitive niche in the postwar market. The industrial design profession helped stimulate corporate visions of the postwar world by seducing (and sometimes intimidating) manufacturers into publicizing unrealizable ideas for reconversion, which thus, in turn, helped raise the public's expectations for postwar progress with images of an unrealistic, fantastic future. Prominent designers Walter Dorwin Teague and Raymond Loewy, especially, were involved in the conservative business community's wartime mandate to undermine the New Deal and reestablish consumer confidence in capitalism. Examining designers' and corporate leaders' complementary postwar planning agendas helps us understand the business motivation behind speculative forecasts for postwar America and the extent to which derailing the New Deal played a tremendous role in shaping wartime marketing aims and strategies.

Because official government war information, like commercial messages, was largely formed and managed by members of the business community, the war and home front duties were explained using the language of business and commercial metaphors tied to America's consumption ethic. *From Submarines to Suburbs* examines war bond advertising as a case in which government information became infused with commercial marketing techniques and rhetoric. Other studies of bond drives have shown how government leaders used established marketing methods to sell war bonds.[40] Sales of war bonds were intended to unite the country while simultaneously building a secure financial bridge toward an individual's material dreams after the war. The marketing "hook" within bond drives also highlights the paradox of the war's loftier moral purpose in that many West Coast Japanese Americans were stripped of their citizenship, their rights, and their material possessions while other Americans were being sold the war as a conduit to greater democratic freedoms, material abundance, and familial/national security. Despite this "fiction of equality," to borrow a phrase from Gunnar Myrdal, the war bond campaign rhetoric coincided with President Roosevelt's aim during the 1930s to democratize higher standards of living.[41] In terms of expanding consumers' purchasing power, business and government were, on the surface, in agreement, yet they definitely diverged ideologically. *From Submarines to Suburbs* looks deep into this ideological rift to show the extent to which business animosity toward the New Deal lurked in advertising fictions of the postwar world—most of which were tied in to war bond sales and savings.

From Submarines to Suburbs also reveals what factors shaped the ideological construction of progress on the home front during World War II. Many wartime commentators were concerned about the Depression's stagnating standards of living, uneven distribution of technology, and a housing shortage left over from World War I. The housing problems exacerbated by the Depression, and the fear of diminishing hygienic standards and proprieties, dominated wartime discourse, from advertising to presidential speeches. As a result of America's backlog of social problems, the war generated a great deal of speculation about ways to radically improve American society and ignite economic prosperity by harnessing wartime lessons in a variety of growth industries, such as plastics, aluminum, medicines, electronics, prefabricated housing, aviation, shipbuilding, manufacturing, and areas of scientific research. Wartime forecasters claimed that if a given product or industry had withstood the test of war on the battlefield, then it could only benefit the postwar consumer. On the whole, the war was looked to as a remedy for irrevocably solving prewar social dilemmas and for assuaging Depression-era fears as they pertained to class disparities, standards of living, and the home.

Competing idioms of dire poverty and technological salvation surfaced throughout the war years and influenced plans for the "world of tomorrow" on the other side of victory. Because the war was marketed as an agent for revolutionizing civilian domestic life, the majority of postwar planning narratives revolved around the symbolic value attached to the single-family suburban home with its streamlined kitchen. The postwar house and its "revolutionary" kitchen grew to grand iconic proportions during the war because they were perceived as the hygienic locus of American progress and the site from which a prosperous postwar economy would spring. Promotional imagery of the mythic "house and kitchen of tomorrow" was used as a means to rally consumer support for the war effort and ignite consumer anticipation for a revitalized America built with the material progress generated through mobilization for war. However, it was not the new domestic products, kitchens, or house designs that would persuade consumers to embrace the business community's commercial plans for the postwar world. Rather, it was the marketing appeal for maximizing efficiency, raising standards of cleanliness, and facilitating a well-ordered world at an affordable price that captured the public's attention.

War, the 1940s embodiment of modern progress, was perceived as a hygienic instrument of social salvation. In light of this thinking, the postwar "hygienic revolution" became celebrated in wartime narratives as a social evolution. Houses, kitchens, and new or improved domestic products were promoted as symbolic escalators leading to middle-class status. Such markers of progress were identified as the critical ingredients for achieving what was literally called a "better America." The war was considered a catalyst for democratizing this form of progress: elevating the hygienic and, by extension, the moral stature of low-income families by bestowing affordable access to the domestic affectations of the white middle class.

But this trajectory into a higher, healthier, and thus improved hygienic spectrum was more than just a manifestation of social mobility. It was a transformation into the normative mold of the "right" type.[42] This progress generated by war was not solely perceived in terms of postwar consumer bounty, but also celebrated as the means to invent a more socially hygienic and rationally designed citizenry after the war. War-born progress was thus positioned, and perceived, as the ultimate social reforming tool.

The appeal of a "cleaned-up" and efficiently running society was not new to the World War II era.[43] Most wartime visions of a "better America" were peppered with a biological, or genetic, determinist edge, masking a totalitarian desire for social homogeneity and control through various manifestations of hygiene and efficiency. This conceptualization of a "better America," I argue, is related to the human-engineering mentality that punctuated the social reform rhetoric popularized in the decades prior to the war.[44] It was during the Progressive Era that engineering and scientific principles were first systematically converted to solving the unhygienic and inefficient foibles of human-made and human-based systems. According to reformers of this ilk, a broad range of human systems were in dire need of a strong dose of rational science and engineering. Adapting scientific and engineering rhetoric legitimized a less than egalitarian impulse to manage the health, hygiene, and efficiency of the social body. Reform narratives were often laden with expressions of an urgent necessity for "betterment," which could only take place after a purging of "threats," such as "unfit elements," "wastefulness," "irrationality," "disease," or "defectiveness." Industrial, racial, genetic, economic, and social issues were often talked about with "survival of the fittest" analogies in which superior and inferior elements battled for dominance. This human-engineering logic sought to streamline mechanisms, spaces, bodies, or practices, subordinating humanity to a "natural law" of rational and impersonal order—all in an effort to safeguard "health," "hygiene," and the "efficient" pace of progress. Reform "betterment" models, such as scientific management, social Darwinism, eugenics, and euthenics, along with related pseudo-sciences used by criminologists, such as physiognomy, promoted "scientific" categorizations of "types" and helped illuminate dangerous differences that could lead to society's downfall.[45] Identifying difference through "scientifically" categorized physical traits, heredity, behaviors, and environs provided the leverage to effectuate social change during the Progressive years by regulating, eliminating, or cleansing anything that strayed from the boundaries of the prescribed normal "type."[46]

From the turn of the century and through the 1930s, virtually every facet of society, the body, domestic life, and labor came under a human-engineering scrutiny and was touched (if not overhauled) by an improvement ethic that, at heart, was guided by the needs of the native-born white middle class. These needs were predicated on middle-class fears that their inherent values were being eroded by the refuse of industrial expansion. Such refuse included the proliferation of unhealthy factories, widespread poverty and crime, dilapidated slums, and epidemics that would often creep into healthy middle-class neighborhoods. Of course the industrial refuse also included the "types" who toiled in the hellish factories and lived in the filthy slums. Peasant immigrants from the "less desirable" enclaves of Europe and African Americans migrating from the rural South were seen as "great unwashed" types in need of a healthy disinfecting. Despite this bias, many reform initiatives had a humanitarian edge, especially those with a focus on family life. Yet such reforms for "cleaning up" immigrant and migrant family life were largely intended to human-engineer the families of the "great unwashed" and coerce their conversion to the hygienic contours of the middle-class normative mold. Regulations on child labor, for example, kept the "great unwashed" children from a life of disease, degeneracy, and ignorance. However, keeping them in school and out of factories ensured that reformers had a captive audience to propagandize the more "healthy" habits of the white middle class. With America modeled on native-born white middle-class values, the country would not only run smoothly and be squeaky clean, but it would also be easier to police.

Advertising copy and illustrations assisted in propagandizing this human-engineering mentality by playing on assumptions about "types" in a way that resembled the social "betterment" models and pseudo-sciences.[47] Throughout the book, I will examine the types shaped by a human-engineering mentality that surfaced in persuasive media messages during the war. Human-engineered types were especially prevalent, as we shall see, in any advertising narrative that conveyed a message about hygiene and conforming to the "right" clean type. Such advertising scenarios were popular prior to the war and continued into the postwar years. Commercial representations of women were especially dependent on such classifications of hygiene, the ideal female type, and the ideal domestic space. Weighty social pressures to "measure up" to such standards added to women's already overburdened days involving caring for home and family and, in some cases, holding down a job. But advertising offered easy solutions for attaining the highest hygienic ideal. Labor-saving designs and devices, as well as cleaning products, were promoted as the sanitary instruments of personal betterment and ensuring one's evolution into the "right" middle-class type. Household technologies were promoted and perceived as stepping stones to higher standards of living—a social status that *demanded* in turn intensified standards of cleanliness and, ironically, spending more time on leisure. *From Submarines to Suburbs* examines the rhetoric and symbolism of hygiene and leisure derived from labor-saving designs and devices that were intended to liberate and sanitize. What sets this book apart from other histories of these concepts is its examination of the ways in which the technological progress of World War II became attached to social meanings of hygiene, leisure, and the ideal middle-class type.

One well-known wartime type, that of "Rosie the Riveter," still exists as a ubiquitous feminist symbol of female strength and women's capability to perform "a man's job." This icon also stands as a popularized testament to women challenging the gender status quo, especially in terms of work both inside and outside the home.[48] As this book explains, however, *conventional* gender identities were perceived as important for the war effort because they helped shore up a sense of stable home and family, despite the obvious social changes created when many white middle-class women entered wartime factory work.[49] Wartime advertising promoted *all* women's reconversion back into the traditional homemaker role and out of the male business of war, even before victory was achieved. Fears concerning the postwar future prompted the same responses. Orthodox gender demarcations were believed to be necessary for a successful postwar reconversion. Such traditional thinking conflicted with the rhetoric of domestic revolution in wartime advertising. New domestic conveniences developed from war-tested products were intended to liberate women from the tyranny of housework—and yet women were *not* expected or encouraged en masse to turn their attention outside the home. This book looks at the commercial representation of women during the war and provides a deep investigation of women's roles in the context of technological progress evolving from the cultural territory of World War II. An extension of this study of women and domesticity involves analyzing criticisms aimed at wartime advertising and promotional literature that marketed the technological revolution geared for the immediate postwar utopia. *From Submarines to Suburbs* explores for whom the visions of effortless hygienic living were an illusion and whether wartime promises for a "better America" came true at all. Well before the war ended, a minority of skeptics questioned and exposed the unrealistic predictions of labor-saving houses and miraculous products intended for the postwar world. Critics in the African American press fell into this category.

New and improved technologies in the hands of a "socially responsible" corporate America were advertised as the key to democratizing progress. Hence, the forecast technological revolution was not simply a domestic one, but a social one as well. Although technology as a galvanizing force for social democracy may have been promised to all, it was not freely given after the war. African Americans found that their country's wartime production "miracle" did not live up to their expectations. The white-dominated business community recognized the rise in the black standard of living during the war, but it never included African Americans in its image of postwar progress publicized in the white mainstream media. Quite simply, blacks did not appear in wartime narratives of progress targeted at white audiences, except occasionally as maids or bellhops.[50] Because a great deal of wartime advertising promoted products that were convenient and efficient to use, black *servants* were not regularly included in visions of postwar progress. The entire premise of such technologies was predicated on enabling a white middle-class housewife to complete the chores effortlessly, alone, and in no time at all. Thus the postwar domestic revolution presumably would make the black servant obsolete.

While researching this project, I investigated whether advertising geared toward an African American audience included narratives of progress similar to those found in the white mainstream press. Definitely, black progress was recognized and discussed in the black press, because the high employment rate during the war put a majority of African Americans on a better economic plateau than most had previously experienced—although their income and opportunities were not exactly equal to those of whites. However, the available wartime documents do not allow for a parallel history. On the one hand, the sources are not readily available.[51] Moreover, the simple fact of the matter is that the black press was not a mirror of the white mainstream media, nor was it intended to be. The degree of advertising (and promotional hype) found in the white mainstream media simply did not exist in media geared to black readers—a disparity on which this book will expound. War bond promotions provided an occasional exception. But there again, concepts of black progress were focused on the collective goal of equality achieved through economic emancipation rather than on dreams of an effortless suburban lifestyle.[52]

African Americans looked to the war as an opportunity to pursue a "Double Victory" (more popularly known as the "Double V"). If the war was being fought, ostensibly, to rid the world of fascist tyranny and make it safe for democracy, African Americans argued that such a fight ought to be first and foremost conducted at home by challenging America's racist status quo. Black Americans manifested this challenge by asserting the rights they were automatically accorded as U.S. citizens, such as the right to participate in the bounty of wartime production. Both mobilization and reconversion narratives taught the public that the war was democratizing progress at a rate that would soon allow all hard-working Americans an affordable means into the hygienic lifestyle of the white, suburban middle class. Plentiful jobs in high-paying industries, war bond savings opportunities, and a paternal techno-corporate order suggested that America was on a new social trajectory toward limitless abundance and higher standards of living for everyone involved. Although such visions of progress were not *advertised* by large corporations in the black press, such issues were certainly discussed by black journalists. African Americans believed that their wartime sacrifices and contributions gave them the right to assume that these corporate promises were also meant for the betterment of their personal lives, too.

An overview of political and economic issues from the early cold war era reveals the social and global consequences of wartime narratives of progress, and whether or not the promises of a hygienic revolution came true as forecast. *From Submarines to Suburbs* shows how cold war realities helped redefine the social meaning of progress and ideas about the postwar "house of tomorrow."[53] During the 1950s, discourse about American progress heralded the arrival of a postwar commercial fallout in which the efficiency, convenience, and plentitude of household labor-saving devices advanced along with cold war military science and technology. As cold war rivalries mounted, advertisers asserted that domesticity had been even further revolutionized by defense-related technologies. This facet of the postwar commercial fallout, though considerably hyped, had a ring of truth to it. The business press readily admitted that civilian product research and development grew from federally financed defense contracts. The propaganda motifs and rhetoric found in World War II-era advertising were recycled during the cold war, and we can find traces of defense- or war-related themes in corporate advertising that sought to simultaneously stimulate civilian spending and undermine Communism with visions of "super-powered" domesticity. The cold war's military-industrial complex became celebrated as America's "winning weapon" that injected greater levels of hygienic progress into the single-family, suburban home. Business *and* civilian consumers alike were encouraged to profit from an economy dependent on the need for conflict.

World War II–era commercial propaganda illuminates how profoundly the current culture of war continues to shape American assumptions about democracy, progress, *and* profits. A recently produced marketing brochure distributed by the company Homeland Investing in 2003 (a rhetorical tie-in with the federal Department of Homeland Security) provides a case in point. Homeland Investing suggests that the *post*–cold war rise in terrorism actually provides consumers with a wealth of personal investment opportunities: "The defense industry is booming," this multipage brochure explains. "Our government spends more on defense than ever before. Read how you can claim your share of the $399 billion market opportunity."[54] *From Submarines to Suburbs* investigates wartime artifacts professing a narrative of progress, just like the one communicated by the contemporary firm Homeland Investing. And the book does so in order to reveal how modern warfare evolved into a sanitary tool for (supposedly) democratizing wealth and progress. Such a thesis is relevant in light of today's increasing levels of terrorist threats and heightened levels of defense/security spending.[55] But perhaps we should be looking *within* as much as we look for conspiracies brewing beyond our own shores. Does technological progress procured from military research and development justify the billions spent, the environmental destruction, the intensified cultural hostilities, and the loss of life in perpetuating a permanent culture of war? Is that the *democracy* for which Americans, and a host of innocent civilians, lost their lives in World War II? What exactly did we "save" from fascism, Communism, and (now) terrorism? When an economy and a government nurtures industries of mass destruction, democracy and freedom are the ultimate casualties. Perhaps exposing a more complete picture of the paradox of war-born progress will reveal how defense and war are ingeniously sanitized, packaged, and justified to the public. It is to be hoped that such an exposure will help popularize the largely ignored critiques of today's military buildup and interventions.

PART ONE

Mobilization

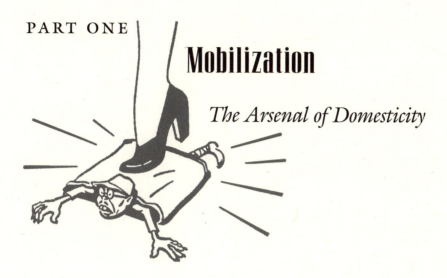

The Arsenal of Domesticity

This is not a fireside chat on war. It is a talk on national security. . . . American industrial genius, unmatched throughout all the world in the solution of production problems, has been called upon to bring its resources and its talents into action. Manufacturers of watches, of farm implements, of linotypes and cash registers and automobiles, and sewing machines and lawn mowers and locomotives, are now making fuses and bomb packing crates and telescope mounts and shells and pistols and tanks. . . . *We must be the great arsenal of democracy* . . . to increase our production of all the implements of defense, to meet the threat to our democratic faith.[1]

America's "arsenal of *democracy*" relied heavily on making an arsenal out of *domesticity*. In his speech delivered late in 1940, President Franklin D. Roosevelt described how Machine Age progress would evolve into democracy's winning weapon against fascism. Manufacturers of every conceivable device from wristwatches to locomotives, he declared, were churning out new lines of goods to equip America's allies for war. From domestic commodities as unwarlike as "sewing machines and lawn mowers" would emerge "the implements of defense."[2] The booklet *War Facts: A Handbook for Speakers on War Production* corroborates Roosevelt's description of preparedness and itemizes the domestic inspiration behind military planes and rafts. "The aluminum for one pursuit plane would make 2,700 average pots and pans. . . . Two thousand, eight hundred pneumatic rafts could be made from the rubber used to make baby pants in just one month last year."[3] *Nation at War: Shaping Victory on the Home Front* likewise relates the ironic liaison between Machine Age consumer goods and military ordnance as companies made the radical switch from producing one line of goods to quite another: "EXAMPLES OF CONVERSION . . . Spark plugs [to] Bayonets . . . Electric driers [*sic*] and heaters [to] Parachute flares; Food machinery [to] Amphibian tanks . . . Motors, fans [to] machine-gun turrets . . . Steel kitchen cabinets [to] Antiaircraft shells."[4] All-out mobilization, we are told, was exceptionally dependent on labor-saving conveniences found in the modernized Machine Age home.

Mobilization realities, however, did not mesh with the cheery descriptions of ease and cooperation illustrated in wartime propaganda. Preparing industry for defense and wartime production was an onerous task to say the least. Exactly what *pains* these companies undertook to retool their assembly lines, reorganize their foundries, and train or hire a workforce is not explicitly explained in the highly publicized wartime accounts. The details of World War II mobilization are a fascinating dramatic mix of struggle, failure, and triumph. The focus of part 1 is not this history, however, but the *glorified picture* of mobilization in wartime propaganda and the reasons for the choices of rhetoric and symbols in mobilization tales. What psychological obstacles were faced and how they were overcome forms the subject of the next three chapters. Before turning to the particular idioms and arguments that formulated mobilization narratives, let us explore some of the *realities* behind mobilization that the propaganda experts decided to omit.

1 Weapons of Mass Disorder

Impediments to Mobilization

If, as historian Richard Tedlow asserts, "business conflict with the New Deal [was] a central theme of the 1930s,"[1] such friction did not automatically vanish when the United States officially began preparing for democracy's defense in 1941. Since reorganizing for war demanded large and swift measures, it naturally involved an expansion of what many business leaders perceived as an already too bloated federal regulatory bureaucracy. Executive branch powers needed control over production, allocation of materials, the financing of new factories, the rationing of food and resources, labor policies, and price setting.[2] R. Elberton Smith, historian of the U.S. Army's economic mobilization, relates that many in business and industry were reluctant to convert their factories in preparation for democracy's defense. Mobilization was hampered by a long-standing suspicion of the New Deal's economic and social recovery agenda and a belief "that the Roosevelt administration was bent on 'socializing' the nation's economy and that it would use the defense program to further this objective."[3] During the 1930s, Roosevelt's recovery and reforming impulse had already assumed too radical a role in the affairs of free enterprise, according to business leaders, by attempting to implement "production quotas, fair prices, marketing codes, and fair labor practices."[4] Organizing "state capitalism" through the National Recovery Administration (NRA), the New Deal had sought to halt "deflation and declining profits"

by consolidating "American industry into a cooperative [rather than a competitive] commonwealth."[5] Old quarrels and mistrust between big business and the New Deal had to be faced if the United States was going to successfully mobilize for defense—and after Pearl Harbor, prepare for total war.

Before manufacturers of sewing machines or automobiles could begin making "shells and pistols and tanks," private industry had to relinquish being 100 percent private, and laissez-faire capitalism had to be content with daily dosages of invasive state "regimentation" and a veritable "nationalizing of industry."[6] Financial underwriting of new munitions plants would make the government an industrial proprietor, curtailing managerial and corporate authority even further. Such a possible limitation *could* make business subservient to its military clientele and the state.[7] And what about profits? How much would an expanded federal presence restrict capitalists' share of wartime wealth? Any hint at a civilian- or federally led "program of national economic planning" that could interfere now or in a postwar future with corporate autonomy stirred antagonisms that caused mobilization to struggle in the face of bureaucratic inertia.[8]

But lack of trust in government planning was not the only impediment to industrial preparedness. Prior to Pearl Harbor, leaders of several large-scale operations exhibited resistance to mobilizing their factories for military output because, quite simply, new growth in the civilian consumer market seemed a safer route out of the current economic slump.[9] A paradoxical upsurge in production to supply Britain and France's fight with the Nazis had increased employment in some sectors of the country. Employed workers embarked on shopping sprees, creating a refreshing demand for goods, and manufacturers would rather oblige that demand than retool for defense.[10] What guarantees did a company have that it wouldn't lose its shirt if it hastily converted to defense production? Fearing risks of heavy debts and empty factories, some business leaders dragged their feet. Businessmen required not only reassurances but also incentives to convert.[11]

If American businessmen needed a financial carrot to coax them willingly (and successfully) into mobilization, it would help if they were led by their own kind. Roosevelt turned to corporate executives' knowledge of the country's industrial and material resources. Such leaders, who were known as "dollar-a-year men," temporarily left their corporations and came to Washington to staff the various mobilization agencies.[12] Roosevelt's National Defense Advisory Commission (NDAC), for example, was run by William Knudsen, president of General Motors, Edward Stettinius of U.S. Steel, and Ralph Budd of Burlington Railroad.[13] Corporate management's distrust of liberal, New Deal Washington, coupled with the liberals' animosity toward big business, was bound to exacerbate tensions and hamper the efficiency of mobilization, not to mention the actual orchestration of the war. In some ways, Roosevelt's need for the logic and expertise of these dollar-a-year men worked against his administration's authority during the war. Final mobilization decisions, as well as reconversion plans, eventually evolved from the interests of corporate leaders rather than Roosevelt.[14]

Wartime business projections about the outcome of a more powerful New Deal shaped the administrative decisions made by the dollar-a-year men and their counterparts among the armed forces' top brass. Historian Brian Waddell states that given a choice between the New Deal or military control over industrial mobilization, "corporate advisors who dominated the top posts of the civilian and military agencies preferred military stewardship of mobilization because the military plan called for extensive reliance on the *private* capacities of corporate America."[15] The War Department had been interacting with major U.S. corporations, business organizations, and corporate executives throughout the 1920s and 1930s, as if anticipating the current political arguments that threatened a successful mobilization.[16] This affinity ran contrary to the New Deal's emphasis on civilian control and an egalitarian contracting system that would have spread wartime production opportunities among several firms, especially small operations. To business leaders, the New Deal's inclusiveness smelled like reform, while the military's procurement practices seemed a safer, more businesslike bet.

The military was apt to give preference to the larger firms with which its officers had established personal ties before the war. This favoritism, though logical to the military and its business contacts, created conflicts throughout the war and, despite military leaders' *prewar* foresight, added to mobilization difficulties. Army and navy procurement officials, many of whom were fresh recruits from corporate America, also tended to award contracts to firms with which they had conducted business or had been intimately connected prior to the war. Other problems emerged when military procurement officials bypassed the authority of Donald Nelson (chairman of the War Production Board), as they usually did, by granting contracts "with little regard for available facilities and the supply of labor and materials, resulting in snarls of priorities, raw materials, and production."[17] Despite the pains it took to plan during the 1920s and 1930s, and despite drawing procurement leaders from corporate America, the military's implementation of its defense needs lacked cohesion. Paul Koistinen, who provides a detailed study of military planning during the interwar years, cites the military's "major flaw" as its "internal operations," rather than its prewar relations with civilian industry and business leaders.[18]

The Roosevelt administration's "internal operations" also diminished the effectiveness of mobilization plans. As shown by accounts of wartime Washington insiders, such as Donald Nelson and Bruce Catton, it seems that frustration abounded everywhere.[19] But irritation was compounded by the limited authority granted to the various mobilization agencies. Roosevelt's defense and wartime offices were accorded mainly advisory roles. However, they were not endowed with sufficient power to execute a swift and efficient mobilization.[20] Roosevelt conducted mobilization with the same experimental zeal behind his administration of the 1930s, tending to scrap existing bureaucratic agencies and establish new ones rather than expand authority or restructure what was already in place. Agency overlap and contradictions (well-established flaws of Roosevelt's 1930s administration) were repeated again throughout the war years.[21]

Manufacturing realities also gravely affected mobilization. Logistical preparations on the factory floor took more grinding effort, sweat, and time than the miraculous assembly-line changeovers described in mobilization narratives.

Conversion did not proceed smoothly even when it was pursued cooperatively, as the *Merlin*'s manufacture illustrates. The contract to mass-produce the British plane engine, the *Merlin,* had been granted to the Packard automobile company of Detroit, Michigan. But before production could begin, specifications in the *Merlin*'s drawings had to be converted from the metric system to U.S. inches. Measurements on twenty thousand drawings had to be recalculated painstakingly—without the aid of an electronic calculator or high-speed computer.[22] The job of mobilization was hardly instantaneous. Donald Nelson puts the dilemma in perspective: "The chief handicap to [mobilization] was possibly the airy belief that any automobile plant or tractor factory could close up shop on Friday and, presto chango! start making the world's best tanks [for instance] on Monday morning."[23] To make matters worse, modeling current mobilization plans on World War I experience was of no help. Nelson observes that America was basically starting the new war from scratch. New battle techniques for the new world war made weapons and equipment just coming off the assembly lines obsolete before they could reach the soldiers.[24] This dilemma was intensified because the U.S. military and its allies contributed to a variety of entanglements and production line inefficiencies, as Nelson further laments:

> The buyer (our Armed Services and the British and French purchasing commissions) knew nothing about mass production or how to adapt manufacture of war equipment to mass production. The seller (American industry) knew all about mass production, but nothing about war or the instruments of war. There should have been a meeting of minds at this point to dovetail the skills and data of the buyer with those of the seller, but unhappily, there wasn't.[25]

Some mobilization hurdles involved manpower. Hiring and training provided their own set of predicaments, but work stoppages by laborers created others. Because conversion entailed construction of new plants or the expansion of existing ones, workers—like their managers—wanted a share of the wartime profits. Organizing strikes on defense production lines, they demanded better pay and improved conditions.[26] Strikes also arose at times from white workers' opposition to the hiring of African Americans.[27] As demands on industry increased, and as more young men were drafted into service, manufacturers were compelled to hire all available manpower, which meant engaging blacks (and women) in jobs traditionally accorded to white males.[28]

Despite the intense need to fully utilize the country's manpower resources, some employers were reluctant to hire blacks outside their customary occupational slots as servants, janitors, and other low-skilled or unskilled laborers.[29] Giving them the same pay as whites was, to many laborers and managers, simply out of the question. Some employers actually argued that the racial status quo was justified because it would keep white workers content and thus ensure that the engines of war moved forward.[30] Long-standing prejudice worked against efficient mobilization and severely hampered American industry's ability to effectively produce.

As the Congress of Industrial Organizations (CIO) labor union's Committee on Racial Discrimination explained, "discrimination against Negroes and other minorities is not only a continuing blot on American democracy, but even more seriously a drag on the total mobilization of all our people needed to win the war against Axis slavery."[31] Although reformers voiced the obvious—that banning blacks from war industry jobs was a "definite help to [the] Axis"—the same racial biases dominated the armed forces.[32] In a war that was being waged to save democratic freedoms from totalitarian despots, American citizens were being denied the opportunity to participate in wartime production and service. Congressman John M. Coffee (D-WA) summed up the paradox in 1942: "Future historians may well ascribe partial blame for British and American defeats and blunders, as at Pearl Harbor, to intellectual deficiencies of our admirals and generals and to their race prejudice. . . . We denounce the racial bigotry of nazism, but permit our industrialists, officers, and officials to discriminate against 13,000,000 loyal colored Americans."[33]

The Roosevelt administration recognized the discrepancy but did little to alter the situation until pressed against the wall—not only by the demands of the war but also by African American activists.[34] Roosevelt finally issued an anti-bias order for any employer with a defense contract and established the Fair Employment Practices Committee (FEPC) to investigate allegations of discrimination. Like many other New Deal wartime agencies with a reforming edge, the FEPC was understaffed and had little power to implement policies and changes. Nonetheless, it at least showed that the administration recognized how racial prejudice was incompatible with full production to total war.[35] The *Pittsburgh Courier* astutely raised this issue in an editorial cartoon titled "If that boy dies, it may be your fault!" In the cartoon, a Washington official labeled FEPC points an accusatory finger at a manager labeled "biased employers and unions," while below him sits "the boy" in jeopardy—a white soldier hidden in the tall grasses of an Asian jungle behind a loaded machine gun.[36]

Marjorie McKenzie, in her *Pittsburgh Courier* column "Pursuit of Democracy," spelled out yet another "fiction of equality."[37] Speaking out against the internment of Japanese Americans in camps for the duration of the war, she said: "We who are so sensitive to an impairment of our own rights have been singularly dispassionate about the war-time fate of Japanese-Americans."[38] Taking a different and surprising view, an earlier article in the *People's Voice* suggested that "Barring Japs in California May Be [a] Boon" for African American workers. With Japanese aliens and naturalized or American-born Japanese being restricted from "vital sections in all the Western states, discrimination of a race more hated than blacks (at least for the duration) may become a land of opportunity for the 90,000 Negroes already living there."[39]

If industrialists balked at the demands of mobilization and the perceived infringements on their free enterprise rights, it is easy to imagine how the average consumer reacted, whether white or black.[40] Mobilization required that almost all of the raw materials used in the peacetime manufacture of civilian consumer goods would be channeled into war production for military use, leaving the public in a lurch. Donald Nelson explained that in 1940, the United States expected to have on hand a greater pool of resources than it actually had. "Raw materials were not quite as encouraging as we had been led to believe. . . . In most of the major raw materials necessary for fighting a modern war we were better supplied than any other nation. . . . [But] there were disquieting lacks. . . . Rubber, of course, led the list. . . . We needed more . . . aluminum, asbestos, cork, graphite, hides, iodine, kapok, optical glass, toluol, vanadium, wool."[41]

From minutia to major durables, consumers were compelled to do without or make creative substitutions.[42] The *Journal of Home Economics* outlined the bad news of mobilization to housewives and domestic engineers. It seemed the only hope was that the war would not threaten a hygienic appearance: "Your next loaf of bread may be delivered in waxed paper instead of Cellophane. . . . The shortage of metal will be most apparent in the kitchen. Metal table tops, drainboards, cabinents [*sic*], and vegetable bins will soon be unattainable. . . . New laundry equipment will not be produced. . . . Floor waxes and polishes will be out of production, but there will be no decline in the output of other cleaning and polishing supplies."[43] A 1943 ad by the National Dairy Products Corporation is a succinct reminder that mobilization meant accounting for even the most seemingly mundane resources (fig. 1.1). Titled "This army was raised to ATTACK!" the ad shows a parade of foods, led by miniature drill sergeants, marching off to the battlefield. Not only were human resources disciplined and drafted for the war effort—but so were apples, eggs, milk, butter, ice cream, and cheese.

Indeed, purchases of basics like dairy products were regulated through the rationing system. Cigarettes were also a scarce commodity, as were meat, sugar, tires, home heating oil, and gasoline—all of which were strictly rationed according to federal guidelines. Changes in eating habits and lifestyle forced by shortages were accompanied by constricted choices and rationing in apparel and accessories. New shoe purchases were regulated through coupon rationing. The use of extra cloth for pleats, gussets, or yoked collars in coats was forbidden; trouser cuffs and patch pockets were outlawed; and no vest could accompany a double-breasted suit. Skirts were not to be fashioned too long or too full. Bone or piano wire had to be used as a substitute for rubber in girdles. Color choices were limited as certain dyes were deemed critical for military uniforms and equipment. Tinfoil, cellophane, elastic thread, metal buttons, zippers, and hook-and-eye sets vanished, too; bobby pins became extinct, though a woman could still do her hair with wooden toothpicks and string. Giving up domestic help and putting up with crowded trains, long lines, and reductions in medical services added to the consumer's new burdens. Packaging also came under government control. Toothpaste tubes were treated almost like money; they had to be returned to the store in order to acquire a fresh tube.[44] Cooking fats from "frying bacon . . . table scraps, [and] meat trimmings" were also collected and turned in for rationing points and pennies: "Remember, you get 2 red points and 4c for every pound of used fat you turn in."[45] Wartime regulations allowed government bureaucracy to intrude into consumers' pantries, compelling Americans to "declare the number of cans and jars of rationed foods—in excess of a certain maximum per person—that they had on hand at home."[46] These and other rationing measures were intended to give all Americans fair access to life's necessities.

This army was raised to ATTACK!

Maybe you've never thought of food as an aggressive weapon of war — *but that's what it is today.*

Food fuels the workers who are making tanks, planes and ships to attack the Axis. Food reinforces the soldiers who launch those attacks. *And food will turn neutrals into friends, friends into fighters, as each new front opens up!*

What's more, service men eat 50% more than they did in civil life. Civilians eat more as they work harder for Victory. And that adds up to a huge order for the folks who raise, process, and distribute food — *folks whose war work is as vital as any welder's.* Last year, America's farmers and food processors set new records for production. This year, the need is greater — and the difficulties under which they work are greater, too.

Every patriotic family will have to pitch in and help — by buying wisely and avoiding waste—by gardening and canning—by making the most of basic, balanced foods.

Food is life — food is hope — and America is trustee for much of the world's supply. That's a big responsibility. A share of it falls on us, as processors of nature's most nutritious food — milk — as well as other dairy and food products. We're glad that our experience and organization equip us to make a real contribution.

Dedicated to the wider use and better understanding of dairy products as human food . . . as a base for the development of new products and materials . . . as a source of health and enduring progress on the farms and in the towns and cities of America.

NATIONAL DAIRY
PRODUCTS CORPORATION
AND AFFILIATED COMPANIES

Originators of the Sealtest System of Laboratory Protection

1.1. Advertisement for the National Dairy Products Corporation (and affiliated companies), *Ladies' Home Journal*, July 1943, 39. Photograph courtesy of The New York Public Library, Astor, Lenox, and Tilden Foundations.

Although price controls were initiated to curb inflation, the cost of everyday goods steadily rose until inflation was finally stabilized in 1943.[47] Inconveniences, regulations, higher prices, and material deprivations were part of the sacrifices made by home front consumers who, for the most part, had not had it so great the previous decade and were looking forward to "the good life" thanks to promises of wartime employment. Wartime consumer limitations, collective cooperation, and the sacrifice of an individual's immediate gratification seemed antithetical to the American Way. Such restrictions on purchasing and ownership were traditionally socialist. Wasn't "consumer choice" a main tenet of American democracy? When they finally had money to spend, home front consumers were denied what seemed a natural American right: "to make and spend money without limit."[48] Conservation and thrift—concepts that were anathema to a Machine Age consumer lifestyle predicated on planned obsolescence—were promoted as patriotic and necessary steps toward victory.

The necessities of total war, combined with engrained attitudes and practices, acted as major impediments to mobilization. But these handicaps to victory were avoided by commercial propagandists who authored mobilization narratives. Although retooling industry for war production would prove monumental in itself, a more cumbersome hurdle involved habituating American consumers to the business of war as battles against the Great Depression were still under way. All-out war following on the heels of a depressed economy called for an intensive ideological conversion. Precise, systematic persuasions were needed to boost American confidence in a lackluster economy and moribund industry and to shape public acceptance of global war in a climate of stern isolationism.[49] Winning such a large-scale war thus called for seducing the public mind—especially because the previous "war to end all wars" had not accomplished the job. Mobilization experts, from government bureaucrats to corporate leaders, advertisers, and PR specialists, tackled this challenge by shaping wartime public perception through symbol management.[50] They sought to cleanse public opinion of any doubt that American industry could swiftly expedite an efficient victory.

Given such a tangled dilemma, which symbols were key to mobilizing public morale and support for the war? How were such symbols conveyed and what arguments were used to counter the ideological remnants of the Great Depression? Oddly enough, the commonplace comforts and conveniences of modern civilization offered an expedient propagandistic solution. Mobilization narratives drew upon the iconic value ascribed to Machine Age civilization. Thus, mass-produced, labor-saving devices played an instrumental role in serving wartime propagandistic needs. "Rational" kitchens, electric toasters, refrigerators, irons, vacuum cleaners, automobiles, radios, and telephones (to name just a few new mechanical gadgets) had increased levels of mechanization in the average middle-class household after World War I.[51] Brand-name processed foods and cleansers, ready-made clothes, and store-bought personal hygiene products, as well as motion picture entertainment, had added to the feel of a lifestyle heavily dependent on machines. Even for the working class before the war, Machine Age mass production had lowered prices on certain comforts and conveniences, putting the tools of modern civilization within the average person's reach. Clearly, as many advertisers had claimed during the 1920s and 1930s, the Machine Age had helped Americans of all classes take a great evolutionary leap forward.[52] Ironically, those comforts and conveniences of the Machine Age, which consumers were asked to sacrifice for war, would provide the propaganda motifs for asserting the logic behind mobilization. The following chapter examines the historical contours of the Machine Age ethos and the role it, and the Depression, played in shaping mobilization messages.

2 Weapons of Mass Persuasion

Mobilization through Symbol Management

"Today," observed Lewis Mumford in 1934, America's "unquestioned faith in the machine has been severely shaken."[1] Mumford, a renowned cultural critic of this era, summed up what mobilization experts also surmised six years later. The symbolic authority of the Machine Age—its institutionalized presence within the American landscape, cityscape, home, and identity—needed desperate resuscitation. Celebration of Machine Age symbols was crucial to effectively harnessing public support for a war that would prove highly technological in nature and deeply dependent on corporate organization and managerial finesse.

The pro-industry rhetoric in Roosevelt's 1940 "Arsenal of Democracy" speech (see page 21) reveals how widespread these assumptions were. In this respect, Roosevelt's semantic choices exemplify the rhetorical inferences we find in mobilization narratives. Roosevelt refers obliquely to the Machine Age as "American industrial genius" and he, like others of his day, understood mass production as not merely a symbol of democracy but also a catalyst for spreading it.[2] Industry, we realize from his words, *is* the arsenal that not only defends but also provides the muscle behind democracy. Both industry and democracy, according to Roosevelt, had never been better, implying that no economic depression had ever sapped America's inherent vitality and acumen. In December 1940, American industry was still "unmatched throughout all the world in the solution of production problems." The mass-produced progeny of this healthy, vigorous Machine Age, Roosevelt tells the public, "has been called upon to bring its resources and its talents into action." Surely a feeble weakling, the public could assume, would never be considered for such a messianic task! Roosevelt's enthusiastic hyperbole suggests that this granite hero, "American industrial genus," had been chosen "to meet the threat to our democratic faith." America's Machine Age simply was, without question, the strongest and the best.

Harnessing the engines of big business for the war effort was publicized as the source of both the brute force and the intellectual finesse needed for American victory on the battlefield. Machine Age motifs and rhetoric were emotive triggers plugged into this propagandistic equation used to glorify mobilization, and their idioms supplied the symbolic fodder for the political and business worlds' sanitized image of modern warfare. These idioms functioned as a means not only to celebrate American industry's revival through war but also to habituate consumers to accepting a stronger corporate presence in the fabric of daily life.

The Machine Age Ethos

Machine Age symbols in mobilization narratives were built upon mechanization's mythological ethos that developed in nineteenth-century America. As a tool for hastening the moral prerogative of progress, the machine, in the form of railroads, automatic rifles, factories, and telegraph wires, combed the "savagery" from America's untamed frontier and civilized it. The machine seemed not only a natural emancipator of "ignorant" and "primitive" traits (supposedly inherent in the Indian and immigrant alike) but also a liberator of the common folk, releasing average citizens from the weary chains of manual labor and elevating them from lowly beast to the disciplined ranks of civilization. The machine would not only enlighten humankind but also make it "free"—and hence more democratic. Moreover, mechanized production created abundance on a mass scale (another democratic feature). It lowered costs for consumers while creating wealth for its industrialists. Though the fat profits mechanization generated went to the few, the machine still offered the democratic promise of social uplift to all who served the competitive capitalist system in which mechanization flourished. It was the ultimate vindication of the middle class's Horatio Alger myth.[3] Self- and social betterment were never easier or more readily at hand. "Better morals, better sanitary conditions, better health, better wages" was Carroll D. Wright's acclamation of the machine as human benefactor when he wrote his essay "The Factory System as an Element in Civilization" in 1882.[4] The machine, like science at this time, became an article of laissez-faire faith, the tireless engine that gave momentum to the American Way. Impersonal, automatic, mechanical, and fast, machines had the power to rationalize the unkempt features of society, transforming every sector of life and leading to greater leaps of progress.[5]

Scientific Management

The machine was not without its detractors.[6] Yet some of the bleak realities of mechanization (especially the frenetic pace, polluting fumes, and monotony of the assembly line) were overshadowed by its rational mystique and the promises of betterment that it was ostensibly bestowing to all. Businessman Edward Filene echoed these assumptions in his 1932 book *Successful Living in This Machine Age*. "Mass production," he tells us, "is liberating the masses . . . from the struggle for mere existence and enabling them, for the first time in human history, to give their attention to more distinctly human problems."[7] Yet during the Depression, many Americans inveighed against the corrosive undercurrents of the Machine Age. And who can blame them? What set the Machine Age apart from earlier industrial transformations was an enhanced emphasis on strict adherence to scientific "laws," engineered efficiency, mechanical systemization, and hierarchies of managerial expertism. Publicly introduced in 1895, Frederick Winslow Taylor's approach to "scientifically" perfecting production methods involved engineering human action, thought, and behavior.[8] Taylorism, as this method was also called, disciplined the foibles of labor and vested greater expertise in management as if both were mere accessories to mechanization.[9] Guided by "thousands of stop-watch observations," Taylor dissected every layer of the manufacturing process, exposing each discrete detail as a way of eliminating waste and thus perfecting motion.[10] His followers were no less exacting. Describing an experiment conducted by his colleague, Frank Gilbreth, Taylor reveals the extent to which common tasks were microengineered to their bare minimum. In the case of Gilbreth's study on bricklaying, eighteen motions were reduced to five: "[Gilbreth] developed the exact position which each of the feet of the bricklayer would occupy with relation to the wall, the mortar box, and the pile of bricks. . . . He studied the best height of the mortar box and brick pile, and then designed a scaffold . . . so as to keep the bricks, the mortar, the man, and the wall in their proper relative positions."[11]

Efficiently timed and "carefully measured tasks" meant greater speeds in production and increased output from the worker.[12] Although he advocated wage incentives as a trade-off for working at demanding speeds, Taylor's emphasis on perfection and efficiency did not mean that the worker met quotas more quickly and thus earned an increase in leisure time.[13] Under Taylor's system, each worker operated at maximum capacity by focusing on one fragment of the entire production process, restricting his movements and concentration to the repetition of the task to which he was assigned. Workers were synchronized and standardized by a logic that presumably they were too ignorant to grasp. The "natural laws" of science and managerial expertise were to perform the thinking (and planning) for them. As Taylor put it, "the workman who is best suited to actually doing the work is incapable of fully understanding this science, without the guidance and help of those who are working over him, either through lack of education or through insufficient mental capacity."[14]

Scientific management techniques arose to fulfill the demands of a new breed of centralized business organization, one marked by both contraction and expansion in its web of power: greater concentration of authority into fewer hands and an explosive growth in bureaucratic systems, standardization, and the quest for maximizing productivity.[15] Mechanized mass production, a synchronistic blend of rational machines, engineered rhythms of assembly, objective science, and expert precision planning, marked the inception of the techno-corporate order. The quickened pace of industrial expansion after the Civil War was largely due to an entrepreneurial elite skilled in the logic of cutthroat competition, which involved strategic planning and maneuvering, centralized power and profits, and institutional organization. John D. Rockefeller wrote, "The growth of a large business is merely a survival of the fittest, the working out of a law of nature and a law of God."[16] The competitive proliferation of large-scale business concerns, such as Rockefeller's Standard Oil, seemed to bear out this ruthless evolutionary truism. The nineteenth century's pantheon of mega-entrepreneurs included the likes of bankers J. Pierpont Morgan and Jay Gould, the steel magnate Andrew Carnegie, and the shipping/transportation mogul "Commodore" Cornelius Vanderbilt. These giants of business and industry were adept at monopolizing markets and taking advantage of the intense rate of technological change as production shifted from steam to electricity during the latter half of the nineteenth century.[17] Thus, scientific management was institutionalized by demands of the modern corporate apparatus, giving rise to the monopoly trust and its need for the efficient flow of facts between its head and its stratified army of managers, engineers, accountants, marketing experts, salesmen, clerical workers, and common laborers. Yet it was also scientific management that cemented the corporation's claim to technological superiority, legitimizing its assumptive expertise over the development and dissemination of technological innovations. By harnessing the unquestionable "facts" of rational "science" to its paternalism, scientific management helped transform industry into more than just "big business." Taylor's methods also organized the business community's administrative reach into a techno-corporate order—the ultimate civilizing machine.

Social Reform and Human Engineering

Searching for efficient solutions to various social problems, many reformers, such as Henry Laurence Gantt, Jane Addams, Charlotte Perkins Gilman, and Margaret Sanger, to name just a few, were drawn to the scientifically managed approach in their efforts to improve American society.[18] Human-engineering tools, like scientific management, offered social reformers a weapon of rational efficiency and managerial expertism in the crusade against filth, germs, and substandard living conditions.[19] Unsanitary and crowded living conditions were perceived as breeding grounds not only for poverty and disease but also for unacceptable types whose behaviors and supposed inclination toward squalor posed a regressive threat to civilization. As one reformer exclaimed in 1890, "Huddled together in miserable apartments in filth and rags, without the slightest regard to decency or health, [immigrants, Italians in particular] present a picture of squalid existence degrading to any civilization and a menace to the health of the whole community."[20]

Progressive Era reformers conceptualized an interconnectedness between epidemics, unsanitary urban slums, and the habits of the "dirty" types who lived there.[21] Difference as much as disease was considered a contagion, and both were threatening pathologies to the "high-grade" gene pool and moral authority enjoyed by the white middle class.[22] An 1895 report published by New York City's subcommittee on public baths and lavatories reveals how some reformers viewed filth as a mark of personal, innate degeneracy and believed that hygiene provided a path to social (and moral) salvation: "To make an habitually dirty man clean is to create in his inmost soul, even if but temporarily, a desire to rise out of the squalor and filth with which he may be ordinarily encompassed."[23] Hygiene was not only the absence of filth, just as health was not simply a matter of being disease free. Social reformers extended the categories of health and hygiene, tying them to social propriety, morality, intelligence, character, and heredity. Just like behavioral and bodily traits, health and hygiene could be inherited, and when operating at their best, they were indicators of an efficient citizen clear of any mental, physical, or moral defects.[24] As one observer noted about immigrants arriving at Ellis Island in 1914, "Steerage passengers from a Naples boat show a distressing frequency of low foreheads, open mouths, weak chins, poor features, skew faces, small or knobby crania, and backless heads. Such people lack the power to take rational care of themselves; hence their death-rate in New York is twice the general death-rate and thrice that of the German [immigrants]."[25] Generally, it was assumed that if the *social* body was more physically, morally, and mentally fit, a healthier environment and hygienic civilization would follow. Such was the message in an elementary school textbook, *Community Hygiene,* published several years later: "Keeping yourselves clean is really the beginning of keeping your community healthy. . . . If you are clean yourself, you will want to live in a clean and orderly house."[26] A disciplined social body was also a hygienic one.

Social hygiene dogma, like the human-engineering tactics of scientific management, found its way into the home through the layers of waste-disposal taboos, cleanliness rituals, and disciplined social affectations. The home was lauded as "part of a great factory for the production of citizens," and, as we can gather from *Community Hygiene,* the home's hygienic management became the locus through which many reformers attacked social chaos and attempted to "scientifically" rationalize society at large.[27] A hyperemphasis on domestic perfection and management aligned modern housework with the professional conceits of science and the mechanized rhythms of mass production. The tortured practices of this "scientific" housekeeping fed the rage for a hygienic propriety. Developed by domestic scientists (also called domestic engineers) at the turn of the century, and conceived as a civilizing strategy during the Progressive Era, scientific housekeeping methods privatized human engineering in the confines of the home under the inquisitional gaze of domesticated "science" and "management." Reformers of the teens such as Ellen H. Richards and Christine Frederick sought to improve society by applying rigorous scientific management techniques to "cleaning up" the home.[28] Hygienic propriety became professionalized into a rigorous discipline through the application of a human-engineering edge.

Social and domestic reform initiatives organized during the Progressive Era retained their impact and reach throughout the 1920s and 1930s.[29] Historian Juliann Sivulka attributes this continuity to the "profit motive" driving advertisers of hygienic instruments such as soap and bathroom fixtures. "Cleanliness," she observes, "had become big business." Although manufacturers of personal hygiene products may have helped Progressive reformers "bolster the virtue of cleanliness" and "messages of moral uplift," it was "the spirit of American enterprise" that ultimately disseminated and institutionalized "a new hygiene consciousness."[30] Sanitizing society by spreading the gospel of scientific housekeeping was not just the prerogative of zealous social reformers with a mania for order. Manufacturers of hygienic instruments not only marketed cleanliness aspirations but also sold the *means* to achieve ultimate sanitary living.

The business practice of proselytizing hygienic propriety, as earlier reformers had done, can be seen in a 1928 advertisement, *"There's CHARACTER—in SOAP & WATER,"* a type of "public service" announcement that expresses the popular hygienic gospel behind the Progressive social uplift mandate (fig. 2.1).[31] Sponsored by a corporate clique, the Association of American Soap and Glycerine Producers, Inc., the ad was directed "to all members of women's organizations in America."[32] It was "one of a series" calling the proper woman's attention to the need for a national "campaign for cleanliness." The association's mission in this regard was "to aid the work of [the] *Cleanliness Institute,*" a scientific-sounding moniker lending the veneer of objective credibility to an otherwise commercial enterprise. While structuring "cleanliness" as the key to enhancing the world's evolutionary progress, the ad's sponsors ascribe a catalytic, civilizing role to the "thoughtful" (i.e., middle-class) wife and mother: "All thoughtful women realize that a cleaner world would be a better place in which to live."[33] Marketing cleaning products en masse, the Association of American Soap and Glycerine Producers reinforced social fears surrounding hygienic propriety, or lack thereof, by playing on the reader's assumed insecurities about her family's evolutionary worth within the social hierarchy: "Do [the neighbors] smile at happy, grimy faces acquired in wholesome play? For people have a way of associating unclean clothes and faces with other questionable characteristics. Fortunately, however, there's soap and water. 'Bright, shining faces' and freshly laundered clothes seem to . . . speak volumes concerning [children's] *parents'* personal habits as well."[34]

Of course, betterment and civilization are not found in low-class slums. The ad is thus situated in a hygienically proper living room of a suburban middle-class family. An anxious businessman, dressed in managerial garb, glances up from his newspaper at his fashionably trim wife, who frets over what sort of impression her rambunctious children are making as they play in the yard. We are implicitly asked to wonder which parent's "routine" is more rational and important—reading the daily news or fretting about what the neighbors think? We learn that the highest mark of civilization is not reading the paper but weighing the consequences of filth and how one's credibility can be blackened by the stigma of dirt. "Questionable characteristics" associated with "grimy clothes" and "unclean faces," according to the Cleanliness Institute, could tell a judgmental public more about

To all members
of women's organizations
in America:

THE advertisement below is one of a series now being widely published throughout the country. All thoughtful women realize that a cleaner world would be a better place in which to live; and to them such a campaign for cleanliness cannot fail to be of interest.

Furthermore these messages should prove a powerful reinforcement to the educational work being done by the Cleanliness Institute, in cooperation with social service organizations, departments of health, and schools, and through group leaders everywhere.

The Offices of Cleanliness Institute are located at 45 East 17th Street, New York City.

What do the neighbors think of *her* children?

To every mother her own are the ideal children. But what do the neighbors think? Do *they* smile at happy, grimy faces acquired in wholesome play? For people have a way of associating unclean clothes and faces with other questionable characteristics.

Fortunately, however, there's soap and water.

"Bright, shining faces" and freshly laundered clothes seem to make children welcome anywhere . . . and, in addition, to speak volumes concerning their *parents'* personal habits as well.

There's CHARACTER — in SOAP & WATER

PUBLISHED BY THE ASSOCIATION OF AMERICAN SOAP AND GLYCERINE PRODUCERS, INC., TO AID THE WORK OF *CLEANLINESS INSTITUTE*

2.1. Advertisement for the Cleanliness Institute, *Ladies' Home Journal*, April 1928, 223. Photograph courtesy of The New York Public Library, Astor, Lenox, and Tilden Foundations. Courtesy of The Soap and Detergent Association—www.cleaning101.com.

the parents than about their children.[35] A crowd of menacing question marks, dancing in the frame below, represents the minds of neighbors who will doubt the social and genetic merit of a family with messy children. The Cleanliness Institute's message emphasizes the purity of one's character (morality, discipline, social efficiency) and one's physical characteristics. Soap may wash filth, but only the elect keep hygienic propriety in the forefront of their daily routine.

The Backlash against Business

We can imagine how those Americans (and immigrants) felt who failed to adequately assimilate the exacting precision of Machine Age cleanliness and "scientific" housekeeping. Those working in factories felt double the pressure, toiling under the unrelenting gaze of a "scientific" managerial eye and its machines that never slept. Louis-Ferdinand Céline, in his 1932 book *Journey to the End of Night,* described a wretched scene of a Ford factory assembly line, where high-speed automation engineers men into the slaves of machines:

> And I came in fact to a group of great squat buildings full of windows, through which you could see, like a cage full of flies, men moving about . . . as if they were contending very feebly against Heaven knows what impossibility. So this was Ford's? . . . One was turned by force into a machine oneself, the whole of one's carcass quivering in this vast frenzy of noise which filled you within and around the inside of your skull and lower down rattled your bowels. . . . The workmen [in the factory] bending solicitously over the machines, eager to keep them happy, is a depressing sight.[36]

Common laborers, as expendable as an interchangeable gear, were, no doubt, unenthusiastic about the techno-corporate system operating the efficient engines of the Machine Age.[37] Lewis Mumford's acerbic jibe at scientific management articulates the disparity aptly: "Saving labor by rationalization was a real improvement which bettered everything but the position of the laborer."[38] The Depression years aggravated labor's discontent and tinged with doubt the middle class's faith in the civilizing benefits of the Machine Age under the leadership of the techno-corporate order.[39] Pessimism about the private sector aside, the common folk could still muster excitement over the machine, perceiving in it a means of technological escapism, as crowds would habitually turn out at airports, train stations, and fairs to greet the latest mechanical spectacles.[40] But the Great Depression magnified mass production's inherent paradox of poverty and progress, to borrow a phrase from historian Alan Trachtenberg, and Americans of various persuasions—not just labor or the poor—wanted an explanation. A generation raised on expertism looked to "the experts" for a solution as well as a shoulder or two on which to place the blame. Public contempt and suspicion were centered less on machines than on the people who ran them from within the feudal corridors of the techno-corporate order. Thus the main hurdle in organizing public opinion for war involved revitalizing industrial management's soured reputation among both blue- and white-collar classes.

The 1929 stock market crash acted as an abrasive catalyst for the traditional enemies of the corporate elite. Labor leaders and their liberal supporters and working-class followers intensified their agitation for a fairer deal, seeking to inject a degree of egalitarianism missing in the bloated coffers of the techno-corporate order. Capitalist monopolies, automation, and unchecked mass production were viewed by many labor-minded liberals and poverty-stricken workers as responsible for the country's dismal economic state. Indeed, increased levels of factory automation had forced many low-skilled (and even white-collar) workers out of jobs prior to the crash.[41] Commentators surmised that overproduction and underconsumption—regressive consequences of the Machine Age—were largely responsible for the widespread economic depression. In short, there was not sufficient mass purchasing power to generate a reliable current of new capital for continued growth and economic development. Consumers either weren't spending their money, or simply weren't making enough money to spend. Roy Sheldon and designer Egmont Arens articulated this widespread belief from the consumer engineer's point of view: "We engineered an adequate supply of goods. We can engineer an adequate supply of customers. Unemployment means underconsumption, and underconsumption means that the consumer is not buying. The cause may be that the goods are obsolete, or merely that the consumer has no money."[42] The contraction of the economy that resulted from this imbalance created a downward spiral precipitating a stock market crash, massive layoffs, unemployment, farm and home foreclosures, and business and bank failures.[43] Something has obviously gone unexpectedly awry despite the business community's zeal for efficiency and rational planning. Capitalism, industry, and corporate management in general were viewed by their critics as guilty of facilitating the Depression's economic woes and shirking social responsibility.[44]

The backlash against business did not stop there, as the authors of wartime mobilization narratives were well aware. The Depression's hardships had intensified American isolationism, and this antiglobal mood was tied to a middle-class public's renewed suspicion of the techno-corporate order and its "gluttonous" profit system.[45] The middle class had a history of doubting the morality of big business. As recently as the Progressive Era, "trust-busting" missions led by turn-of-the-century reformers attempted to purge the capitalist system of monopolistic dominance and return to it a sense of middle-class decency, if not democracy. During the 1930s, this Progressive trust-busting ethos was revisited by investigative groups who examined the suspicious profits reaped by the munitions and arms manufacturers during World War I. "War . . . is the health of the machine," lamented Lewis Mumford in 1934, and to many Americans, war contributed too readily to the fiscal health of certain members of the techno-corporate order.[46] It was widely speculated that large corporations and financial institutions conspired to stir up global wars in order to enrich their coffers. Giant aggregates, whose profits depended on military contracts, goaded nations into aggression against each other, then charged exorbitant prices for their wares in a time of crisis. Wars were thus created for the profit of the corporate elite at the expense of the common citizen. This "merchants of death" theory gained credence during the Depression years when antibusiness sentiment was already running high—as was the public need to unearth strong evidence that corporate greed had led to the current economic disaster.[47] Reformers, consumers, and even government officials thought they had found that evidence buried in the mobilization maelstrom of World War I.

Merchants of Death

Belief in a merchants of death conspiracy spread as war clouds began to form over Europe, triggering fears of American entanglement in another global conflict. A public gravely disillusioned with the failure of "the war to end all wars" and the 1929 collapse of the techno-corporate order proved a receptive audience to any news sanctioning assumptions about a merchants of death collusion. The Nye Committee led the investigative charge in a federal attempt to uproot the specific villains and discover who was responsible. Operating between 1934 and 1936, the Senate Special Committee Investigating the Munitions Industry, chaired by Senator Gerald P. Nye (R-ND), sought to prove allegations of wartime profiteering and fraud among companies benefiting from the manufacture and sales of munitions before, during, and after World War I. Significantly, DuPont (seller of powder and explosives) and the J. P. Morgan Company (financier and purchasing agent for the Allies) were prime targets. The Nye Committee could not substantiate any real evidence of an evil conspiracy to foment war for the sake of corporate profit. But the public relations damage was done. Coupled with other sensationalized reports of the period, such as Helmuth Engelbrecht and Frank Hanighen's best seller *Merchants of Death,* such negative press further deteriorated the public's attitude toward big business, the Machine Age, and the impersonal, greedy engines of the techno-corporate order.[48] Donald Nelson explains the consequences of this theory for interwar defense industries: "There was a strong feeling in this country against the 'merchants of death,' and after World War I we cracked down on the 'munitions barons.' . . . The biggest rifle manufacturing firm in the world . . . was swept away. Half-finished ships rusted and rotted. . . . Machine-gun plants and the beginnings of a promising military-plane industry disappeared."[49]

The merchants of death publicity of the mid-1930s weakened the ideological foundations of the Machine Age and corroded the authority of its institutional presence in American thought and life. Experts who scripted ensuing mobilization narratives in the 1940s realized that Americans, especially those Progressive-minded members of the middle class, needed reassurances that the Machine Age was not only alive and well but also ethical. Symbolic distinctions between the "heroes" and the "enemy" had to be firmly drawn and repeatedly communicated. There could be no "bad guys" on the American team, no vestiges of the earlier allegations of war-related fraud and profiteering. The techno-corporate image needed to be purged and sanctified if America was going to effectively mobilize for war.

If consumer belief in the democratic promises of technology (and its rulers) had slipped, would it be such a stretch for them to question the sanctity of the American Way? The belief in the mythical power of mass production as a democratic panacea — rather than as an oligarchic tool used by merchants of death — had to be reinstalled during the war if Americans were to believe that their country could defeat the established war machines of Germany and Japan.

Evidence of Machine Age Failure

Mobilization experts of the 1940s found the published facts of Machine Age failure hard to overcome. The Depression's unsanitary shantytowns, looming like industrial plagues on vacant lots, confirmed suspicions that the Machine Age had not lived up to its industrial potential. It was clear that technology in tandem with the American Way had not completely democratized progress as popular mythology had claimed that it would.[50] Widespread substandard living conditions in urban and rural settings influenced the rhetoric and symbols woven into the war's mobilization narratives, and, as we shall see in subsequent chapters, such records of social devolution also shaped the war's reconversion propaganda.

Documentary photographs of the Depression years bore witness to technological defeat and raised questions about the American Way. In a 1932 *Architectural Forum* editorial entitled "No Rent—No Taxes—No Work," vestiges of Machine Age progress peek through the social refuse of a town made of rickety wooden shacks, built with the debris cast off from Manhattan's West Side (fig. 2.2). The stovepipes protruding from unstable walls lend a mere pretense of modern comfort. Electrical wires crisscross above the makeshift shacks, and water towers cast a cold shadow over the decrepit town. Such modern amenities seem to bypass the destitute citizenry below. The "mayor" of the dismal community, in his tidy, three-piece suit, poses a stark, middle-class contrast to the haphazard sheds. The picture subtly inveighs against the system that brought this man so low — despite his clinging to a managerial appearance that has been unable to save him or his surroundings.

According to newspaper stories printed early in the Depression years, many Americans were not only living in shacks made from the refuse of modern consumer culture but were also subsisting off its garbage. Chronicles of American citizens standing in lines at dumps, rather than at grocery stores, were common:

> About twenty-five men and boys and one woman stood in two rows all day, all the way down to the garbage hill waiting for that load to come down. And then, like a flock of chickens, they started to scratch in that smelly pile, and pick out certain things, which they deposited in baskets. . . . Apples seemed most popular even when half rotten away. Carrots, potatoes, and bread also found their way into the baskets. . . . Most of them admitted that it was for their supper.[51]

NO RENT—NO TAXES—NO WORK

A "HOUSING PROJECT" of improvised shelter built by and for the unemployed on a vacant lot in New York, at 12th Avenue and 40th Street, known to its tenants and the police as "Shanty Town." At the left the "mayor" rings his bell announcing the communal meal. Industrialized housing to produce large-scale, planned communities may contribute to the solution of the problems of both unemployment and housing

2.2. Irving Browning, *Architectural Forum,* July 1932, 80. Shantytown built by unemployed men along the Hudson River, 12th Avenue and 40th Street, New York, New York. Collection of The New-York Historical Society.

Like the *Architectural Forum* photo, Dorothea Lange's 1930s picture of an Oklahoma mother and her three children (fig. 2.3) underscores the disparity between established hygienic proprieties and abject poverty. Unlike the subjects of Lange's other popular photographs, this woman was allowed to clean herself and her children up a bit before posing for the camera. In both figures 2.2 and 2.3, the juxtaposition between vain attempts at "keeping up appearances" and the dilapidated shacks in the background exposes the fallibility of the promises implicit in the American Way gospel. Emphasis on attempts to appear clean and neat according to middle-class codes of decency and hygiene show assertions of a "civilized" character amidst social and economic decay. According to established Machine Age mythology, failed progress was perceived as irrational, contradicting the white-collar elite's value conferred on the logical, disciplined, and efficient. In essence, American civilization was threatened with devolution and stagnation when standards of living declined so drastically.

The shantytown mayor and the unfortunate mother in Lange's photo have an air of the modern consumer about them. Their cognizance of hygienic propriety, like their clothing, appears store-bought, a ready-made commodity that connects them to the modern pipelines of Machine Age "normalcy," that is, rational science and engineered efficiency in tandem with mass-produced civilization and mass-consumed convenience. Their "high-grade" appearance, however, certainly refutes any assumption that they are unfit or undesirable types. Although their world may be defective, they cleave tenaciously to classifications of well-born and well-bred. The power of these images, for us and for their original audience, lies more in the familiar resonance with the ethos of the consumer, a citizen civilized and sanitized by the Machine Age, struggling against the irrational tide of antiprogress.

The Cleanliness Institute of the late 1920s would have been thoroughly appalled by a rather eye-opening 1939 report about migrant farmers' housing near Sacramento, California. Written on the brink of the war, this account, extracted from a larger federal survey, paints an even more dismal picture of the wretched living conditions caused by economic decline during the Great Depression:

> Entire families, men, women, and children, are crowded into hovels, cooking and eating in the same room. The majority of the shacks have no sinks or cesspools for the disposal of kitchen drainage, and this, together with garbage and other refuse, is thrown on the surface of the ground. . . . Many families were found that did not have even a semblance of tents or shelters. . . . One water tap at an adjoining industrial plant was found to be the source of the domestic water supply for the camp.[52]

President Roosevelt had exclaimed in an oft-quoted speech of 1937 that he saw "one third of a nation ill-housed, ill-clad, and ill-nourished." He actually turned out to be off by about 10 percent. When the Treasury Department's U.S. Public Health Service reported its 1935–36 National Health Survey in 1938, it revealed that 40 percent of the nation lived in substandard, unhygienic housing. The scarcity of progress was actually much worse than the government had realized.[53]

The photographs and reports documenting the detritus of the Depression years do not simply underscore the breakdown of the American Way; they show us a yardstick for what civilized progress should have provided by revealing its antithesis. Roosevelt recognized the public relations potential behind such polarizing narratives and put them to work for his administration during the 1930s. Photojournalists working for the New Deal's Resettlement Administration (RA) and its successor, the Farm Security Administration (FSA), disseminated images

2.3. Dorothea Lange, "Family of Rural Rehab Client. Tulare County, California." Photograph, no date. Courtesy of The Bancroft Library, University of California, Berkeley (1942.008; Folder 108:6).

such as Dorothea Lange's, exposing the Depression's disturbing effects across geographic boundaries and class lines. RA and FSA photographs were part of a massive publicity campaign launched by the Roosevelt administration in order to visually justify the existence and expense of its social programs and plans for the American economy.[54] The RA/FSA photographs were able to command a wide audience (especially among the middle class) because the Photography Section's director, Roy Stryker, funneled copies of the prints directly into the public domain, where they appeared in general-circulation magazines such as *Life, Look,* and *Saturday Evening Post.*[55]

However, the RA/FSA photographers were also part of the New Deal's hygienic solutions for combating the Depression. Photographers were instructed to document when certain New Deal programs *succeeded* in order to visually demonstrate how public moneys could help reverse dire poverty. Lange and other

RA/FSA photographers not only visited makeshift shantytowns, but also toured government-operated work camps for migrants, which offered clean and orderly places of refuge with bathing and laundering facilities. Both the "before" and "after" images documented by the RA and FSA were intended to illustrate how government could efficiently restore order and a sense of progress through tax dollars and centralized bureaucratic power.[56]

Roosevelt's Reforms and the Ultimate Hygienic Solution

The New Deal's recovery efforts were not limited to making temporary shelter more hygienic and comfortable for migrant workers. In the long run, the New Deal sought to democratize progress by advancing consumer purchasing power.[57] Roosevelt aimed to raise American standards of living across the social spectrum by bringing modern power sources and their conveniences within reach of communities where such technological progress had not existed before.[58] This did not simply mean creating temporary jobs with public works projects that the government would fund; rather, his plan entailed making economically viable communities by modernizing rural areas with electricity. Since four-fifths of the United States in the early 1930s had not been upgraded to the twentieth-century standards enjoyed by the middle class, Roosevelt's plan encompassed an enormous untapped market. Modernization, he argued, would generate wealth and abundance because consumers with electricity in their homes would want to upgrade outmoded shelters and would purchase utilities and appliances (especially radios), thus feeding a variety of industries across the nation by fulfilling rural electrical needs.

Roosevelt's intent was not just a material betterment of everyday life, but a moral improvement as well. The emphasis he placed on the role of technological progress as a catalyst for uplifting the character of society classifies New Deal aims in this case as a hygienic solution to a chaotic social mess.[59] New Deal hygienic solutions threatened corporate conceits about the oligarchic role of business as paternal dispenser and financier of modern progress to the common folk. Never mind that business leaders had a history of intentionally overlooking working and rural classes as a market for durable goods and modern conveniences.[60] The point was that consumers were fuel for the capitalist system, an economic structure resting on the bedrock of *private* industry, not public.

The bombardment of publicity that juxtaposed the tragic "before" with the heroic "after" that resulted from government action surely did little to boost the public's confidence in the ability of big business to do a similar if not a better job. Business leaders realized that skepticism toward corporate competency and honesty had to be countered by stimulating public belief in big business as the moral patriarch of technological progress. Bruce Barton, founder of the advertising firm BBDO, articulated this realization in a cogent statement published in a 1936 issue of *Economic Forum,* where he chided industrial management (referred to as "Industry") for losing its public relations edge to the Roosevelt administration: "Industry and Politics . . . are competitors for the confidence of the same patron, the public. Politics knows it; industry, for three years, has acted as if it did not."[61] Yet Barton was not the only one who realized that business would need to wrest the mantle of public savior from the New Deal. Starting well before the war, the corporate elite inaugurated its own hygienic solutions designed to simultaneously gain public favor and counterattack the New Deal.

Business's Hygienic Counterpoint

The 1939 New York World's Fair (NYWF) is perhaps the most memorable of these corporate hygienic solutions, and, in terms of our examination of wartime narratives of progress, is the most apt.[62] Planners of the fair devised the theme, "Building the World of Tomorrow," as a way of focusing the public's attention on the benevolent role of big business as the ethical engine of progress—the leader in crafting "democratic" solutions to a devolving social order. Designed as a futuristic spectacle, the fair was geared to stimulate public lust for technological escapism, but it aimed especially to turn public apathy and suspicion into an unquestioning enthusiasm for the inventive vitality of the techno-corporate order. Business sponsors offered to solve social problems with a superficial, commercial outlook, attempting to showcase the moral fiber underlying the faceless corporation marked with a less than honest reputation.[63] Although earlier world's fairs invoked an ideological component that was "educational" in scope, the 1939 NYWF was distinguished by the business community's united focus in streamlining public opinion toward a specific ideological goal, one in which corporations acted in the paternal role of generating progress as a means of saving the American Way.[64] Consequently, the fair as an image of future progress became part of the business community's arsenal for counteracting the hygienic solutions prescribed by the New Deal.[65]

The fair's corporate pavilions embodied the confluence of scientific management with a hygienic imperative—streamlining, a rational design ethic.[66] "Streamlining," whether applied as a stylistic motif or a tool for rationalizing the public mind, was a method employed by human-engineering experts of various sorts to "clean up," rationalize, standardize, and enhance efficiency in the home, the factory, the market, or society. In both its visual and verbal contexts, streamlining was synonymous with exacting order out of chaos and was co-opted by reformers, designers, advertisers, managers, engineers, government officials, and even housewives. Streamlining embodied the managerial impetus of human engineering and the hygienic contours of a healthy society: comfort, convenience, efficiency, and control. As a stylistic method, streamlining went beyond mere surfaces because its idioms of rounded corners, aerodynamic shapes, and smooth lines were ascribed the power to rationalize whatever they came in contact with.

There are fewer more apt examples of the streamlining method as a style and ideological tool than the General Motors (GM) "Highways and Horizons" pavilion, which featured designer Norman Bel Geddes's "Futurama" (fig. 2.4). Bel Geddes's design for the "Futurama" entailed an urban/suburban diorama of the "City of 1960," where clean, wide-open spaces and integrated highway arteries

2.4. Norman Bel Geddes, model of the "Futurama" for the 1939 New York World's Fair. In Norman Bel Geddes, *Magic Motorways* (New York: Random House, 1940), 240. Harry Ransom Humanities Research Center, University of Texas. Courtesy Estate of Edith Lutyens Bel Geddes.

were intended to facilitate physical and social well-being.[67] In Bel Geddes and GM's utopian conception of the future, spacious avenues have cleared a clean, direct path through the once slum-ridden city for the private automobile. Evenly spaced model cars suggest a lack of stress in a future world where the automobile industry would dominate and organize the external environment. Such predictions about the future also revealed concerns about the present and packaged them in streamlined containers representing perfected, sterilized progress.

The GM exhibit highlighted the social benefits of the automobile and the frictionless public spaces that highway planning would presumably facilitate. Such a harmonious image was ironic in light of the intense labor conflicts that had plagued the automobile industry during the Depression.[68] Nonetheless, the GM exhibit constructed an ideological and economic agenda, like other corporate-sponsored exhibits, by masking past discord with futuristic fantasies about the omnipotence of the machine and the social benevolence of capitalism, which implicitly promised to democratize progress for all. The smooth, frictionless appearance of streamlining was intended to soothe the tensions between rich and poor and between labor and capital, by suggesting that a harmonious, slum-free society could be sustained by ever-advancing developments in commercialized science and technology. The underlying message was that big business would universalize standards in health, cleanliness, and hygienic living without compromising free enterprise.

Bel Geddes's design reads like a hygienic how-to manual in which both society and the environment are streamlined to perfection. Such streamlined narratives of progress are not without their human-engineering subplots, and the "Futurama" is no exception.[69] If Lange's and *Architectural Forum*'s photographs are the Depression's quintessential expression of progress derailed and diseased, then Bel Geddes's streamlined future is squalor's healthy antithesis.[70] The "Futurama" stresses the purity and efficiency of forms attributed to the streamlined style. Such rational hygienic features boldly eschew Depression poverty and decay, thus equating the "Futurama's" sponsor, General Motors, with social betterment and America's unhampered evolutionary trajectory into the future—a messianic image no corporation was about to share with the New Deal. Clean, efficient design and technological progress created under the expert aegis of the corporation are cast as the remedy for uplifting the acceptable types of Americans out of the dregs of the Depression.

With the NYWF as a precedent, it was easy for corporate-minded mobilization experts to position the war as America's *new* Machine Age. Couching social uplift metaphors in corporate-sponsored streamlined designs, as Bel Geddes did for General Motors, would prove a useful public relations tool in America's ideological mobilization for war. Mobilization narratives, as we shall see, stigmatized the Depression years as a time of stagnation and social inertia while heralding America's involvement in the war as a natural outgrowth of progress. Mass production, mechanization, and the assembly line, guided by managerial expertise, would once again be celebrated as the panacea for economic and social ills. Corporations, by extension, would gain credence as saviors of the American Way.

3 Positioning Machine Age Heroes and Wartime Types

Corporate displays at the 1939 New York World's Fair were an attempt to publicly identify the true heroes in America's struggle to resuscitate its economy. Mobilization provided business with an extension of this earlier marketing strategy. But war did not mean that business's public relations battles were over. As the National Association of Manufacturers (NAM) realized, the necessities of the conflict certainly opened new vistas for positively positioning the techno-corporate order:

> The war has enabled American industry to provide the most dramatic demonstration ever of what it can accomplish, given the chance . . . and the goods have been delivered by a brilliant application of mass-production "know-how" which for so many years has been smeared. . . . In other words, if the public believes in the competence of business leadership . . . most of the threats which have concerned us in the past will be on the way to handling themselves.[1]

Written in 1943 as a positioning plan for the NAM agenda, these remarks reveal an amazing amount about the corrosive resentments stewing beneath the new big business/big government dynamic that developed during the 1930s. Not only was the war perceived as a springboard to prosperity, as illustrated here and in subsequent chapters, but corporate leaders also embraced the war's upheaval as a welcome relief from the federal blister that had been irritating big business for nearly ten years. The NAM's 1943 positioning plan provides a classic example of the clash between the New Deal agenda and the conservative managerial elite as it had festered through the 1930s.

What do all the NAM's buzzwords mean, especially in light of the Depression and war? If the leaders of "American industry" possessed "mass-production 'know-how'" that was brilliantly applied, why would such tremendous ability have been smeared "for so many years"? Even the NAM's New Deal nemesis, Roosevelt, acknowledged management's "industrial genius, unmatched throughout all the world" (see p. 21). So who exactly did the "smearing"? What "threats" had weighed heavily on business leaders "in the past," and how would they "handle themselves" in the future? Indeed, "the past" is just as mysteriously referred to as "the future."

First of all, "American industry" is a catchphrase referring to management, not to labor.[2] Used in this context, which it often was during the war, "industry" is a reflection of management's image of itself as the great rational machine—the ultimate expression of impersonal engineering efficiency, logic, and perfection. Peppered with defensiveness, the NAM's comments suggest that the expertise inherent in American industry (i.e., management) had been unfairly "smeared" "for so many years." Second, from the business perspective the problem with government expansion and its bureaucratic zeal for perfecting every category of society was *regulation*—one of the "threats" from "the past" alluded to by the NAM. Many New Deal reforms of the 1930s were aimed at business practice or organization.[3] New Dealers were critical of the corporate status quo but were not, on the whole, necessarily antagonistic toward the system of capitalism. Nonetheless, Roosevelt's administration challenged the established structure of laissez-faire corporate capitalism, and in so doing looked for flaws in the paragons of perfectionism and efficiency. Liberal advocates, within and outside of government, believed that America's social ills were largely caused by defects inherent in the hierarchical system of the techno-corporate order. The very system that championed and subscribed to rationality, science, and engineering was blamed for infecting society like an irrational contagion. Government reforms meant that managers were being managed by a system of control mirrored after their corporate image! Surely an elite fleet of experts could have governed themselves—as the NAM implies in its defense of management's superlative "know-how."

As many reformers saw it, the main scourge was bigness—corporate monopolies with large-scale centralizations of economic and industrial power. Attacks on monopolies were another of the "threats" from "the past" to which the NAM refers. Ironically, government's "bigness," from the corporate perspective, was yet another. Federal size and regulatory measures seemed to swell disproportionately, allowing government's reach to penetrate deeply into corporate territories, influencing matters of the economy and the masses within it. By and large, where reforms touched consumers' lives was where government's bigness stung big business to the core.[4] Consumers, like labor, were corporate turf.

Herein lies a major reason for much of the NAM's defensiveness: regulations and looming government presence in the economy, it suggests, had fettered and stymied "American industry's" optimal potential. But "given the chance" to perform at its peak during the war, it was not only able to "deliver the goods" but also to make "the most dramatic demonstration ever of what it could accomplish." And how was this feat achieved? The war grew and entrenched federal bureaucracy—but, unlike the 1930s, wartime exigencies also expanded big business's presence and influence within government circles. The New Deal desperately needed corporate America's managerial "know-how" in order to win the war. The phrase "given the chance," while deriding government bigness and paternal regulation, celebrates the corporate role in effectively managing the war from Washington, D.C., where businessmen steered the United States toward victory overseas and, in terms of industrial growth, a financial victory at home.[5]

The NAM positioning plan reveals a near-universal wartime imperative to dissolve the public's Depression-era perception of big business, reinvigorate public trust in mass production, mechanization, and technology, and stir feelings of unquestioning affinity for managerial expertise and corporate authority.[6] The war, as the NAM points out, was helping business leaders achieve a reversal in their public image because wartime industrial output countered an avalanche of negative publicity and suggestions from "the past." Though it may seem vague to us, "the past" to business leaders included a variety of well-known and well-defined "threats," including (but surely not limited to) Roosevelt's efforts to enhance consumer spending power and his popularity among the common folk; government bureaucratic and regulatory expansion; the reforming mood of the times culminating in damaging press such as the Nye Committee's report; and the general poor public image of large-scale business in reaction to the catastrophic financial fallout of a lengthy depression.

Aside from business's "smeared" reputation and its clash with the New Deal, another issue facing business at the onset of the war was fear of losing consumer brand recognition as a result of mobilization. Holding their market shares was on the mind of NAM leaders just as much as the "threats" from "the past." Keeping a business name alive for the duration of the conflict was just as important as creating public faith in the techno-corporate order, and mobilization narratives served this overlapping purpose. Mobilization stories were just that: the story of how a particular industry or specific business had retooled its products and resources for military consumption. From toasters to tuna fish, manufacturers of every sort apprised the public of their products' absence from store shelves. For example, Van Camp, the company behind Chicken of the Sea tuna, explained that their "large tuna clippers are in the Navy for the duration," but they were "working overtime to supply" grocery stores all the same.[7] These "off to battle" tales were essentially "tie-in" advertisements, linking a known product line with an essential task necessary for victory. They were meant to retain public recognition of American brand names and trademarks and lay a foundation for a robust postwar economy.[8] The

NAM's focus on generating public belief "in the competence of business leadership" referred not only to how management conducted industrial mobilization and production but also to how it could simultaneously win a war and successfully anticipate the reconversion process for peacetime.

Positioning Roosevelt and the New Deal as two of business's "threats" from "the past" was one way the NAM vilified the liberal agenda as a wartime enemy to both consumers and industry alike. Making it clear who the "enemy" was became a significant focus for not only the NAM but also authors of mobilization narratives. One way to make this distinction was to leverage racial and ethnic stereotypes in order to contrast the "good guys" from the "bad." The category of "enemy" was asserted through a spectrum of genetic types.[9] During the war years, the Germans and Japanese fell to the bottom of this spectrum, as Dr. Francis Dieuaide of Harvard University tells us: "We cannot do otherwise than believe that the Germans for the time being are off the path of social and political progress. . . . It is no mere superficial conclusion that many Germans are in a mentally disordered state much of the time. . . . The Japanese . . . [are also] out of the line of progress."[10] Before Italy's capitulation in September 1943, the Italian enemy was also derided in a similar fashion.[11] The popularization of such stereotypes as "scientific facts" made it easy to educate Americans about who was a wartime hero and who wasn't. Because such genetic determinist truisms were tied to concepts of social and racial progress, they proved exceptionally powerful in mobilizing the public mind for winning a global war—despite more than a decade of economic stagnation.[12]

The racial and ethnic stereotypes in mobilization narratives were not immune to fantasies of racial hygiene. A 1943 logo for a scrap salvage campaign illustrates one way in which a racial hygiene narrative was woven into mobilization propaganda (fig. 3.1). Created by the government's War Production Board (WPB) and Office of War Information (OWI), in cooperation with the business community's War Advertising Council (WAC), the image reveals how overt were hierarchies of race at this time. In the logo, the Japanese solider is pictured intentionally as a subhuman pathology, and his physical defects seem to justify his humiliating defeat by a middle-class housewife's high-heeled shoe. Compared to the classical perfection of the white woman's shapely leg and foot, the Japanese soldier's scrawny arms and legs are too thin, his head and hands too large; his mouth and teeth are too big for his face; and his clawed fingertips curl like a monster's. From a genetic determinist point of view, he represents the disfigured and deformed type, certainly out of step with the norm. Categories of racial superiority versus animalistic inferiority, like those depicted in this logo, were also common to the visual arguments made by followers of the pseudo-science of physiognomy, in which character was measured through the shape, size, proportion, and national origin of facial traits.[13] Though physiognomy as a serious area of study had declined in popularity by World War II, advertising still relied on the visual clichés classified by this pseudo-science in order to quickly convey a message with the least wording and the simplest graphics possible. The Japanese soldier in the tin can exemplifies this visual communications technique. His exaggerated facial features suggest a sinister and hence inferior type. In vilifying the enemy through such stereotypes,

STEP ON IT

SAVE TIN CANS

Official WPB and OWI material, prepared under direction
of the War Advertising Council, paid for by industry.

3.1. War Production Board, Office of War Information, War Advertising Council scrap salvage campaign logo, n.d. Courtesy Advertising Council Archives, New York (Ad #248, WAC Folder).

mobilization experts' appeal for patriotic participation became essentially a call to arms in defense of racial hygiene.[14]

However, it was hard to argue that the enemy was naturally inferior or unfit while America foundered in the Depression. Another ideological hurdle that mobilization experts had to face was the superlative militarization efforts of the Axis powers. With steely determination behind their quests for global dominance, Germany and Japan had harnessed a Machine Age ethos for war while the United States remained embattled by economic disorder.[15] Newsreel footage, newspapers, and magazines heralded triumphant tales about Germany and Japan's military development during the interwar years. By comparison, Donald Nelson painted a grim (and frightening) picture of America's lack of preparedness during the late 1930s:

> German munitions plants were working twenty-four hours a day. . . . Yet the United States . . . had an army inferior in size to that of Poland, which had been ground into the dust by the Wehrmacht in less than a month. . . . At the beginning of 1940 our munitions industry was only a token. . . . Compared with the munitions giants of Germany . . . it was a pigmy. . . . During the last half decade of the 1930s Germany was not only building tanks and organizing tank brigades, but was motorizing its whole army . . . beyond anything ever before heard of in the science of war. . . . In normal times [arms and munitions] appropriations were not even generous enough to finance experimental work.[16]

It would have been hard for the public not to see the contrast between the Nazis' industrial output and America's, which was proportionately quite bleak. Because America had not engaged in substantial or highly publicized military buildup after World War I, this seeming impotence threatened efforts to convince the public that American industry was fit to enter, let alone win, a new world war.

What else did mobilization narratives argue? Naturally they countered skepticism by asserting that America did possess the industrial might and resources to fight the military machines of Germany and Japan. But with what was America fighting? According to mobilization narratives, everything—including the kitchen sink.

The Machine Age Goes to War

In its attempt to mobilize the public mind, *War Facts: A Handbook for Speakers on War Production* projects the indisputable aura of expert authority through the rational, objective "fact":

> Everybody knows that the United States has the greatest capacity in the world to manufacture an almost limitless variety of products. . . . Phonographs, radios, refrigerators, vacuum cleaners—all the comforts and conveniences of modern civilization . . . In short, the country has enormous resources of raw materials and matchless industrial plants to turn these materials into finished goods. But we could not fight Germany and Japan with ice boxes and automobiles; our tremendous industrial power had to be shifted from peacetime production to war purposes. . . . Automobile manufacturers—and one of them alone can fabricate more metal than all Japan—are making tank engines and plane engines and antiaircraft guns. Machines to make vacuum cleaners have been shifted to making weapons. . . . It was confidently forecast well along in 1942 that we would produce 45 billion dollars' worth of munitions during the year—more than the total national income in 1932, the low point of the depression.[17]

Issued by the Office of Emergency Management sometime during the war, *War Facts* voices a buoyant confidence in American industry that seems to defy the devolution of the Depression years. Opening with a rather gossipy tone—"everybody knows"—each phrase is designed to construct confidence in America's industrial might and nullify any public doubt about the health and vigor of America's Machine Age. Mass production, the reader can assume, is alive and well—in *fact,* never better.

War Facts attempts to revive the rational ethos of the Machine Age with metaphors of unsurpassed progress and perfect working order. Phrases such as "greatest capacity in the world," "almost limitless variety," "enormous resources," and "matchless industrial plants" organize a picture of virile abundance—as if the Depression had never interrupted the Machine Age's evolutionary trajectory. And why, *War Facts* suggests, fear the Axis powers, who had spent the 1930s honing their industry for military production, when one U.S. automaker in Detroit "can fabricate more metal than all Japan"? Such potent statistical data took the form of an imaginary graph highlighting the inherent supremacy of American industry: "in 1942 . . . we would produce [in just munitions] . . . more than the total national income in 1932, the low point of the depression." In these data points, pulled from the language of business, the Depression is worn as a battle scar of distinction. *War Facts* argues that America is so inherently fertile that it could surpass the Axis even during a period of intense economic stagnation and decline.[18]

The persuasive rhetoric in *War Facts* does not stop with the elevation of America's rank on the evolutionary scale of modern industry. *War Facts* also celebrates

America's industrial merit with the miraculous results of that progress: the "comforts and conveniences of modern civilization." The true measurement of American superiority was partially contained in its seemingly unlimited strength and resources—its bigness—but even more so in the way this "tremendous industrial power" brought the Machine Age home, organizing and "retooling" housework into an efficient, smoothly running machine. Voicing a modern assumption about the measuring rod of cultural superiority, *War Facts* suggests that the balance of power in the world did not hinge entirely on innate resources, numbers, or managerial expertise. World industrial leadership fell to those countries who placed an emphatic value on *leisure:* those "comforts and conveniences" and the climax of modern civilization. The ability *and* drive to transfer the burden of household drudgery to various labor-saving devices—from toasters and washing machines to canned soup and quick-dissolving soap—were the genetic markers of an elite nation, inborn traits that even a temporary bout of economic depression could not eviscerate.

Rhetorical juxtapositions of "American civilization" and "Axis barbarism" were intended to identify and cement polarizations of superiority versus inferiority, thereby segregating the American factory system and its industrial management from the category of "enemy." Civilization/barbarism comparisons relied on assumptions based in genetic determinism, where categories of inferior and superior physicality were cemented in a scientific framework of indisputable facts. This superior/inferior dichotomy that we find in mobilization narratives was articulated with binary metaphors of modern vs. primitive, healthy vs. ill, efficient vs. wasteful or drudging, and in some cases, as evidenced in figure 3.1, clean or hygienic vs. dirty or unfit. The obverse of "superior" was always present in a mobilization narrative, whether specific inferior traits of the "enemy" were spelled out or not. And the "enemy" was not always limited to the Axis, but included (at times) snide references to the Depression, liberal reformers, and the New Deal.[19] In mobilizing the public mind for all-out war, big business also reconceptualized its own image, thereby creating persuasive connections between itself and innate superiority as well as an association between the corporation and victory.

Although, as *War Facts* tells us, "we could not fight Germany and Japan with ice boxes and automobiles," mobilization narratives actually professed otherwise. The civilization/barbarism dichotomy was reinforced with the theme of common household objects—especially modern labor-saving devices—marching off to war. Juxtaposing civilian life and domesticity with the battlefield was the main polarization strategy applied in mobilization narratives, and it was deployed usually to underpin an obvious "before and after" story line. Embedded within such tales was a counterattack against both the public impressions of devolving progress and any negative associations with big business, management, and industry that had been spawned by the Depression.

American Magazine's 1943 editorial "Why We Must Do Without These Things" provides a didactic "before and after" plot that maps out what the consumer needs to sacrifice on account of the war while simultaneously stressing the country's boundless productivity and abundance (fig. 3.2). Data are strategically organized in overlapping rectangles stacked in two equal vertical columns. Arrows emphasize

WHY WE MUST DO WITHOUT THESE THINGS

Out of our homes and into the battle . . . a picture story of weapons
forged from everyday peacetime articles now rationed or discontinued

MOTORCARS
The steel used in one auto will make a 75 mm. howitzer.

NEW TIRES
Seven auto tires use enough rubber for one bomber tire.

CUFFS
Wool in the cuffs of 21 men's suits will make one army uniform.

STOCKINGS
The nylon and silk from 136 pairs of stockings will make one army parachute.

WASHING MACHINES
Steel in one washer will make six 3-inch 75 mm howitzer shells.

TOYS
A 3½ pound toy locomotive uses enough copper and brass for six 30-caliber bullets.

NEW RECORDS
The shellac in one phonograph record will make a signal flare.

BICYCLES
The steel contained in a junior-size bicycle is enough to make one 30-caliber machine gun.

GOLF CLUBS
The steel used in a set of golf clubs will make 30 hand grenades.

RUGS
An average 9'x12' rug contains jute enough for 32 sandbags and wool for two army uniforms.

STOVES
An average wood-burning stove contains enough iron for a 500-pound aerial bomb.

BEDSPRINGS
Steel in a set of bedsprings will make two 4-inch 105 mm. shells.

FURS
A lady's mouton coat will provide the lining for an aviator's jacket.

FURNITURE
Wood in an average desk will make three boxes to hold 3,000 rounds of 30-caliber ammunition.

GASOLINE
An average car consumes gas enough in six months to run a Flying Fortress for one hour.

JUKE BOXES
A juke box contains plastics for one pursuit plane's cowling.

ALUMINUM
The aluminum in a coffeepot will make a large incendiary bomb.

RADIO
A radio phonograph contains copper enough for army field radio.

GIRDLES
200 girdles require the rubber needed for an army gas mask.

REFRIGERATORS
One refrigerator uses steel enough for two 3-inch trench mortars.

GRAPHS BY PICTOGRAPH

3.2. "Why We Must Do Without These Things," *American Magazine,* October 1943, 53. Photograph courtesy of The New York Public Library, Astor, Lenox, and Tilden Foundations.

the story's managerial voice by mimicking a corporate flowchart, anchoring the reader's eye to various data points. Within each box, simple graphics pair "everyday peacetime articles" with their military counterparts—visual facts that support the statistical captions beneath. Such a picture assumes that an economic defect had never threatened American industrial fecundity.

The majority of civilian consumer goods illustrated in "Why We Must Do Without These Things" would certainly have merited inclusion under *War Facts'* "comforts and conveniences of modern civilization." Borrowing from the rational ethos of the Machine Age, *American Magazine* assured its readers that the machines of war lay just beneath the surface of mundane artifacts found in everyday life. If Americans possessed automobiles, refrigerators, washing machines, jukeboxes, radios, aluminum coffeepots, steel bedsprings, nylon stockings, phonograph records, and rubber girdles, and indeed they did, then surely it would take only a small leap for these goods to evolve into machines for war: howitzers, parachutes, shells, bullets, bombs, airplanes, gas masks, and grenades. The rudiments of modern civilization, *American Magazine*'s story suggests, were the inherent ingredients for victory against the Axis—who, as such stories implied, no doubt had less.

This home front/front line juxtaposition recurs in a Reynolds 1943 *Fortune* ad, "The Crackle that Grew to a Roar!" (fig. 3.3), in which battlefield heroics are paired with a mundane household product. However, it is not the soldier risking his life, nor the housewife sacrificing her aluminum foil, who is the hero of this story. Dominating the ad is a gigantic godlike hand—the elite fist of managerial power, not labor—that crumples a wad of Reynolds aluminum foil.[20] From this disposable domestic product erupts a squad of fighter planes, speeding through the air on a mission, perhaps a bombing raid. The image implies a "before and after" narrative in that the warplanes of "today" have evolved from the domestic product of "yesterday." In the copy, Reynolds situates its readers (in this case mostly businessmen) within the context of wartime scarcity: "Remember the crackling of the aluminum foil that was used to package and protect so many products in daily use? You don't hear it any more, do you? It's gone . . . until the boys come marching home."[21] Then the copy shifts to a celebration of Reynolds's managerial prowess in the "science" of forecasting and rational planning: "Long before Pearl Harbor, Reynolds—the world's largest aluminum foil producer—foresaw a shortage of aluminum. . . . So we put all of our foil plants on a war basis." Climaxing in the rhetoric of success, the ad asserts that the real hero of the war is the American corporation: "All of our precision experience . . . [went] into the war effort. . . . Today, with hundreds of millions of pounds of finished metal already produced, Reynolds Aluminum flies into battle in virtually every American plane now clearing the skies of Nazis and Japs."[22] In Reynolds's case civilization is saved through the efficiency not only of its product but *especially* of its corporation. Here, the corporation assumes dual responsibility for victory on the battlefield and in the "survival of the fittest" struggle, by the triumph of efficiency, rationality, and calculated productivity over Axis savagery.

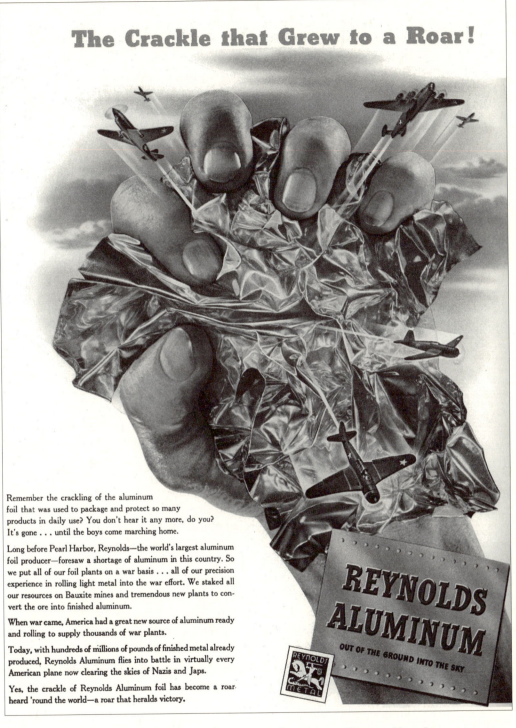

The Crackle that Grew to a Roar!

Remember the crackling of the aluminum foil that was used to package and protect so many products in daily use? You don't hear it any more, do you? It's gone . . . until the boys come marching home.

Long before Pearl Harbor, Reynolds—the world's largest aluminum foil producer—foresaw a shortage of aluminum in this country. So we put all of our foil plants on a war basis . . . all of our precision experience in rolling light metal into the war effort. We staked all our resources on Bauxite mines and tremendous new plants to convert the ore into finished aluminum.

When war came, America had a great new source of aluminum ready and rolling to supply thousands of war plants.

Today, with hundreds of millions of pounds of finished metal already produced, Reynolds Aluminum flies into battle in virtually every American plane now clearing the skies of Nazis and Japs.

Yes, the crackle of Reynolds Aluminum foil has become a roar heard 'round the world—a roar that heralds victory.

REYNOLDS ALUMINUM
OUT OF THE GROUND INTO THE SKY

REYNOLDS METAL

3.3. Reynolds Aluminum advertisement, *Fortune,* September 1943, 74. Courtesy Alcoa, Inc.

The hand in the ad tells us much about the dominant beliefs and concerns within the corporate stratum at this time. It is a man's fist, to be sure, and its aggressive size completely overwhelms the composition in a full-page, full-color ad; the fighter planes are dwarfed by its gargantuan presence. It appears anything but enfeebled by a mere economic depression or by excessive government regulations; rather, it assumes a genetic superiority. Similar in shape to a lion's paw (i.e., king of the jungle), it exudes a masculine vitality that erases any doubt about the fecund powers of Reynolds or of American industry. This genetic determinist theme of might—vibrant health and indisputable strength—also surfaces in Reynolds's reference to its prewar production of aluminum foil for domestic use: "aluminum foil . . . used to package and protect so many products in daily use." The word "protect" underscores the assumed paternal facade of the corporation, an image that big business had tried to secure long before the war.[23] The word also supports the omnipotent father-protector image embodied in the unchallengeable fist.

A similar, if perhaps softer, set of corporate assumptions is made in a 1943 *Ladies' Home Journal* ad for Brillo in which a young soldier sits beneath a canopy of camouflage netting—a Norman Rockwell–like picture in all respects, except, of course, for the accoutrements of combat (fig. 3.4). The helmet and fatigues the young soldier wears nearly mask his body entirely within his artificial "natural" surroundings, but the camouflage can't hide his boyish face as he looks up at the viewer (presumably a woman in this case). The letter he is writing home nostalgically begins, "Dear Mom: I know where your Brillo went . . . because they are using [it] for camouflage in the Army—*bales* of it—painted green like grass!"[24] The familiar "before and after" narrative strategy surfaces in the home front/front line comparison, which in Brillo's case refers to the military adaptation of a mass-produced square of steel wool formerly used by thousands of mothers to cleanse America's pots and pans.

Would the simple Brillo pad, one might wonder, fit *War Facts'* criteria for the "comforts and conveniences of modern civilization"? As a labor-saving device, though not a mechanical one, the little square of steel wool certainly would have alleviated the ritual drudgery of purging grime caked onto cooking utensils. Typical of mobilization narratives, this black-and-white, half-column ad (subdued, compared to the Reynolds ad) takes the most unassuming household product and stretches it to heroic proportions. The meager Brillo pad can claim ownership of American superiority and victory, like Reynolds Metals can, because of its association with the triumph of efficiency and hygiene. If such a product is victorious in peacetime over filth, drudgery, and wasted time, is it such a vast leap to imagine that its military application would prove at least equally successful in purging the world of the Axis's mess? The superlative hygienic powers of the Brillo cleansing pad were not limited to the small square itself but also extended to the image of the corporation. The more a domestic product could be positioned as a hygienic victor in the civilization/barbarism dichotomy, the greater the enhancement of the corporate mind that spawned it.

Industries that perfected the female form took their share of credit for an efficient Allied victory as well. Intimate apparel manufacturers were just as likely to

Dear Mom:
I know where your
BRILLO went . . .

"Maybe your pots and pans are black
and burned but *we* are bright and
protected because they are using Brillo
for camouflage in the Army—*bales* of
it—painted green like grass!"

* * *

The makers of Brillo are sorry about your
pots and pans, Mom, and we hope you will
wait for us until the war is over. You still
can have Brillo polishing soap, though—
you know it's swell for making your aluminum shine.

BRILLO

3.4. Brillo advertisement, *Ladies' Home Journal,* September 1943, 151. Courtesy Church &
Dwight Company, Inc. Photograph courtesy of General Research Division, The New York
Public Library, Astor, Lenox, and Tilden Foundations.

3.5. Real-Form Girdles of Grace advertisement, *Woman's Home Companion,* September 1943, 101. Photograph courtesy of General Research Division, The New York Public Library, Astor, Lenox, and Tilden Foundations.

claim that they contributed as essentially to the victory equation as did automobile manufacturers such as Cadillac, who produced engines for tanks.[25] In its 1943 *Women's Home Companion* ad, "Military Needs Come First," Real-Form, makers of "Girdles of Grace," approaches the "before and after" narrative structure and its home front/front line juxtaposition a bit differently than in those about Reynolds or Brillo (fig. 3.5). No matter how intense wartime shortages might become, mobilization narratives from the glamour and beauty industries stressed that ideal femininity would be preserved at any cost. Following this cultural logic, Real-Form's ad exhibits both an apology for changed conditions and a promise that femininity would not be compromised as a result of the war: "Real-Form is devoting most of its Raschel knitting machines to [the] vital military need [for camouflage nets], while making a limited number of girdles and panty girdles. You'll continue to find Lastex in Real-Form as long as our supply lasts. Please be patient if your dealer can't supply you at once."[26] Real-Form's contribution to the battlefield is tied to its mission to safeguard the well-molded female form for the duration. It is as if ideal femininity is as much a military priority as camouflage nets or other bits of matériel.

Real-Form's one-column ad reveals an explicit genetic twist to the wartime superior/inferior dichotomy and the corporate revival of modern civilization's Machine Age ethos. Not far removed from Reynolds's masculine fist, the heroic protagonist is a half-clad blonde, who turns her head toward the viewer while sensuously licking a ration stamp. Her Aryan features and attenuated form echo genetic determinist models of superior physicality. This model of femininity, rhetorically engineered and celebrated by white racial hygienists, also overlaps with a modern managerial ideal. She is pared down to the essentials, streamlined or Taylorized, like modern business; aerodynamic in form like the shape of a modern machine; tall and thin like the modern skyscraper. Her contours are smooth, precise, and lean. Hence, her perfections are thus also efficient: there is no excessive fat or waste. She is the model of social hygiene in that she is racially and genetically pure.[27] Not only does she epitomize the ideal modern female consumer through her streamlined form, but she also exhibits traits of maximized efficiency and mental accomplishment by adhering to wartime rationing standards. She may be glamorous and sexy, but she is anything but feebleminded or dumb. Her heroic contribution to victory is thus twofold: she sustains the apex of feminine beauty while effectively managing her household's wartime consumption.

Mobilization narratives reveal how the war's conceptualization was shaped as a bureaucracy of interchangeable parts—aluminum foil for planes, steel wool for camouflage, a girdle for a gas mask, an auto for a howitzer, and so on. An archaeology of the routine bits and pieces of consumer goods unfolds—the discrete details of their materials or manufacture being dissected, scrutinized, then resurrected through symbol management. This process reveals that each minute shard has *some* ideological contribution to make toward mobilizing the public mind in favor of all-out war and the corporation's assumed command within it.

Bombers Can Begin in the Strangest Places

During the war, the streamlined woman's image stood as a testament to American industrial might and managerial inventive acumen. Mobilization narratives thus broke an established middle-class taboo about unabashedly focusing public attention on the ideal sexual attributes of the genetically superior female type. At the same time, however, these stories echoed established myths about labor-saving progress and used these assumptions to buttress big business's wartime political agenda.

The streamlined woman was the biological apotheosis of Machine Age progress. So efficient were the rational labor-saving products spun from "scientific" factories, emerging under the watchful eye of expert engineers and managers, that, finally, womankind's feminine charms need not deteriorate under the taxing demands of household drudgery. Store-bought cleansers, ready-made clothes, processed foods, electrified gadgets and appliances, and sanitary plumbing fixtures not only helped eliminate unwanted filth and odors, kept foods fresher longer, and made clothes cleaner, but, according to advertisers, also preserved women's youth and delicate femininity. Modern conveniences—the hallmarks of hygienic civilization—promised to save women from a fate of aging unnaturally due to old-fashioned, inefficient housework that sapped energy and drained housewives of attractive vigor.[28] Designed to more easily manage work in the home, labor-saving products allowed women to take the enviable evolutionary leap to their higher purpose: leisurely focusing on family health and character while perpetually reveling in youthful sex appeal and hygienic beauty.[29]

Mobilization narratives, however, made it clear that the streamlined woman did not get that way without the aid of the techno-corporate order. The icon of the streamlined kitchen conveyed this concept in one neat package, and advertisers of any sort, whether they made kitchens or not, borrowed the symbolic value ascribed to this ultimate labor-saving and civilizing "machine."[30] Wartime advertisements featuring streamlined kitchens asserted the idea that not only did the modern middle-class household rank as the apex of hygienic civilization, but this proper home also provided the key technological components for America's successful industrial production and its victory. War, like the streamlined kitchen or woman, provided an opportune marketing stratagem that promised to popularize a given company's contribution to victory and tie its brand name to the unhampered trajectory of modern progress.

The "scientific" advent of the streamlined kitchen occurred during the "efficiency craze" of the Progressive Era.[31] The principles of space and time-motion management, popularized by experts such as Frederick Taylor and Frank and Lillian Gilbreth, were not adapted to "women's work" until the publication of Christine Frederick's series "The New Housekeeping," which appeared in a 1912 *Ladies' Home Journal* and was published in book form the following year.[32] These experts helped popularize the image of the middle-class housewife as a "home manager" who was simultaneously supervisor and laborer in her own household. Following the efficiency precepts of Taylor, the Gilbreths, and Frederick, subsequent domestic scientists and industrial designers applied a rational and scientifically managed aesthetic to the kitchen as a whole. "Streamlining" in kitchen design meant that appliances, cabinets, and countertops were "cleaned up" or standardized in height and width to create a continuous, uninterrupted work surface. Poorly arranged kitchens that had not been "streamlined" wasted one's energy on unnecessary steps between appliances, storage areas, work surfaces, and eating areas built too far apart. The tools of the civilized housewife needed compact arrangement so that her efficiency would be maximized and any unnecessary movements minimized, much like the arrangement of a factory assembly line. The perceived rational aesthetic of the streamlined kitchen design scheme was also intended to show that such an organized plan would automatically facilitate an efficient flow of work with minimal to zero drudgery. Because such a seemingly logical design was imbued with the aura of scientific calculations, the hygienically smooth and white aesthetic of the streamlined kitchen also bore a strong resemblance to a laboratory.[33]

The streamlined kitchen's "efficiency aesthetic" provided a sanitized instrument through which mobilization experts discussed the dirty business of war and, for those with brand names to promote, an excellent marketing opportunity. A 1943 *Business Week* ad placed by Owens-Corning, "Bombers can begin in the strangest places," spins a mobilization tale around the efficiency inherent in its insulating material, Fiberglas, used in modern ranges and refrigerators but also handy for producing better bombers and warships (fig. 3.6). Owens-Corning, like other mobilized corporations, suggests that the modern kitchen provides a wealth of resources for upgrading America's military machine, implying that through household technologies, the Allies can match, if not surpass, Germany's and Japan's head start in war production:

Odd as it seems, materials for bombers have also originated with refrigerators or ranges. For it was a certain insulating material used in refrigerators

Bombers can begin in the strangest places

ONE OF THE usual sources of materials for bombers is in Alabama, where some aluminum, used in bombers, is mined.

Odd as it seems, materials for bombers have also originated with refrigerators or ranges. For it was a certain insulating material used in refrigerators and ranges that led to a saving of aluminum by the Navy. *Already enough of the material has been used to release enough aluminum to build more than 350 four-engine bombers!*

Here's the story.

In pre-war America, there were hundreds of thousands of ranges and refrigerators equipped with a modern insulation . . . an insulation of glass in fibrous form called Fiberglas.*

This Fiberglas insulation is highly efficient. When used either as springy wool blankets for range insulation or in semi-rigid form for refrigerators, it doesn't settle, even when oven

or refrigerator doors are repeatedly slammed shut. It doesn't leave "holes" through which heat can leak in or out.

Of course, it's firesafe. And from a manufacturer's point of view, it is easy to install.

In this combination of Fiberglas qualities, the Navy saw several outstanding advantages for warships.

For the Navy demanded a *highly efficient, lightweight* insulation for living quarters and other important places on its ships. The Navy had to have *fire safety*, too. And of course it had to have an insulation which *wouldn't settle* under the vibration of pounding waves or gun fire. Fiberglas wool met all these requirements and was used widely aboard many types of ships.

But of even greater importance was this: The Navy saw how it could eliminate the aluminum facing, formerly needed to keep insulation in place, by using an

adaptation of the semi-rigid type of Fiberglas which needs no metal facing.

This is just another instance of the Navy's imagination and alertness in adapting a peacetime product to a wartime use.

One day, Fiberglas will again be available for household equipment. But till then 'round-the-clock plant operation and the skill of our workers are devoted to supplying increasing quantities of Fiberglas for wartime uses where it is the most suitable material for the job. *Owens-Corning Fiberglas Corporation, Toledo, Ohio. In Canada, Fiberglas Canada, Ltd., Oshawa, Ontario.*

OWENS-CORNING

FIBERGLAS
*T. M. Reg. U. S. Pat. Off.

3.6. Owens-Corning Fiberglas advertisement, *Business Week*, 17 April 1943, 65. Courtesy Owens Corning.

and ranges that led to a saving of aluminum by the Navy. . . . In pre-war America, there were hundreds of thousands of ranges and refrigerators equipped with a modern insulation . . . Fiberglas. This Fiberglas insulation is highly efficient. . . . It doesn't settle. . . . Of course, it's firesafe . . . [and] easy to install. . . . The Navy saw several outstanding advantages for warships [in Fiberglas]. . . . Fiberglas wool met all [the Navy's] requirements and was used widely aboard many types of ships. . . . This is just another instance of the Navy's imagination and alertness in adapting a peacetime product to a wartime use.[34]

The focal point of the ad is not the managerial prowess of the navy or Owens-Corning, as in other mobilization narratives. Rather, the crux of the ad's message hinges on two icons: the streamlined housewife and her streamlined kitchen. Our attention is drawn to the significance of these icons by a senior naval officer, who assumes a look of "the Navy's imagination and alertness." It's as though we have caught him in the moment of inspiration. "Ah, yes" is the look on his face as he considers the best place from which to fight the war. The kitchen, he imagines, provides an essential ingredient for producing superior war machines—a "fact" described to us in detail. But, as this navy officer also realizes, American industry's potential for victory is measured by a different criterion, its management's successful role in the making of a smiling, satisfied housewife, whose domestic work is so effortless that she can perform it in high heels.

In the Owens-Corning ad, we see the middle-class twin of Real-Form's Aryan pinup.[35] Both represent genetic efficiency and success. The "nice girl's" apron ties around a slim, attractive waist; her looks are youthful and relaxed; her legs are shapely, her nails polished, and there isn't a hair out of place. But, according to Machine Age mythology, it's the leisure built into her modern kitchen that boosts her up the evolutionary ladder of civilization and plants her securely in the middle class. The streamlined kitchen's symbolic role as the pinnacle of progress resided in its ability to award sanitary comfort and hygienic leisure through effortless, antiseptic housework. Such a kitchen claimed to purge domesticity by removing not just the filth but especially the class stigma of manual labor. Electric, built-in appliances and sterile-looking cabinets presumably facilitated a cleaner kitchen through "scientific" design and offered to take the "dirty work" of household maintenance out of the middle-class housewife's hands.

The Norge company's mobilization ad placed in *Ladies' Home Journal* of 1943 echoes many of the "facts" asserted by Owens-Corning to readers of *Business Week* (fig. 3.7). Like the majority of ads from this period, both are aimed at a middle-class audience. But the readership of these two magazines could scarcely be more different, and yet the themes, symbols, and rhetoric we see in these two ads are very much akin. The Norge ad is set within a middle-class streamlined kitchen, complete with continuous white cabinets and an uninterrupted countertop surface. The chrome countertop and handles on the cupboards and drawers shine like the sterile counters one might find in a laboratory or doctor's office. If the chrome and white surfaces aren't enough to convince us of this household's hygienic propriety, then the slim, blonde, Aryan housewife surely is.

This is how a
NEW 1943 NORGE
would look in your kitchen

Startling, isn't it? But here is the new 1943 Norge Rollator Refrigerator which you are doing without.

The American behind the pair of guns can swing his turret completely around as swiftly as you can point your finger. In a flash, he can tilt his sights up to the sky or dart them toward ground or water.

No foe in air, on land, on sea is fleet enough to elude his searching aim. The target found, he can check his motion in a hair's breadth and, in the same split instant, can loose a shattering stream of fire.

Such is the new Norge for 1943. It embodies more than the actual steel and other critical materials which would have gone into your refrig-

erator. Into it have gone, too, the bold imagination, the conscientious skill, the mechanical deftness, the "know-how" which have made Norge refrigerators so fine in the past and which would have made your new Norge the finest ever built.

Your reward for doing without your new Norge is the knowledge that you, too, have helped to speed the day of Victory and Peace.

When the guns are stilled, you can be sure that Norge thinking and Norge skill, stimulated by the stern school of war, will bring you even greater satisfaction, greater convenience than you have enjoyed before.

NORGE DIVISION BORG-WARNER CORPORATION, DETROIT, MICH.

NORGE HOUSEHOLD APPLIANCES

ROLLATOR REFRIGERATION · ELECTRIC RANGES

WASHERS · GAS RANGES · HOME HEATERS

3.7. Norge advertisement, *Ladies' Home Journal,* June 1943, 105. Courtesy of Maytag. Photograph courtesy of General Research Division, The New York Public Library, Astor, Lenox, and Tilden Foundations.

Norge's example is very blunt and dramatic about its conversion by depicting its 1943 Rollator Refrigerator as a rotating machine-gun turret. Apparently, this poor, unsuspecting housewife has just walked into her civilized kitchen to encounter a brutish soldier about to fire his guns—right where her refrigerator once stood. The picture of war does not fit her neat middle-class paradigm or the hygienic contours of her streamlined kitchen. So startled is she over this bizarre juxtaposition that she recoils in horror. Thankfully, her equally genetically superior husband (just on his way to or back from the office) is there to catch her. But he can hardly believe his eyes, either.

Like other mobilization narratives, Norge applauds the prowess behind the techno-corporate order. Using managerial rhetoric typical of wartime commercial propaganda, the ad conveys that Norge's industrial management possesses an innate mental superiority ("imagination . . . skill . . . deftness . . 'know-how'") that, according to the list of superlatives, seems to border on absolute genius. How else could the techno-corporate order take the parts of a refrigerator and turn them into an efficient war machine?

> The American behind the pair of guns [seen in your kitchen] can swing his turret completely around as swiftly as you can point your finger. In a flash, he can tilt his sights. . . . No foe . . . is fleet enough to elude his searching aim. The target found, he can check his motion in a hair's breadth and, in the same split instant, can loose a shattering stream of fire. Such is the new Norge for 1943. It embodies more than the actual steel and other critical materials which would have gone into your refrigerator. Into it have gone, too, the bold imagination, the conscientious skill, the mechanical deftness, the "know-how" which have made Norge refrigerators so fine in the past and which would have made your new Norge the finest ever built.[36]

However much we'd like to think that the heroic gunner is the focal point of the ad, it is really the attractive housewife and her kitchen. Norge's mobilization story, though lengthy in its self-congratulatory prose, actually revolves around the "shock to the consumer's system" theme. From the standpoint of the mobilized corporation, "consumer shock" was a mental and physical condition peculiar to middle-class housewives. Unable to purchase any commodity when she pleased, the middle-class housewife subjected to mobilization and rationing would surely go into a histrionic tailspin. If not addressed early in the war, "consumer shock" could worsen into "brand-name amnesia." Hence, much wartime advertising included a "consumer shock" plot in which the corporation gallantly assumed the paternal responsibility of assuaging the middle-class housewife's despair by educating her on the hard "facts" of mobilization. Usually, the "shock" to her system was softened by a series of reassurances: not only should she consider her material lack a patriotic contribution, but after victory, the goods she craves will be better than ever—thanks, of course, to the company's mobilization for war:

Startling, isn't it? But here is the new 1943 Norge Rollator Refrigerator which you are doing without. . . . Your reward for doing without your new Norge is the knowledge that you, too, have helped to speed the day of Victory and Peace. When the guns are stilled, you can be sure that Norge thinking and Norge skill, stimulated by the stern school of war, will bring you even greater satisfaction, greater convenience than you have enjoyed before.[37]

The streamlined kitchen maintained the health of the perfect body, the perfect class, the ideal citizen, the consummate homemaker. But in many mobilization stories, the perfect machine's presence was simply implied by the level of sexiness conveyed by the woman in the illustration. At times, we are shown only a single well-sculpted feature of the well-born female type, which speaks volumes about the racial and class assumptions shared by the intended audience and these images' makers.

In a WPB fat salvage campaign ad, produced by the New York advertising firm J. Walter Thompson, the perfect machine/perfect body equation is summed up by a colossal feminine hand (fig. 3.8).[38] Godlike in proportions, similar to Reynolds's masculine hand, the woman to whom the hand belongs embodies the ad's slogan: "A war job only a WOMAN can do!" We get the impression from this large yet rather glamorous hand that the woman attached to it must be equally well-manicured, polished, and attractive. But it's a messy job she has, pouring nasty cooking grease from a frying pan into a howitzer.[39] The incongruity of the model hand with the dirty chore of saving grease makes it hard to believe she indulges in this kind of manual labor very often. If she does, though, one surmises that the rest of her kitchen must be so automatic that it largely performs the cooking and cleaning for her.

The 1943 logo for a scrap salvage campaign reproduced in fig. 3.1 revealed only an attractive leg attached to a woman's high-heeled pump. No kitchen, no blonde hair, no trim waist—but their absence does not deter the association of this leg with a superior genetic type. The logo not only shows the story of the streamlined kitchen's triumph over drudgery but also imparts a story of the war's underlying commitment to racial hygiene. We know that this woman represents the stereotypical hallmarks of civilization discussed before, because with a mere toe, she crushes a vilified caricature of a Japanese soldier. Like an insect, he is squashed, not by the machines of Western civilization, but by the moral strength behind its hygienic beauty. His humbling defeat is further asserted by his placement in a used tin can—refuse that would have been expendable in peacetime. Middle-class domesticity and racial purity are asserted over the enemy, making the collection of garbage into a glamorous patriotic duty—for both country and genetic purity. Trash will be transformed into weapons for war that will literally crush the enemy, thus eliminating the foreigner's threat to middle-class America's hygienic propriety.[40]

Although the streamlined woman represented a democratized form of leisure, civilization in wartime could not come off as being too "soft." The reality for most wartime women (no matter what class or race) was far from leisurely or comfortable.

3.8. Kitchen fats salvage advertisement by the War Production Board, *Advertising & Selling,* December 1943, 28.

Holding down demanding full-time jobs, they also performed all their household chores, which were made more challenging by rationing, salvaging, and shortages.[41] Mobilization experts thus created the "nice girl's" aggressive twin: a resourceful and resilient housewife who would counter the peacetime image of the leisurely woman dependent on electric appliances: "American women have had many things to make life easier for them . . . but it hasn't made them soft," argues an ad for Hoover vacuums. In response to the implied insult, a blonde, cherub-faced housewife wearing a frilly apron looks out sternly at the viewer as she rolls up her sleeves, preparing for hand-to-hand combat with her household dust and dirt: "Nobody's going to call me a Softie!" Coinciding with its message that the American housewife was more than capable of holding down the home front, Hoover avoids showing the woman comfortably using its product, as it would have done before the war.[42]

Images of ideal feminine glamour dominated wartime mobilization narratives. The April 1945 cover of *American Magazine* suggests that women's wartime activities complemented femininity and that war did not absorb a woman's time spent at her toilette. To illustrate this point, a wartime vixen, clad in army khakis and helmet, holds a compact mirror and pauses, raising the tip of her lipstick tube to her mouth. She looks up from her important makeup duty at a viewer, who has just interrupted her serious pursuit of victory.[43] The emphasis on traditional feminine identity as a woman's essential patriotic duty was especially tied in to ads from the makers of feminine hygiene products. Women's deodorants, for example, promised to "defend daintiness" no matter if a woman was "engaged in war work . . . or the important job of being a woman."[44] One advice columnist in *True Story* (a working-class woman's magazine) called her readers to attention like a drill sergeant: "Beauty Up! . . . Don't forget to accentuate femininity, when donning a new uniform. . . . Even the girl on the assembly line . . . must keep her hands soft and smooth. . . . Daintiness is more than ever a 'must.'"[45] Military recruitment brochures likewise stressed that femininity would not be lost if women joined the services. A 1944 brochure entitled *Women in the War . . . For the Final Push to Victory* claimed that female military recruits would be motivated to work on enhancing "poise and charm" once they had signed on, primarily because military dress code permitted the use of cosmetics.[46] Indeed, the Marine Corps instructed women that "lipstick and nail polish should match or blend with the scarlet hat cord [of the uniform]."[47]

Ads depicting pretty streamlined housewives and pinup types, toiling effortlessly on wartime assembly lines, littered the pages of business magazines targeted at men. This is not surprising given the number of women who entered manufacturing jobs for the first time during the war. According to historian George Lipsitz, there was a staggering 140 percent increase in such female laborers between 1940 and 1944.[48] Air Reduction's 1944 *Business Week* ad, "Seamstresses of steel," with its conventional gendered idioms, seems to cushion such shocking statistics—and their social implications for male managers (fig. 3.9). On the one hand, "Seamstresses of steel" takes the streamlined woman out of her kitchen and plants her squarely in the male domain of industry. But the presence of women's traditional domain—the kitchen—is implied because the streamlined woman's role in the factory was to be a mirror of what she had done at home. Wartime recruitment labor literature (largely aimed at middle-class housewives) asserted equations between modern domesticity and traditional male jobs in defense-industry plants.[49] A Women's Bureau pamphlet titled *What Job Is Mine on the Victory Line?* describes the assembly line as a natural extension of modern streamlined housework. The mechanization to which middle-class women were accustomed at home was akin to the automation they would find in the munitions factory, aircraft assembly plant, or shipyard:

> If you've sewed on buttons, or made buttonholes, on a machine, you can learn to do spot welding on airplane parts. . . . If you've used an electric mixer in your kitchen, you can learn to run a drill press. . . . American women, more used to mechanical gadgets in their homes than any other women in the world, are fortunate in having experience to help them make a record as soldiers of production in war work.[50]

Husbands and male employers resisted the idea of hiring women (particularly white middle-class housewives) to perform roles in heavy industry. Advertisements such as Air Reduction's attempted to reassure the menfolk that women could do a "man's job" for the war's duration and still remain essentially feminine—especially if they already were the ideal type.[51] In the ad, one welder's streamlined nature is obscured by her bulky coveralls. That the worker is a woman is only revealed through the name, "Vera," painted on her headgear. A co-worker in the background looks up from her blowtorch, revealing a pretty face and pinup's physique. So genetically and socially superior is the perfect streamlined woman that her makeup doesn't run despite the heat of a blowtorch—nor can men's coveralls obscure the inherent attractiveness of her physical form.

What we learn from mobilization narratives is that victory is dependent on the technology behind modern civilization: the comforts, conveniences, efficiency, and leisure found in the middle-class home. This technology, whether in the home or on the battlefield, aids in perpetuating a highly evolved, superior race and class. Such an argument, in which the perfect body is paired with the perfect machine, is made time and again in wartime narratives of progress; we shall see this suggestive coupling in reconversion advertising as well. Juxtaposing the efficient machine with the efficient body type was typical of a human-engineering agenda. Whether mobilization experts openly ascribed to human-engineering practices or not, they insist that the correlation between streamlined perfection and efficiency lies in the site of civilization's cradle—the middle-class home—and its womb—the ideal female body. The housewife's glamorous, streamlined appearance and the absence of hard labor reflected her top-ranking social and genetic status, and this stature in turn reflected the triumph of the machine and the techno-corporate order. According to the ads, this superiority certainly would manifest itself in the form of an Allied victory. As Lewis Mumford told us earlier, "War . . . is the health of the machine." And indeed, according to wartime

Seamstresses of steel ....

Using the dazzling electric arc for a needle...molten ribbons of metal for thread, women welders in war industries everywhere fashion sturdy steel battle-dress for fighting machines.

Today their traditional feminine dexterity—and their modern steel-sewing implements—are meeting a crucial need of the nation. Tomorrow this war-proven fabrication method will realize important savings in time, cost and materials in the manufacture of countless metal products.

Modern equipment for this improved fabricating process is but one of many products of Air Reduction.

★ BUY UNITED STATES WAR BONDS ★

AIR REDUCTION SALES COMPANY
MAGNOLIA AIRCO GAS PRODUCTS CO.
NATIONAL CARBIDE CORPORATION
PURE CARBONIC, INCORPORATED
THE OHIO CHEMICAL & MFG. CO.
WILSON WELDER & METALS CO., INC

AIRCO   **AIR REDUCTION**
60 EAST 42nd STREET   NEW YORK 17, N. Y.

OXYGEN, ACETYLENE AND OTHER ATMOSPHERIC GASES • GAS WELDING AND CUTTING APPARATUS • CALCIUM CARBIDE
ARC WELDING MACHINES AND SUPPLIES • CARBON DIOXIDE • "DRY ICE" • ANAESTHETIC AND THERAPEUTIC GASES AND APPARATUS

3.9. Air Reduction Company advertisement, *Business Week,* 30 September 1944, 91. Reproduced by permission of The BOC Group, Inc. © The BOC Group, Inc. 2005. All rights reserved.

advertising, war would lead to even "healthier" products for advancing middle-class civilization.

By showing how domestic products were facilitating higher levels of efficiency for the Allied military machine, the business community met three major objectives. First, it stirred American patriotic fervor by demonstrating how commodities generated by the techno-corporate order possessed the power to win the war. As a result, big business was able to restore America's battered faith in Machine Age progress and build the public's confidence that the Allies, with the aid of home front management, would triumph. In so doing, business leaders were able to capitalize on this revived faith in mechanized progress, thereby accomplishing their second objective—to reconstruct the techno-corporate order's tarnished reputation. By aligning trademarks and brand names with particular war matériel, manufacturers showed their civilian customers and manufacturing clients how generous was their industrial sacrifice toward victory. With renewed public faith in American progress and business, manufacturers were also able to satisfy their third objective: to restore public acceptance of an economy run according to tenets of the techno-corporate order, as opposed to the state capitalism proposed by Roosevelt and the New Deal. In so doing, manufacturers sought to restructure the public perception of American progress and lay the groundwork for the much-feared but plausible scenario of postwar depression. If free enterprise, industry, and big business could win the war, then they could also build a successful bridge toward higher standards of living and democratize progress for all the "right" American types.

The business community's sanitized mobilization narratives were not free of hype. Accompanying the details of how the parts of refrigerators or girdles could give the Allies the advantage was a great deal of patriotic baggage that cloaked corporate ulterior motives. The conflict compelled a symbol management strategy in which domestic progress was depicted as a weapon of war in order to excite public patriotism. Such a link between the products of the home and their contribution to the battlefield also attempted to build bridges of consumer loyalty and thus were intended to ignite a consumer buying frenzy once victory was achieved. These narratives sometimes implicitly but often openly argued that consumer products that had proven their superiority in battle could surely increase levels of domestic convenience, comfort, and efficiency once they had returned from their military jobs overseas. As a result of wartime advertising, the techno-corporate order would have a public record of its contribution to victory and would be celebrated, along with its domestic products, as the heroic engines who helped the Allies win the war.

The home front battle over who would control the postwar economy and the war's commercial fallout—business or government?—would be largely waged in wartime narratives about the reconversion process. Although mobilization narratives pointed to the progress of the past, reconversion narratives offered a tantalizing future of domestic improvements resulting from the war. Manufacturers and the industrial design profession (along with colleagues in the advertising field) played a prominent role in showing how visions of the postwar world could be used to the business community's advantage and to the detriment of the New Deal. As subsequent chapters show, some manufacturers and industrial designers used the concept of the postwar "world of tomorrow" as a weapon to secure the business community's ascendancy over the New Deal and its reform agenda.

PART TWO

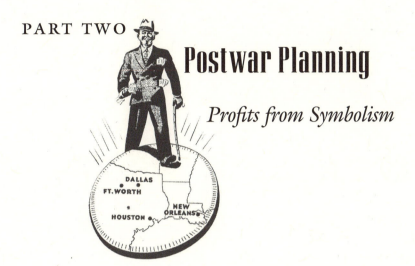

Postwar Planning

Profits from Symbolism

One of the perpetrators of the [postwar] dreamworld, of course, was the advertiser who had no current consumer goods to sell . . . and yet was charged with the responsibility of keeping his company's name fresh in the public memory. The adman had a budget beyond his wildest dreams. . . . After he had said what there was to say about war bonds many times over, he had nothing to talk about but the future, and in so doing he naturally followed the functional line of his craft—the creation of desire.[1]

The author of "What Happened to the Dreamworld?" lobbed this scathing critique in 1947. Speculations about postwar living, he tells us, blossomed uncontrollably across the pages of wartime magazines, newspapers, and promotional books. Despite the outrageousness of some postwar plans, envisioning a "dreamworld" was certainly better than harping on economic catastrophe and a postwar depression, which many Americans, even business leaders, feared. It seems that the war was ancillary to the motives behind reconversion narratives that promised a miraculous "world of tomorrow," an assessment with which the author of "What Happened to the Dreamworld?" would most likely have agreed.

What prompted business leaders to pay so much attention to postwar markets well before victory? Weren't mobilization and the present war keeping them busy enough? With their industries heavily committed to war production, manufacturers had only two things to sell—their roles in the present war and the future peace. *Advertising & Selling* articulated the dilemma in 1942: "With nothing to sell the public, advertising must concern itself with intangibles."[2] Reconversion narratives went a step further than their mobilization counterparts. Although mobilization ads were about "war information," and both types of narratives were intended to keep trade names and brands alive, reconversion tales associated a given product or industry with winning the war while crafting a spectacular "world of tomorrow" based on a company's wartime contributions. Such advertising fictions did not simply recoup business's public reputation by highlighting its corporate patriotism, as mobilization narratives did; they focused on building an intimate future with the consumer. Sustaining a competitive edge while wooing "Mrs. Postwar Consumer" sparked the struggle for winning a postwar reputation during the war. A 1944 ad, "How to Kill a Business Without a Word," sums up the way in which consumer engineers coerced prospective business clients into publicizing speculative plans for the postwar future. The ad illustrates a chilling rejection of the postwar businessman who had failed to advertise during the war: "Are you going to be a stranger to Mrs. Tomorrow? Are you going to wait until peace to let her know about the things you want her to buy? Do you think it's smart to come cold to your biggest market and try to crash it, when competition will be so tough? Mrs. Tomorrow should get to know you today."[3] In the ad, a colossal feminine hand (with a delicate bracelet at the wrist) reaches out of an ominous, black background, and, as in the legend of Caesar at the Coliseum gladiator games, she turns her manicured thumb down with impunity on the unplanned postwar future.

Similar to mobilization narratives, "world of tomorrow" forecasts were used by the techno-corporate order to further its own political, social, and economic agendas.[4] Reconversion narratives spun by forecasters and commercial propagandists traversed a rhetorical pattern similar to the stories about America's "miracle" mobilization—both were described in terms that evoked a technological sublime. The symbolic contours of postwar progress were controlled and their underlying meanings manipulated not only for reasons of financial gain but also to secure a more influential position for corporate authority in shaping the parameters of American life. Profit and class motives merged with a wartime propagandistic function, allowing the managerial elite to prosper both financially and symbolically.

4 Glimpses into a "Better America"

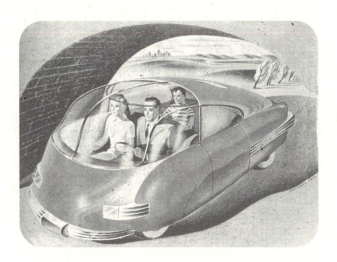

The coming year [1943] will be filled with violent conflict—yet with *high promise of better things.* . . . Two years ago I spoke in my annual message of *four freedoms.* . . . *The third freedom—freedom from want* . . . means that . . . when war production is converted to the economy of peace, [the men and women overseas] will have the right to expect full employment. . . . *They do not want a post-war America which suffers from undernourishment or slums—or the dole.* . . . In this war of survival we must keep before our minds not only the evil things we fight against but *the good things we are fighting for.* We fight to retain a great past—and we fight to gain a greater future.[1]

What did Roosevelt mean when he said that the war would yield the "promise of better things"? For what "good things" were Americans fighting? Here, Roosevelt, in a speech made early in 1943, hints at the revolutionary effect that wartime production promised to make on postwar standards of living. The outward signs of poverty, such as substandard housing, unbalanced diets, unsanitary conditions, and the social diseases they accompanied, would be eradicated because the "miracle" of war production would usher in a new era and fully democratize a middle-class standard of living. This "world of tomorrow" was dependent on the time "when war production" was "converted to the economy of peace," and would begin churning out not simply the new and improved but also the more affordable refrigerators, washing machines, automobiles, dishwashers, garbage disposals, plastics, synthetic fabrics, and prefabricated houses at an unprecedented rate.

Both mobilization and reconversion narratives encouraged the belief that Americans were fighting for unfettered access to hygienic propriety and the ensuing social betterment that such revolutionary changes were bound to generate. Postwar forecasters and commercial propagandists argued that if war production could be channeled into peace, it could easily solve material inequities (as recounted by Roosevelt) and secure a more orderly and hygienic world free of irrational drudgery, vulgar filth, unscientific housing, and social decay. Thus, the ideals behind why Americans should support and fight the war were cemented in the pursuit of a "better America," made more efficient, rational, and clean through the material progress that would win the war and simultaneously generate a social evolution during peacetime.

In December 1940, about two years before Roosevelt's speech, designer Walter Dorwin Teague had proclaimed that the ultimate hygienic revolution lay far in the future. Although dreams for social uplift were never scarce, Teague explained, the manufacturing processes, infrastructure, and materials needed to democratize hygienic propriety were prohibitively expensive, and put the "world of tomorrow" well beyond the reach of those whom it was meant to liberate: "Our better world may be expected to make equally available for everybody such rare things as . . . emancipation from drudgery and a gracious setting for daily life . . . bodily well-being and mental equanimity. But since even such simple conveniences as modern kitchens and bathrooms have not yet become general in America, attainment of these more difficult objectives by a majority of our people is *far in the future*."[2]

Why, shortly after Teague's pessimistic forecast, did many Americans—from the president to the average person—believe that a social utopia lay just around the corner? American production was concentrated on winning a war on foreign soil, rather than on solving poverty, drudgery, substandard health, poor housing, and "mental equanimity" on the home front. The answer lies in the fantastic details of mobilization narratives, whose authors gave the general impression that the war had kindled an industrial metamorphosis, accelerating manufacturing's evolutionary leap. Praised as incarnating a herculean "miracle" virtually overnight, America's factory output was described as surpassing former production records.[3] Between 1939 (the year Germany invaded Poland) and 1945 (when the war ended), America's gross national product (GNP) more than doubled from $91 billion to $214 billion. Naturally, the wartime GNP was based on production geared for military consumption, and the proportion of war-related manufacturing soared from 2 percent of the GNP before the war to 40 percent by 1943, when the total GNP was $193 billion. The industrial yield behind these numbers fattened each year by more than 15 percent; by comparison, yearly production had increased by only 7 percent during World War I.[4] The amount of goods (albeit slated for military consumption) underscores the impressive wartime GNP data, as shown in table 4.1.

Wartime propagandists claimed that military demands had stirred America's inherent ingenuity, which had lagged during the Depression but was certainly not extinct. Mobilization had miraculously accelerated experimentation and invention, expediting the birth of new materials and new assembly methods. In some cases, mobilization had induced a radical tabula rasa, in which companies retooling for war production abandoned old machinery made obsolete by the unusual needs of modern warfare. Complete production lines were often redesigned and new facilities built from scratch. The entire process acted as a rejuvenating stimulus to American manufacturers, increasing their efficiency and productivity by thoroughly modernizing assembly methods and standards. Such a utopian industrialization was once seen as a small point on the distant horizon and as the scientific spectacle of world's fairs. But now this imagined future was racing toward the present.

Hindsight reminds us of the extent to which romanticized commercial hype inflated the accomplishments of wartime production. John Jeffries, in his 1996 book *Wartime America,* demythologizes the enthusiastic assumptions. Wartime industrial "miracles," Jeffries reports, primarily evolved because "underutilized productive resources" and labor were finally put to work. The much acclaimed increase in inventive genius and productivity—a substantial 25 percent—was gained by "new technologies and capital equipment, economies of scale, better management of productive resources, and the sense of common cause."[5] Yet it was the *celebration* of mobilization "miracles," Jeffries concedes, that enhanced faith in America's economy, business, industry, institutional authorities, and large bureaucratic organizations.[6] A buoyant attitude, it seems, was even more critical to victory and a successful reconversion than any monetary or material gain. Wartime

Table 4.1. Wartime Production Figures

Airplanes	300,000
Ammunition	41 billion rounds
Bombs	6 million tons
Landing craft	80,000
Large artillery weapons	370,000
Machine guns	2.6 million
Merchant ships	5,600
Military trucks	2.4 million
Small arms	20 million
Steel	434 million tons
Tanks and armored cars	100,000

Data quoted from John W. Jeffries, *Wartime America: The World War II Home Front* (Chicago: Ivan R. Dee, 1996), 45.

commercial propagandists seemed to have sensed this and were quick to capitalize on America's renewed optimism in its Machine Age.

It is not surprising that such unbridled confidence—so antithetical to the Depression years—intensified among business leaders and consumers. Consumers' expectations for access to fatter paychecks, abundant job prospects, and higher standards of living were fueled by the momentous rate of wartime employment. Although modernizing and building one's dream home were on hold for the duration, mobilization was achieving victory not only on the battlefield, we are told, but also in the pocketbooks of the lower classes—a segment engulfing a large chunk of the population. Tessie Agan in her 1939 domestic science textbook gives the percentages of Americans living below what she ranked a "comfortable" level. According to the 1934 statistics she cites, just over 40 percent of the U.S. population was living at subsistence and poverty levels. Only 35.7 percent ranked at "minimum comfort," while a mere 13.7 percent hovered at "moderate circumstances." Less than 10 percent enjoyed "comfortable" to "wealthy" lives.[7] Employment, modern amenities, and basic necessities, which had been hard, if not impossible, for many poor Americans to attain during the Depression, were now increasingly available because of the desperate need for labor in war production facilities. C. W. Stuart of General Electric's Home Bureau alleviates Agan's bleak picture somewhat, stating that "only 65.4 percent of the population" in the United States "lived in electric-lighted houses" in 1932. By 1942, however, this "percentage had increased to 80.3."[8] War was already delivering a better America for millions of workers and their families whose prewar lives had been substandard.

Such a dramatic change in the population's economic status made businessmen take notice. Like manufacturers, architects were scanning the postwar horizon and sniffing the economic winds. Kenneth Stowell, the editor in chief of *Architectural Record*, presents us with an optimistic assessment, not quite a year after Pearl Harbor, of what postwar business could expect: "Even our President has forecast 'lower standards of living' for Americans for the duration. . . . Yet there are millions now who are earning more than they have in years, enjoying relative prosperity, saving through War Bonds as added security for the future. . . . I believe there will be, and already is, a 'higher standard of living' in America."[9]

Perceptions in the moment sometimes eclipse critical facts. As the economic historian Robert Higgs asserts, John Jeffries challenges the assumption that mobilization was a source of genuine prosperity. The high production, payroll, and employment figures were not substantive signs of economic well-being. The economic "bed of roses" associated with the war did not occur until soldiers (included in wartime payroll and employment statistics)[10] were mustered out of service and into civilian jobs, thereby raising the rate of "supply and demand" employment, as opposed to "command" employment geared to meeting military needs. Despite popular assumptions, the wartime economy, as Higgs and Jeffries tell us, did not typify *true* prosperity, especially since consumers were assailed with "hidden inflation" such as the black market or government price controls; "deteriorating quality" of services, consumer choice, and everyday commodities; "scarce goods" due to rationing and substitution; "long working hours"; and "wartime incon-

veniences" such as long lines, blackouts, and geographic and familial "disloca-
tions."[11] The war may have invigorated the GNP, but it also increased the cost of
living by 30 percent.

Discomforts aside, mobilization indeed produced a higher yield of potential
consumers by raising wage levels. But it had also stifled consumers' ability to immediately spend what they had earned. To forecasters and commercial propagandists, this meant that prospective buyers of the "world of tomorrow" now extended well beyond the parameters of the middle class. This realization of the
presence of a new mass market roused the techno-corporate order's hopes for
consistent demand and greater profits in the postwar economy. Designer Walter
Dorwin Teague explains to us that years of economic depression, stagnant industry, and material want had primed Americans' faith in the possibilities for postwar
progress. Fresh markets were just waiting to be tapped once victory was won:

> In addition to the backlog of needs created by the war, there is a far
> greater backlog accumulated through the years of depression, and one
> still greater created by the inability of a large part of our population ever
> to attain what we like to think of as the American standard of living. . . .
> Much more than half of our population has permanently gone without
> many of the things we think of as necessities. . . . The market for goods in
> America is far greater than we have yet realized.[12]

By 1943, with American war production in full swing, Teague revised his time-
table for the "world of tomorrow's" arrival. Progress, as the heroic progeny of the
war, would undoubtedly make the dream of mass-produced prosperity, social
harmony, and domestic utopia attainable:

> We're discovering and perfecting new arts and new techniques every day,
> and when they have served to blast our enemies off the face of the earth
> they can be used to make the earth blossom again. . . . We shall end this
> war with our hands full of means for the building of a new world beyond
> anything we ever dreamed of in our most exalted moments. . . . This war
> is the end of an old world and the beginning of another.[13]

Along with commercial propaganda about the wartime renaissance in American industry, forecasters assumed that the technology experienced by women in
modern production facilities would galvanize female aspirations for advanced
comforts in their homes. *Science Digest* reveals to us how factory automation and
the modern industrial work environment encouraged defense-plant workers to
expect domestic versions of the machinery responsible for the "miracles" of war
production. Mobilization had habituated female consumers to such higher levels
of technology that they would soon demand the same efficiencies for their postwar
homes: "Time spent in working in air-conditioned, fluorescent-lighted war plants,
for instance, will create new acceptance for the same conveniences at home."[14] *Science Digest* also tells us how mobilization transformed the female consumer into a

professional efficiency expert, whose war-won edification would keep designers and manufacturers scrambling to perpetually improve labor-saving devices and convenience products: "Some gain in women's mechanical-mindedness as a result of war-plant experience, plus wartime lessons gained from keeping a job and home going simultaneously, assure greater demand for automatic, time-saving, labor-saving equipment."[15]

Glimpses into a "better America" galvanized patriotic support for the war effort, which had become symbolically tied to the heroic image of corporate America and its power to raise the average consumer to the top of the hygienic hierarchy. Consumer confidence in the future was thus nurtured by the fertilizing promises of the fast track to social evolution, and it was wartime technological advances that were credited as the key to democratizing this evolutionary ascent.[16] Because all American industries had made moderate to substantial investments in their mobilization, it behooved them to contrive an image of reconversion in which the past was characterized as a stultifying pathology, distanced in the evolutionary spectrum from the ideal: the future. At the same time, however, this future would be engineered to accommodate traditional assumptions, especially existing racial and gender biases. Thus, those manufacturers with industries heavily committed to the war effort would attempt to secure postwar sales by showing how corporate benevolence would channel war-proved products into the postwar mission of elevating the average consumer beyond current standards while rigorously maintaining the social status quo.

Reconversion and the Military Endorsement

The techno-corporate order believed that the test of war would provide an excellent merchandising tool. Parker James, writing for *Advertising & Selling* in 1943, reinforced the enthusiasm behind this promotional concept when he wrote, "A product which has stood up during wartime has earned its right to postwar popularity."[17] The main argument behind such reconversion selling points was that the "miracles" credited with winning the war had freed Asia and Europe and thus could easily emancipate the American housewife. Thus, a product's military endorsement was usually underscored by a host of hygienic household benefits. A 1944 article in *Better Homes and Gardens* typifies the hygienic imperative in reconversion narratives where the war was conceptualized as a messianic soap expected to erase all traces of filth, disorder, and inconvenience. Despite improvements since the turn of the century, the author writes, "we're still battling the age-old problem of dirt, disorder and inconvenience. Now, through application of many wartime discoveries to peacetime living, we homemakers will be able to purge our lives of clutter and useless routine."[18]

The hygienic imperative in reconversion narratives was often attended by obsessions with an effortless future. A 1943 *House Beautiful* article, "Are You Learning the Language of Tomorrow?" instructs the consumer on the lessons of leisure to be gained from the war. The author, John Sasso, personifies the war as a paternal manager, leading the befuddled consumer through a magic fairyland of war-developed products. It seems as though progress has advanced faster than civilization, leaving the lives it was meant to improve awash in confusion and in need of accelerated learning: "The changes that will come in our lives after the War is over are going to be greater than our minds are now able to grasp. . . . Do you know where these new products and sciences will alter your life, your home, how they will serve you?"[19] Sasso is typical of forecasters and commercial propagandists who scripted the war as a means of improving one's imperfect and burdensome lifestyle. Regardless of one's class, life in the present was obviously inferior compared with the future. Sasso's didactic tone is also typical of reconversion tales. Despite casting the reader as a dependent schoolchild, Sasso insists that wartime developments promised to engender her future independence and make her world easy to discipline and control. As Sasso tells us, wartime "miracles," spun from laboratory secrets, would facilitate a worry-free world in which the consumer's authority over her personal environment would increase while her domestic workload and anxieties would diminish.

Casting wartime developments in the role of servant was often a means to weigh the past against the future and characterize the war as an enhanced stepping-stone in civilization's evolutionary climb. In the promotional book *Miracles Ahead!* Norman Carlisle and Frank Latham assumed that the wartime "servant problem" was ubiquitous to their readership. Servants for middle-class households, they inform readers, were scarce because domestics could find better-paying jobs and improved working conditions in defense plants. The servantless household was the anticipated norm in reconversion narratives—despite the fact that most Americans did without paid domestic labor anyway. Nonetheless, this dilemma would be solved with war-tested electronic "servants," making all drudgery (either the maid's or the housewife's) obsolete in the postwar future: "In the home there will be more than a dozen swift, silent electronic 'maids' at the beck and call of the homemaker, freeing her from the drudgery of housekeeping."[20]

J. D. Ratcliff, writing for *Woman's Home Companion* in 1943, avoids the class issue of the "servant problem" altogether by picturing postwar products as cooperative and efficient attendants. Such automatons' sole purpose is to dispel the pathologies of drudgery and discomfort so that the postwar consumer might logically advance to a more leisured lifestyle: "You must be thrilled by the comfort-making labor-saving devices planned for your home of tomorrow, just waiting [for] the war's end to move in. . . . The good-by to the drudgery of dusting, while an air cleaner does it automatically; the end of cold draughty houses as electron tubes warm your family, even with all windows open."[21] Ratcliff assumes that the reader is already primed for postwar progress—even as early as July 1943, almost a year before the Allied invasion of Europe. The statement "You must be thrilled" implies that the wartime consumer has her attention focused exclusively on the future with just one aim in sight: *her* personal victory over the fascist demands of scientific housework.

Discussion of products planned for postwar consumption also typically ascribed to them the power to make other industries extinct. *Science News Letter,* in its 1943 article "Post-War Promises," reported that expendability was an extraordinary bonus born from wartime research and development. Fabrics that required less cleaning ultimately would lead to unparalleled efficiency in the development of disposable clothing and the obsolescence of the Laundromat: "All of us may be wearing glass fiber textiles in a post-war world. . . . Glass fiber is an important war material. . . . We may even come to the day when we can have new fresh clothes whenever we wish to change such synthetic 'linen.' . . . Present laundries might give way to clothing factories that have speedy production lines for stamping out by the millions such expendable outfits."[22] Such "miracle" fabrics, which had proven their superiority in war, possessed an indestructible power over most forms of decay and filth and therefore would make doing laundry an inconvenience of the past:

> Rayon and nylon are the pioneers of a great number of synthetic textiles which will compete strongly with natural fibers in coming years. . . . And these chemically treated clothes will be creaseproof, waterproof, fire-proof, verminproof, and even stainproof. Farewell to moths and cleaning bills! . . . The use of melamine resins and other plastics may give us paper shirts and other articles that will be attractive but so cheap that we can throw them away when soiled.[23]

Perhaps unconsciously, but noticeably, reconversion narratives pit progress against antiprogress through language culled from a popularized evolutionary model. In this case, rayon and nylon are the sturdy "pioneers" that "compete strongly" with their ancestors, "natural fibers," which they ultimately surpass in the evolutionary and cleanliness spectrums. Science is portrayed as the heroic protagonist: "chemically treated clothes" are not only physically superior ("creaseproof, waterproof, fireproof" and "attractive") but they also deflect the contagions wrought by vile pests such as vermin and moths, as well as stains. Nature certainly comes under fire in reconversion narratives where sterilized science rules the "world of tomorrow" and where wartime laboratories purge the future of any social maladies or physical imperfections.

Plastic World in the Making

Plastics manufacturers were anxious to win the favorable appreciation of designers and other industrialists responsible for adapting new "miracle" synthetics to various domestic and manufacturing markets. Promotional narratives tried to persuade wartime readers that a plastic future was far superior to the present and certainly exceeded the defect-riddled past. However, many home front consumers, having used synthetic products as substitutes for scarce wood or metal, had discovered that plastics' reputation for perfection was flawed. Despite wartime publicity trumpeting the unsurpassed "miracles" of plastics, certain synthetics cracked, melted, or discolored, thus exposing the overblown nature of their manufacturers' claims and laying the groundwork for postwar consumer rejection.[24] As a result, propagandists for the plastics field were compelled to counter the negative experiences of many wartime consumers, for whom the words "plastics" and "synthetics" had become synonymous with "lemon."[25] Manufacturers and designers (especially packaging engineers) sought to generate a mass postwar demand for their new synthetic products and inspire consumer confidence in an industry that (at least on the home front) had not lived up to its claims.[26] In spite of their uneven performance, wartime substitute materials made of plastic were promoted as performing better than the wooden or metal products they were intended to replace for the duration of the war.[27]

Propagandists for plastics catered to a human-engineering value system, adopting a persuasive rhetoric similar to that used by forecasters in other fields. They painted a picture of a "new and improved" America in which sterilized artificiality, proven superior to the natural world, would revolutionize domesticity and guarantee one's ascent into hygienic propriety. Wording that praised traits of maximized comfort, convenience, and control was included among the descriptions of the "miracles" intended to improve life in the postwar world. But showing how *ultimate* cleanliness and optimum levels of sanitation could be won from the war was the most popular rhetorical formula used by forecasters in the plastics industry.[28] This war-tested material would make it easier for households to stay clean and for the housewife not only to maintain but to surpass current middle-class standards of living.

Carl C. Austin, in a 1944 *Modern Plastics* article, certainly applies standard hygienic metaphors in his story of plastics' qualities, but he highlights the healthy signifier of stamina, which was almost more important than the ability to repel the scourge of dirt:

> Not long after our men began fighting in the Pacific area they discovered that they were facing not one enemy but two. . . . [A] screen cloth was needed which would withstand the rigors of tropical climate and yet have strength and durability. . . . The answer . . . was finally found in a plastic insect cloth which has become an important weapon of war in many U.S. outposts. . . . In developing this screen for domestic use after the war, it is believed [that] its [light] weight . . . flexibility . . . [and] smooth surface [which] does not collect dirt easily, and . . . can be quickly washed off with ordinary soap and water [will prove to be strong assets for the postwar consumer].[29]

Austin eschews simply stating that the plastic screen is durable. Instead, he composes a picture of masculine strength in its prime, fighting off the intense, yet still irrational, climate of the primitive jungle ("withstand the rigors of tropical climate"). Surely, this is a product that has earned a high place in the evolutionary spectrum! That such a plastic would deem to become a mere household article after the war is a miracle in itself.

Plastics were clothed in guises other than that of heroic supermen. Columbia Plastics in its 1945 ad "After Mars . . . A Rendezvous with Venus" renders the mystique of plastics in a feminine, erotic aura and promises to revolutionize glamour and beauty with its war-won knowledge in the plastics field (fig. 4.1). The sanitary and durable traits of Columbia's plastics (produced in "unrivaled facilities") will create a "world of tomorrow" free of the hazards, ugliness, and imperfections wrought by (feeble) nonplastic products. Unlike other reconversion narratives that juxtapose the battlefield with the postwar future,[30] the Columbia ad depicts only the end results of its wartime research along with the promise to "pioneer the road to new perfection." Here, a slender, outstretched hand offers a perfect world of sterilized, unblemished beauty (the hygienic spoils of victory) to a seductive brunette, who seems to look at her colorful postwar trophies with aloof interest. In this case, the promises of plastics are geared toward improving the female physique by maximizing glamour, which will transform the average consumer into a feminine ideal—purportedly as depicted in the ad. Unlike other feminine icons in reconversion advertisements, however, this alluring protagonist is a brunette vamp; usually the first choice for the ideal feminine type was blonde.[31] This diversion from the normative mold of the tall, thin, pale-skinned blonde causes us to intensify our critique of the ideological implications behind this selection. Though the blondes in other ads are rendered sexy, this brunette vamp's seductiveness is far more dark and primal along the evolutionary chain of womanhood.[32] She is the femme fatale: her sex appeal borders on the sinister and thus the improper, the unrespectable, and the unhygienic—definitely not representative of the middle class. Is it possible to imagine this Jane Russell look-alike slinging a mop in the name of scientific housekeeping? Not at all! Perhaps the depiction of the glamour of plastics in a rather primordial and dangerous light was accidental. Or did it matter? After all, the publication in which the femme fatale appeared was geared for an industrial clientele and male-dominated trades, rather than housewives.[33]

The wartime image of a plastic postwar world echoed desires for not only hygienic, durable beauty but also familiarity and control. In Goodyear's plastic "world of tomorrow," war-developed Pliofoam expedites healthy home ownership in the suburbs (fig. 4.2). Pliofoam, a featherweight insulating material, forms the building blocks of a socially hygienic future. Not only is this building material safe and clean, but also, compared to bricks, cement, and lumber, it is so light and easy to use that even a child can handle it like a toy. Goodyear tries to persuade other manufacturers that its plastic is the means toward hygienic propriety, not simply in terms of its clean application, superlative durability, and ease of use, but also because it can expedite the building of *single-family* homes.[34] Social evolution into the middle class demanded this ideal building type, separated from commerce by the subdivision and from neighbors by a bucolic lawn. Goodyear underscores this anti-urban sentiment and cements it with its choice of the ideal little girl: the Shirley Temple type, innocent, playful, and white with wavy golden locks.[35] The Shirley Temple icon also stresses the "normality" of a house built with unfamiliar plastics. In this regard, Goodyear attempts to make the unknown and fantastic features of postwar utopia seem realistic and inviting. Emotional appeals to traditional childhood play, safely segregated environments, and doll-like icons make the transition into the "world of tomorrow" much smoother.

4.1. Columbia Plastics advertisement, *Modern Plastics,* March 1945, 24.

It's less than 8 times heavier than air!

ANOTHER REASON FOR GOODYEAR LEADERSHIP

Meet the new lightweight champion of the insulation world. It's an amazing new plastic called Pliofoam. A whole cubic foot of it weighs considerably less than a pound.

Born in the Goodyear Research Laboratory, Pliofoam is already at war. For one thing, it is being used as a wing filler in airplanes. It is placed around the bullet-puncture-sealing fuel cells. If enemy bullets rip through these tanks, Pliofoam instantly soaks up the few drops of gas that might leak out before the tank seals the bullet-hole.

Pliofoam—T.M. The Goodyear Tire & Rubber Company

Because of its astonishing light weight — and its proved efficiency as a heat, cold and sound insulator — Pliofoam is destined for many important post-war uses. You may be finding it in homes, refrigerators, railroad cars, airplanes, automobiles, buses.

The development of Pliofoam is another dramatic demonstration of how Goodyear Research works constantly — in widely diversified fields — to bring Americans — in war or peace — new, more efficient, more economical, more useful products.

A pioneer in rubber, Goodyear for a long time has been a busy worker in many other vital fields—plastics, metals, textiles, chemicals, aircraft . . . and from the new Goodyear Research Laboratory "the best is yet to come."

BUY WAR BONDS AND BUY FOR KEEPS

THE GREATEST NAME IN RUBBER

4.2. Goodyear Pliofoam advertisement, *Business Week,* 26 August 1944, back cover. Used with permission of The Goodyear Tire & Rubber Company.

Such images of the future argued that if clean, convenient products such as plastics were used to achieve higher standards in design and efficiency, then a secure and lasting world order would ensue. The frictionless, sterilized surfaces of plastics would automatically engender a healthy, smoothly running household and society. V. E. Yarsley and E. G. Couzens in their 1942 *Science Digest* article "The Expanding Age of Plastics" articulate for us the sentimental values that manufacturers affixed to a material not many Americans had used. Departing slightly from typical rhetorical formulas that patronized the reader's intelligence, Yarsley and Couzens narrate a vision of the future as seen through the experience of a confident protagonist of the plastics age. The virtues of plastics are embodied in the highly evolved character of "Plastic Man." Descriptions of his world imply that life in 1942 is far more primitive than the hygienic postwar future where every object (and even humans) has been genetically improved by the science of plastics:

> Imagine a dweller in the "Plastics Age" that is already upon us. . . . "Plastic Man," will [be born] into a world of color and bright and shining surfaces . . . [with] no sharp edges . . . [and] no crevices to harbor dirt or germs. His parents will see to it that he is surrounded on every side by tough, safe, clean material. . . . He sits in a new kind of school room . . . at a moulded [*sic*] desk, warm and smooth and clean to the touch. . . . The windows of this school, curtained with plastic-faced cloth entirely grease- and dirt-proof, are unbreakable. . . . Like his home, too, the plastic floors are silent and dustless. . . . Outside the home, the same universal rule of plastics holds . . . because of its durability, surface attractiveness and eminent suitability for clean smooth design. . . . In how much brighter and cleaner a world he has lived than that which preceded the plastics age.[36]

Plastics' value is enhanced by their possession of both male and female characteristics. Yarsley and Couzens feminize the smooth, warm surfaces with "no sharp edges," gentle like a mother's touch, while plastics' masculinity is revealed through their toughness and safety, like a father's protective embrace. Indeed, the authors give Plastic Man parents—familial icons of cozy security in a highly artificial and foreign environment. Despite its unknowns, this is a world one can trust: it's unbreakable, and it's universal, equally applied inside and out. Yarsley and Couzens, writing only one year after Pearl Harbor, composed a scenario that completely contrasts with the previous years of economic depression and hardship. With the war years looming before them, home front readers could be expected to respond positively to the comforting metaphors and utopian promises of a hygienic future ruled by plastics.

Given the past to which all postwar products were compared, we should not be surprised that plastics were imbued with the power not only to revolutionize the household, office, and factory, but also to liberate the world from rivalries over natural resources—tensions that give rise to war. According to Yarsley and

Couzens, the universal application of plastics would raise the standard of order and civilization throughout the entire world, as if scientific housekeeping's exacting practices had been applied to organizing the global economy:

> [The world of Plastic Man] is a world free from moth and rust and full of color, a world largely built up of synthetic materials made from the most universally distributed substances, a world in which nations are more and more independent of localized national resources. . . . When the dust and smoke of the present conflict have blown away . . . we shall see growing up around us a new, brighter, cleaner and more beautiful world, an environment not subject to the haphazard distribution of nations' resources but built to order; the perfect expression of scientific control, the Plastics Age.[37]

Although efficiency was lauded by forecasters as the most desirable quality of any postwar product, Yarsley and Couzens emphasize the authoritative role of "scientific control" in expediting an efficient world. "Haphazard distribution" of resources, such as verminlike "moth and rust," are the tainted artifacts of an unfit society—rightly headed for extinction—thanks to the plastics born of war.

Echoing Yarsley and Couzens's emphasis on the powers of science in the "Plastics Age," Dow Chemical in its wartime advertisement for Saran Film suggests to us that its plastic wrap is endowed with the revolutionary ability to save the world from global chaos, just as it promises to safely deliver the machines engineering the Allied victory (fig. 4.3). In this case, the earth and a machine gun, encased in clear plastic wrap, are shown as enduring and surviving (thanks to Dow) the stress of a frightening torrential downpour, presumably a metaphor for the apocalyptic nature of war.[38] Dow's ad conveys the idea that the universal application of its protective Saran Film will dispel confusion and mess by extracting order, clarity, security, and durability from hygienic technologies developed for war.

Likewise, DuPont, in a 1945 ad for Cellophane, highlights the benefits of a sterile, plastic-wrapped world in which goods are shielded from the natural (but messy) process of spoilage and decay (fig. 4.4). The ad is directed to packaging engineers and other businessmen with the intention of compelling them to consider the postwar housewife as an exacting superconsumer who, like any practitioner of scientific housekeeping, will demand pristine clarity from a product's package: "How does the Post-War shopper fit into your package? . . . She will want to make certain just what she is getting . . . what color, what size, what quality." Although DuPont argues that the female consumer controls the destiny of future postwar sales with her critical eye and finicky pocketbook, the ad suggests otherwise. DuPont shows how its manufacturing clients can gain the upper hand over the wily female shopper, despite her managerial powers, by packaging her, along with her groceries, in Cellophane. Like other wartime promotionals for a "better America," these advertisements portray plastics as part of the orderly

4.3. Dow Chemical advertisement, 1945. Courtesy Post Street Archives, Dow Chemical Corporation.

How does the Post-War shopper fit into your package?

WARTIME rationing and substitutions will make the shopper in the post-war era more value-conscious than ever before. Will your package do its part to satisfy her exacting requirements?

SHE WILL WANT TO SEE. She will want to make certain just what she is getting . . . what color, what size, what quality. With self-service becoming more prevalent, she will depend on her *eyes* to provide this assurance. The product packaged in transparent Du Pont Cellophane will permit her to *see* what she buys.

SHE WILL WANT PROTECTION. The post-war shopper will expect and demand products in their original quality—clean, sanitary, unimpaired by loss of freshness and flavor. The products packaged in moistureproof Du Pont Cellophane will appeal to her because she knows from experience that Cellophane provides superior protection.

YOU WILL WANT LOW PACKAGING COST. Because the post-war housewife will want more for her shopping dollar, your product will have to be priced to appeal. This will mean lower distribution costs and will require attention to packaging economies. In Du Pont Cellophane you get the desirable combination of *transparency* plus *protection* at *low cost.*

Back of every sparkling square inch of Du Pont Cellophane stands Du Pont research, constantly at work to develop and improve types of packaging film for greatest efficiency.

Military demands now limit the civilian supply of Du Pont Cellophane. We hope the day is not far off when again there will be enough Du Pont Cellophane to fill all your needs.

E. I. du Pont de Nemours & Co. (Inc.), Cellophane Division, Wilmington 98, Delaware.

**BETTER THINGS FOR BETTER LIVING
. . . THROUGH CHEMISTRY**

DuPont Cellophane

Shows what it Protects—at Low Cost

4.4. DuPont Cellophane advertisement, *Business Week*, 13 January 1945, 25. Courtesy of Hagley Museum and Library, Wilmington, Delaware.

pipelines of modern progress, whether on the battlefield, in the grocery store, or at home.

Secret Weapon Today, Electronic Betterment Tomorrow

The war . . . has given a tremendous acceleration to the development of all things electronic. . . . Housed within [the R.C.A. Radio-Electronic Laboratories] are one hundred and fifty laboratories where the secret weapons of today are being developed to win the war, and where new electronic wonders will become handmaidens of tomorrow's miracle world.[39]

The rhetorical formulas found in narratives about postwar electronics echoed the accolades preached about plastics. War-developed electronic technologies, forecasters claimed, would infuse the postwar house with the power to regulate its own order by monitoring levels of cleanliness and maintaining itself. Like plastics and synthetic fabrics, electronics would generate access to maximum sanitary living, thereby accelerating the national standard of cleanliness, but at the same time promising that this evolutionary leap into the middle class would require very little effort.[40] Walter Adams, in his 1943 *Better Homes and Garden* article aptly titled "Mystery Weapon Today—Your Servant Tomorrow," describes the "untold wonders" of electronics. Fairy-tale magic, paradoxically, enhances science's superlative rationality, endowing the postwar consumer with an unprecedented care-free life: "Electronics . . . magic secret weapons of war now, a new wonderland for you at war's end . . . untold wonders of ingenuity and comfort, convenience and entertainment . . . cook a roast in six seconds . . . heat your house electrically . . . phone your wife while flying over China . . . the electron promises to 'change the whole aspect of our lives.'"[41]

Along with the eradication of fascism, one of the most widely heralded achievements of the war was the increased ability to annihilate germs and dangerous bacteria—the unseen scourge of even the most precise scientific housekeeper, as Adams explains: "[Electronic tubes] can . . . filter hay-fever pollens and even bacteria from the air."[42] The promise of these pollutants' demise in the postwar house was a welcome feature. Propagandists and forecasters in the electronics industry announced that not only would the future house be maintenance-free, but new wartime developments in the electronics field would liberate the postwar family from the embarrassing contaminants of disease-causing germs and bacteria and safeguard against poor health: "The fluorescent lamp . . . gives off powerful germ-killing ultraviolet rays which will keep your home free of harmful bacteria. . . . Electronic controls will make possible germ-free air, to guard against disease; electronic devices will preserve food, guarding against contamination. Electronic irradiation of food will store more and more sunshine into what we eat."[43]

Significantly, features of electronics and electrical products promised to not only replace unhealthy drudgery with comfort but also remove the stigma of rotten garbage and grime that housekeeping, especially kitchen work, entailed. Wartime promises about future scientific housekeeping offered to make it possible for middle-class housewives to avoid the menial, filthy chores of scullery maids because electronic automation would do the dirty work for them:

> Admiral Corporation is turning out its Dual Temp refrigerator equipped with . . . a Sterilamp, the ultra-violet-ray device that retards the growth of mold and bacteria. . . . Westinghouse, General Electric and Edison General Electric (Hotpoint) . . . will bring out new models [of dishwashers] that will spray, wash, rinse and dry the dishes with one push of the button. . . . Perhaps the nearest thing to a dream appliance . . . is the electric waste disposal unit that fits in the kitchen sink, and does away for good and all with the ancient nuisance of scraping dishes and emptying garbage pails.[44]

Avoiding contact with germs and bacteria, readers were advised, would keep the housewife pure, rank her housework at a managerial level, and maintain an ideal feminine attractiveness. A 1943 ad for Republic Electric Furnace Steels in *Business Week* further illustrates scientific housekeeping's taboos about touching soiled or contaminated surfaces (fig. 4.5). In Republic's ad, electric furnace steels have manifested the postwar hygienic revolution. The future takes place in an antiseptic middle-class household where perfection is virtually automatic and is never sullied by offensive remains from the natural world:

> [Republic's] ENDURO Stainless Steel . . . a material with the high strength of steel and the cleanliness of glass. Because it is inert to fruit, vegetable, meat and dairy products, it neither affects nor is affected by foods. Its hard, smooth surface is sanitary and remarkably easy to clean. A mere wiping with a damp cloth usually restores all its beautiful silvery lustre [*sic*].[45]

In the ad, "tomorrow's better world" is realized through hermetically sealed and sterilized "ENDURO Stainless Steel," a name that suggests heroic force and trustworthy durability. A picture of perfect domesticity, Republic's kitchen possesses only smooth surfaces and uninterrupted flush fronts, not only eliminating the potential for stains but also offsetting the buildup of grease, crumbs, dust, and other unmentionable refuse that might fall unnoticed into crevices. No one will ever see this filth, of course, but just to *know* it is there is enough to make any proper housewife swoon from embarrassment or fear of hidden filth infecting her family. Republic has ingeniously resolved this middle-class horror. All open spaces between appliances, countertops, and cabinets—from floor to ceiling— have been purged by Republic, leaving only one solid complete unit, a variation on the mechanical core ideal popularized during the 1930s—a feature covered in chapter 6. Republic's main hygienic solution to the kitchen crevice dilemma was

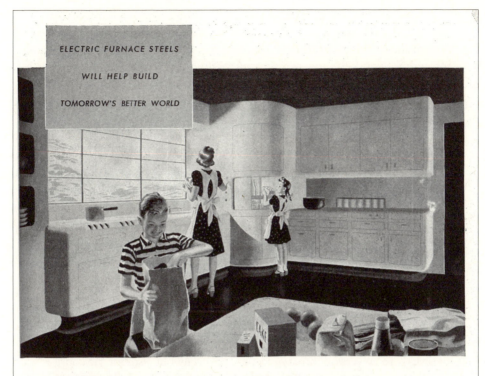

ELECTRIC FURNACE STEELS

WILL HELP BUILD

TOMORROW'S BETTER WORLD

A Dream Comes True Tomorrow

When a peacetime dawn dispels the dusk of war, the American housewife will find a new joy in living in the kitchen of tomorrow. It will be bright, cheerful, efficient — because steel, and especially stainless steel, will make it so.

Designers and engineers already are using their ingenuity in producing plans. And with the coming of peace they will be able to use the fine steels which the greatly increased capacity of Republic's Electric Furnaces makes available to them.

Outstanding among Republic Electric Furnace Steels is ENDURO Stainless Steel—the metal of ten thousand uses —a material with the high strength of steel and the cleanliness of glass.

Because it is inert to fruit, vegetable, meat and dairy products, it neither affects nor is affected by foods. Its hard, smooth surface is sanitary and remarkably easy to clean. A mere wiping with a damp cloth usually restores all its beautiful silvery lustre.

It lasts indefinitely—because it resists rust and corrosion—because it is solid stainless steel all the way through with nothing to wear off.

ENDURO Stainless Steel is only one of the "targeted steels" made possible by electric furnace processing in Republic mills. Others—each made to perform its specific task— are proving in wartime use how precise control in the electric furnace enables them repeatedly to hit exacting marks established by product or fabricating specifications.

Tomorrow holds the prospect of better things to work with and to live with—in the home—in industry —on the farm. Your product may be one of these better things—something that can be designed with enhanced sales appeal and manufactured by economical methods of mass production through the application of Republic Electric Furnace Steels. Republic Steel Corporation, General Offices—Cleveland 1, Ohio. Export Department: Chrysler Building, New York 17, N. Y.

REPUBLIC
ELECTRIC FURNACE STEELS
alloy... stainless..."aircraft quality"

—also open hearth and Bessemer steels—cold drawn steel bars, sheets, strip, plates, tin plate, pipe, tubing, bolts, nuts, rivets, farm

fence materials, wire, nails, shelving, lockers, windows and other steel building items, and many modern fabricated steel products.

4.5. Republic Electric Furnace Steels advertisement, *Business Week*, 17 July 1943, 99.

to design a cylindrical refrigerator from which the countertops, stove, oven, and sink radiate as a clean and orderly collective into the surrounding sanitary space. Health and vitality emanate from this picture just as brightly as the sun streaming through the window. However, we must ask why, if "tomorrow's better world" is such an improvement over yesterday, are the women in most of these progressive pictures (like Republic's) still wearing aprons? Wouldn't such high-tech, hygienic solutions make aprons obsolete?

Forecasters of postwar progress wove their "fairy tales" about the "miracles" of their wartime developments around a middle-class domestic paradigm. Capitalizing on the middle-class moral aversion to coming in contact with potential contagions, they borrowed human-engineering metaphors to reinforce their claims. Upgrading and transforming scientific housekeeping through war-inspired product engineering represented the ultimate wartime benefit because it addressed conventional middle-class aspirations toward maximizing hygienic propriety.

Streamlined Strategies for Tomorrow's World

Advertisers in trade, business, and women's magazines used the streamlined style to suggest America's alchemical transformation into a pure and hygienic society free of friction and chaos. Smooth corners and curved edges symbolized not only an orderly reconversion into a peacetime economy but also, for the consumer, an effortless evolution toward higher standards of living. Streamlining, as discussed in chapters 2 and 3, was a design technique used to "clean up" surfaces, standardize forms, and enhance efficient productivity.[46] Whether the streamlined style (aptly known as the "efficiency aesthetic") actually facilitated a hygienic and more orderly environment is debatable. Its ideological role seemed as vital as its ideal appearance because streamlining was part of the visual lexicon of human engineering. And its "clean" look was a natural fit for the sanitary conceit of scientific housekeeping.

Wartime forecasters and propagandists realized that one way to rationalize the postwar future was to streamline it. Following this trend, Cooper-Bessemer cast its General Purpose vehicle as the streamlined car leading to perfect postwar transport (fig. 4.6).[47] In its 1943 ad "Paging the Jeep's Nephew," the boxy military jeep—unsightly, but cheap and efficient—is depicted in a tiny frame below its postwar progeny, a teardrop car of the future, complete with an aerodynamic bubble top and speedlines encircling a rounded chassis. As in other reconversion tales, military proficiency is infused into the middle-class family (in this case its automobile) and provides frictionless travel for the suburban commuter.

Western Brass, in its reconversion ad from 1943, compares its wartime contribution—a torpedo—with the postwar application of its metal casings: a gleaming, streamlined toaster, which has just perfectly browned a slice of bread (fig. 4.7). The torpedo's streamlined shape, which makes it so efficient as a weapon, also validates its future application in the postwar kitchen. Here, the comparison between toaster and torpedo is also concentrated on the quality of each one's performance, suggesting that wartime torpedoes will lead to higher standards of

LOW COST POWER...TO WIN THE WAR NOW...AND THEN THE PEACE

Paging the Jeep's Nephew

THE jeep owes a lot to Cooper-Bessemer compressors. It bounds along on synthetic rubber which starts in a compressor. Compressors aid in refining its fuel. It is equipped with compressor-born plastic parts and accessories.

And to the compressor, the tear-drop car of the future—the jeep's nephew—will owe even more. It may have a small but powerful motor hidden under the rear seat, made of magnesium and aluminum alloys, fueled with high-octane gasoline. Tires of synthetic rubber will roll up new-record mileages. Cushions of synthetic foam-rubber will bring the luxurious riding ease of the airplane. Fixtures, accessories, surface finish will be of jewel-like plastics.

Magnesium, plastics, synthetic rubber, high octane gasoline . . . all are products of compression.

Today, compressors by Cooper-Bessemer are making these products for war . . . in steadily increasing volume.

But most of our 110 years have been devoted to building engines for peace. So we shall welcome Victory when we can turn again to building engines and compressors for peacetime necessities, conveniences and luxuries which "The American Way" enables us all to enjoy.

THE
Cooper-Bessemer
CORPORATION
Mt. Vernon, Ohio • Grove City, Pa.

4.6. Cooper-Bessemer advertisement, *Business Week*, 14 August 1943, 25. Courtesy Cooper-Bessemer, a registered trademark of the Cooper Cameron Corporation, who is still providing compressions today.

When its TOASTERS *instead of torpedoes*

As the pendulum of war swings on toward peace and reconversion, Western brass will again be used in products designed for service—utility—convenience—beauty—and comfort.

Post-war industry will want Western brass—in sheet or strip, drawn or stamped parts —because it is easy to form, draw, buff and plate, and because it will be "tailored" to meet **exacting** specifications. That's the way we like to do the job . . . as we are now doing it to meet war requirements. Western mills at East Alton, Ill. and New Haven, Conn. are *experienced* in producing nonferrous metals *to exactly suit the job.* We will welcome the opportunity to demonstrate our ability to meet your specifications . . . now or post-war.

Western BRASS MILLS

Division of WESTERN CARTRIDGE COMPANY, *East Alton, Ill.*

4.7. Western Brass Mills advertisement, *Business Week,* 16 September 1944, 93. Courtesy Olin Corporation.

"service—utility—convenience—beauty—and comfort"—traits of hygienic propriety embodied in the streamlined toaster.[48]

Firestone stresses that war production offers a streamlined avenue toward higher standards of living in peacetime. But streamlining was not limited to postwar products. Even the future housewife was molded in an efficiency aesthetic. In Firestone's 1944 ad (fig. 4.8) the personification of the "world of tomorrow" is in the form of an attenuated blonde who (not coincidentally) fits the genetic ideal of American beauty. The combined traits of long legs, wavy yellow hair, blue eyes, ample bosom, and an extremely narrow waist were thought to be the prescription for maintaining racial, social, and moral hygiene.[49] Considered the pinnacle of civilization, such a type, businessmen believed, also constituted the genetic stock of the "average" consumer, who would lead society into a hygienic and prosperous future. Firestone's two-page ad shows us a soldier (a hygienic masculine type obviously possessing discipline, strength, and stamina) with bayoneted rifle standing guard above the "war front," which consists of tanks, jeeps, and other army transport vehicles presumably headed in the direction of victory. This superman's postwar counterpart, the streamlined housewife, strides above the "home front"— a suburb, complete with a child riding a tricycle and a streamlined car motoring into the future on a smooth, clean highway. Above these settings float Firestone's

4.8. Firestone advertisement, *Business Week*, 22 July 1944, 60–61. Courtesy of Bridgestone Americas.

wartime contributions and their by-products in peacetime, like a constellation of stars in the night sky. Firestone announces that its wartime work will "set new standards of quality, durability, comfort and economy," and suggests that the progress of war leads to better girdles, brassieres, ranges, tires, washing machines, and other conveniences for the postwar home and body. Here, "producing for war" and "preparing for peace" are paralleled as two sides of the same evolutionary trajectory.

At heart, streamlining the "world of tomorrow" provided a way to salvage wartime investments, and advertisers did so utilizing the current beliefs and known symbolism at hand. Manufacturers and designers in the aeronautics field were especially lured by the visual metaphor of streamlining, because their products already embodied aerodynamic efficiency—the hallmark of the streamlined style, even for stationary objects.[50] Forecasters apprise us that air force pilots, once

"Put my groceries in that blue helicopter"

THE new clerk at the village market will soon learn that Mrs. Kimball's helicopter is blue—and that Mrs. Peters' is the bright red job. Almost all the shopping housewives now make use of the plane-parking lot across from the market.

It is interesting to think about this town—Anyplace, U. S. A.—after the war. And helicopters aren't the half of it.

There'll be new kinds of stores, amazing new products on the shelves . . . and new, more efficient packages for the products.

4.9. "'Put my groceries in that blue helicopter,'" from *Glimpses into the Wonder World of Tomorrow* (Wilmington, Del.: E. I. du Pont de Nemours, 1943), 9. Courtesy of Hagley Museum and Library, Wilmington, Delaware.

mustered out of the service, would launch widespread demand for personal commuter aircraft. The anticipated avalanche of streamlined airplane and helicopter sales would eventually make the automobile market obsolete. In visions of the future, the postwar skies were littered with rounded aluminum and Plexiglas airplanes or helicopters. In DuPont's 1943 promotional booklet *Glimpses into the Wonder World of Tomorrow,* teardrop-shaped helicopters conveniently buzz from shopping centers to their rooftop hangars in the suburbs (fig. 4.9). Postwar rush hour traffic would smoothly take to the air and presumably alleviate earthbound bottlenecks in crowded cities and on congested highways.[51]

Laboratory test tubes and beakers—like aircraft, torpedoes, attenuated blondes, and teardrop cars—constituted yet another manifestation of the streamlined style and expressed streamlining's hygienic, rational connotations. International Minerals and Chemicals acquaints us with the postwar product reconversion process in a 1943 ad, which depicts the products of tomorrow arising from laboratory research (fig. 4.10). In "Treading on the Heels of Tomorrow," the new technologies resemble the efficiency of the lab equipment in their physical appearance:

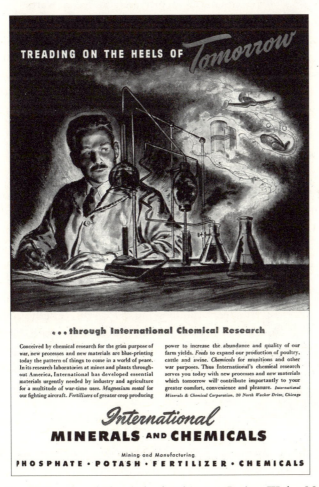

4.10. International Minerals and Chemicals advertisement, *Business Week*, 8 May 1943, 81.

There's a Great Day Coming!

WAR-INSPIRED RESEARCH PROMISES *New Wonders* **FOR THE HOME**

Today at Delco Appliance, nothing except precision products for our armed forces is being produced. All of the well-known Delco Appliance peace-time products—automatic heat, water systems, light and power plants —have gone to war.

For the American home a great new future is waiting . . . a future that will swiftly become the present as soon as Victory is ours. Newly developed materials, processes and machinery will combine to give to Americans even finer home appliances than they enjoyed before the war.

During the past year, Delco Appliance's mass production of precision war products has reached an all-time high in efficiency. This same skill will bring you the new things of tomorrow, quickly, when peace comes.

Delco Appliances include Automatic Delco-Heat (oil-coal-gas), Delco Water Systems, Delco-Light Power Plants and Delco-Light Ironclad Batteries

DELCO APPLIANCE GM

DIVISION, GENERAL MOTORS CORPORATION, ROCHESTER, N.Y.

Victory Is Our Business

a cylindrical refrigerator (with speedlines), an aerodynamic airplane/helicopter combo, and a bubble-topped car (rendered in an aircraft motif) float upward in a haze emanating from laboratory beakers, under the gaze of a Clark Gable–like scientist.[52] Likewise, Delco Appliance underscores the idea of reconversion as streamlined alchemy in its 1943 ad (fig. 4.11). Here, a jeep, tank, and airplane gestate in a test tube under a scientist's gaze, transforming from embryonic weapons into mature "New Wonders" for the postwar household. Ironically, the scientist in the International Minerals and Chemicals ad, geared for a business audience, evokes a macho Hollywood aura, while the researcher in the Delco ad, placed in a women's magazine, appears quite ordinary by comparison.

The ads for Delco and International Mineral and Chemicals depict men in secret wartime laboratories concocting a "new and improved" America. The Utah Radio Products Company employed a similar scenario, complete with a studious scientific type (fig. 4.12). In its 1943 ad "Utah Engineers Stay Up Nights Thinking About Her . . ." the present and the future are not only gendered but also identified in terms of federal and consumer power: "Today our boss is Uncle Sam—tomorrow the American housewife."[53] In this example, a Utah engineer is wrapped in an atom, a symbol of his scientific mystique—as well as the war's. He contemplates his fantasy, who looms above him like a thought bubble: a contented Mrs. Postwar Housewife, who sighs blissfully from her pink, streamlined, electronic kitchen, complete with appliances built into the walls and cabinetry—a host of comforts and conveniences she has gained from the progress of war. The streamlined aesthetic here suggests that postwar housework will be a cheery, fulfilling pursuit. In this orderly, sanitary world, rational design rules in a sterilized domestic space where neither appliances nor cords litter the countertops; glass-door cabinets reveal only regimented stacks of plates; and no burners or deep crevices exist that could possibly trap menacing dirt. Not only are the dictates of scientific housekeeping underscored, but so is maximum

4.11. Delco Appliance advertisement, *Better Homes and Gardens,* March 1943, 62. Courtesy of Delphi Energy & Chassis.

UTAH ENGINEERS STAY UP NIGHTS THINKING ABOUT HER...

TODAY Utah's plants are working 100% on electrical and electronic devices for tough hombres winning a high-speed, fast-communications war under even tougher bosses. ¶ When those tough hombres come back from making war they will find a new boss — a pretty one — making peace in a new home, run on new principles in electronic equipment. ¶ Today our boss is Uncle Sam — tomorrow the American housewife. ¶ Since radio broadcasting began, more than half of these American housewives unknowingly listened to their favorite programs through a Utah speaker, whatever the make of their complete sets. Tomorrow they will hear for the first time of Utah in a new and exciting way. ¶ *Already Utah's engineers and technicians are working overtime charting the future, preparing the scientific groundwork to supply Mrs. America with new, improved and different products in the electronics field.* ¶ Utah was ready to go into a new kind of war production for our high commands, the day Pearl Harbor broke. It will be ready to go into a new kind of peace production for American housewives, the day folks start throwing the ticker-tape to celebrate victory.

utah
RADIO PRODUCTS COMPANY
CHICAGO, ILLINOIS

4.12. Utah Radio Products Company advertisement, *Fortune,* December 1943, 104.

control through automation. Presumably the focus of the Utah engineer's research is an electronic console with levers, push buttons, and a timer: the postwar version of the domestic servant and the source for middle-class women's liberation from the illogical tyranny of unscientific kitchens and irrational improper filth.

Ultimately, streamlining answered the needs of both scientific housekeepers and wartime propagandists because the style *appeared* to exact rational, hygienic order out of a wasteful, defective mess. Scientific housekeepers and wartime propagandists shared the same intent: they sought to sanitize their objective. For propagandists, that included sanitizing war information and postwar prospects. Thus, the streamlined style provided a convenient visual vocabulary that resonated with the desire to help a more hygienic America evolve smoothly from the dysfunction and destruction of war.

The Ultimate Democratizing Machine

Because revolutionary improvements for domesticity could not materialize until after the war, forecasters offset disappointment by assuring consumers that when "miracles" finally started flooding into stores, the promised hygienic revolution would be affordable. Patriotic patience would be rewarded with lowered costs. J. D. Ratcliff explains how manufacturers could democratize the price tags for revolutionary miracle products so easily:

> But you ask . . . "Won't all these scientific miracles be prohibitively expensive?" . . . The answer [is] decidedly no . . . [because of] the tremendous productive capacity America has built, and is building, for the war effort. . . . Take for example two of the largest manufacturers of electrical goods. The biggest volume of their business today is making electronic devices for the armed services. Tomorrow they won't want to junk their machines, skills and knowledge. They will make these war-born devices your peacetime servants.[54]

Wartime scientific research and product development in tandem with high production held the key to lowering the cost of the long-awaited hygienic revolution. But what Ratcliff emphasizes here are options determined by *managers*. Consumers would have the techno-corporate order to thank for putting postwar wonders within their price range. Although commercial propaganda fueled the assumption that the war was the ultimate democratizing machine, the brains behind those supposedly egalitarian engines belonged to the managerial elite. War alone could not equalize access to higher standards of cleanliness, comfort, and convenience without the superlative "know-how" and industrial acumen of corporate decision-making machines.

Interestingly, the techno-corporate order's postwar planning decisions had an unexpected corrosive effect on the consumer color line. As the purchasing power of African Americans rose, the white managerial elite began to take the black consumer more seriously.[55] Realizing that African Americans had value as a *market,* the techno-corporate order began to adapt a marketing approach that would, inadvertently, assist blacks (and other minorities) in their quest for equal access to democratic freedoms.[56] From the records of wartime advertising, it is difficult to recognize this dynamic in a pictorial sense, because African Americans were not featured *as consumers* in reconversion narratives, and their appearance in mobilization advertising was generally limited to their traditional and stereotypical roles as porters, cooks, or maids, when they appeared at all.[57] The white business press represented the only *mainstream* media to publish reconversion advertising depicting African Americans as recipients of the progress generated by the war. In a 1944 *Advertising & Selling* ad promoting the "Negro Market," black participation in the postwar world is described as an untapped gold mine for postwar sales (fig. 4.13). The ad, placed by the black newspaper the *Houston Informer,* explains that African Americans had experienced a rising standard of living during the war like their white counterparts: "The Negro Market . . . is many times richer today than at any time in its history. . . . And it's a SPENDING market NOW, with War Bonds providing the spending power for tomorrow."[58]

Despite the growing business fixation with black purchasing power, advertising in women's and general-circulation magazines did not picture African Americans enjoying the forecast hygienic revolution—even though such progress was ostensibly democratized for all consumers. Given that black physical features were perceived as failing to fit the racial hygiene standards of the white normative mold at the time, blacks' depiction in mainstream advertising was intentionally omitted by wartime symbol managers, forecasters, and propagandists. African American images in any advertising venue, even the black press, were generally less than complimentary and attest to the resiliency of a racially based genetic determinism in

A market bulging with new wealth!

THE NEGRO MARKET of these four INFORMER cities is many times richer today than at any time in its history. Individual and family incomes have reached undreamed-of peaks. And it's a SPENDING market NOW, with War Bonds providing the spending power for tomorrow.

These bulging pockets . . . and pocketbooks, too, are reached by the INFORMER, with the largest Negro circulation in the South. Your message in the INFORMER reaches eager spenders, gets prompt response, establishes tastes and desires that will continue into the future, when sales will be harder to make. Write for free particulars!

THE HOUSTON INFORMER
2418 Leeland   Houston, Texas

The INFORMER Group

NEW ORLEANS, HOUSTON, DALLAS. FORT WORTH

Circulation over 38,000
— All at One Low Cost!

4.13. The Informer Group advertisement, *Advertising & Selling,* February 1944, 126. Courtesy the Houston Informer.

the United States—ingrained assumptions that were demonstrated throughout the war years. Advertisements of products for lightening black complexions and taming black hair textures heavily populated newspapers geared to an African American audience. Advertisers of these personal grooming products seduced black consumers with promises of appearing less African, thus inadvertently confirming the assumption that their economic and social success was based on how "white" they could look. Such ads also reinforced the misconception that the "norm" consisted of strictly stereotypical Aryan traits to which all minorities aspired.[59]

The Negro Market mascot in the Informer Group advertisement is actually typical of ads including African Americans, and we find similar stereotyped models in advertising illustrations published in the black press. These ads depicted African Americans with European-looking facial features and wavy, not kinky, flowing locks of hair. Many times the skin of these "black" protagonists was lightly shaded, similar to the skin of the man representing the Negro Market. Such shaded features meant that the ad's protagonists were intended to speak to a black, rather than white, readership. A wartime ad in the Harlem, New York, paper the *People's Voice* also illustrates this paradox (fig. 4.14). An "Irresistible Beauty," a woman, is paired with "Dynamic Power," a tank—a juxtaposition similar to the home front/front line contrast we saw in mobilization advertising. The newspaper's tie-in of its publicity service with the "dynamic power" of a war machine is typical of advertising in any publication of this time. It capitalizes on a wartime icon to stress its strength, determination, and aptitude. This radical black newspaper also references its superior capabilities in the form of a seductive female, but the irony is that she has been rendered with conventional white features and a shaded face.[60]

A brief look at advertising in two popular wartime black papers, the *Pittsburgh Courier* and the *Baltimore Afro-American,* reveals to us the extent of this paradox. Ads for skin bleach and hair straighteners were prolific; they touted products such as Dr. Fred Palmer's Skin Whitener, "La-Em-Strait" for smooth, silky hair, Snow White Hair Beautifier, and Murray's pomade and pressing cap used to set extremely curly hair close to the scalp.[61] In an ad for New Nix Liquid, which "Lightens Skin," advertising's standard "before and after" motif is at work. Here, a black woman with African features is the model; half of her face is depicted white, the other shaded dark.[62] Nadinola Bleaching Cream, unlike most others of its kind, used photographs of black women but, like New Nix, only ones with light skin.[63] The makers of Slick Black also applied the "before and after" motif in their ad showing a black woman with one side of her hair kinky and the other side smoother and tamed, while Madam Lillian's hair straightener made the sexual appeal that "Long, Smooth Hair *Attracts* Men!"[64]

The manufacturers of Sweet Georgia Brown hair pomade published ads featuring episodes in the romantic life of a young black woman who was constantly losing her man to a girl with distinctly white features. The ads' copywriters chastised readers with the line, "If it's kissin' you're missin', Get a can of Sweet Georgia Brown." The same young black woman was pictured in every ad, and her

DYNAMIC POWER and IRRESISTIBLE BEAUTY —

A rare combination.....

Matchless in creating reader response to the products and places advertised in this newspaper. . . . Our prime motive is to give the reader
and advertising client, alike, service superior to any similar publication . . . to create a distinctive market of intelligent readers who sha"
buy wisely. . . . Our every effort shall be toward a steadily-rising stan
ard of editorial policy . . . enhanced by unsurpassed beauty.

The **VOICE** PEOPLE'S
AMERICA'S GREATEST NEGRO NEWSPAPER

4.14. *People's Voice* advertisement, *People's Voice,* 21 February 1942, 8. Photograph courtesy
of General Research Division, The New York Public Library, Astor, Lenox, and Tilden
Foundations.

kinky hair and African features were accentuated each time. In one episode after
another, she watches in astonishment as a young white playboy plants a healthy
kiss on an equally Aryan-looking "dame."[65] The ads suggest that, clearly, the black
girl would be the one getting the "kissin'" if she would only Aryanize her hair
with Sweet Georgia Brown. In so doing, the ad actually implies that her African
facial features will also "normalize" when her hair is tamed to fit the white standard of female beauty.

Although the *Houston Informer*'s Negro Market ad in *Advertising & Selling*
(fig. 4.13) spotlights blacks' significance as consumers, thus situating their dollars
on the level of white Americans, stereotypes still prevail. The Negro Market mascot seems a bit overdressed, as if to emphasize his nouveau riche status, which
does not quite fit him. One hand and his pockets are stuffed full of bills, as he
strides with a newfound pride across a shiny coin, sporting a cane, a large fedora,
and a double-breasted tweed suit (a banned "luxury" in wartime). The suit seems
a bit loose and recalls the extravagance of the urban zoot suit, which in this case
has been tamed.[66] In such a getup we imagine he must be wearing spit-polished
patent leather shoes, too. Moreover, we're told that the black market "bulges"
with wealth, a reference to the assumption that black men possessed a "natural"
heightened virility and primitive sexuality—a trait also ascribed to black women,
and which some white Americans argued was one reason why poor minorities
had more children than they could afford.[67]

Although Robert Weems in his 1998 study *Desegregating the Dollar* contends
that more corporate advertisers began buying ad space in black papers during the
war, it seems that Roi Ottley's wartime findings do not fully agree. Ottley asserted
in his 1943 book *New World A-Coming* that the advertising published in black
media consisted "largely of sucker items such as loadstones, zodiacal incense
[and] books on unusual love practices."[68] There was "little profitable advertising
in Negro newspapers," Ottley observes, but that also gave the black press wide
editorial liberties to speak out against racial injustice, especially during the war,
when cooperation was demanded through threats of censorship.[69] Dwight Brooks's
1991 study "Consumer Markets and Consumer Magazines" bears out Ottley's position. Brooks maintains that black magazines were often short-lived because,
unlike white magazines that profited from high advertising revenues, African
American publications "relied on institutional support such as the church and
education for their economic base" or "subscriptions, local advertising from small
Black businesses, and the solicitation of shares in stock companies." This made for
a "weak financial base" and smaller circulation figures that could not provide
enough incentive to attract national advertisers. Brooks cites two prewar black
magazines with high circulations "and a presumed affluent readership" that did
draw "a few national advertisers." These were *Colored American Magazine,* which
claimed a circulation of 17,000, and *Voice of the Negro* with 13,000. However, the
national advertisers in such black publications were limited to manufacturers of
"liquor [and] tobacco . . . railroads . . . and book publishers."[70]

Despite the national circulation of local papers such as those cited above,
major national corporations did not advertise superfluous postwar visions in black

publications, an observation borne out by Ottley's book and a 1987 study published in *Journalism Quarterly*.[71] According to the latter's survey of the *Pittsburgh Courier*, advertisements sponsored by large corporations were virtually nonexistent in the black press prior to the war. After Pearl Harbor, the excess profits tax encouraged businesses to pour an unprecedented amount of advertising dollars into the black *business* press. However, according to the study's findings (which are similar to Ottley's observations), these advertisements were mostly for low-budget necessities, such as personal grooming supplies or food, as well as alcohol, soda, life insurance, gum, cigarettes, travel, and health care.

Ottley contended that wartime African Americans "wanted tangible assurances that the loud talk of democracy [was] in fact meant to include them."[72] The black vision of postwar progress did not primarily consist of streamlined kitchens, "miracle" plastics, and suburban houses; rather, it resonated with the war's deeper purpose: the end of totalitarian infringements on freedom, whether at home or abroad.[73] The wartime ideal of democratizing progress through access to higher standards of living, from the black standpoint, certainly meshed with the Double V objective. But would such promises turn out to be more hyperbolic than substantive?

African American leaders before the war had taught their communities to take steps toward empowerment by conscientiously choosing the ways in which they spent or withheld their money.[74] Supporting black businesses and boycotting stores that upheld racist practices formed part of the prewar strategy to insist on the right to full American citizenship.[75] Interestingly, the techno-corporate order maintained a somewhat similar mindset because its core value—free enterprise—perceived the growth of capital as a natural extension of American liberty. During the war, the techno-corporate order framed patriotism and the fight for democratic freedoms in terms of consumer bounty made available to the "masses." Both groups—the black community and the white managerial elite—understood that "progress" could advance through expanding mass consumer purchasing power.[76] Though corporate ideology and intentions certainly differed from African Americans' moral crusade, the white managerial elite's profit motive and blacks' strategies for empowerment met in the crucible of consumerism.

Perhaps it was better to be seen as the color of money, rather than being identified only by the color of one's skin. One could argue that the social stigma of blackness was swapped for the monotonous identity of the universal consumer. To many African Americans, it seemed that such a compromise would at least garner them a respect that was virtually absent in America despite the promises of wartime production. "The Negro," wrote black columnist George E. Schuyler in 1945, "will get respect and consideration in the degree that he acquires economic power."[77] For African Americans, breaking the color barrier by penetrating the techno-corporate order *as consumers* would prove to be the most effective route toward significantly democratizing progress.

5 Home Front War

The Campaign to Save the American Way

We come now to the need of defining the part which advertising should play in this undertaking. . . . It needs to sum up, by implication, the impression that the future will be better for all if reliance is placed on the enterprise of individual citizens, than it will under the *masterminding of an all-powerful State.* . . . [Such advertising needs] to put the NAM and business generally in the position of holding forth *hope for the future.* . . . Accordingly, the advertising phase of your 1944 program should take [this] form.[1]

Beneath the optimistic vision of the postwar world lay speculations that were far more pessimistic and reached deep into territory beyond consumer spending habits. "World of tomorrow" narratives, which held out "hope for the future," covertly harbored big business's animosity toward the New Deal and its belief that the liberals in Washington would stifle the postwar economy with excessive regulations, more taxes, and plans for state capitalism. The ad executive Arthur Kudner, who is quoted above, was not alone when he voiced his disdain for the New Deal in his advertising recommendations of 1944. Many business leaders who expressed anxiety over wartime government controls doubted the survival of free enterprise, democracy, and the American Way in the postwar future. Historian Roland Stromberg refers to this anxiety as corporate "misgivings." The New Deal's potential invasions into economic matters during the war, he observes, "were magnified into an almost hysterical fear" of government's role in the future.[2] Although it would be narrow-sighted to call the business community "monolithic" in its thinking at any time, historians recognize that wartime corporate leadership did come close to an unprecedented unanimity in its opposition to Roosevelt and the New Deal.[3]

Government regulation (perceived as interference) was one factor contributing to this near unanimous opposition. Wartime federal commercial holdings and a vast national debt formed yet another. Because of the necessary haste of wartime mobilization, financing for much of the wartime industrial development was federally sponsored; consequently, the U.S. government owned one-third of the war production facilities.[4] Historians Roger Beaumont, James Olson, and Stuart Brandes reveal how government and business interests became entangled in war plants and defense contracts. Washington, they relate, wound up owning a sizable chunk of the techno-corporate order's industrial infrastructure through the Defense Plant Corporation, which was initially intended to finance new manufacturing construction.[5] Under the aegis of the Defense Plant Corporation, 2,300 factories were built and outfitted with the necessary tools and machinery. Olson and Beaumont explain that such plants backed by the government were leased to private corporations "for a nominal fee," while "the title stayed with the government."[6] Washington would only "share modestly in any profits" but would "assume all the losses."[7] Businesses were encouraged to expand for war production with "generous incentives" such as "full tax write-off on equipment and plant in five years."[8] But many members of the techno-corporate order saw federal, as opposed to private, ownership as a dangerous precedent steering the United States in a direction antithetical to the traditional principles of free and private enterprise. "State capitalism" through the activities of the Defense Plant Corporation, though beneficial to wartime business, was too reminiscent of the New Deal's reform agenda of the 1930s, which to many conservative businessmen was essentially un-American. The colossal size and reach of the Defense Plant Corporation also bred concern. Historian Stuart Brandes calculates that the "federal inventory of machine tools was so large that it amounted to about twenty-five years of peacetime production of the American machine tool industry."[9] By war's end, the vast New Deal industrial holdings and investments made the Soviets look like amateurs in the art of state-run economies.

These concerns, it appears, weighed heavily on the techno-corporate order, judging by a 1943 *Nation's Business* series of articles enumerating the hurdles that industry was apt to face after victory. In mid-1943, the war's end did not seem to be in sight, and as history would bear out, it wasn't even close. Nevertheless, management's planning ethos was spurred into action. A. H. Sypher, author of the *Nation's Business* series, explains how government, as part or full owner of war production facilities, was basically developing into another business competitor. The American Way was seriously in jeopardy under these conditions and could easily become a casualty of the reconversion process if government did not remove itself immediately from industry as soon as victory was in sight: "After the war, everyone's job, everyone's future, will be affected by what the Government decides to do with its tremendous industrial holdings. . . . There is serious doubt that the traditional system of private companies engaged in free enterprise could long exist in competition with a Government in business on such a scale and scope, and with regulatory powers over all other business."[10]

Although federal borrowing and financial support helped expedite victory, business leaders agreed that it was in the best interest of the free enterprise system to teach the public that federal commercial holdings only led to disaster for the American Way. Washington bureaucrats were considered unreliable at best in commercial matters, and state ownership of war-related industries posed an ominous threat to democracy.[11] Business advocates argued that government control of production facilities and machinery after the war would not only hasten the demise of the American Way but also contradict all the claims of postwar progress that advertisers had been circulating throughout the war years. Sypher articulates the assumptions stimulated by the federal presence in war industry:

> Post-war prosperity and the future of all American enterprise depends on the Government's handling of war contracts after peace is declared. . . . It is America's post-war problem No. 1—and until it is done there can be no great surge into post-war markets. Instead, there may be deep depression; or possibly a new kind of government that would quiet the spirit that has made America great. . . . Present government trend indicates that government terms would include rigid lines of control. If that takes place, Government will have stepped into "partnership" with business, and free enterprise will become something of the past.[12]

Postwar problem no. 2 could certainly have included the New Deal's progressive reconversion agenda intended to offset a postwar depression, namely the proposed Full Employment Bill.[13] Certainly, businesses wanted to sustain the momentum of wartime production levels into the postwar future, but not through government legislation dictating social reform through the mandatory creation of jobs. Surely, such a demand was counter to the corporate liberties for which the war was fought. African American columnist George Schuyler, writing in the black newspaper the *Pittsburgh Courier* in 1945, inveighed against the totalitarian scent wafting from the liberal agenda for full employment. According to Schuyler, coercing the techno-corporate order would sabotage democracy's freedom of opportunity, rather than preserve or enhance it:

> The American people ought to know that full employment is not synonymous with either economic security or freedom. . . . The clamor for sixty million jobs would not get such a big audience if the people understood the implications of it: i.e., the controls, regimentation, taxation, and compulsion necessary for the Government to put such a program

into operation. . . . The whole business is a slavish borrowing from Germany and Russia. . . . Every one of these so-called liberal programs is aimed in the direction of dictatorship whether the advocates know it or not.[14]

Business groups, committees, and institutions rallied in response to the business community's postwar planning concerns. The Committee for Economic Development (CED) was one such organization. Formed by business leaders in spring 1942, within months after America's formal entry into the war, the CED aimed for bipartisanship in crafting realizable postwar economic goals.[15] Historian Robert Collins observes that the CED was devised by "the Business Advisory Council of the Department of Commerce and . . . unaffiliated businessmen who wanted the federal government to play a positive role in stabilizing the economy."[16] The CED's aims were not as conservative as other postwar planning agendas, because the committee envisioned how government could be "cooperative" instead of "oppressive" by partnering with business in reconversion. Nonetheless, the CED was about making sure that business controlled the flow of the economy and the government's role in it, as Collins explains: "The CED sought to devise governmental economic policies which would . . . allow natural adjustments under the laws of supply and demand and under the incentives of the profit system, rather than efforts by direct regimentation."[17]

It was one of the most conservative and reactionary of American business institutions, the National Association of Manufacturers (NAM), that took the reins of wartime symbol management and channeled business fears into a formidable public relations weapon.[18] In offering a way to halt the dreaded spread of wartime government into postwar industry, the NAM crafted a marketing campaign to engineer public favor for *business's* vision of the "world of tomorrow" as opposed to the New Deal's.

Rhetorical Formulas for Derailing the New Deal

The NAM's campaign was a two-pronged persuasive education program aimed first at mobilizing the entire business community against the New Deal. The second prong provided business leaders with the marketing tools necessary to habituate the public to wholeheartedly embracing corporate America's autocratic power and its ideological biases. The NAM's public relations arm, the National Industrial Information Committee (NIIC), served the business community, especially manufacturers, with guidelines for "selling" the public on the corporate definition of American democracy. A double-sided promotional flyer entitled *Re-Selling the American Way to America* illuminates the types of marketing messages that the NIIC used to solicit new recruits and inspire NAM member cooperation. The flyer also details the media channels that the NIIC used to reach the public (fig. 5.1). Radio programs, industrial films, booklets, pamphlets, billboards, in-house publications for employees, and press releases are shown as some of the venues through which the NIIC circulated the NAM agenda. Although this particular flyer was

5.1. National Association of Manufacturers/National Industrial Information Committee, promotional flyer to solicit NIIC members, "Re-Selling the American Way to America." NAM Accession #1411, Series III, NIIC Box 848. National Association of Manufacturers collection. Courtesy of Hagley Museum and Library, Wilmington, Delaware.

printed during the defense period and was largely a response to Depression-era issues, its strategies and content were also articulated during the war years.

In late 1943, *Newsweek* announced the NAM's persuasive education program in an article entitled, "'A Better America' is Banner of Industry's Postwar Program." So closely does the wording in this article mirror other NAM messages that one wonders if the NAM, or the NIIC, might have written this "news" itself. Nevertheless, the *Newsweek* article is exemplary of the way the NAM sought to unify the managerial elite and, in turn, convince the public that corporate authority was best equipped to handle the complexities of postwar reconversion. At the same time, the NAM conceptualized any planning or controls on the part of the government as a serious taboo:

> What did emerge [from the NAM's Second War Congress] was a platform calling for *removal of elements of regimentation* in American life, and *preservation of the free private competitive* enterprise system . . . a new business banner: "A *Better* America"—a banner heralding a plan of action aimed at creating a prosperous postwar America by *individual effort* as

contrasted with *government fiat*. This program is the springboard from which the NAM next year will launch a vocal and wide-spread educational program of action to show America why it was that free private competitive enterprise could *win the war* and why the NAM believes this system is *necessary* to *win the peace*.[19]

Although the business community's animosity toward the Roosevelt administration was cloaked by ebullient advertisements about postwar progress, the NAM's distaste for the New Deal was anything but hidden. In the *Newsweek* announcement the New Deal and liberals are typed as unfit "elements" that require swift "removal." In an intended parallel with Axis totalitarianism, the New Deal is conceptualized as a sinister menace, a correlation also made by Arthur Kudner when he referred to the "masterminding of an all-powerful State" (see p. 114). The words "regimentation" or "fiat," when used in conjunction with government, are codes for totalitarian or socialist contagion, here and as in other NAM messages.[20] Such language inveighed against the federal government as if it were an out-of-control epidemic contaminating the free enterprise system, thus jeopardizing the health and vitality of democracy. By comparison, words such as "individual," "private," "competitive," "initiative," and "free" were metaphors for the business construct of a healthy and pure American Way, and were commonly deployed idioms in NAM messages. (Kudner's reference to the "enterprise of individual citizens" is an example of this strategy too.)

The hyperbole in the *Newsweek* announcement is loaded with a sense of urgent necessity. The business struggle against the New Deal is thus structured as if it were a type of natural selection ("preservation"). The battle to "win the war" and "win the peace" was a competition that (in a Darwinian melodrama) only the fittest would survive. This morally superior position discernible in the *Newsweek* announcement is also noticeable in the NIIC's presentation of its 1943 positioning plan for the NAM (see chapter 3):

> What can we do, starting now, to convince the public that, in the postwar period, business can provide America better economic leadership, with better results for the average man, than can be had from politicians and bureaucrats? . . . The threat is that this country . . . will choose or have chosen for it a collectivist economy under which initiative would be stifled under a permanent blanket of government control.[21]

As this extract from the NIIC's presentation attests, NAM rhetoric conjured prophetic scenes of democracy's extinction through ideological infection. Phrases such as "permanent blanket of government control" evoked images of a postwar America arrested ("stifled") in its rightful progressive trajectory by the deadly contaminant of a "collectivist economy." Often in NAM publications, the word "control" referred to unwanted government regulations that presumably would negate democracy's guarantee of liberty, especially free enterprise. Business's moral duty was to ensure that the postwar future did not inherit any defects from the

New Deal generation and to "convince the public" of business's innate "leadership" supremacy over "politicians and bureaucrats."

The use of "better" and "initiative" as highly evolved features of business and capitalism implied that those who championed the American Way's system were, at the very least, intellectually superior to those who supported socialism, collectivism, or the New Deal—generally cast in NAM narratives as "the threat." Sometimes expressed as plural, "the threats" included consumers and blue-collar workers who had developed animosity or distrust toward the techno-corporate order during the Depression—an illness, business leaders believed, spread by consumer groups and labor unions, who were also numbered among "the threats." Comparisons between economic ideologies implied that free enterprise was healthier than a "planned economy" and was thus more fit because its natural strength ("vitality") stemmed from a laissez-faire gene pool that gave rise to leaders born with an inherent American pioneer spirit. As the NIIC in its 1943 presentation claimed: "The New Deal believes in 'planned economy.' Free enterprise takes its vitality from the resourcefulness, initiative, imagination, and daring of many individuals free to work out solutions and meet challenges in their own way."[22] According to James Adams, president of Standard Brands, Inc., and NIIC vice chairman, the higher standard of living enjoyed by "the average man," on which the Allied victory depended, was due to management's natural ability to bring about technological progress, virtually single-handedly: "We have not built America or our standard of living for the average man either from the hand-out of government or under the direction of the bureaucrat."[23] In this speech, published in 1943 as *Working Together for Postwar America,* the "we" to which Adams refers stands for the private sector. Adams more than suggests that America's abundance and prosperity were born of business acumen only and had no kinship with the inferior character inherent in government bureaucrats.

The NAM's rhetorical arsenal also exhibited traces of a Taylorist ideology that reveal the prerogatives of modern managerial style and a white-collar conceit. From the business point of view, wartime mobilization succeeded because of the competency, efficiency, organization, and rational prowess of corporate America's managerial elite. This belief is echoed by Adams in his 1943 speech: "How is it that we have accomplished the gigantic job of war production with such breathtaking speed and efficiency? It is not the Government bureaus that have wrought the miracle of mobilization, of production of war materials."[24] Where corporate bureaucracy excelled, government bureaucracy was pictured as perpetually fumbling and muddying the waters when it came to industrial planning—either during war or peace. Though structured hierarchically like a corporation, government was inherently irrational in matters of mobilizing the country's commercial infrastructure. Its ineptitude also generated waste, which acted as a parasitic drag on America's progress and freedom. As the NAM complained at its Second War Congress in 1944: "Let's get rid of red tape and all the clutter of stuff that has gathered around us during the war, and let us free America."[25]

A managerial machismo echoes throughout the NAM's commercial propaganda. Despite the fact that wartime mobilization could not have been achieved without labor, in NAM narratives, the class awarded credit is management—the leaders—who (in the manner of Taylorism) alone are privy to the mystique of production "know-how."[26] Mass production metaphors evoked an aura of technological and intellectual perfection for which management was solely responsible. In both the trade press and consumer media, wartime management was lauded as functioning with the precision of a machine, and we saw illustrative references to this correlation in mobilization ads such as Reynolds's (see fig. 3.3). Narratives of flawless mobilization presumed that corporate authority was also perfect. The idiom of "industry" (as quoted below and throughout other NAM-related documents) may encompass all contributors to production, but it is management at the helm of the "spectacular achievements" that, according to James Adams, justified business control of the postwar future:

> Its spectacular achievements in making America the production arsenal for democracy have convinced the public that it has the "know-how" of full production. Industry's greatest public relations responsibility today is to provide the vision, the leadership, and the program for applying that production "know-how" to the public's postwar needs.[27]

Big business's "greatest public relations responsibility" involved not only engineering public perception of "industry's" contribution to the war but also cementing public acceptance of corporate autocracy. Seizing the credit for victory and disparaging the New Deal's role in matters of industrial mobilization, it was believed, would validate managerial hegemony, business's ideological agenda, and the corporate role as familial mediator between the public and an intimidating postwar future. Government's role (and controls) in everyday life would be replaced with an invisible but tangible corporate influence.[28] Gaining public trust through a stronger corporate presence in everyday life would lay the groundwork for successful (and profitable) reconversion as planned by business, rather than by government. The NAM offered a remedy for business's wartime public relations dilemma. As the NIIC explained in its 1943 presentation, the NAM would supply the necessary paternal organization and "guidance" that would induce the public to see business leaders as managerial supermen, "the men who can get things done":

> Such organizations as the NAM can of course provide inspiration and guidance. . . . But it will be even more difficult to make your answers effective unless the public is more willing to heed and respect your leadership than it has been in the past. . . . Once business leadership is trusted—once people come to look to you as "the men who can get things done"—whatever you have to say in future will receive proper credence.[29]

Taking credit for victory (before the war was over) and smearing government's wartime performance was one aspect of the NAM's strategy to regain public trust and make consumers "more willing to heed and respect [managerial] leadership."[30] Much of the wartime commercial propaganda, especially advertisements, highlighted this "triumph," which was widely publicized in trade journals and in women's and general-circulation magazines. Evans Products, for example, in its business-to-business (B2B) ad from 1944, explained how the hastened necessity of wartime emergency had accelerated the development of chemical research and production processes from which new industries seemingly sprang up overnight: "Out of the crucible of war will come many great new industries, with products that are destined to provide mankind with a new freedom, a new joy in living."[31] In support of its claim, Evans Products illustrated American industry's recent renaissance as a newborn universe, fashioned by the hands of a nude, allegorical figure like a cosmic vision of William Blake's (fig. 5.2). The ad suggests that manufacturers so successfully converted their factories, resources, and products for war that they were simultaneously able to create unprecedented freedoms and joys for the postwar future. Although such persuasive messages did not name the New Deal directly, their insistence on the efficient heroics of business implied that government bureaucracy was not only ill-equipped to win a war by itself but also too inept (i.e., inferior) to launch a viable reconversion. This idea of management's vitality and superiority is underscored by the Aryan model of manhood in the Evans Products ad—it is as if the perfect corpus (i.e., corporation) is both progeny and creator of the perfect machine. Any industry aligned with this heroic and anatomically flawless supernude surely embodied an above-average ability to "anticipate the needs of tomorrow."

In accordance with their anti–New Deal platform, business leaders and manufacturers attempted to discredit liberal Washington, and the Roosevelt administration in particular, by charging it with impeding the reconversion process to the detriment of national progress. NAM officials argued that laborers and consumers had sided with the business plan for the postwar economy, but that constipated government bureaucracy threatened the vast progress that lay on the other side of victory. Such persuasive arguments built support for the business community's postwar plans and publicly demonstrated that if government held onto its war plants and regulatory powers, a "better America" may never materialize after victory.

Building a "Better America"

What, specifically, is it we want the public to believe? . . . There are few things which could do more to allay fear of a postwar depression—than a steady stream of inspiring announcements regarding postwar prospects. . . . What should this advertising say and how should it say it? . . . The most interesting headlines and pictures will be those which seem to portray to the public what others are beginning to think. . . . Faith in the future—and faith in industry's ability to make a brighter future come true.[32]

"*Vision to Anticipate the Needs of Tomorrow Creates New Industries Today*"

Out of the wealth of experience comes ability to create the new. And out of the crucible of war will come many great new industries, with products that are destined to provide mankind with a new freedom, a new joy in living.

For nearly a quarter century, Evans Products Company has pioneered the development and use of new products, each of which has contributed a new utility, new economy and new benefits to the American public and those basic industries serving it.

In transportation—automotive, aviation, rail and marine; in home building; in wood products and plastics; in domestic appliances—heating and ventilating; in organic chemistry; Evans Products Company is a producing force, fashioned to serve the needs of tomorrow.

PRESIDENT

BUY MORE WAR BONDS

EVANS PRODUCTS
COMPANY
DETROIT

Evans War Products: Machine Gun Mounts • Tank and Automotive Heating and Ventilating Equipment • Evanair Water Heaters • Aircraft Engine Mounts • Airplane Landing Gear Beams • Battery Separators • Prefabricated Houses • Molded Plywood Products • Skyloader • Utility Loader • Auto-Loader • Auto-Railer • Auto-Stop • Stampings • Evanair Domestic Heating Equipment

5.2. Evans Products Company advertisement, *Business Week*, 29 July 1944, 47. Courtesy Evans Industries.

The key to engineering public perception was to flood it with "world of to-morrow" narratives, as outlined by the NIIC in its 1943 presentation of its positioning plan for the NAM. The NAM strategy included building consumer confidence in the commercial future and instilling in Americans the belief that big business could smoothly and efficiently lead American society through the uncertainties of postwar reconversion, thus erasing any notion that government could do as well or better. Advertising "headlines and pictures" about the postwar world were central to mobilizing the public mind and were intended to create a symbolic totality in which management and the corporation were equated with a "brighter future."

Appearing to follow its own advice, the NAM launched a nationwide newspaper advertising campaign in 1944 entitled "How Americans Can Earn More, Buy More, Have More." The main concept in the ads from this campaign appears to answer the question posed in the NIIC's 1943 positioning plan above and also shows how animosity toward New Deal power and reforms was woven into messages about postwar prosperity. Designed by the ad agency Kenyon and Eckhardt, the full-page ads (usually unillustrated) announced to the American public: "The time has come when we must look beyond military victory—to make sure that we will have, in peace, the kind of world for which we are now fighting. *Postwar Prosperity for All*. . . . In this undertaking American business . . . will play a major role. For it is primarily to business that . . . the American public turn for a higher standard of living. . . . The 'process of prosperity' can be put in motion and lasting jobs created. They can't be made through government hand-outs—which only increase public debt and raise taxes still further. . . . These messages are published to make clear the steps that must be taken to assure the American people of an economy of abundance in the postwar world." At the bottom of each ad was printed a New York City address to which the public could write for a free booklet of the same title and the assurance of "A Practical Guide to Postwar Prosperity."[33]

The NIIC distributed *A Time for Action: The Job That Industry Must Do Now*, which described and illustrated the NAM's 1944 newspaper advertising campaign. This B2B booklet also included stock advertising samples (with illustrations) that business leaders could use as models to "inform the public of the specific things you are doing to provide postwar employment." The booklet encouraged business leaders to advertise their product plans for the postwar world as a tangible demonstration that there was indeed a better America on the horizon—and to tie this future to concepts of free enterprise:

> You can make your advertising meaningful . . . by translating free enterprise into terms of the jobs, wages, and better living conditions your own business will help provide. Perhaps you have new products now in the laboratory or on the drafting-board, awaiting postwar introduction. Let the public know—specifically. Or discuss some of the improved production and distribution methods you intend using after the war. . . . Many companies are using such approaches now, but a greater use of them and continuing emphasis on *the way in which they are helping Americans*

"to earn more, buy more, and have more" will add immeasurably to the [overall nationwide advertising] program. . . . Specimen advertisements, which *are not meant for use* . . . but which point out ways of utilizing some of the various themes, will be found on the following pages.[34]

In marketing visions of the postwar world, the NIIC suggested to NAM members and other businessmen that they also "sell" the country's corporate/capitalist infrastructure, and we can see this pitch made throughout the NIIC's "Re-Selling the American Way" flyer (see fig. 5.1). The thrust of the NAM's "forceful public information program in behalf of all business and industry"[35] was also summarized in James Adams's 1943 speech, *Working Together for Postwar America,* which positioned the NAM plan for propagandizing free enterprise: "SELLING THE PEOPLE WHAT THEY WANT . . . Whether you sell a manufactured product [or] a service . . . you sell the producer or the company behind it. Why not, when an opportunity offers, sell also the system under which it operates? Why not join with us in our fight for economic freedom?"[36]

"World of tomorrow" narratives, like NAM positioning plans and campaigns, thus presented a picture of business engaged in the "socially responsible" role of saving American democracy and free enterprise from the perceived meddlesome interference of the New Deal in order to clear the way for postwar progress and prosperity. Such a message would be carried out in advertising narratives that illustrated what types of "new and improved" products manufacturers had planned for the postwar future. The subjective details of these products and the sales rhetoric supporting them were meant to rationalize the consumer through nonrational appeals. The real motive behind "world of tomorrow" narratives was to "educate" the public about the contrasts between the economic insecurities and restrictions they would suffer with the New Deal at the helm of the U.S. economy, as opposed to the unfettered prosperity offered by the techno-corporate order—a concept articulated by Arthur Kudner in his advertising recommendations of 1944 (see the opening of this chapter). *Newsweek* recapped this polarizing strategy in its 1943 announcement about the NAM's plan for postwar industry: "'Today . . . Production for Victory . . . Tomorrow . . . Opportunity, Jobs, Freedom' . . . The American system is individualistic—not collectivist. . . . Free, private competitive enterprise brought the world's highest standards of living to America and is the only means for still further advancement."[37]

Although the NAM plan for a "better America" consisted of "Opportunity, Jobs, Freedom," what else did it include? Not only would corporate leadership engender a prosperous economy, but its "better America" would bring about a social evolution. In the business plan for reconversion, prewar comforts and conveniences for the few would translate into commonplace amenities for the many. A 1942 ad from Armco Sheet Metals, published in *American Home,* exemplifies how the war was depicted as the catalyst that ushered a hygienic middle-class standard of living into the average working-class market (fig. 5.3). The ad's copy suggests that its content could have been influenced by NAM marketing suggestions. "Yours for Victory!" points to postwar rewards for consumers' patriotic patience:

Yours for Victory!

Courageous, aggressive, resourceful, this determined youth symbolizes the indomitable spirit that has won every war America has had to fight.

To help serve him and his millions of comrades, practically our entire production is going into *special-purpose* iron and steel sheets for warplanes, ships, combat cars, tanks and jeeps . . . hundreds of vital things to save lives and win victories.

When peace comes the ARMCO Stainless Steel in your kitchen sink, in your pots and pans will be stronger and tougher from its battle lessons. Your porcelain enameled range, refrigerator and other sheet metal equipment will be better for wartime research.

It is this standard we're all fighting for — everything we have that stands for America. The American Rolling Mill Company, 1291 Curtis Street, Middletown, Ohio.

A STANDARD OF LIVING
WORTH FIGHTING FOR

5.3. Armco Sheet Metals advertisement, *American Home*, May 1942, 3. Courtesy A. K. Steel. N. W. Ayer Advertising Agency Records, National Museum of American History, Behring Archives Center, Smithsonian Institution.

the "standard we're all fighting for—everything we have that stands for America."[38] The emphasis on fighting for the American Way echoes the NAM's messages conveyed to both business and the public (see fig. 5.1). In the Armco ad, a pilot, dashing off to a bombing mission, smiles cavalierly at the viewer, as if to imply that modern comforts and conveniences were indeed the reason for his wartime sacrifice and duty. This confirmation is underscored by the hygienic icons of civilization below: a streamlined kitchen of Armco steel cabinets and countertops, lined with an electric mixer and other labor-saving devices. This standard of living was the version of American democracy that corporate leaders hoped to affix to the cause of the war and profit from after victory.

Advertisers took up the wartime battle for the postwar consumer through the promotion of government war bonds. Such campaigns, initiated under Henry Morgenthau, secretary of the treasury, were promoted through private entities such as the War Advertising Council and through government bureaus that were dominated by business leaders, such as the Office of War Information. Businesses contributed to these campaigns by paying for advertisements that included war bond messages—not only to keep their trade names afloat for the duration of the war, but also to earn tax incentives, which sweetened business participation.[39]

War bond advertising offered business leaders a government-sanctioned means of promoting their postwar plans and speaking directly to their future markets— despite the scarcity and sacrifice demanded by the war. Capitalizing on the "world of tomorrow" concept, businessmen turned public support for the war into an incentive to vastly enrich one's standard of living—a marketing trend promoted by the NAM. Buying war bonds was a show of patriotism, and advertising claimed that this form of national loyalty would lead to individual betterment. A 1943 article in *Better Homes and Gardens* articulates the connection between war bonds and a consumer utopia in the "world of tomorrow": "That's what war-bonds bought today will buy you tomorrow—better products and more of them."[40] Such messages conveyed the idea that wartime savings would augment the public's ability to consume, and wartime production would provide jobs and lower prices, putting higher standards of living within reach of millions.[41]

Business was not alone in conceptualizing war bonds as a conduit to economic uplift and social evolution.[42] Under the leadership of Morgenthau, the New Deal goal to extend consumer purchasing power and democratize modern amenities was woven into the marketing policies behind government war bond campaigns.[43] The Roosevelt administration saw in the war "an opportunity to create social harmony," and Morgenthau's war bond campaigns pulled together the New Deal's complementary agendas for universalizing modern standards of living *and* manifesting a more egalitarian America aligned with democratic principles.[44] Thus, government policy behind war bond campaigns intentionally brought together collective participation and individual financial gain. War bond appeals blended "patriotism with economic prosperity" and democracy with consumerism. Cementing victory to the competitive, free enterprise ethic and democratic idealism was perceived as a way to alleviate class and racial tensions during the war and pull the nation together in a common, equitable effort toward defeating the spread of fascism. Emphasizing that *all* Americans were invited to buy war bonds collapsed artificial class barriers. Through this egalitarian agenda, national identity shifted to "a shared aspiration of middle-class materialism" and the potential for social evolution through material gain.[45] Middle-class standards of living could be universalized for anyone willing to participate in the war by buying savings bonds. Naturally, it was easier to save during a period when there was little to purchase and when paychecks were steadier and higher than in the previous decade. Still, Morgenthau believed that highlighting the consumer and class incentives behind war bonds would encourage average Americans to eagerly support the war.[46] Selling shared "sacrifice" as a stepping-stone to abundance would help offset any home front opposition to the war or civilian regulations.

The inclusive consumerism and equal opportunity messages of the war bond campaigns seemed to openly invite ethnic and racial minorities to cooperate wholeheartedly in the war effort. Advertisers hoped that the inferences behind such a message would also deter activists from using the emergency to leverage social reform—an accusation perpetually lobbed at wartime Washington. But the emphasis on the United States as a collective of consumers with shared material aspirations contradicted the unfair treatment experienced by blacks barred from defense jobs, housing, or military service and by Japanese Americans interned for the duration of the war. Although war bond campaign messages implied that minorities were invited into mainstream American society, in reality that was not the case. The federal government may have called for an egalitarian society where everyone had the opportunity to live freely and leisurely as part of the middle class, but it did little to activate that goal. The New Deal rhetorically rallied a united front behind the fight to preserve American "freedoms" such as consumerism, single-family home ownership, and private competitive enterprise. But Washington's collusion with standard racial injustices in business, housing, the armed forces, and manufacturing made it difficult for minorities, especially African Americans, to genuinely believe that they would ever be part of an equal and free nation.[47]

The banner of black wartime "unity" differed drastically from the concept of "unity" forged within white society. When comparing the black press with the mainstream media, it often seems that there were two completely different wars being fought. African American leaders articulated that "unity" was key to victory overseas. And for blacks that "unity" also meant forming a collective front at home in order to secure democratic freedoms denied to nonwhite minorities here and abroad. This dual objective was institutionalized in the black press as the Double V.[48] Educator and activist Mary McLeod Bethune informs us that "what we seek are the prerequisites of complete national unity. America—our America—needs that unity to achieve victory."[49] Bethune does not tie wartime "unity" and "victory" to egalitarian consumer incentives as would have been the case in the New Deal–inspired war bond agenda. Nor does she associate wartime participation with the potential for personal financial gain. Instead, her message is for black Americans to embody the example of genuine democratic cooperation by "point[ing] the way toward a united America. . . . Un-American prejudices, discriminations, and exclusions have no role in the world today. That is why we are fighting Hitler,

Mussolini, and Tojo. That is why we must present a united front in insisting on these same prejudices, discriminations, and exclusions being wiped out in America."[50] It is interesting that the NAM newspaper ads stressed equal opportunity in the postwar world. Part of the NAM's better America equation was "an America in which everyone has the right to get ahead."[51] Could the NAM simply have been referring (as usual) to freedom from government bureaucracy and fiat? Or was it pitching a form of the Double V objective? Another of the ads from the NAM's newspaper campaign asked the public: "Is war the only common cause that can unite us?" suggesting a greater democratic social objective.[52]

Ironically, corporate advertising strategies overlapped with New Deal interest in equalizing access to higher standards of living through war bond savings. However, the business intent behind war bond advertising was hardly a duplicate of the New Deal's populist aspirations for economic and political equity. The techno-corporate order, in contrast, illustrated war bond purchases with objects of persuasion that visually defined democratization as a process of individualistic conspicuous consumption. Sales rhetoric explained that consumers' postwar social mobility would be smoothly expedited by purchases made possible through war bond savings and that this democratization of consumption was the reason for making personal sacrifices during the war. Although New Dealers perceived war bonds as a heroic bridge toward unifying the country for war, and thus ultimately manifesting social harmony, business leaders' idea of unification was certainly more profit and power oriented.[53] A collective outcome for war bond savings had no place in the techno-corporate order's marketing agenda. This bias was spelled out in NAM guidelines to business on how to educate Americans about the American Way through wartime advertising appeals.

Following the business emphasis on individual (over collective) betterment, Hotpoint's campaign helped popularize war bond sales through the tempting promise of a "new and improved" domestic future after victory (fig. 5.4): "We figure the sooner we put every last cent we can in War Bonds, the quicker this war will be over—and we'll be able to have that new Hotpoint Electric Kitchen we want."[54] The "freedoms" for which the war was waged are rhetorically connected to the liberties gained from a labor-saving kitchen with automatic appliances and clean, streamlined cabinets. Another Hotpoint ad states, "Buy War Bonds Today—Electric Kitchens Tomorrow . . . Every dollar I spend for War Bonds gives me a great big thrill of satisfaction! I figure I'm not only helping win the war but hastening the day when I'll be able to own the kitchen I've always dreamed about."[55] Stockpiling war bonds was advertised as a necessary step toward hygienic living. Like the allure built into Hotpoint's electric kitchen, General Electric's new house was a means of social evolution—both of which were the rewards of supporting the war effort with bonds.[56] In its 1943 ad "Hope Chest . . . '43 Style!" GE emphasizes how financing the war was a natural segue into a middle-class lifestyle (fig. 5.5). Blueprints for a postwar dream house are locked away in a box with war bond receipts like pirated treasure.[57] War bonds were typically illustrated as metaphorical transport into a future middle-class status. In a 1943 ad for Kalamazoo Stoves and Furnaces, a family glides into its postwar streamlined kitchen

We're On The BOND WAGON NOW!

WE'RE rolling down that good old Victory road—full speed ahead! We figure the sooner we put every last cent we can in War Bonds, the quicker this war will be over—and we'll be able to have that new Hotpoint Electric Kitchen we want! That's why Joe and I are stretching the budget to invest even *more* than ten per cent of his pay in War Bonds. The more money we have in Bonds, the more of that thrifty, time-saving equipment we can buy for our Hotpoint Electric Kitchen when Hotpoint makes home appliances again instead of war materials!

Some Day We'll Have The ELECTRIC KITCHEN That Bonds Bought!

FOR HOMES COSTING $6,000. The **Meadow Lark Kitchen** illustrated is designed for homes costing as little as $6,000 and is completely electric, with Hotpoint Range, Refrigerator, Dishwasher, Sink and Hotpoint Steel Cabinets.

FOR LOW COST HOMES

FOR HOMES COSTING AS LITTLE AS
$4,000

Hotpoint Electric Kitchens including Range, Refrigerator, Sink and Steel Cabinets have been installed in numerous homes costing only $4,000.

Tomorrow Is Worth Saving For

THERE'S a whale of a lot of incentive for you to make every sacrifice you can today! For after the war—with all the new appliances that are being perfected—the homes of America will be *finer* and cost *less* than you can imagine! Cooking will be done by Hotpoint Electric Ranges that require no watching. Electric refrigeration will be improved beyond belief ... All these miracle-working conveniences can be yours —when the war is won. So speed the day of Victory—save wherever possible in order to buy more and more War Bonds.

BUY WAR BONDS TODAY—An Electric Kitchen Tomorrow!

• Kitchen hours will be cut down considerably with an automatic Hotpoint Electric Range to do the pot-watching! Vitamins and minerals will not be cooked away!

• Built to provide plenty of storage space—and keep foods at flavor peak far longer—the Hotpoint Electric Refrigerator will save time and money!

• A Hotpoint Automatic Electric Dishwasher and Disposall eliminates your most disagreeable, time-taking household tasks! Turn a switch—and your chores are done for you!

The Cost of a Hotpoint Electric Kitchen Averages About 10% of Home-Building Costs

HOME PLANNING FILE

PLAN TODAY FOR TOMORROW'S electric kitchen. Hotpoint's Home Planning File is perfect for saving ideas for your new home. Size 9 x 12 inches, of box board, ten divisions, folder for recording War Bond purchases. If your dealer cannot supply you, send 25 cents in coin or War Stamps.

Edison General Electric Appliance Co., Inc.
5625 W. Taylor St., Chicago, Illinois

Enclosed find 25 cents for which please send **Home Planning File.**

Name _____

Address _____

City _____ State _____

ELECTRIC **Hotpoint** KITCHENS

5.4. Hotpoint advertisement, *Better Homes and Gardens,* June 1943, 16. Used with permission of General Electric.

on a war bond rendered as a magic carpet (fig. 5.6). The family's middle-class rank is emphasized by the father's managerial uniform. A variation on the transport metaphor appears in another GE advertisement from 1943. In "U.S. Victory Highway 1 . . . to the Home of your Dreams!" war bonds pave an easy path, free

5.5. General Electric advertisement, *Better Homes and Gardens,* June 1943, 3. Used with permission of General Electric.

"**Magic Carpet**" – that will carry you into an enchanted kitchen of cooking thrills

AFTER VICTORY–

...**Wonderful new products in cooking and heating will come to improve your way of living**

While Kalamazoo factories hum with war work, Kalamazoo designers and engineers are quietly developing in our research laboratories such far reaching improvements in cooking and heating as to make your present war-weary equipment far behind the times. Invest in War Bonds today— enjoy the conveniences and comforts of new Kalamazoo products tomorrow.

KALAMAZOO STOVE & FURNACE COMPANY
Kalamazoo, Michigan

Kalamazoo
Stoves and Furnaces
QUALITY LEADERS SINCE 1901

of obstacles, to suburban home ownership (fig. 5.7).[58] Lying side by side, the bonds are composed in the manner of a "yellow brick road" leading directly to a single-family house in the background. Just like the father's suit and tie in the Kalamazoo ad, the single-family suburban home is a visual clue that this future bought with war bonds takes place in the middle-class stratum.

Images of a future filled with streamlined kitchens and quaint, clapboard houses seduced potential bond buyers with visions of ascending to a flawless family life.[59] The democratic values for which the war was supposedly fought were associated with consumer purchases through which one could evolve into a higher social plateau. Social evolution as scripted in "world of tomorrow" narratives involved the freedom to make consumer purchases and the liberty to acquire a white middle-class standard of living. War bond savings thus promised those outside the white middle class access to the products that would affirm their evolutionary worth through cleaner and more efficient, comfortable, and convenient lives.[60] This mass leap into the middle class, then, also represented a hygienic *revolution*. The war was thus conceptualized as a messianic catalyst for disseminating these vestments of proper civilization and progress.

5.6. Kalamazoo Stoves and Furnaces advertisement, *Ladies' Home Journal,* August 1943, 134.

And this shall be our Victory:

In a free nation—as the birthright of every American

—each home shall be a shrine of freedom.

...*to the Home of your Dreams!*

THERE'S a new home at the end of this Victory Highway, where it climbs to meet the horizon— *your home of tomorrow!*

It isn't built yet, and can't be until this war is won— 'til peace. But you can plan for it today.

And what a home it will be! It's going to be friendly, inviting, chock-full of comfort—with electrical conveniences that will make it a far more livable home than you ever thought possible. Your Victory Home of tomorrow will have *better living built in!*

Take the shortest way there—the sure road to happiness and security for yourself, to peace and prosperity for your country—buy War Bonds!

DEDICATED TO THE SERVICE OF AMERICA'S HOMES

The General Electric Consumers Institute at Bridgeport, Conn., is devoted to research on such wartime home problems as: Nutrition · Food Preparation · Food Preservation · Appliance Care · Appliance Repair · Laundering · Home Heating and Air Conditioning. Bulletins and booklets are available through your G-E Appliance Dealer, or from G-E Consumers Institute, Dept. AH5-3.

Tune in on Frazier Hunt and the News every Tues., Thurs., Sat. evenings over C. B. S. On Sunday night listen to the "Hour of Charm," over N.B.C. See newspapers for time, station.

GENERAL GE **ELECTRIC**
CONSUMERS INSTITUTE

WAR BONDS WILL BUILD NEW VICTORY HOMES TOMORROW

5.7. General Electric advertisement, *American Home,* May 1943, 3. Used with permission of General Electric.

African Americans realized they were not especially included in the "equal opportunity to consume" messages that saturated wartime advertising. Appeals for purchasing war bonds were certainly marketed to black communities, as Lawrence Samuel's 1997 study points out, and black consumers were encouraged by columnists and activist leaders to perceive war industry jobs and bond savings as a way to empower their race economically.[61] But war bonds for blacks were not merely an escalator into freedoms and equal citizenship via consumerism, but a way to underscore the less-than-democratic contradictions inherent in American society. In the African American paper the *Pittsburgh Courier*, the war bond logo with the tagline "For Victory" was included in cartoons criticizing American injustices. In 1945 the illustrator "Holloway" depicted a scene titled "The Convenient Accused," in which a thug (rendered as a menacing white gangster) has just clobbered Uncle Sam in the head. The gangster, with his club hidden behind his back, points accusingly at a young black news carrier holding papers with the masthead "The Negro Press." A stunned Uncle Sam looks helplessly at the young news carrier, who is about to become the gangster's next victim. An appeal for buying war bonds, illustrated with a Revolutionary War minuteman figure, is tacked to the wall behind the scene where "The Negro Press" is about to be silenced for speaking up in defense of American democracy—the principles for which American independence was initially fought and the freedom for which the current war was ostensibly being waged.[62]

Marketing the war through consumer incentives certainly distanced the effort from the justice sought by black Americans. The concept of the "world of tomorrow" bought with war bonds ironically helped connect class aspirations and conspicuous consumption with winning the war, thus diluting the fight for worldwide democracy down to little but superfluous rhetoric. However, "world of tomorrow" narratives were not limited to selling American consumers on the idea that their lives would improve from the war. Little did white Americans realize that the "gangster's" reach, as illustrated in the *Pittsburgh Courier*, was not restricted to impinging on liberties in black communities.

Building a Docile America

A "better America," according to the business community's plan, meant avoiding hindrance not only from New Deal bureaucrats but especially from disgruntled labor unions. Business would attempt to undermine the New Deal by associating it with a failed "world of tomorrow," lower living standards, no jobs, and thus a bad deal for labor. Managerial controls or plans were identified as the efficient Taylorized saviors in the NAM postwar narrative and were never cast as nefarious (or virtually barbaric) like those of the New Deal were. This paradox surfaces in James Adams's 1943 speech:

> Those who favor bureaucratic control over our economy will hesitate at nothing. Already we can see that the bureaucrats are claiming credit for the war production job. . . . If business falters in its responsibility, the

public reluctantly will accept the bureaucratic approach of threat, regimentation, and the bribery of deficit spending. . . . Above all, if we are to
continue America's 150-year-old record of a rising standard of living . . .
through constantly lowered unit costs, with resulting constantly lower
prices relative to the consumer's income, we must maintain the efficiency
which comes only through free enterprise.[63]

If business could make a more feasible promise for delivering the goods in
peacetime, as it had delivered the goods for war, then it could offset the growing
collectivism in the country by focusing labor's attention on the easier acquisition
of middle-class status, complete with the latest appliances and postwar "miracle"
products. Corporate-sponsored studies, the NAM claimed, had shown that the
public sought higher standards of living and associated the end of the war with
achieving them: "All Americans hope for advances in our standards of living, security and economic justice when the war is over."[64] Obviously, the advertising
campaigns were working.

Despite the emphasis on saving the free enterprise system from the collectivist clutches of the New Deal, the postwar hygienic revolution would not come
for free. There was a catch to the business postwar plan: no handouts—unrestricted production did not mean a free ride into middle-class social standing.[65] As
was the case with business's plan for recovery during the Depression,[66] postwar
prosperity would be delivered only if the public (and especially labor) preferred
management, mass production, and mass consumption to solve social problems
instead of relying on government-backed programs. Just as business had sought
to resuscitate the public's faith in its ability to win a global war, so too would consumer confidence in spending have to be rebuilt, and the idea instilled in the public mind that a higher standard of living in the postwar world could be had by all
if Americans would only accept the business equation for a successful reconversion: that is, consumption plus production equals American democracy. Thus,
the business plan emphasized that postwar prosperity and democratized progress
depended not only on a compliant labor force but also on a commercial commitment from the average consumer to unfreeze war bond savings and spend—an
assessment acknowledged by the Kenyon Research Corporation in its 1944 synthesis of public opinion on "the subject of post-war problems and planning":

It is obvious that if full employment is to be realized after the war people
are going to have to "unfreeze" their savings. Spending is a function of
confidence. It is industry's job to instill that confidence by presenting to the
public now the story of what they are doing to solve the unemployment
problem after the war. . . . Unless given this [economic and leadership]
confidence, however, the public will, in all probability turn to public
works, relief, etc. with its inherent high taxes and governmental controls.[67]

The NAM encouraged advertisers to promote a vision of the postwar
world demonstrating how consensual consumption, upheld by the corporate

infrastructure, would solve economic problems, as well as labor discord, and universally raise standards of living, which, in its estimation, government could not and had failed to do.[68] A postwar depression, disgruntled labor, and a stronger New Deal could be avoided if consumers were convinced that a commercially viable and thus "better America" awaited them in the postwar era.

Although corporate patriotism revealed the "unselfish side" of business and built consumer goodwill, ads and articles envisioning the postwar world were intended to cement the paternal relationship between the corporate establishment and the average consumer with the temptations of a "better America." Thus, publicity about the postwar world, which revealed what new products and improvements were in store for consumers, was intended to profess that business had the only "proper" and "democratic" strategy for creating jobs and sustaining wartime prosperity after victory.[69]

In its attempt to remove the New Deal from its postwar equation, the techno-corporate order contrasted its promise of higher standards of living (resulting from high production and consumption) with a frightening vision of American decline and socialism resulting from the corporate perception of New Deal bureaucratic incompetence and pathological control. Ironically, the corporate program for a "better America," especially as crafted by the NAM, exhibited as many undemocratic and taboo controls as business leaders perceived in the New Deal. Business leaders' postwar commercial agenda harbored strategies for institutionalizing a corresponding social agenda as well. Engineering a "better America" involved an intensive psychological assault on the public mind, consisting of disciplining consumers to believe that the corporate way was the authentic (and more hygienic) American Way.[70]

Styling Corporate Plans for the Postwar World

Industrial design very definitely means more, and means something else than decoration. . . . Design means deliberate, organized planning. . . . It aims at better products at lower costs, achieved through the means of efficient planning. It aims at higher standards in appearance values through means of imaginative planning . . . and it bases such planning upon the findings of modern science and technology. . . . Efficient, imaginative, creative planning—does it sound like something that has no place in time of war?[71]

On the eve of World War II, the industrial design profession enjoyed a respectable reputation within the business community due to its association with managerial planning and organization.[72] Often perceived (and promoted) as a logical extension of modern scientific methods, mechanization, engineering, and mass production, industrial design was recognized as integral to making business run more smoothly through efficiently designed products, spaces, and equipment. Certainly designers thought of themselves this way, as Antonin Heythum of the California Institute of Technology tells us in his 1940 article quoted above, in which he describes the design profession's perfect fit in wartime mobilization. Given the variety of projects that designers engaged in during the war, it was obvious that government, military officials, and business leaders concurred.[73] The mobilization of furniture designers to wartime production is especially telling of how "stylists" were able to adapt their design techniques and materials knowledge in order to maximize the efficiency of the Allies' war machine. Charles and Ray Eameses' work in molded plywood furniture and their study of organic forms made this couple especially valuable for solving the wartime need for "efficient, imaginative, creative planning." In addition to the molded plywood splints and stretchers for the navy, which needed a more comfortable and hygienic solution to its metal leg splints, the Eameses and their colleagues produced glider nose cones, aircraft stabilizers, and pilot seats.[74]

As a result of their adaptability to wartime production needs, designers did not face the ad men's desperate quandary of finding a "legitimate" or "useful" wartime role upon America's entry into World War II (see introduction). Although ad men also relied heavily on the "science" of human engineering and had woven the language of Taylorism into their ad copy, the design profession did not have to defend its purpose as did the ad industry, because "efficiency design" (a managerial and more macho-sounding label for "styling") was recognized as not merely necessary for the war effort but especially imperative to secure a prosperous postwar economy. Heythum tells us how critical designers were to efficient and effective postwar planning, a role they would perform throughout the war: "Some production centers now fully occupied with wartime jobs are calling on industrial designers to work on projects involving problems which will arise from the latter shifting from war production back to civilian production."[75] With their wartime niche well established and their managerial reputation intact, the industrial design profession embarked on two major objectives for profiting (both symbolically and financially) from the war effort.

Like ad men, industrial designers were not immune to the business community's struggle for a successful reconversion. Their clients' factories, tooled for war production, provided the postwar industrial infrastructure on which the much-heralded "world of tomorrow" would be built. How the government responded to the war plant reconversion problem was crucial to whether designers and their clients would be able to see their blueprints for the "world of tomorrow" become profitable postwar realities. But according to one of the most prominent designers of the day, Walter Dorwin Teague, more than profits was at risk in determining the direction of the postwar economy. A socialist or collectivist future lurked on the horizon for those businesses that left the postwar future to chance. As if following NAM publicity guidelines, Teague in 1943 called upon management to preserve the free enterprise system and "our democratic way of life" by wresting postwar planning decisions from government:

When it comes time to go back to consumer production [after victory] . . . on the rightness or wrongness of the decisions hang stakes that are just about the biggest that can be imagined: not merely the prosperity of individual businesses, or even national prosperity—but the continued existence of our system of free enterprise, and the preservation of our democratic way of life. . . . The responsibility is squarely up to industrial management. . . . The government can't do it—under our system. The alternative is for industry to do it, and prove that our system is as good as we think it is—or run the risk of another system being tried.[76]

It was, therefore, in the best business interest of designers to follow the dominant corporate plans for reconversion, which included dismantling the New Deal's power and popularity. Another influential designer of the era, Raymond Loewy, in a 1942 *Art & Industry* article, espoused an anti–New Deal platform and expressed fears of the collapse of traditional business practices as a result of the collectivist tendencies installed to win the war. By implementing and publicizing plans now for product reconversion, Loewy claimed, manufacturers could offset this dangerous scenario lurking on the horizon:

> Another trend which is affecting design through business is the increasing danger—to the large manufacturing corporations—of Government operation. In order for private industry to avoid such an eventuality it must demonstrate clearly to the public that no other set-up [than private industry] could possibly do a better job. Distinctive design at minimum cost, reflecting imagination and taste, is the best, single advantage that private industry has over Government-manufactured products. By designing now for days of peace the designer is preparing with industry for the immediate economical conversion of plant activities into peace-time efforts.[77]

Likewise, Teague proposed, again in 1943, that the New Deal, and any socialist governments that might emerge anew after the war, could be undermined through corporate product planning, which would resuscitate consumption and stimulate reconversion in the direction of a capitalist-driven prosperity. In Teague's estimation, "styling" was the answer to battling regimented, overbureaucratized government, because human nature craved the consumption of attractive and efficient products. Therefore, according to Teague, design could function as propaganda for American free enterprise and corporate postwar interests by associating freedom of product choice and variety with democracy:

> Above all else, [we should] see that . . . good things are accomplished through the will of the people . . . and that they are not handed down from above by the fiat of a wise, beneficent Government. . . . Reform by regimentation won't work anyhow, because people are naturally cussed and bitterly resent being forced to accept what they don't choose for themselves. . . . Human progress is not accomplished through benefits conferred by force, but through the growing and spreading desire for better things with the means at hand to satisfy that desire. You think that

isn't a design problem? But it is. It is the job of creative design to make the good things so attractive, so useful, so desirable that the wanting of them will grow irresistibly in every mind . . . Above all, it is the designers' business to open more and more eyes to the vision of the fair and orderly world that we shall have [after victory].[78]

Both Teague's and Loewy's polemics recall many of the rhetorical strategies utilized by the NAM. In Loewy's example, "Government operation" is demonized by highlighting how private industry is naturally capable of doing a "better" job in the business of reconversion—a point Teague also makes. Idioms such as "distinctive," "minimum cost," "imagination and taste," "orderly," and "creative design" emphasize, once again, the superior traits born of the corporate efficiency ethic—which inferior "Government-manufactured products" obviously lacked. Teague depicts a paternal omniscient government as a coercive menace; "regimentation" and "reform" are, as in the NAM's rhetoric, codes for the New Deal's supposed totalitarian contagion. Teague, especially, writes of the inherent dangers to social evolution ("human progress") when laissez-faire competition and consumption (i.e., "choose for themselves") are eclipsed by government programs and plans (i.e., "benefits conferred by force"). Progress naturally unfolds, according to Teague, when the "desire" for social evolution ("better things") is met by a business-controlled industrial reconversion ("the means at hand").

Although Teague and Loewy concurred with the NAM's anti–New Deal platform, as is evident in their statements quoted here, they also took advantage of business anxiety about the postwar future to further their own professional agendas. Yes, they agreed, the New Deal's heavy presence in wartime industrial and economic matters posed a significant threat. But designers positioned themselves as the antidote, and in their wartime articles they attempted to monopolize the cure for postwar socialism and depression. Although any copywriter might be able to spin a "world of tomorrow" narrative, it was the industrial design profession that had the knowledge and experience to make such hyperbole tangible. In fact, it was the designer's job, his very raison d'être (i.e., "Above all, it is the designers' business to open more and more eyes . . ."). What manufacturers needed to "demonstrate clearly to the public" was the value of the free enterprise system, and what better way to do so than through design? Stimulating desire for a postwar social evolution and having the material goods to "satisfy that desire" was the key to harnessing public favor for corporate plans and leadership rather than the New Deal's.[79]

Although stimulating public interest in the "world of tomorrow" could build goodwill with consumers *during* the war, what about *after* victory? Designers argued that manufacturers would be forced to deliver the progress they had held out as an incentive for supporting business leaders' postwar agenda. Postwar narratives would need to become concrete realities. After all, business had shown how the New Deal plan represented a failed "world of tomorrow" even before the war ended. The renewed consumer faith in business may collapse if no new products were available soon after victory. Once again, designers held the antidote for this problem: planning now (through product development) would salvage business's reputation and help it sustain the authority it had restructured for itself during the war. Utilizing dystopian scenarios, Leo Rich of Teague's firm compelled anxious businessmen and manufacturers to plan realizable postwar products during the war by hiring experts in product styling:

> It's one thing to resume production with old models because of factors beyond one's control, and quite another to resume production with old models because the producer expects a seller's market in which anything goes. There may be considerable resistance to these old models if the public [primed for progress] feels the manufacturer is holding back. . . . Instead of a wild scramble, the public will exercise its freedom of choice when it has time to spend its wartime savings. . . . Preparing the regular products of a company for the postwar market is just as important as the development of new products. . . . The industrial designer can offer invaluable assistance in shaping postwar products to postwar markets.[80]

Although consumers needed a boost to their confidence in the American Way, Rich argued that their desire for higher standards of living required no stimulation. This put business in a precarious situation if it failed to harness this desire and, instead, let government regulation take over by default: "The desire of the people for better things is symbolic of their hope for a better world. Will it be necessary for them to secure these things through governmental authority or will we in industry [i.e., management] be able to get more and better goods into the hands of a greater number of people, thereby maintaining employment and raising the standard of living?"[81]

Designers also took responsibility in their rhetoric for convincing business that a prosperous postwar economy was contingent on full employment. Citizens with jobs were consumers who would spend their paychecks and wartime savings on newly designed goods. According to Teague, providing an incentive for consumption with steady employment and new postwar products would put business, not the New Deal, in the reconversion driver's seat and thereby stave off the demise of the American Way:

> [If we can accomplish full employment after the war,] the people employed will have the means to consume the goods they produce. . . . If industry can make the American public understand and appreciate its program, the atmosphere necessary to a successful trial will be induced. If it can show that it is on the way to solving the problem of full employment and high productivity within the frame of our own system of free enterprise, the reasons for government domination and revolutionary change [i.e., socialism] will be removed.[82]

Thus, the corporate vision of postwar America, which the consumer engineering professions helped shape and disseminate, attempted to abolish New

Deal collectivism by associating the American Way with victory on two fronts: the battlefield and the postwar economy. The entire livelihood of "consumer engineers" and "stylists," and of the whole design profession, was dependent on consumer confidence in spending and less government interference in business. Although designers had found a ready and welcome niche for their expertise in the war effort, they recognized that uninhibited, private enterprise and a consumption-driven economy, stimulated by perpetually new styles and products (i.e., planned obsolescence), provided the salient and—in their estimation—only remedy to their profession's growth after the war. Thus, while the advertising trade scrambled to endure and override the criticisms lobbed at its credibility in a wartime economy, designers leveraged the commercial obfuscation of the war years to plot their strategies for helping clients fashion a postwar world dominated by unbridled mass production and voracious consumption. Designers like Teague and Loewy not only adopted NAM-like rhetoric but also emphasized the corporate practice of planned obsolescence, which they wove into design propaganda that disparaged the New Deal and simultaneously habituated businessmen to the idea that hiring a "stylist" was the critical ingredient to a profitable reconversion.[83] Such members of the design industry used schemes to make prewar models obsolete as part of their frontal attack on wartime socialist/collectivist practices that posed an unwelcome (perhaps exaggerated) threat to the consumption-driven economy. By equating democracy and freedom—the causes for which the war was supposedly fought—with a utopian postwar world of unprecedented consumer choices and access to affordable higher standards of living, the techno-corporate order, with the assistance of industrial designers, was able to ensure that a "business-dominated social and economic order" would prevail over wartime collectivism and New Deal regulations.[84]

6 Hygienic Solutions for the "House of Tomorrow"

Despite our twentieth-century realism and scientific advances, the average home possesses few comforts. Suffocatingly hot in summer, drafty and unevenly heated in winter, badly lighted in all seasons, cluttered with too much furniture and equipped with old-fashioned appliances that function poorly or not at all, our homes reflect few of the engineering and designing achievements of our generation.[1]

As postwar forecasters Norman Carlisle and Frank Latham lamented, housing had not adequately advanced to mid-twentieth-century standards before the outbreak of the war.[2] *Rational* domesticity, in the form of efficiently designed spaces, universal electric standards, and automatic appliances, they claimed, still eluded many Americans. Too hot, too cold, too cluttered, and inefficient in every regard, the average contemporary abode seemed to have been overlooked by Frederick Winslow Taylor's ethos of standardization. What was common to science, business, and the factory, Carlisle and Latham suggested, seemed far removed from most American households. Statistics confirm this assertion. In 1941, as the United States mobilized for war, inadequate living standards remained the unfortunate norm: eleven million houses lacked running water, fifteen million were deprived of private indoor flush toilets, and seventeen million were wanting in private baths.[3] With little construction implemented during the 1930s and with wartime developments in housing, technology, and science limited to military or defense-plant use, hygienic propriety lay beyond a large fragment of the social body.[4]

Built-in Better Living

The paucity of rational housing in the early 1940s was not for want of trying.[5] Domestic scientists at the turn of the century had attempted to tackle the problem by rationalizing the average household. Influenced by the efficiency craze spearheaded by Frederick Winslow Taylor, these domestic scientists restructured household space and chores around the perceived logic and order of the factory assembly line.[6] Their insistence on making a science of domesticity institutionalized the civilizing craft of scientific housekeeping. The kitchen and bathroom received much of the reformers' attention because in these rooms, higher standards in design and efficiency, as well as lowered costs, would automatically instill an internal, self-regulating ethic.[7] Scientifically managed bathroom and kitchen designs were intended to naturally induce hygienic living practices. Ultimately, household reform through modernization and scientific housekeeping was another conduit for social control.

Such socially hygienic goals, many reformers believed, could be reached only by redesigning the house around its power and sanitation sources. Radical domestic reformers espoused the idea that affordable electricity and running water should enter the bathroom and kitchen facilities through a scientifically planned, factory-assembled, utility service unit—or "core." Architect and designer R. Buckminster Fuller led the charge for supporters of the prefabricated "core" concept. In 1927, Fuller introduced his "scientific" building type, the Dymaxion, which consisted of standardized, built-in appliances, such as a machine-stamped, central engineering facility (the "core").[8] Designed to control each house's climate, lighting, sanitation, and water supply, the Dymaxion core was equipped with its own power generator and water recycling system, thus eliminating dependence on public utilities and solving the problem of their absence in rural areas. Because this utility core would be factory-made and easily transported, Fuller insisted, it would also be inexpensive and available to urban and rural citizens alike.[9]

Variations on the service core concept dominated the 1930s ideal of the curative "house of tomorrow," revealing the continuity of Progressive Era prescriptions for sanitizing society through scientifically managed reforms. By the war years, the idea of prepackaged kitchen/bathroom units in the hygienic form of mechanical service cores, as Buckminster Fuller proposed, had evolved into standard lore within housing reform narratives found in the manifestos penned by some modernist architects/designers as well as the recommendations promoted by kitchen equipment, flooring, and cabinetry companies. Standard reform narratives of the 1930s also involved discussions about the hygienic features of built-in appliances (designed to be flush with cabinet surfaces), uninterrupted built-in furniture modules, and standardized movable panel walls.[10] These progressive design features

were offshoots of the popular streamlining impulse to "clean up" surfaces and
spaces through simplification, standardization, and prefabrication. Elaborate decorative features, it was argued, were "unscientific" and wasteful because they absorbed too much time and energy on cleaning dust-collecting nooks and crannies.[11]
Corporations and modernist architects promoted these "cleaner" design plans as
the ultimate "scientific" solution because they seemed to lack "irrational" (unhygienic) ornamentation.[12] The hygienic powers ascribed to rational design and scientific planning were not limited to streamlining health and aesthetics, but were
also imbued with the ability to rout poverty and cure the social ills that substandard housing naturally bred.

The 1930s housing reform debate, like its predecessor in the Progressive Era,
was permeated by a less-than-democratic undercurrent. A 1939 cartoon titled "We
Hope You'll Be Gone With the Slums" conveys the urgency for social control
through housing reform and reveals key prejudices underpinning the movement
for rational design and scientific planning (fig. 6.1).[13] The visual idioms in this cartoon, which appeared in the *New Orleans Times-Picayune,* express common human-
engineering assumptions that housing type and appearance were barometers for
measuring the health of human character and genetic traits. In the cartoon, degrees of innate health and aesthetic beauty are contrasted with degrees of inborn
ugliness and degeneration—the socially permitted versus the repulsed and forbidden. The heroic protagonist looks remarkably similar to a youthful Franklin Roosevelt. He is the proper and healthy specimen of Anglo-Saxon masculinity (the
racial "norm"), and he smiles self-righteously as he shows his arsenal of reform to
"Delinquency," "Disease," and "Dispiritedness," happily communicating these un-
desirables' deserved demise.[14] The miscreants, about to be leveled along with
their dilapidated house, have been rendered with faces riddled with aesthetic defects that underscore the badges of ill health and poor character that they wear. All
three have exaggerated long noses (deviations from the racial norm) that reflect a
backward genetics and inborn social defects that are the root cause of such types'
predisposition to manifest the unhygienic conditions in which they reside.[15] The
nose on "Dispiritedness" is bulbous at the end—an indication of alcoholism. The
mongrels' roster of physical flaws include scrawniness and, for "Disease" and
"Dispiritedness," sagging jowls and masses of hair as unkempt as their surroundings. Even the shape of the chin acts as a measure of character. "Disease's" chin is
disproportionately pointy, while that of "Dispiritedness" has sunk into his face—
both indicators of poor breeding and an inferior genetic stock that will never
measure up to the high standards of the "best" Americans, like the cartoon's Roosevelt look-alike.[16] Clearly, the picture suggests, these undesirable denizens are as
much a lost cause as their slum housing.

The houses in this hygienically directed narrative also array regularities against
irregularities, paralleling the physiognomic story of the human specimens and
underscoring the moral of the tale: that the "best" possess a stamina that will ultimately triumph over the unfit. Everything about the slum house is feeble and
derelict: the shutters are uneven and appear to have come unhinged (signifying to
us lack of care and attention from the people therein) and the bricks seem to

6.1. Political cartoon by Keith Temple, "We Hope You'll Be Gone With the Slums," 1939. © 2005 The *Times-Picayune* Publishing Co. All rights reserved. Used with permission of the *Times-Picayune*.

We Hope You'll Be Gone With the Slums

crumble from the weight of inefficient health, defective morals, and ill-bred minds. Across the street from the slums is the hygienic answer to this pervasive social dilemma: single-family houses. As if to highlight the evolutionary disparity between the two housing types, the slums are rendered in black (the negative end of the spectrum), while the single-family houses are depicted in "pure" white. Like the specimen of Anglo-Saxon racial superiority, the single-family house was perceived as the best and most healthy type of house. As euthenic supporters asserted, the "racial norm" and the "housing norm" were engaged in a reciprocal reinforcement: they were inseparable, and deviations from either were considered lower and less deserving on the evolutionary scale of progress.[17]

Tessie Agan's lessons in her 1939 textbook parallel the social, racial, and ethnic beliefs that pervade the New Orleans cartoon of the same year. Following along the lines of euthenic beliefs, Agan's remarks imply that substandard housing and overcrowded conditions are tied to character. Moreover, the contagion that such conditions bred was not limited to the people and places where it began; hence the need for social planning in order to protect the health and well-being of those living outside the slums:

> Undoubtedly, [poor housing] is one factor in producing disease and degeneracy. It is so often linked with other injurious circumstances such as poverty, ignorance, vice, and uncleanliness, with the accompanying

consequences of unsatisfactory food, scanty and ineffective medical and nursing service, monotonous or difficult labor, unhygienic personal habits, noise, bad air, dust [etc.] . . . It is generally recognized the effects of poor housing on health are not confined to the slums. . . . Originating there, these effects may spread out through the community, and beyond to state and nation, affecting the health and happiness of persons seemingly remote. . . . Overcrowding or lack of room . . . has long been . . . one of the most common conditions in substandard housing. It may be caused by shortage of housing, poverty, or ignorant racial habits.[18]

The legacy of a social reform ideology that associated "proper" housing with "proper" character and genetic destiny can be traced throughout wartime discourse on the postwar house. Walter Dorwin Teague's 1943 treatise in *House Beautiful,* "A Sane Prediction," provides a glimpse into reconversion narratives that focused on evoking social reform through healthy environs and communities:

If a house is dilapidated, ramshackle, not equipped properly according to modern standards of living, it will be obliterated ruthlessly as we now illuminate any other plague spot. We shall insist that human dignity and the racial welfare require decent and adequate shelter for everybody, on the same grounds that we insist with growing firmness on proper education, diet and health service for everybody. . . . At last the means will be available for maintaining such a standard.[19]

Echoing the assumptions of earlier reformers, Teague believed that efficient housing design and rational planning were no mere physical necessities but were essential for attaining societal health ("racial welfare"). In "A Sane Prediction," poor-quality houses ("dilapidated, ramshackle," and ill-equipped) are cast as "plague spots" that are "illuminated" by the righteous spotlight of scientific reform and annihilated like germs. "Proper" houses reflect civilized order and control over chaos as well as the perpetuation of the "best" character. Teague, like other wartime forecasters, claims that the war is an instrument for bettering society by liberating access to the tools necessary for attaining hygienic propriety (he states, "At last the means will be available for maintaining such a standard"). If the war is being fought to rid the world of fascism, then the lessons of wartime housing design and construction make designers and architects morally obligated to transform their wartime work into a vehicle for eradicating the visible, socially debilitating blight of poverty: substandard housing.

Teague's belief in the curative powers of standardization and modular units was widely expressed in other reconversion narratives of the day. Wartime reformers and forecasters generally agreed that prefabrication and mass production provided manageable and thus efficient alternatives to current construction practices. Teague championed prefabricated movable wall panels that promised speedy assembly and the exponential growth of home ownership: "I believe that the successful [prefab construction] system will reduce the house to a small assortment of moderate-size panels which can be quickly assembled into hundreds of different plans."[20] For Teague, as well as for other housing specialists from the conservative to the liberal, it was important to assert that mass production facilitated the healthy evolution of individuality, rather than its stagnation and ultimate demise. Prefabricated modular units, though fashioned from a single mold, could produce "hundreds of different" design plans. Moreover, artificial plastic materials could do the same thing, thus surpassing costly and dwindling natural resources in their ability to manifest a wide range of design choices. Such consumer liberty in housing was usually reserved for those who could afford expensive custom designs. But this exclusivity would change (ironically) through standardization: "The principal materials used [in construction of the postwar house] will be synthetic [and] can give the low-cost, prefab house an aesthetic range and richness which only the wealthy have been able to enjoy in the past. . . . The dynamic trend will be toward better and better houses at lower and lower costs, until we reach a balance between income and the price of shelter."[21]

The market for which the standardized, mechanized "house of tomorrow" was intended had to be convinced that wartime innovations would fulfill not only basic necessities but also aspirations to, at the least, *appear* middle class. Thus, standardized built-ins, plastic prefab parts, and factory-stamped mechanical cores were shown to uphold the innate moral values that composed hygienic propriety: neatness, cleanliness, taste, and orderly control. Commercial forecasters for the housing industry were speaking to this audience of middle-class pretenders, and, as a result, the solutions they offered had to realistically fit this market's ambitions, not to mention its wallet.[22]

Wartime articles about R. Buckminster Fuller's Dymaxion House blended democratic idealism with conformity to middle-class norms. Fuller's Wichita Dymaxion, as his postwar model was called, offered a presumably rational means by which low-income families could enter the symbolic realm of middle-class identity and even surpass its ideal hygienic standards. Drawing on plans from his 1927 Dymaxion, Fuller professed his ability to solve postwar housing and employment shortages by reconverting the wartime aviation business into a prefabricated housing industry (fig. 6.2). Thanks to advances in war production, his postwar Dymaxion could conceivably be implemented at low cost for the postwar home buyer by creating a house with preexisting aircraft parts and aeronautic assembly methods using bolts and "blind" rivets.[23] Fuller's postwar plan, like his 1927 version, organized single-family living around a centralized household unit. Fuller's service core made managing family life virtually effortless and, best of all, affordable: "Electricity, heat, light, water and air services are centrally placed in a controlled system offering the shortest radial distance to each of the rooms thus providing the most economic use of energy sources. . . . Based on planned production of at least 50,000 units per year, the house will sell for no more than $6500."[24]

Promotional articles about the Wichita Dymaxion assert that Fuller's "scientific" plans made it easier to achieve hygienic propriety through household designs and machines that annihilated dirt and disorder automatically. Fuller demonstrated his model of futuristic scientific housekeeping in diagrams showing

6.2. R. Buckminster Fuller, "Wichita Dymaxion House," model. Courtesy, The Estate of R. Buckminster Fuller, Santa Barbara, California.

6.3. R. Buckminster Fuller, "Wichita Dymaxion House," cutaway drawing. Courtesy, The Estate of R. Buckminster Fuller, Santa Barbara, California.

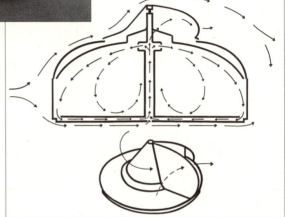

a progressive ventilation system that would suck "healthy" air in and flush "bad" air out (fig. 6.3). The Dymaxion's built-in scientific "housekeepers" would create a tidy appearance and sanitary household instantaneously without the need for paid servants or much labor from the housewife: "Photographs taken in the Fuller House . . . show why housewives are enchanted. . . . The ventilator draws air from the house changing the air inside every six minutes if desired and carrying away dust, odors, and germs."[25]

The rejuvenated American industries and newly developed materials and processes derived from the war made it possible for reformers, architects, designers, and household equipment companies to implement their ideal "world of tomorrow." Although they painted a picture of a utopian America in which few would suffer from the inadequacies of unsanitary living conditions and faulty housing, they advised their prospective consumers that this utopia was not offered for free with no strings attached. "Scientific" comfort, convenience, and hygienic propriety could be democratized by fully developing the wartime housing lessons into domestic use in peacetime—but only at a price. This human-engineering version of American "democracy" was actually a process of cultural homogenization that would assist the "proper" classes, religions, ethnicities, and races in smoothly assimilating into the hygienic ideal of the native-born, white middle class. The postwar hygienic revolution, then, would reach far beyond the cleaned-up contours of new household products to "streamline" the social body into an acceptable middle-class mold.

Authors of reconversion narratives commonly linked human engineering to the benevolent by-products of American freedom and democracy. Walter Dorwin Teague, in a 1943 article for the British industrial art journal *Studio International,* exemplifies this rhetorical pattern, which many times reflected an anti-urban (and thus anti-nonwhite) sentiment. Teague espoused a vision of a sterilized postwar world in which the inner city would be purged of its "unscientific" inefficiency and transformed into a hygienic arena for the business transactions of the managerial class. Factories and old buildings that did not fit the new hygienic norm would be dismantled and replaced with facilities for "airborne automotive transport," which would fly commuters to and from their safe, sanitary enclaves in the suburbs: "Here are some of the things we shall have to do [after the war]: . . . Rebuild our cities for airborne and automotive transport . . . [and drain] most of the residential population out of them and [transform] them [urban spaces] into spacious, *cleanly marts* where people come together for the transaction of business."[26]

In the process of this urban cleanup, many working poor and minorities who populate these areas will be evicted and uprooted—all for the sake of progress. But Teague turned a blind eye to their needs, classifying them, by implication, as subhuman due to their substandard environs. After all, Teague assumed that if these urbanites were the proper types, they would not be living in slums in the first place. Nonetheless, Teague's planned utopia reads like a housing bill of rights—despite his earlier emphasis on manifesting social control through a perfected environment:

> Provide for all the people housing that shall be as efficient, as attractive, as cheap, as easily acquired, and as readily renewable as the cars they ride in now . . . It means the replacement, largely, of our old-fashioned building craft by a scientifically directed factory craft [i.e., scientifically managed prefabrication and assembly-line production]. . . . See that every house in the country has a modern bathroom, a . . . modern kitchen, and those appliances that take the drudgery out of housework.[27]

Every body and every space will be expected to conform, in an orderly fashion, to the "best" standards, and thereby the cultural ethics, venerated by the white middle class. The only time Teague deigns to dirty himself, it seems, is while democratizing the means of hygienic propriety. Universally purging aesthetic defects ranks equal with sanitation and comfort: "The full-time, thrilling, sweaty job of the future will be in the . . . putting of bathrooms and central heating and electrical washers and cleanliness and colour [*sic*] in every home, the creation of order and the elimination of ugliness throughout the land."[28]

Teague's democratization of comfort and convenience was no socialist or New Deal collectivist doctrine. On the contrary, in Teague's estimation, modern housing design offered a means of saving free enterprise: "Unless we have luxuries to admire and work for, where will be the fun in effort? The Russians have proven that there won't be any. . . . By our own less dictatorial but in the end more effective methods we should set about giving reality to that basic ideal of democracy."[29] Indeed, his reference to the Russians is a metaphorical stand-in for the New Deal's state capitalism and public reforms. The postwar promise of effortless living, according to Teague, represented the very essence of the American Way, because such a luxury would instill in the working-class consumer a desire for ever higher standards of living and make him or her work competitively for them. But democratizing that progress by creating inexpensive, prefabricated, efficient housing would transform those dreams into affordable realities. Teague expressed this sentiment elsewhere in his article, as shown earlier, but in terms of postwar housing, this concept underscores his anti–New Deal bias with an analogy of the evolutionary distance between capitalism and Soviet Communism.

Normalizing the "House of Tomorrow"

> It is one of the major ironies of human history that modern war has contributed so much to material progress. . . . There are many more new inventions and processes of almost equal importance now being employed for war production . . . that will later mean greater comfort and convenience than we have ever dreamed possible. . . . We will enjoy the benefits of new processes that can now transform . . . paper into weatherproof panels for the walls of houses, glass so resilient that it can support the weight of an elephant. . . . The mass-production techniques now being employed for gargantuan quantities of war material will later be used to turn out, by the thousands . . . prefabricated homes equipped with modern lighting, plumbing, and air-conditioning units (homes fit for kings).[30]

Carlisle and Latham's observation quoted above represents a synthesis of the main "miracle" features ascribed to the "house of tomorrow"—the most important of which were "mass-production techniques . . . used to turn out . . . homes fit for kings." But what did "homes fit for kings" look like in the postwar world? Most forecasters did not agree on the extent to which the progress of war would revolutionize and transform the external *appearance* of the postwar house. Or at least, depending on the intent of the advertiser, two types of formulas for "tomorrow's house" prevailed. In business and trade magazines we can usually find the "house of tomorrow" designed along the line of typical popular science predictions, world's fairs exhibits, and modernist demonstration prototypes, in which fantasy and experimentation overruled what was possible, practical, or even desirable to the public—though there were rare exceptions.[31]

Firestone's 1945 ad published in *Business Week* demonstrates the fantasy formula. The ad's scenario centers on a postwar suburban neighborhood in which white, middle-class families live in flat-roofed dwellings punctuated with an eclectic array of details borrowed from a modernist architectural vocabulary: curved walls,

6.4. Firestone advertisement, *Business Week*, 4 August 1945, 110. Courtesy of Bridgestone Americas.

cantilevered rooflines, and terraces anchored by a central mass chimney (fig. 6.4).[32] Firestone's illustrator has chosen progressive fragments that recall Frank Lloyd Wright's 1935–36 house "Fallingwater" (fig. 6.5).[33] The model house's horizontal windows are also reminiscent of Richard Neutra's "Health House" of 1927–29 (fig. 6.6), and the round addition at the back looks like a cousin of George Keck's solar "House of Tomorrow" constructed for Chicago's 1933 Century of Progress fair (fig. 6.7). Across the street, a family greets its guests from a balcony enclosed by tubular railings, echoing the ocean-liner sundeck motif found in Keck's house and the "outdoor living" concept built into the Neutra "Health House."[34] In the Firestone ad, the visiting family alights from their helicopter, with its protruding fins, streamlined

6.5. Frank Lloyd Wright, "Fallingwater. The Edgar J. Kaufmann House." View from southwest as seen from downstream. Fayette County, Pennsylvania. Photograph. Library of Congress (HABS, PA, 26-OHPY.V,1-3).

6.6. Richard Neutra, "Health House for Dr. Lovell." View from below. Los Angeles, California. Photograph. Courtesy Department of Special Collections, Charles E. Young Research Library, UCLA. (Collection 1179, Box 837, Folder 1, LO-E-5).

6.7. George Keck, "House of Tomorrow for 1933 Century of Progress Exposition, Chicago, Ill." View from carport deck roof, from east to west. Moved from Chicago to Beverly Shores, Porter County, Indiana. Photograph. Library of Congress (HABS, IND, 64-BEVSH, 9-9).

detailing, and, of course, Firestone tires. Fantasy designs and scenarios were not intended to solve the anticipated postwar housing crisis but rather to align company brand names with the presumed technological "miracles" that were winning the war. Such fantastic images suggested that in the future, a longstanding company and its product would not easily become obsolete.

Bohn Aluminum and Brass Corporation consistently employed popularized modernist idioms in its formulas for the future. Its 1943 ad published in *Fortune* presents a "new design for living." A radical, streamlined abode made of Bohn aluminum sports modernist clichés of glass walls and a cantilevered roof (fig. 6.8). This single-family house of the future, which even has an internal carport, appears so aerodynamic that it is about to fly off its suburban lawn. Bohn employed streamlined modernist motifs again in another 1943 ad, this one published in *Business Week* (fig. 6.9). The company's utopian postwar city recalls models like Futurama

6.8. Bohn Aluminum and Brass Corporation advertisement, *Fortune,* August 1943, 28. Courtesy Citation Corporation.

FORECASTING BY BOHN

Today America's manufacturing processes are concentrated solidly on war materials for Victory. From this gigantic effort will spring many new developments of vast economic consequence to the entire universe. The City of the Future will be born—startling new architectural designs will be an every day occurrence! New alloys—new materials—new applications—designs engineered by Bohn will be an important contributing factor in making possible a world of new products. Remember the name Bohn. Our advanced knowledge will be most helpful to many manufacturers in redesigning their products of tomorrow.

BOHN

BOHN ALUMINUM AND BRASS CORPORATION, DETROIT, MICHIGAN
GENERAL OFFICES—LAFAYETTE BUILDING
Designers and Fabricators—ALUMINUM • MAGNESIUM • BRASS • AIRCRAFT-TYPE BEARINGS

6.9. Bohn Aluminum and Brass Corporation advertisement, *Business Week*, 13 March 1943, 60. Courtesy Citation Corporation.

from the 1939 New York World's Fair (see fig. 2.4). The ad suggests how Bohn is planning a streamlined "world of tomorrow," new and improved with the metal alloys it developed for Allied military campaigns.

Streamlining was an unarguable sign of optimism and a fast, frictionless trajectory into a better tomorrow. As America's efficiency aesthetic, it was perceived as somehow more scientific—and thus more logical and rational—than other styles. In terms of the postwar house, an aerodynamic look suggested an abode that embodied the lessons of scientific housekeeping and thus facilitated hygienic propriety. We can read this or any other style in a manner similar to the investigative methods employed by the pseudo-science of physiognomy, in which the human face functioned as an indicator of internal character. Indeed, the documents we have examined thus far suggest that reformers, designers, and forecasters of the era interpreted the look of shelters with a similar bias or approach. The smooth contours, aerodynamic curves, speedlines, and round chromed surfaces of the streamlined style indicated the "character" of the house—which included the mental, moral, and physical attributes of the people who presumably resided therein.[35] Streamlined traits in a house, like those in a kitchen, suggested an efficient, flawless, clean, attractive, and intelligent family type. Although imaginative, futuristic structures such as Bohn's did not share the architectural idioms common to standard middle-class houses, the streamlined style was perceived as a visual tag for the pinnacle of civilization—no matter to what object or body it was applied.

The other formula for the "house of tomorrow" is rooted in conventional middle-class idioms derived from period styles. But the traditional "house of tomorrow"—an oxymoron if ever there were—signified the postwar future and evolution toward ultimate hygienic propriety as much as modernist fantasies and streamlined designs. Trimming the "house of tomorrow" with conventional, quaint architectural features was common to war bond advertising that sought to link consumer support for the war effort with strengthened family security and middle-class values. For example, in a 1942 ad sponsored by thermostat manufacture Minneapolis-Honeywell Controls, featured in *Better Homes and Gardens,* a war bond is pictured as the foundation on which a suburban dream home has been built. Despite claims in the ad's copy that the "house of tomorrow" will be advanced with wartime innovations, the postwar house bought with war bonds (which also carries a Federal Housing Administration endorsement) exhibits rustic clichés, including a chimney, dormer windows, a pitched roof, and a roughened stone facade.

Orthodox housing models were more likely to surface in women's and general-circulation magazines, as in the previous example. But exceptions did exist, and any company that wanted to emphasize exactly how its facilities had been converted to producing wartime ordnance generally juxtaposed the battlefield with the desired status quo. United States Rubber in its 1945 *Business Week* ad succinctly reveals the content of such a formula in the heading "From submarines . . . to suburbs . . ." (fig. 6.10). Here, progress, left over from ocean battles, promises to maximize comfort and convenience for commuters between the city and their cozy suburban houses. A submarine—the site of United States Rubber's wartime

From submarines...

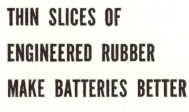

...to Suburbs...

THIN SLICES OF ENGINEERED RUBBER MAKE BATTERIES BETTER

You may never see engineered rubber in your battery.

But you may know when it isn't there . . . when you step into your car, only to find it won't start because the battery went dead.

Well, dead batteries had no place in our wartime submarines. The chief cause of battery failure—the buckling of ordinary separators—had to be eliminated.

It was—with engineered rubber. "U. S." scientists and engineers developed wafer-thin rubber separators, with over 1,000,000 tiny holes per square inch...plus high resistance to abrasion and chemical reaction. What's more, a battery could be charged, drained of water and acid, shipped or stored without losing its life.

This development of the U. S. Rubber Engineer means the end of one of the expensive and annoying battery troubles. It means batteries that last longer—and give sure starting in any kind of weather . . . through engineered rubber.

US ENGINEERED RUBBER

Serving Through Science

UNITED STATES RUBBER COMPANY

1230 Sixth Avenue, Rockefeller Center, New York 20, N. Y. • In Canada: Dominion Rubber Co., Ltd.

6.10. United States Rubber Company advertisement, *Business Week*, 27 October 1945, 31. Courtesy Michelin North America.

contribution—floats above a sentimental domestic scene: mother and children have just come home from the grocery store. They unload their bags from a vehicle standard for the time—not a futuristic helicopter or bubble-topped car. Though the house is not shown, the reader can tell from the garage that the family lives in very conventional and familiar surroundings. No streamlined future is involved. And yet such a juxtaposition was intended to show how the present war acted as a proving ground for future comforts and conveniences in suburbia. As in many ads from this era, the pairing of weapons of war with pictures of normal middle-class family life was not perceived as anomalous but rather natural. War, as a fuel for progress, was promoted as a guarantee for social evolution once victory was achieved.

Like advertising, articles in women's magazines and general-circulation media also tended to couch the "house of tomorrow" in socially acceptable clichés. Such staid structures were considered authentic postwar houses, unlike Bohn's and Firestone's flat-roofed designs, which had their marketing purposes but would not realistically be built on a mass scale. Nonetheless, both types of postwar models—whether streamlined or quaint—signified rational order, comfort, convenience, and efficiency—major ingredients of hygienic propriety. Walter Dorwin Teague, who helped popularize the streamlined style during the 1930s, offers us a conservative estimate about the "house of tomorrow's" appearance in "A Sane Prediction." The article opens with a bird's-eye glimpse into the suburb of tomorrow where standard, middle-class architectural idioms overshadow modernist references—there are no streamlined fantasies like Bohn's. In Teague's future suburbia, stately single-family houses (clearly intended for a middle- to upper-middle-class price range) encircle a tree-lined cul-de-sac (fig. 6.11). The central house that dominates the sketch sports a huge stone chimney and a Regency-style roof. All but one of the houses on the cul-de-sac are cast in pitched-roof, conservative modes. The sole flat-roofed model (with its progressive windows and terrace for California outdoor living) is nearly squeezed out of the picture.[36]

The text of Teague's article contradicts the decorum of acceptable suburban types that adhere to the normative mold. Although the exteriors of Teague's postwar suburban houses echo tradition and established middle-class affectations (even the flat-roofed California model has its acceptable qualities), the interior conveniences reveal a house of quite antithetical proportions. Teague describes a plastic, prefabricated future complete with built-in features and mechanical service cores—the futuristic mode of scientific housekeeping: "The heart of the house will be its service section. In the lowest cost brackets, this will be a compact [prefabricated kitchen and bathroom] unit. . . . All bathroom fixtures, sink, and plumbing will be molded of lightweight synthetic materials."[37] Thomas Holden in the 1944 book *New Architecture and City Planning* reveals that this polarity was not uncommon. New materials (like those developed in wartime) were usually seamlessly assimilated into conventional-looking houses, thereby discouraging any compulsion to produce new exterior designs that reflect the interior conveniences described by Teague:

6.11. Walter Dorwin Teague, "A Sane Prediction About the House You'll Live in After the War," *House Beautiful,* August 1943, 48–49. Drawing by George Cooper Rudolph. Photograph courtesy of General Research Division, The New York Public Library, Astor, Lenox, and Tilden Foundations.

> While the utility and value of modern labor-saving devices and producers of household comfort are beyond measure . . . they have not . . . necessitated radical changes in the design of houses. . . . Adoption of modular design, use of standard sizes and lengths of structural materials, and . . . use of site-assembly methods [are all possible now]. Most of these houses . . . have been quite ingeniously fitted into the currently popular Cape Cod cottage exteriors. The reason . . . is that the houses are built to sell and the buying public has a highly developed sales resistance against houses of unconventional appearance.[38]

Predictions about realistically applying wartime lessons in synthetics, prefabrication, built-in features, and mechanical service cores were as varied as forecasts for the appearance of the postwar house. Responding to the not-so-stellar reputation of prefab housing (a plight that had plagued the industry prior to the war), businessmen packaged their innovative housing materials and construction techniques in an orthodox middle-class format. Architects, designers, and manufacturers applied traditional architectural idioms—rather than radically modernist ones—in an attempt to appeal to the conservative taste of the middle class and those aspiring to be in it. New appearances, materials, devices, and construction techniques (even those proven in war) posed a tough sell to potential home buyers, despite all the hype about the "miracles" of household comfort, convenience, and affordable leisure that forecasters claimed would be available after victory.[39] Consequently, companies capitalized on conventions and established expectations, while they tried to forge innovative paths in shelter materials, equipment, and construction.

Purging the Stigma from Prefabrication

During the 1930s, innovators in prefabrication made many claims about the infallibility of their factory-assembled and standardized products.[40] Yet in several cases, houses labeled "prefabricated" failed to live up to their manufacturers' promises to dispel the mass-produced shelter's low-class, low-quality stigma.[41] Despite standardization, prefab "houses of tomorrow" were usually still priced beyond the economic range of the most needy, and members of the middle class eschewed prefabricated parts and assembly for traditional construction methods and period-style designs. In 1934, *Architect & Engineer* made a rather sour prediction:

> No practical art has made less progress through the ages than home building. . . . There have been attempts in experimentation and research by some individual manufacturers. . . . The general purpose of these experiments has been to reduce costs, but to my knowledge few, if any, have accomplished this purpose. . . . Those who are experimenting with pre-fabricated houses are, in most cases, departing from the conventional designs, but the home buyers are not ready to depart materially from the conventional. They still want a brick exterior, in an English, a Colonial, or some other current design.[42]

Sears Roebuck had sold "ready-cut, stock plan" houses for several years prior to the Depression, but not all prefabricated or mass-produced housing enterprises were as successful. By the late 1930s, several companies had gone under.[43] Housing visionaries of the 1930s stymied in their attempts to commercialize their prefabrication experiments confronted several obstacles, but none more daunting than their impracticality. The size of the United States made national distribution of finished, ready-made houses next to impossible. Moreover, huge amounts of capital would be needed to retool industry for mass-producing new forms of housing and built-in appliances—a necessity that economic uncertainties of the Depression made unfeasible. Some prefabricators did manage to get a few of their model houses on the market by the mid- to late 1930s, but the restrictive economic situation, the polarized political views in the housing industry and in government, the houses' not-so-low cost, and the social stigma of mass-produced housing projects inhibited their widespread construction. Prefab companies such as Stran-Steel sold units for the relatively high cost of $9,000 each, while American Houses, Inc., offered an array of prices between $1,975 and $15,000. Such housing costs were still prohibitive for low-income Americans. The 1939 median monetary income of male farm laborers was $373 per year. Craftsmen that year earned $1,309, while male managers (middle-class professionals) earned $2,136. Female

managers made about half that in 1939, grossing $1,107, and women clerical work-
ers earned $966. White male workers in 1939 earned an average pay of $1,112,
while their black counterparts fared much worse at $460 that year.[44] If the
cost/wage differential put a damper on the prefab industry, the Federal Housing
Administration (FHA) completely undermined it. The FHA's disapproval of
mortgage insurance on prefabricated houses did little to alleviate the public's
skepticism. This discouraged prefabricators from launching large-scale housing
developments, which might have lent them the experience to prove their claims.
Thus, on the eve of America's involvement in the war, prefabricators were still
saddled with a rather shoddy public image that needed to be reversed if wartime
contracts, and postwar profits, were to come their way. In 1940 *Architectural Forum*
voiced the skeptics' dubious faith in the future of prefab houses:

> On the other hand, [national defense needs] may disprove Prefabrica-
> tion's long and loudly voiced claim that it alone holds the answer to
> many a U.S. housing problem. . . . A few leaders have actually fulfilled a
> few of these boasts in a few isolated projects [including American
> Houses, Inc., at Dundalk, Maryland, and Gunnison Housing Corp. at
> New Albany, Indiana], but the unconvincing accomplishments of the in-
> dustry as a whole have prompted many observers to rhyme prefabrica-
> tion with prevarication.[45]

Like many other obstacles to victory, the problems arising from quartering
soldiers and defense-plant workers harbored potential threats to the Allied cause.[46]
Providing adequate shelter for thousands of American soldiers bivouacked in climates ranging from African deserts to South Pacific jungles, and building low-
budget houses for workers pouring into small, overcrowded towns with new,
booming production facilities, presented an unprecedented housing emergency
that needed to be addressed quickly without jeopardizing the well-being of the
military and home front labor pool. The need for reserving critical materials, such
as iron and steel, to build ships, tanks, and munitions worsened the wartime
housing crisis. As a result, architects, designers, and builders were encouraged to
plumb the depths of their imaginations for innovative shelter solutions and substitute building materials.[47] For the struggling prefabricated housing industry, the
critical wartime need for expediting inexpensive construction with as little skilled
labor as possible and with nonpriority materials appeared the most promising
means to launch a successful—and profitable—housing revolution.

In response to the shelter emergency, architect Wallace Neff of Los Angeles
devised a quickly constructed "Bubble House" out of concrete, which was sprayed
onto an inflated balloon covered with a reinforcing mesh. *Popular Mechanics* informs us that Neff's "buildings are blown up, not constructed in the ordinary
sense. . . . A balloon is inflated . . . so that concrete and insulating materials can be
shot over the form by air pressure. When they harden, [the] form is removed."[48]
Neff sought to align his concrete domes with all the comforts of "normalcy" and
"home." Despite the "Bubble House's" igloolike appearance, Neff added fireplaces

adorned with neoclassical molding, while pianos with fluted legs were fit snugly into arched rooms of concrete. Yet these cozy and familiar trappings failed to erase the stark contrast between staid middle-class decorum and a cheap, concrete solution—despite the universal privations of war. Neff's attempt to normalize his innovation by giving it the trimmings of a middle-class identity typified prefab promoters' strategy of purging the stigma attached to unconventional housing plans.

The makers of Homasote (pressed wall panels made with the pulp of old newspapers and weatherproofing materials), however, were undaunted by the prefabrication industry's universally bad press. Corporate leaders of the Homasote Company, who launched their firm in 1909, perceived the war as a profitable means by which to merchandise their product. The company's vice president, F. Vaux Wilson, Jr., explains to us that the success of prefabricated housing would not lie in its potential practicality but rather in its public image: "Neither technological improvement, nor lower cost solves the housing problem—proper merchandising will."[49] Following this corporate dictum, Homasote launched a two-pronged marketing attack on their industry's inferior reputation. Part of Homasote's plan to expand the marketability, and thus the acceptance, of its product included promoting a four-hundred-page book geared for architects, contractors, and lumber dealers and titled *Tomorrow's Homes,* which provided details about its materials research and prefabrication method, called Precision-Building. The other half of the plan involved tapping into the $250-million defense housing budget offered by the federal government.[50] In 1940, Homasote invited members of the Defense Department's housing administration to witness a demonstration of the company's prospective solutions to wartime shelter needs: "Homasote . . . completely erected during [Government officials'] one-day visit the first Precision-Built Jr. house. By nightfall the untutored labor had laid the last shingle, had cemented the last concrete block. . . . And, two days later, true to predictions, the house was ready for occupancy. . . . Total cost—everything but the lot: $2,137."[51]

Government administrators and the public at large were not the only ones needing a persuasive education on the superlative values of Homasote. The article quoted above, titled "Old Newspapers to New Houses," was published in the December 1940 issue of *Architectural Forum,* thus addressing the elite class of professional architects—one year before Pearl Harbor. Homasote houses would not become postwar realities without the approval of architects and management in the building trades. Still early in the war, the makers of Homasote sought attention from a broader business and construction clientele in its 1942 *Business Week* ad (fig. 6.12) in which it describes how "Precision-Built" housing would not only secure profits but also eradicate social ills associated with urban decay: "prefabrication will bring quality homes within reach of new millions of people."[52]

Following a social hygiene argument along the lines of "We Hope You'll Be Gone With the Slums" (see fig. 6.1), Homasote implied a euthenic line of thought in its 1942 *Business Week* ad. The storyboard sequence of the ad supports Homasote's claims that its product is geared for effective "slum clearance." The ad's first frame introduces a run-down urban block—a degenerate neighborhood overrun

New construction methods
tap new markets

Prefabrication has won a major victory—through the sudden, immediate need for housing thousands of war workers. Today, on Defense Housing projects throughout the country, this new method of construction is proving its worth. It is also proving that when the emergency is over, prefabrication will bring *quality* homes within the reach of new millions of people.

The proof is now on record*. It is the natural result of the speed and control of construction—made possible by mass production methods.

Homasote Company foresaw this new market when, in 1935, we pioneered with our first Precision-Built Home. Millions of dollars worth of Homasote Homes have been built and countless improvements have been made since that time. We know that we will continue to improve Homasote Homes—and to lower their costs. But the records to date of thousands of machine-perfect, doubly-insulated homes show that the way has already been found to

tap new housing markets all over the country.

At present, all our facilities are of necessity devoted to Government work. When this picture changes, fabricating plants throughout the country will be ready to supply you with Homasote Homes of any design or size—for employee housing, realty developments, slum clearance and many similar projects. Write today for full details. HOMASOTE COMPANY, Trenton, N. J.

500 Houses in Missouri in 49 working days
977 Houses in California in 73 working days
5000 Houses in Virginia to be built in 5 months

REALTORS...Write us for complete details on Homasote Precision-Built Homes—*your* best means of converting idle property into profitable homesites.

H O M A S O T E
Precision-Built
H O M E S

6.12. Homasote Precision-Built Homes advertisement, *Business Week*, 11 April 1942, 79. Courtesy The Homasote Company, West Trenton, New Jersey.

with young hooligans, fighting and playing in the streets. Aesthetic defects in environment and abode point to the inferior stock and character of the occupants, whose deviance is underscored by the darkness of the urban rowhouses and their feeble, unsanitary construction materials: wood and brick. Suggesting that prefabricated housing could offer a hygienic solution to such squalid environs and the improper habits they presumably bred, the epitome of urban blight is transformed into single-family suburban houses made of Homasote. In Homasote's affordable suburbia, white (and thus untainted) prefabricated houses with pitched roofs and quaint shutters encircle a healthy grassy park with swings and a seesaw. Here, children play in an orderly fashion and social calamity is subsequently dissolved.

Housing reform narratives (whether discoursing on what was proper or on what was poor) were usually loaded with a human-engineering emphasis bent on social redemption through the benevolence of the private sector. As it did in its narratives on reconversion, business went out of its way to illustrate how government was too inept to effectively plan housing developments. When it did, many in business argued, the results were shoddy or were markers of the country's descent into Communism. Bror Dahlberg, president of Celotex and chairman of the board of Certain-teed roofing products, distinguished the prefab units constructed by the government for war workers (a collectivist trend) from the single-family dwellings targeted for middle-class suburbia. Such a distinction was intended to discredit the New Deal by associating government prefabs ("standard design") with enforced regimentation, socialism, and stagnation: "What we are building now in the housing projects surrounding our war plants should not be taken as the complete pattern for the future. When you have to build a thousand dwellings in the greatest possible haste, the only way to get them done is to use a standard design."[53]

Government-sponsored standardization in housing was somehow ideologically (if not also morally) suspect, even though standardization was prevalent in privately owned industry and was heralded as the key to democratizing progress while increasing profits. But Dahlberg nonetheless expressed the common assumption that some "strains" of standardization were inherently superior to others: "But when homes are built individually and with less need of haste, they can be as different as the people who occupy them. . . . Already the architects and designers are developing hundreds of new designs for private homes, using exactly the same materials that are going into regimented housing projects, but turning out as many different plans as there are designers. A 'machine house' need not be a standardized house."[54]

Wartime standardized housing built by government agencies was maligned as inferior and overcrowded, echoing traits of urban slums and the social, moral, and ideological decay that an unhygienic environment presumably tended to breed. Stigmatizing government-sponsored houses as the breeding grounds for an unhealthy society would halt any plans the New Deal had for getting into the housing business after the war.[55] From the conservative viewpoint, single-family home ownership, built by the private sector, signaled the happy return of American individualism, another facet of the anticipated hygienic revolution.

The Stran-Steel Corporation also sought to carve out a substantial postwar niche market for itself with the durable, noncorrosive steel, arch-ribbed framing it had provided for the popular defense structure known as the Quonset Hut.[56] Easily stocked, transported, and erected with minimal skill (like the Homasote house), the Quonset Hut was even more adaptable to several shelter requirements. Despite its low cost and obvious efficiency, which made prefabricated structures attractive for military use, the Quonset Hut's public image as temporary emergency shelter needed to be reversed. Its stellar wartime reputation was an ironic detriment to the Quonset Hut's suitability for civilian homes in peacetime. In an attempt to erase its stigma as tract housing for military personnel, Stran-Steel "rebuilt" the Quonset Hut in the form of familiar structures (fig. 6.13). It was critical for prefab companies (as well as plastics and electronics—anything new) to convince decision makers in manufacturing, construction, and design to adapt their new merchandise to postwar civilian use. Otherwise, such relatively untried methods or products would never see the civilian market. In its *Business Week* ad from 1944, Stran-Steel shows Uncle Sam (a metaphor for the wartime use of Stran-Steel's products) symbolically removing the khaki military shell from the buildings that promise to be the Quonset Hut's civilian counterparts: a barn, a school, and a single-family suburban home. Color symbolizes the structure's reconversion, as if it were a demobilized soldier removing his khaki uniform and donning colorful civilian clothes. Stran-Steel metaphorically suggests that when the Quonset Hut loses its drab military uniform, a brighter and better solution to postwar construction will emerge, fit for middle-class suburbia.

Like most narratives heralding the achievements of prefabricated housing, publicity about Fuller's Dymaxion tried to downplay its industrial appearance. Its origins in an airplane factory were softened by adding ornaments of suburban decorum (see fig. 6.2). Shrubbery and a rustic stone sidewalk were icons of acceptability placed around the house's exterior, while the interior was replete with even more codes of hygienic propriety: a baby grand piano, fireplace, and conventional armchair with dust ruffles—a feature totally obsolete in a house designed to automatically dust itself via an air cleansing system. Fuller's advanced heating system also made the fireplace a decorative dinosaur. Despite the mix of anachronisms, emphasis on familiar middle-class affectations set in industrial forms was an attempt to ascribe the trait of "normalcy" to housing concepts that were radically removed from most Americans' expectations, aspirations, and experience. Following this necessity, promoters of prefab, standardized housing illustrated their futuristic homes with would-be buyers who fit the normative white middle-class mold. In an article on Fuller's postwar Dymaxion appearing in *Architectural Forum* (April 1946), a well-dressed couple of the managerial class are introduced to a model of the Wichita Dymaxion by a dapper realtor. The couple's clothing types them as conservative in character—responsible and rational consumers inherently incapable of wasting their money on a socialist or far-fetched experiment. The prospective male client wears a manager's suit and tie, while his wife sports a netted pillbox hat and a high-necked blouse with a Victorian ruffle. These orthodox codes of middle-class respectability suggest that the industrial

When the Quonset Huts take off their uniforms

When the needs of war lessen . . . when the use of Stran-Steel is permitted for home-front construction . . . then, the rugged strength and permanence of quality steel framing will be available within the price range of even the small farm building or industrial warehouse.

Today, Stran-Steel, in war-front barracks, hangars, hospitals, shops—in arctic blizzards and steaming jungles—

STRAN-STEEL

has set an amazing new standard of building efficiency. Easy to ship, stock and handle, and speedily erected *with ordinary carpenter tools*, its economy is obvious. And its use in famous Quonset Huts all over the world attests its remarkable resistance to deterioration.

If saving time and money is *important* then Stran-Steel is a "must." It's adaptable to almost any style of architecture or type of collateral material. It's a "world of tomorrow" development, here today—extensively tested—conclusively proved—an answer in steel to better building and reduced construction and maintenance costs . . . Keep your eye on Stran-Steel.

 GREAT LAKES STEEL CORPORATION
STRAN-STEEL DIVISION, PENOBSCOT BLDG., DETROIT 26, MICH.

UNIT OF NATIONAL STEEL CORPORATION EXECUTIVE OFFICES: PITTSBURGH, PA.

6.13. Stran-Steel advertisement, *Business Week*, 30 December 1944, 72.

Dymaxion could be marketed not only to the needy masses but also to the "best" types.[57]

Advocates of prefabricated housing realized that their industry had long been stigmatized as anti-individual, bordering on the communistic. The prefab's champions sought to turn this image around by showing potential postwar home owners how buying a factory-assembled house would be no different, and therefore no less individualistic and American, than purchasing an automobile in a dealer's showroom. If postwar prefab houses were to be made affordable to everyone as promised, then they needed to be not only assembled like cars but also sold like them. Teague gives us a glimpse into this production possibility: "You will be able to call at your dealer's showroom and from a number of models pick out the complete kitchen and bathroom you want, just as you picked out your car . . . [and your factory-made home will be] ready to be connected to the services in an hour's time."[58]

A 1947 ad by Stran-Steel exhibits the lengths to which the prefabrication industry went in its attempts to purge prefab standardization of any association with regimentation. In this ad, which was directed to the postwar newlywed market, Stran-Steel pictures the Quonset Hut as a unique, "smartly styled," architecturally designed house by trimming it with civilized idioms such as a bride and groom (as opposed to bachelor soldiers), curtained picture windows, and suburban landscaping (fig. 6.14). Furthermore, by renaming the Quonset the "Brighton" model, an echo of romantic English estates, Stran-Steel, like other housing developers, sought to lend an aristocratic cachet to its mass-produced "$35. a month" solution.[59] Naturally, the bride and groom are just as important selling points as the house's pretentious moniker. We see that the couple is a "modern" and "attractive" type like the Brighton model. With their movie-star looks—white, blonde, and thin (one could argue they are "streamlined")—they position the Quonset Hut in the normative mold.

The stigma of Communist-like conformity attached to "scientifically" managed prefabrication was hard to erase, even for a designer as renowned as Walter Dorwin Teague. His treatise "A Sane Prediction," examined in part before, brought the new "reality" of prefabrication and standardization to the female consumer market. Teague, like other prefab apologists, conceived of a spectrum of prefabricated types in housing's evolutionary development. In order to persuade potential postwar home buyers that wartime prefab techniques enhanced individuality, he characterized American postwar standardization as the most humanized, flexible, and rational approach to middle-class housing. To lend an emotive appeal to his point, he cast the modernist International Style as a housing villain, derived from foreign aesthetic stock. Characterized as possessing an inflexible starkness and boxy rigidity, which Teague labels "aggressive," the International Style displayed a factory-assembled aesthetic that, in Teague's eyes, bordered on fascism. Richard Neutra's "Health House" from 1927 (see fig. 6.6), with its factorylike look, may have been the type of modernist example on Teague's mind when he maligned the International Style:

6.14. Stran-Steel brochure, "Modern, Attractive, Well-Built Homes that sell for $4,000 to $6,000!" 1947. Albert Farwell Bemis Foundation Records, 1926–1954. AC 302. Institute Archives and Special Collections, Massachusetts Institute of Technology Libraries, Cambridge, Massachusetts.

Most of our designers of the aggressively modern school have devised their houses like mathematical equations, so rigidly planned . . . that if you move an ashtray or turn a chair . . . the whole composition is spoiled. . . . [T]he postwar house will be something mellower than the rectangular and aseptic offerings of the International School. It will preserve the functional approach . . . [b]ut it will be humanized.[60]

Teague's strategy was to redirect the focus of prefabrication's stigma to a "foreign" nemesis. Given that this article was written in 1944, one wonders if this foreign stylistic contaminant he mentions is not a reference to the Axis enemy—Germany, one of the European countries where the functionalist tenets of the International Style were nurtured before the war.

Designer Norman Bel Geddes in his 1941 *Time* magazine ad for Revere Copper and Brass offered his own solution for reversing prefab housing's negative public image by cloaking the picture of sameness in the rhetoric of variety (fig. 6.15). The "pros" of standardization are defined as a universal level of quality combined with the sense of individuality: "We who are planning these homes [of tomorrow] know that Americans do not want standardized designs. So the basic parts of this [prefabricated] house are made so that they can be assembled in various ways to form no less than 11 distinct homes—all different."[61] The language of individuality contrasts with the images of assembly-line sameness in the ad. Despite claims that consumer choice is enhanced by prefab, standardized design, all the homes look alike—from the artist's illustration, to Bel Geddes's desk model, to the picture of his house fragmented into its individual parts. Moreover, the design of these mass-produced abodes bears a remarkable resemblance to the degenerate foreign "enemy" style denounced by Teague. Much of Bel Geddes's design echoes the International Style's modernist vocabulary: flat-roofed with windowed walls and no traces of period-style moldings or conventional suburban quaintness. (The central-mass chimney is more reminiscent of Frank Lloyd Wright's modernism.) Bel Geddes tells us that his standardized house enhances opportunities to express individual taste (an American trait) with movable panel walls. Forecasters generally agreed that modular devices and units were an affordable means toward articulating one's personal aesthetic voice and expressing freedom of choice.[62] They were also a way to conveniently redesign a house's layout in order to fit a growing family's future needs, suggesting that even the most modest residences would never become stylistically obsolete.[63] Such an argument is an inherent part of Bel Geddes's housing plan with its interchangeable parts and eleven variations.

The only detectable "variety" appears in the individual faces of the neighbors standing before three of Bel Geddes's mass-produced houses. Nonetheless, the three people pictured represent the cultural homogeneity of the white middle-class normative mold. These are *not* types waiting to be assimilated—they are already in the mainstream, as we can see from the sign "Main Street," which lends an air of normalcy and convention to this otherwise unorthodox type of standardized, mass-produced community more reminiscent of Communist collective housing than American-style dwellings geared for the middle class.

We see Bel Geddes hovering over a tiny model of his prefab innovation. In the copy he elaborates on the interior features, which are also factory assembled and completed before arriving at the residential site. The houses possess a machine-stamped mechanical core for the kitchen and bathroom. Though their origin may be antithetical to consumers' current experience, Bel Geddes reassures his readers that these factory-made cores look "just like those you see in the magazines."[64] In order to further calm the readers' imagined (and probably likely) apprehension, Bel Geddes asserts the physical and social suitability of his prefab houses: "Here is

For us the living...better homes

"Americans want 'living', not 'housing'. We want homes with telephones, radios, automatic heat, mechanical refrigeration, air conditioning. In short, Americans want more copper in their homes, for more copper means better living. That is why industrial research and the new developments in copper now taking place in Revere's laboratories can bring us far greater comfort and pleasure in days to come.

"So, no matter what else results from the all-out effort our country is making, one thing seems certain. When it is over, real enjoyment of life in our homes can be greater, can be available to millions more. For in this great emergency, new standards are being created. Industry is experimenting with new processes. Revere is working out new things in copper. Architects are inventing new methods of building.

"Here is one conception by the famous designer, Norman Bel Geddes. It shows the deep comfort, the complete convenience, the dignity of living which American production methods could easily provide."

Donald Dallas
President

NORMAN BEL GEDDES says—"Through our inventive and productive genius, we Americans enjoy more comfort, more freedom, more fun than any other people on earth because these things are built into our homes. That's the secret of our famous standard of living. But we are still back in the dark ages in the way we construct a house. If we got as much house for our money as we do in a modern radio or automobile, even the lowest income could buy living fit for a king.

"The way to do it is to build our homes as we build the other good things of life—not just a few at a time, but by the thousands, using our mass production methods.

"Here is a home I have designed which, if built on such a scale, would cost you less than $2000. It is a home with much more copper in it, because it is full of the new conveniences which copper alone can bring.

"When you once realize how spacious and attractive such a home can be, how luxuriously livable, how free from repairs—and how much individuality in shape and design it offers—I think you and all America will want homes built this way.

"Imagine a house with only 27 basic parts, which can be delivered at your building site in the morning and assembled into a finished home ready for you to move into by dinner time! Here you see the 27 units as they would come off the production line. But we who are planning these homes know that Americans do not want standardized designs. So the basic parts of this house are made so that they can be assembled in various ways to form no less than 11 distinct homes—all different.

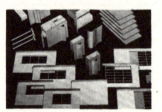

"The kitchen, complete with modern range, sink, mechanical refrigerator and steel cabinets, looks just like those you see in the magazines. But what you don't see is that this kitchen is formed in one piece by machine, without costly hand work. On its opposite side is a modern bath, built the same way. And its interior encloses the hot water and heating systems.

"Here is a place for a healthy, happy family to grow up—in spacious rooms flooded with light from large windows. Fresh air is brought in from outdoors, washed, heated in winter, and circulated all year 'round. These are only a few of the many features in this home which modern production methods can bring within your reach."

NORMAN BEL GEDDES

Largely through copper, the modern house has 200% more living in it than that of a generation ago. For the more copper you get per building dollar, the better the home to own or sell. In this way Revere adds value to houses from roof to cellar. Heating units with Revere Copper cut down service costs. Plumbing of Revere Copper saves on installation and upkeep. Revere Copper guards against wind, damp, cold, insects.

Today, the copper industry is working for Uncle Sam, and copper is restricted for general use. But meanwhile, in Revere's laboratories, research is constantly developing new copper alloys, new uses for copper, new forms for copper. We are working today to be ready for your housing needs tomorrow.

*　　*　　*

Naturally, it is impossible for Mr. Geddes to give full details about his house in this space. We have prepared an illustrated folder describing it fully. We will be glad to send it to you on request. Just write to:

REVERE
COPPER AND BRASS INCORPORATED
Executive Offices: 230 Park Avenue, New York

6.15. Revere Copper and Brass and Norman Bel Geddes advertisement, *Time,* 15 September 1941, 31. Courtesy of Revere Copper Products, Inc.

a place for a healthy, happy family to grow up." In Bel Geddes's postwar world, like that of other forecasters, standardized, factory-built prefabs are the seeds of a rationally controlled environment that promotes a mentally and physically healthy family. However, although other predictions eschew the natural or deem it entirely irrational, Bel Geddes's artificial abode attempts to show how nature is perfected in his superior model of future hygienic propriety: "Spacious rooms [are] flooded with light from large windows. Fresh air is brought in from outdoors, washed, heated in winter, and circulated all year round."[65] Despite its robotlike qualities, it is surely a home bestowed with stamina and efficiency, able to control nature, sanitize and regulate the family's air supply, and protect the home's health from outside contagion. Bel Geddes's emphasis on the healthy benefits of light, space, and air distance his inexpensive prefab units from shoddy structures. But his concepts were not unique. Poor ventilation, insufficient sunlight, and overcrowding were the abhorrent attributes of not just substandard dwellings but especially slums. The same prescriptions for family vitality are evident in Tessie Agan's 1939 textbook. Agan specifically directs scientific housekeepers to the purifying properties of sunlight in the home, which aids in health, cleanliness, and the killing of microorganisms and acts as "an effective bacterial agent."[66]

If one reads between the lines of wartime housing reform narratives, one notices how the predictions were inherently contradictory. Propagandists for mass-produced standardized housing and mechanical cores tried to convince the public that their prefabricated, standardized future was a symbol of democratic freedom—not of fascist regimentation. Access into the middle class through prefabricated and mechanized houses was defined as a barometer of civilized progress, although, in hindsight, we could argue it nearly guaranteed cultural homogenization. Housing reformers and forecasters tried to dispel fears of conformity by affixing metaphors of not only expansiveness but also social evolution to the features of the prefabricated "house of tomorrow." Paradoxically, postwar standardization was characterized as an open door to variety, originality, and individualized choices, while at the same time its advocates denied that it also could breed slavish obedience to conventional standards.

In an effort to establish a receptive postwar market, supporters of prefabrication attempted to make the prepackaged, standardized "house of tomorrow" appeal to *desires* for automatic access to a higher social stratum. By effortlessly eliminating household drudgery as well as dirt, dust, odors, and germs, the prefab "house of tomorrow," with built-ins, movable walls, and a mechanical core, promised the working-class housewife the elevated appearance of professional, "scientific" cleanliness.

Like other manufacturers who promised to deliver war-proved efficiency to the postwar consumer, prefabrication innovators publicly labeled and defined their hygienic revolution as a beneficial by-product of war. And yet this public perception did not automatically result from the fact of war; rather, it was the result of calculated publicity geared toward building consumer confidence in mass-produced houses. Those companies, architects, and designers with war-proved experience who promised to not only ease the cost of acquiring a house but also erase the stigma attached to prefabrication possessed the best chance for financial success in the anticipated frenetic postwar economy. Not coincidentally, while they masked the limitations of prefabrication by espousing its features as the key to revolutionary freedoms and ultimate hygienic propriety, advertisers and designers in the housing field also denied the fact that the higher standards of household efficiency and cleanliness, which promised to liberate the housewife from irrational drudgery, were actually forcing her to give more of her attention to household chores, not less, and were boxing her into orthodox feminine roles.

The promotional literature devoted to raising expectations about reconversion all used similar seduction tactics to convince consumers (and business clients, too) that American industry was more than capable of winning a global war because it could simultaneously plan for revolutionizing domesticity after victory was achieved. But the blueprints for postwar America functioned as a multipurpose myth and as a double-edged propaganda sword, which could be used by any faction (manufacturers, architects, or designers) to further its own agenda. Consequently, when the war ended and reconversion got under way, the hype surrounding the visions evaporated, leaving in their wake only the great expectations and the uncertain hope that a "better America" had indeed emerged from the war.

PART THREE

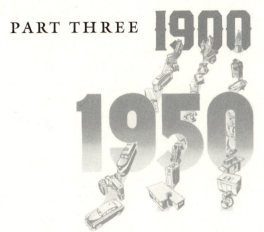

1900
1950

Postwar Progress

Myth or Reality?

A good part of the current [wartime] paper shortage might be laid to the ads and articles describing the marvels in houses and household equipment waiting only for Victory, and to other ads and articles demonstrating that there aren't going to be any marvels at all.[1]

Were the corporate visions of the "world of tomorrow" realistic? Could they come to fruition? The success of wartime production suggested that a controllable world could arise out of conflict, death, and destruction. Inspired by this unprecedented productivity, the postwar dream offered a means of accounting for the mess of the past and accordingly prescribed an antidote for it. Yet there was an appalling lack of consensus among postwar forecasters and commercial propagandists, an observation made by Miles Colean, a former federal housing administrator, who laments this schism in his article "The Miracle House Myth." Writing in December 1944, he informed his *House Beautiful* readers that postwar planning involved more rhetorical conflict than action. But given the seductive array of hygienic solutions examined in the last three chapters, Colean's pragmatic message could easily have been drowned out by the very panoply he criticized.

In hindsight, it is apparent that Colean was right. Indeed, experts argued bitterly over the extent to which war-tested methods and "secret weapon" development could be channeled into civilian markets. In their attacks on swollen postwar predictions, skeptics not only tried to show the unfeasibility of the overblown forecasts but also emphasized the ambivalent commercial motives of advertisers who released unsubstantiated hints about war-born "miracles." The author Eric Sevareid, writing in the intellectually elite *Saturday Review of Literature* in 1944, called this propagandizing trend among consumer engineers "super-dupering the war," claiming, "Too many advertisers have put self-interest ahead, if not of patriotism, at least of reality."[2] Granted, the impracticality of visionary designs had been overlooked in the excitement generated by American industry's accelerated preparation for war. But Sevareid's criticism reveals that the "world of tomorrow" was not the innocent daydream it seemed. Although he called wartime forecasts a "battle of adjectives," the real conflict lay in advertisers' competing for postwar dollars before finishing the business of war. His accusation suggests that profits were put before patriotic sacrifice, and that fighting to save democracy was lost in a maelstrom where the war was leveraged to shore up the corporate bottom line.

Some consumer engineers agreed with Sevareid's denunciation of their industry's culpability in "super-dupering the war." Well before victory was in sight, skeptics realized that the "world of tomorrow" theme had snowballed out of proportion. The postwar hyperbole was described as a rollercoaster careening out of control, a risky escalation that could ultimately plunge the entire business community into disaster. Reporting on the American advertising scene in 1943, W. B. B. Fergusson of the British firm Masius and Fergusson Ltd. implicitly cautioned his readers against emulating the recklessness behind the American mode of postwar planning: "[The critics] say that the impression given is that the war has only to be won and immediately afterwards the world will become an easier place to live in through the benefits of plastics, electronics, air travel and television. Advertisers are warned of the harm that this undue optimism may do to trade in general and to their businesses in particular."[3]

Skeptical consumer engineers feared that if inflated consumer expectations went unfulfilled and the promised vision failed to live up to reality, the wartime honeymoon between the public and the techno-corporate order would be over. Designer Raymond Loewy articulated this opinion in a 1943 article in the *New York Times Magazine*. Loewy opened his argument by admitting that postwar planning had its merits because "with American industry in the war effort 100 per cent, it became necessary to talk of the future."[4] Nonetheless, postwar planning, he found, had grown toward the illusory instead of the practical. He publicly scolded those unwitting "designers, salesmen, and manufacturers" who "may have contributed to the myth that wonderful new things may be forthcoming in the salesrooms of the country."[5] In what turned out to be a rather futile attempt to curb unbridled fantasies, Loewy argued that promoting a better America, "trembling upon new thresholds of improvement," may be detrimental to postwar sales rather than stimulating. Resentment would be visited upon manufacturers and salesmen alike:

> To the scrap heap of discredit but once popular theories . . . please add another, the immediate Post-war Dream World. . . . Lately it has become apparent that the public is being misinformed systematically about the wonders that await them. . . . The American of today sees a better product, a better home, a better appliance, just one model after the war—our current barrier [to the future]. . . . The man who expects to turn his war bonds into a packaged home may have to wait longer than he now supposes. . . . If this customer isn't forewarned it may take years to knock that chip off his shoulder.[6]

Loewy did not count himself among such unscrupulous consumer engineers, unlike car body designer Carl Sundberg, a harsh critic of overimaginative forecasters (including himself). Sundberg, of the industrial design firm Sundberg-Ferar, made a public plea for forgiveness in a 1945 article published in the trade journal *Modern Plastics*. Expectant designers were guilty of being tempted by romantic fantasies and letting their imaginations run amuck. "We designers," he cries, "are guilty too—guilty of each new development announced by the plastics industry up to and beyond the fullest limits of its possibilities."[7] Sundberg's appeal for atonement begins by incriminating the military in fomenting postwar hyperbole. If only those military secrets hadn't slipped out, postwar planners would have had nothing to speculate about in the first place: "As rumors and reports of amazing advances in all industry have filtered through the screen of military secrecy, they have been pounced upon by the postwar prophets and translated into promises of every type of super-super product."[8]

Despite their lust for progress, Sundberg felt that he and his fellow sinners were not wholly to blame, for they had been seduced by the "Eves" of a wartime technological Paradise—the molded plastics used in Flying Fortresses and Liberator Bombers:

Always casting about for new ideas, we have sometimes given in to the temptations offered by plastics—particularly some of those mysterious things war production has been doing with various materials and about which we know a little but not enough. Because the pictures we have drawn are sensational and good to look at, they have been published and have contributed to the misleading of the public. . . . Transparent noses, gun turrets and blisters on war aircraft have also proved too great a temptation to many prophets.[9]

In searching for "good" to emerge from the war, forecasters and commercial propagandists had been too eager to attribute miraculous powers to war production, despite its herculean achievements. Wartime narratives credited the war with pulling Americans not only out of economic depression but together as a nation. Such narratives suggested that if these united classes, races, religions, and ethnicities could identify with a national cause and produce enough to defeat two of the greatest war machines in history, then surely this social power—according to some wartime forecasters—could be harnessed to create order, democratize abundance, and secure permanent peace. Wartime forecasts of the "world of tomorrow" carried within them an idealistic quest for social harmony, betterment, and uplift. But because they were largely rooted in plans to improve the world artificially through consumer spending, such projections were doomed to outstrip existing manufacturing and construction realities.

Critics suggest to us that the postwar dream world, impractical and irrational, should have stayed in the forecasters' heads. As the skeptics had anticipated, reality never lived up to the dream. But as the following three chapters reveal, there was more to realizing the "world of tomorrow" than just limitations in production or manufacturing infrastructure. Social desires for returning to the status quo seemed to be the largest factor in stifling plans for democratizing progress and fashioning a truly "better America" out of the crucible of war.

7 Wartime Skeptics and the "World of Tomorrow"

The "house of the future" is the spoiled darling of the editorial and ad writers these days. Magazines bristle with projections about the house of 194X. Each tries to be more startling than the other, in a race to be different.[1]

Plans for the "house of tomorrow" received the brunt of wartime skeptics' flak, as Walter Dorwin Teague informs us. In his 1943 *House Beautiful* article, he voices disdain for the unmitigated gall exhibited by forecasters and commercial propagandists who made outrageous, misleading predictions about postwar domesticity. The title of the article, "A Sane Prediction," suggests that other forecasts, unlike Teague's, of course, were based on irrational speculations, rather than on sound managerial planning.

Wartime opinion polls revealed that many consumers were not entirely seduced by blueprints for the postwar "miracle" house, either. In their 1943 "Kitchen of Tomorrow" contest, *McCall's* contrasted a "modern" kitchen of "established design" with a "revolutionary" one, an experimental, fully automated, glass and open-plan kitchen sponsored by Libbey-Owens-Ford (L-O-F) (fig. 7.1).[2] Although many consumers recognized favorable convenience features in each kitchen, 62.6

7.1. Libbey-Owens-Ford promotional still, "Kitchen of Tomorrow," 1943–44. Designed by H. Creston Doner. Photograph. Courtesy Ward M. Canaday Center for Special Collections, William S. Carlson Library, University of Toledo.

percent of 11,887 contestants selected the "Tried-and-True" kitchen of prewar design over L-O-F's "Day-After-Tomorrow" model. Those consumers who rejected L-O-F's more technocentric features were attracted to the nostalgic appeal of the prewar model. As the director of this contest, the architectural editor, Mary Davis Gillies, commented: "Some of the erstwhile traditionalists imagined this kitchen as 'a place for building memories like my grandmother's kitchen.'"[3]

Despite the torrent of "world of tomorrow" publicity flooding newspapers and magazines since at least the 1939 New York World's Fair, symbols of traditional, steadfast home life remained viable contenders against newfangled Dymaxions and mass-produced mechanical cores. And contrary to some forecasters' criticisms of conventional building types and their obvious limitations, these familiar forms represented psychological anchors to order and stability in a world thrown into chaos, as Gillies reports in her findings: "The contestants who choose the traditional living room regard it as a symbol of a comforting, sheltered mode of life. It seems to them secure and lived-in. . . . The traditionalists are far more anxious to protect their families against violent post-war changes. They . . . feel that continuity of a decorating trend will be a stabilizing force for post-war America."[4]

Cautious postwar forecasts for mass-produced housing showed that prefabrication contractors would be responding to this popular traditionalist trend. Such estimates revealed that the postwar house would in actuality remain fairly close to the conventional prewar version. A year after the *McCall's* contest, Miles Colean, a former federal housing administrator (see introduction to part 3), cautioned readers not to "count on a spectacular, out-of-this-world house of tomorrow. Instead, get acquainted with the best prewar planning practices."[5] Like Teague, Colean smolders with the conceit of the expert confronting an irrational nemesis. We can almost see him still shaking his finger at a flamboyant future after all this time.

Who else but a catalogue publisher for the housing industry would know what would *really* happen to the "house of tomorrow"? Starting in the 1930s, the F. W. Dodge Corporation published custom-designed home owners' catalogues for individual contractors wishing to publicize layouts, features, and facades.[6] Company president Thomas S. Holden gives his expert opinion in a 1943 *Architectural Record* article titled "Postwar Realism vs. Romance." He grants that new techniques in wartime prefabrication, slowly implemented, would improve building methods. Still, the "house of tomorrow" will not materialize, as predicted, on the day after victory: "It is reasonable to expect that the vast war construction program, with its stringent requirements of speed, of economy in use of materials . . . will have contributed improvements of lasting value to the construction industry. . . . [But] they will not change the fundamental functions of buildings; nor are they likely, I believe, to come to the front so fast as to render all past procedures and existing buildings obsolete overnight."[7] Higher incomes and increased savings, as a result of accelerated wartime industry and savings bonds, represented the "revolutionary" changes to emerge from the war, not the "miracle" house of tomorrow. Holden continues: "If, as is generally expected, national income continues in the postwar period at much higher levels than in the poverty decade, the number of families able to buy or occupy houses in the middle price ranges will be vastly larger than in the 1930s."[8]

Kenneth Stowell, *Architectural Record*'s editor in chief, confirmed Holden's conclusions in an article from that same year. Conservatives in the architecture and building trades assessed how prefabricators might apply their lessons from wartime construction to domestic housing, and they concluded that they would base their mass-produced designs on historical, hand-crafted structures, presumably just what their buyers wanted: "The results [of consumer surveys] seem to indicate certain conservative desires, in spite of 'miracle house' publicity. They seem to indicate a sentimental rather than an intellectual approach, on the part of prospective home builders. . . . The evidence of this is further seen in the activities of most of the prefabricators who are preparing to merchandise new homes to meet the public demand."[9] Stowell alleges that pitched roofs, ornamental pilasters, and other period-style idioms will make up the much-heralded postwar inroads in low-cost prefabrication, rather than plastic walls, removable panels, and roof-top heliports: "[The prefabricators'] designs, for the most part, are hardly revolutionary. The fact is, they stem largely from Colonial-with-variations, and the home buyer can select such 'architecture' as pilasters, quoins, shutters, and 'Dutch hoods' from the catalog at so much above the base price. And the operative builders, with sales uppermost in their minds, are working with the designs that sold best before the war, [embellished] with new gadgets . . . of course."[10]

A 1944 Alan Dunn cartoon parodied the fantastic visions promoted by wartime housing forecasters, including reformers and propagandists. In Dunn's satire of the future, the prefabricated "house of tomorrow," delivered to suburbia from the showroom, looks suspiciously like the conventional counterpart forecasters said it would supplant (fig. 7.2). In a depiction that resembles skepticism voiced by the conservative wing of the housing industry, Dunn's "Home of Tomorrow" appears to have wood siding and quaint hourglass window curtains—hardly an accessory one would expect in Firestone's or Bohn's futuristic models (see figs. 6.4, 6.8, and 6.9). Underscoring the "normalcy" of literal "home delivery," Dunn includes a satisfied white middle-class couple who calmly watches the "Zip-Its Up" company set their new home down on its flooring, as if this is just the way everyone builds a home nowadays. How do we know they are from the middle class? By the typical icon of social respectability: a man dressed in a suit.[11] Dunn situates traditional façades of a middle-class mentality right in the center of postwar forecasting rhetoric. The resulting absurdity suggests that the prefabricated postwar world was more symbol than substance.

But were nostalgic attachments to conventional building types at odds with the "scientific," hygienic living also promised by postwar forecasters? Like *McCall's*, *House Beautiful* conducted studies about the standards of cleanliness and automation that the wartime consumer would demand for her postwar house and discov-

7.2. Cartoon by Alan Dunn, "The Home of Tomorrow," in "Utopia—1955," *Saturday Evening Post*, 30 December 1944, 37. Courtesy of *Saturday Evening Post*.

ered that utility, efficiency, and "cleanability" were the high-ranking ambitions: "House Beautiful asked its readers what they thought ought to be made to produce a better world after the war. . . . They want things to work better, last longer, be more cleanable [and have] INCREASED UTILITY. . . . Greater cleanability ranks high on the wanted list. . . . Durability . . . Intelligent use of space . . . Scientifically planned . . . The expression of distaste for handling very dirty objects was a pattern running through all the letters."[12]

Both "traditional" decor (albeit via prefabricated moldings) and higher standards of efficient, "scientific" cleanliness symbolized esteemed social hallmarks of middle-class stature. Thus, although the two different household features— functional utility and maximized sanitation versus decorative vestiges of the past— seem incompatible on the surface, wartime improvements in prefabrication and mass-produced, "miracle" products promised to bring them within the price range of the working class, offering rational design and a higher standard of living at low-income costs. The desire for status (via prefabricated period styles) as well as higher standards of household efficiency and cleanliness represented different patterns cut from the same fabric, but both were intended to garnish their wearer with the illusion of having arrived in the middle class.

Thus, even before the war ended, astute forecasters realized that a mixture of the past and the future would distinguish the postwar "world of tomorrow," not only in response to consumer taste but also, as designer Raymond Loewy claimed, because the imagined hygienic revolution would be more costly to undertake than was first thought. As early as 1943, Loewy predicted that financial realities would outweigh even the strongest urge to make the utopian "world of tomorrow" materialize after victory. Under the duress of war, he relates in the *New York Times Magazine,* no expense had been spared to facilitate progress toward victory. The same rash desperation would not apply in peace: "War, we know, has compressed much research into an abnormally concentrated period. . . . By a process of rationalization it has been said that all these benefits, the by-products of war effort, can be extended to peacetime production. It is not so simple. . . . War is costly. Since there is no alternative, methods are permitted that would be unthinkable if a civilian buyer were loser by the deal. Therefore, the matter of economy, no issue in wartime, rears its familiar head [in peacetime]."[13]

H. A. Smith seconded Loewy's assessment in 1944. He foresaw the discrepancy between industrial limitations and the fantastic pictures of products that promised to revolutionize domesticity. Smith's *Advertising & Selling* article titled "Don't Promise the Public Too Much—Too Soon" explains how far removed the illustrations were from "present standards" and capabilities: "It is a far cry from working up a bright picture of what Mrs. Joe Doakes' postwar kitchen will look like to actually creating all the fancy gadgets she has been promised in plastic and glass. . . . Many of the illustrations present designs which are impossible from present standards—and may remain so for many years—because their execution would far exceed known manufacturing and material limitations."[14]

Even if the much-demanded postwar housing "revolution" could be launched as planned, would consumers wholeheartedly embrace the radical "new and improved" intrusions into the "sacred" spaces of their private family homes? As the *McCall's* survey found, the "house of tomorrow" was perceived by the majority of wartime American consumers as a means to express and establish order, control, and stability. Although the Dymaxion's mechanical core could have satisfied middle-class concerns about universalizing higher standards of sanitation, Fuller's "revolutionary" *form* failed to answer the pressing psychological need for securing a traditional haven in the wake of unprecedented global destruction and irreversible social change.

To some wartime critics, the world of the present—despite all its domestic flaws, discomforts, and inconveniences—appeared much more inviting than the forecasters' future world of plastic order and artificial leisure (fig. 7.3). Miles Colean's wartime article "The Miracle House Myth" includes a pictorial parody of the postwar house with butlers and hostesses borne aloft by miniature helicopters and assisted by a domestic escalator. Outdoor living is taken quite literally: every flat, horizontal surface of the house offers an opportunity for rooftop leisure, including multiple terraces, a heliport, and a pool. Even the barbecue has supplanted the indoor kitchen. Next door to the postwar "house of tomorrow" the neighbors have erected a Dymaxion-like abode with curved walls and horizontal bands of windows. A bewildered home owner pokes his head outside his dwelling contraption, perhaps to gain some control over a rooftop "mechanical core," which, in this case, appears to have generated more work than it has saved. Assuming that the "house of tomorrow" could become a reality after victory, Colean asks his readers if maximum comfort and lack of effort, as promised by postwar forecasters, poses a difficult psychological adjustment best avoided: "Let's examine this super-electronic, radio-activated, solar-energized miracle house of tomorrow. No-

7.3. Illustration from Miles L. Colean, "The Miracle House Myth," *House Beautiful,* December 1944, 78–79.

body works here . . . not even the servants. All that stuff is done by electric eyes and levers and things. . . . Meals cooked by polarized atoms roll right out to you in a mobile kitchen. . . . Could you stand it?"[15] Apparently, some consumers could not. The promise of postwar domestic emancipation also carried with it more limitations and tended to compromise personal freedoms rather than saving them.

The Myth of Labor Saved

Chapter 6 explored the ways in which features of the "house of tomorrow" aligned with the precepts of scientific housekeeping and its discourse on the triumph of hygiene. Efficiency fought waste, cleanliness conquered filth, and the healthy ideal surpassed the unfit. Is it surprising then that such human-engineering ideology filtered into wartime promotions for "tomorrow's kitchen," where promises of efficient bodies, easy class ascendancy, and the flawless social face were sold? The purpose behind new labor-saving kitchen designs and devices, according to commercial propagandists, was to evolve toward a more leisurely, and thus middle-class, standard. But the goal of "leisure" in the postwar kitchen was actually a manifestation of marketing rhetoric and the social staging of proper "health," rather than a relaxing reality.

Publicity for the postwar kitchen raised hopes for more than just a social evolution, because it offered a means toward ultimate hygienic propriety. In the case of designer William Hamby's "kitchenless" plan, the imperfect housewife is not merely improved but molded to flawless perfection through advanced kitchen automation and extreme streamlined design (fig. 7.4). In Hamby's scenario, the woman's physique is absorbed into her "machine for living," to borrow a phrase from the functionalist architect Le Corbusier. Ironically, the postwar kitchen's heightened efficiency was intended to liberate housewives from the servitude of monotonous drudgery, but because such plans overlapped with the exacting standards of scientific housekeeping, the "kitchen of tomorrow" wound up entrapping the female body in woman's own labor-saving machines. Thus, in the postwar kitchen, domestic labor is encapsulated and policed by a tyrannous regime of efficiencies, instead of being "rescued" (i.e., "liberated" and "saved"). The postwar woman, like her kitchen, would evolve into a self-regulating, mechanized assembly line, keeping her locked into the gender status quo. In the future, bodily form would follow domestic and social function.

In Hamby's November 1941 *Saturday Evening Post* ad, sponsored by Revere Copper and Brass, the efficient housewife was the by-product of a work space designed around recipes that were literally built into the kitchen's interior plan. The housewife's cooking preparations would follow logically in an assembly-line manner, because all tools, appliances, and ingredients would be placed within reach from one position. Here, "location" and "space" are transformed into labor-saving devices just as physical movement is human-engineered around the ingredients of each household task. By following this plan, Hamby claimed, cooking, meal serving, and dish washing would become effortless and virtually extinct: "What! A house with no kitchen? . . . If, by a kitchen, you mean that place where a woman

"What! A house with no kitchen?"

"IT ALL depends on what you mean by a kitchen", says the noted architect, William Hamby, in telling about the better, lower-cost homes which tomorrow holds in store. "If, by a kitchen, you mean that place where a woman wears herself out stooping and stretching to get things out of cupboards, where it's hard to be quick or tidy, where she works early and late washing and scouring—then this house I've designed has no kitchen, I suppose.

"A house is not merely a shelter—it is a place to work and play. The way to make it better is to improve it for the one who has the most to do—the woman. So I conceive the house of tomorrow as a place to increase the entire family's enjoyment by lightening a woman's work. Beginning with the kitchen, it would be planned around the household tasks a woman does—cooking, serving, cleaning, laundering. And it develops that such a house, without being actually larger, would have much more room in it for living.

"I have started with an entirely new idea, in which the kitchen is not just a room for cooking, but is a perfect place for preparing the recipes you and your family like. It would be *planned* around recipes, with everything you need right at your finger-tips, with plenty of elbow and table room, with refrigeration, cooking and storage arrangements all in straight, handy rows, and with nothing behind your back except a spacious dining area.

"There would be a long horizontal arrangement of counter, sink and cupboard space, in which the staples and heavy utensils are just below shoulder height, with all the lighter dishes and plates on the shelves above. The whole length of the counter would be used for food storage, with compartments that hold each food at its own ideal temperature and humidity, including frosted foods and cereals.

"Everything would be grouped so that an entire recipe could be prepared, from start to piping hot finish, from one spot without stooping or stretching. There would be no range—you would both cook and serve in electric utensils, each located according to recipe. Dish washing would be cut almost in half. Not only would this kitchen be a work-saver, but a pleasure and living center too, because it is really the end-wall of the dining room.

"Of course an arrangement such as this permits a whole new organization of the house. So I have gone on to visualize such a house, planned to make housework fun instead of drudgery. Many of its important parts would be made of copper to prevent rust, leaks and repairs. Using our mass manufacturing techniques, such a house could be built complete with its 'super' kitchen and its laundry for little more than $3,000. In this way we can easily have homes tomorrow that will provide better living for millions."

WILLIAM HAMBY

America's creative and productive genius is preparing to offer us a way in which the many can have better homes. Talented architects and engineers have been developing new designs, new materials, new building techniques for today's housing emergency. Afterward, these can be available to build homes for all.

It is too soon to predict exactly what form such homes will take. But it is certain that more people than ever before can have real comfort, beauty and convenience in their homes. And in these homes copper is sure to play a vital part.

Already, Revere copper has given our homes protection against wind, rain, snow, termites—has provided us with clear, rust-free water, has helped to heat our homes more comfortably with less fuel, and has cut down both repairs and depreciation. Architects and engineers know that the more copper there is in a house the better it is to own or rent or sell.

That is why, in their plans for better homes, they are relying more upon copper, are using copper in new places for new purposes. Today, the copper industry is working for Uncle Sam, and copper is restricted for general use. But meanwhile, Revere research is developing new alloys and new forms of copper, new uses for copper, to help prepare the way for the better standard of living to come.

Naturally, Mr. Hamby was unable to describe all the fascinating details of his conception in this limited space. No blueprints are available, so instead Revere has prepared a complete illustrated folder which we will gladly send to you, free. Just write to:

★ ★ ★

REVERE
COPPER AND BRASS INCORPORATED
Executive Offices: 230 Park Avenue, New York

7.4. Revere Copper and Brass and William Hamby advertisement, *Saturday Evening Post*, 22 November 1941, 85. Courtesy of Revere Copper Products, Inc.

wears herself out stooping and stretching to get things out of cupboards, where it's hard to be quick or tidy, where she works early and late washing and scouring—then this house I've designed has no kitchen. . . . The way to make [the home] better is to improve it for the one who has the most to do—the woman."[16]

Hamby's "kitchenless" plan implied that the absence of this common room dissolved the work that was done in it. As in typical housing and domestic reform narratives, the unfit element (here, the kitchen) has been eliminated and supplanted by the engineered ideal. Despite his intent to impose an elevating logic onto the deviance of unscientific housework, Hamby (and his corporate sponsor) overlooked the inherent irrationality of this plan. Lost in the battle to eliminate waste, Hamby failed to mention the fact that the entire kitchen assembly line would require extensive retooling if any recipes were added or changed. Although certain drudgery elements of housework would be reduced by the utopian "kitchenless" plan, constantly adapting recipes in accordance with Hamby's strict format would require more busywork and greater domestic management skills. In order to keep up with the demands of such a space, the housewife in Hamby's "anti-kitchen" would have to evolve into a mechanical extension of the family's mealtime assembly line.

The contradictions increase when Hamby's illustration of the anti-kitchen is examined further. Despite his "kitchenless" claims, individual electric toaster and coffeemaker appliances sit on Hamby's countertops. Moreover, a pitcher and bowl reside where the sink would have been—under a picture window. In a close-up view, the model housewife takes a large Revere pot out of a cupboard—a *metal* utensil that we assume would have been rendered obsolete by Hamby's built-in appliances in which cooking and serving, he claimed, would be done in the same *glass* dish. We see one such built-in glass appliance to the left of the picture window. Some sort of roast or duck ringed with vegetables cooks beneath a glass dome. A final inconsistency is the "kitchenless" housewife herself. If her work is now so effortless, why does she need to wear that antiquated mantle of domestic drudgery—an apron?

Like Hamby and Revere's plan, the L-O-F kitchen was designed to be drudgery free—not free of the need for women's labor.[17] The 1943–44 L-O-F "Kitchen of Tomorrow," designed by H. Creston Doner, was perhaps the most widely publicized postwar vision advertised during the war. Featured in magazines and newspapers across the country, it was also mass-marketed through a Paramount film short. More than 1.6 million visitors viewed the fantasy in person via one of the three models traveling around the country (see fig. 7.1). The irony of postwar kitchen design rhetoric was that ease and relaxation were emphasized in the context of routine work. Despite its radical design, the L-O-F "Kitchen of Tomorrow" (also known as the "Kitchen of the Day-After-Tomorrow") was not so different from yesterday's standard domestic plan, primarily because it was merely a new cosmetic veneer pasted over the same old chores. Hygienic glass provided the cosmetic upgrade, covering the storage cabinets, built-in oven, and a built-in refrigerator consisting of drawers: "Generous use of glass enables the housewife to see through the oven door and cook pots, into icebox and cupboards."[18] Though L-O-F promotional stills depict model housewives in standing positions, descriptions of the "scientifically" calculated countertops explain that these work surfaces were placed lower than usual so that meals could be prepared while seated: "Bending and stooping are reduced to a minimum because counters and utensils are at proper working level."[19] The counters were also curved inward to accommodate the presumed hourglass physique of the "average" housewife: "Fronts of counters and drawers beneath working surfaces are slanted in so that the housewife has knee room when she sits at her work."[20] And the sink and stove were designed with hinged tops that concealed their presence, thus allowing for a truly uninterrupted counter surface and further facilitating work flow.

After the war, efficiency zealots followed the wartime impulse to human-engineer a "better America" through its kitchens. Applying Taylor-like acknowledgment of the expert's conceit, Fritz Burns's postwar kitchen of 1946 eliminated wasteful and unscientific domestic prewar devices and practices, mainly the need for the housewife to think. Electronic push-button managers were designed to perform the tiring task of thinking for her. In a kitchen so smart that it had a "household nerve center," all a woman needed to perform her duties was a well-manicured finger:

> The kitchen of the Burns house is a big, highly mechanized household factory. . . . Near the middle of the room is the household nerve center. It is the hub of the inter-communication system from which a person can talk to [nearly any other room in the house by remote radio control; there were five loudspeakers total]. From this point, too, electric controls switch on lights, tune in the various radios, open and close doors and turn on the lawn sprinklers.[21]

Fritz Burns, a Los Angeles contractor, built this experimental dream house for his wife after the war. The kitchen alone was "equipped with 2,000 pounds of machinery to make cooking and housework easy." Burns purged all mental effort and physical exertion from domesticity. No energy would be spent that the house's "dozens of push buttons" couldn't handle remotely. So utterly robotic, toilets would "flush automatically" and garbage was handled by a push-button "disposal unit." Was the housewife even necessary in a home that was purified with artificial ventilation, an "electronic dust eliminator," and "germicidal lamps" that automatically kept bacteria at bay?[22]

Whether it was push buttons or glass, the "kitchen of tomorrow" promised to utterly sanitize domesticity by removing not only the filth but especially the stigma of hands-on labor. Electric, built-in appliances and sterilized structural materials facilitated a cleaner kitchen by design, thus eliminating the "dirty work" of household maintenance and replacing what essentially remained manual labor with emblems of a leisured, high-class patina. This "revolution" in postwar domesticity would have nothing to do with altering women's social roles and the middle-class ideal of the private family household.

Not surprisingly, design flaws within the "house of tomorrow" bubbled to the surface well before the war ended. Avid critics pounced on the irrational shortcomings, noting that the effort- and time-saving features of "kitchenless" houses and war-proved "miracle" products were well-garnished myths. According to wartime skeptics, advocates for the "kitchen of tomorrow" had failed to consider the extra attention their new designs and mechanical gadgets would require. Most schemes for "improving" postwar domestic progress would generate more housework, not less. Jean Austin, writing in *American Home,* complained about such indulgent theories of postwar planners "gone frenzied over the wonders of our postwar kitchens." In her 1944 article aptly titled "Postbaloney," Austin enumerates the charms of "all these wonderful gadgets I read about that will do everything but diaper the baby," and pointedly asks, "who's going to keep 'em clean?"[23] Designers did not seem to actually operate the space-saving built-in appliances, such as those dreamed up for the Hamby and L-O-F kitchens. Austin laments: "Somebody ought to tell them that too much compactness makes for more work, not less." In her estimation, the glass house was the housewife's modern nemesis, not her salvation. Admittedly, it looked highly civilized and hygienic, but Austin astutely argues that "first they've got to find a way for me to keep it clean. . . . And, until they invent a gadget to make window washing easy, an all-glass house is not my idea of a house for the little woman to keep clean singlehanded."[24] Austin raises the sore issue that women were the intended housekeepers of the future, and as usual they were imagined as keeping house alone, even with a household full of machines. Advertisers and designers, on the other hand, turned this "lone woman" aspect of modern housekeeping into a selling point, stressing that the middle-class housewife could easily conduct all the household chores at the highest standards if they purchased the "right" appliance and had the "right" interior design.

Shelby Davis had criticized this "lone woman" concept two years earlier when she lamented that paid "household servants" were "gone forever." Household technology may have promised to eradicate the burden of domestic labor, but in reality it could do no more than alleviate some of the hassles of drudgery, and in many cases it would increase it:

> Will streamlined housing and mechanical inventions eliminate the postwar need for servants? I doubt it. . . . With too many gadgets you soon reach a point of diminishing returns where the time spent in taking them out of cupboards, plus cleaning and replacing them after use, often outbalances any increase in efficiency over doing the job the old-fashioned way. . . . Even the home of tomorrow is going to demand constant attention to keep it decently clean.[25]

The postwar "domestic emancipation" issue was taken quite literally in the black press. Discrimination on the job and education fronts had historically relegated African American women to domestic servant roles in white-owned houses—an occupation that most blacks considered a low-paid extension of slavery. Columnist Marjorie McKenzie asserted in the African American newspaper the *Pittsburgh Courier* that the high degree of automation and hygienic plastics planned for the "world of tomorrow" would clearly make the perennial black maid an obsolete fixture in white family households: "It is not necessary to sacrifice Negro women workers to the maintenance of American homes. American ingenuity is already at work developing commercial cleaning, cooking, and laundry services which will be cheaper and more efficient than the efforts of unwilling household drudges."[26]

McKenzie takes the postwar hygienic revolution a step further by arguing that the war had inspired new industries that would handle the white middle-class housewife's domestic needs, freeing black women to pursue careers with vastly improved pay, conditions, stature, and opportunities. McKenzie's logic that the comforts and conveniences of modern civilization would completely eliminate the black maid aligns to a great extent with promotionals for the "kitchen of tomorrow" and postwar miracle products, such as plastics. But unlike manufacturers, McKenzie seems to realize that a certain breed of homemaker is not going to want to lift a finger in her own home. Push-button gadgets and hygienic plastics aside, McKenzie points to postwar job opportunities *outside* the home, not improved washing machines and electric dishwashers, as the answer for black women's *final* emancipation from white households.[27]

Gender definitely drove the debates about who would get stuck with the dirty work in the postwar world. Alan Dunn's 1944 postwar house raises questions as it satirizes the "miracle" labor-saving devices forecast for consumers after victory (fig. 7.5). At first glance, we might laugh at this ridiculous picture. But after a closer look, surely we feel some empathy for the lone woman in Dunn's cartoon. Dunn's postwar housewife is clad in a kerchief and work overalls as if she is back at the shipyard or war plant assembly line—a place, according to surveys taken at the time, she may not have wanted to leave.[28] Frowning, unlike the smiling, contented housewives starring in reconversion ads, she drives around her house on a mobile vacuum cleaner unit, kicking up dust clouds along the way. Above her head floats a lamp fixture shaped like the planet Saturn—an ancient symbol of melancholy or a sign of the future?[29] Dunn stresses the dichotomous nature of the postwar hygienic revolution by including an old-fashioned brick fireplace, which presumably should have been replaced by some cleaner, automatic, built-in appliance. Certainly, the

7.5. Cartoon by Alan Dunn, "The Vacumobile," in "Utopia—1955," *Saturday Evening Post,* 30 December 1944, 37. Courtesy of *Saturday Evening Post.*

woman's work clothes and the "vacumobile" signify possible postwar changes on the horizon. However, the quaint fireplace she cleans indicates that the *look* of housework has evolved but not the content. The future would not be immune from dust, grime, and the need for women's domestic labor.

Indeed, a 1947 article on the labor-saving benefits of plastics inadvertently supported the suspicion that war-born designs and products would not relieve women of their socially ascribed domestic duties after the war: "Plastics are here to free you from drudgery. . . . They are proving themselves on the testing ground you know best—the housekeeping arena, where the traditional battle with dust, grime, stains, scratches, and shabbiness has made the housewife's profession synonymous with slavery."[30] We see that despite the Allied victory over fascism, housework is still a "profession" presumably conducted by married women (i.e., house*wife*). The postwar hygienic revolution promised to win the "traditional battle with dust, grime, stains, scratches, and shabbiness," altering the image of housework from that of a series of drudgery chores "synonymous with slavery" to chores associated with comfort, convenience, and leisure. As in most postwar narratives of domestic progress, it is simply the rhetorical emphasis that has shifted, not the reality.

Were the exacting demands of scientific housekeeping alleviated with plastics, or did products that were cleaner by design heighten the domestic standard that women were expected to emulate? From the same 1947 *House Beautiful* article quoted above, titled "This New Era of Easy Upkeep," the hygienic properties of postwar plastics are described as buffers between the home and the defective enemies that threaten perfect family life:

> Plastics give you home furnishings that are constitutionally averse to stain-ing, scuffing, and deterioration: . . . a shower curtain which is inherently so moisture-proof that mildew can't even begin to exist on it . . . wallpa-per [which] is impregnated with resins that anticipate almost every con-ceivable type of household staining . . . [and a] lampshade [that] simply cannot be permanently grayed by dust because its plastic surface is natu-rally so smooth and unporous that dust cannot become imbedded in it. . . . And when you have a chair upholstered . . . in a material that refuses to absorb stains, in a color that won't fade . . . upkeep problems are solved before they begin.[31]

Perhaps the stain-resistant surfaces of plastics meant fewer items to keep clean, but did their engineered purity and efficiency shine so brightly that their presence made everything else seem defective or unfit by comparison? Did the plastic "type" provide a model of hygienic perfection to which the rest of the house (and those in it) were to aspire? In this respect, perhaps, plastic labor-saving surfaces subtly urged more time and laborious attention to be spent on sanitizing every-thing surrounding the plastics, rather than less.[32]

Unmoved by wartime skeptics, the postwar plastics industry intensified its propaganda deluge. It almost seems as though it was in the corporate interest to keep women psychologically chained to the exacting demands of scientific house-keeping instead of truly liberating them to pursue careers, like men, outside the home. Certainly, if such a social shift occurred, it would also mean less need for porters, cooks, and maids, and more African American women and men would be "liberated" to hold positions of higher pay and status. If housework were completely eliminated by postwar comforts and conveniences, and if the social stigma attached to "dust, grime, stains, scratches, and shabbiness" was nullified by new materials or designs, indeed a "better America" would emerge. But wouldn't a lot of companies be forced out of business by such radical change?

Wild forecasts for "revolutionary" domestic progress outnumbered the insightful criticisms, primarily because there was more financial motivation to raise the wartime consumer's expectations than there were incentives to remain realistic in advertising rhetoric. And it appears that the demands and fears of the war years themselves inspired more fantasy than practicality when it came to "family," "home," and a "better America." Consequently, exaggerated visions of the postwar world received less flak than perhaps they normally would have in peacetime because they were published for a variety of sentimental reasons, but mainly to uphold complex social and economic agendas in an era of grave uncertainty. Manufacturers who wanted to keep their trade names before the public during the war tied their visions of future utopian kitchens and houses to advertising for consumer purchases of war bonds. Such a scheme allowed businessmen to channel their excess war profits into advertising for their own benefit instead of turning financial gains over to the government in the form of taxes to help support the war—or worse, New Deal social welfare programs. Further, inviting consumers to plan for the future by investing their money in war bonds ensured that a pool of customers would be ready with not only great expectations but also actual money to spend. Lastly, postwar forecasts about the "house and world of tomorrow" functioned less as a means to get the consumer patriotically active in the war effort and more as an educational tool to channel consumers' postwar enthusiasm into embracing big business's conception of the future, thus rejecting any government plans for a state-run economy after the war. In this context, then, we see why the business community on the whole had more reasons to generate unrealizable blueprints for a postwar utopia than to systematically criticize or prohibit them. Despite some of their outrageous predictions for the unprecedented degree of effortless living after victory, the most widely publicized visions for a "better America" were not radically different from the status quo, and as a result, such visions fit well with popular wartime desires for stability and family unity, just as they shored up traditional assumptions about women's roles and work in the home.

Beneath the utopian picture of ever-advancing household technology lies the conventional gendered division of progress, in which progress is defined as the work of men, creating leisure for women through the products they buy. This paradox of progress, which on the one hand "liberates" women, also denies them an inventive role equal to that of men. The contradiction forces us to ask: what happened to the image of strong, independent women wielding welding torches and the like on the World War II home front? Statistics tell us that women supplied the labor behind the "miracle of war production," to borrow a popular phrase of the time.[33] If the legacy of postwar prosperity is rooted in World War II, would it not seem natural for women's domestic and social liberation to evolve at an equally speedy pace? Recognizing women's strength in wartime and their contribution to victory could have fueled the *real* revolution in domesticity by liberating women from traditional gender stereotypes and their second-class status in the American workforce. The same could be said for African Americans, and the real "servant" problem, that is, race-based employment and stereotypical roles, could have been eliminated by offering genuinely equal opportunities for social and economic advancement. Yet, as we shall see in chapter 9, the female image of "strength" after the war was white and defined by the power a woman mustered with the latest detergents and the control she administered with push-button washing machines. The advertising of the World War II era set a precedent for depicting victorious women, but during the cold war years, such motifs translated into an image of feminine "superpower" enhanced by the latest vacuum cleaner, frozen dinner, or self-cleaning oven. Consequently, a woman's role in postwar victory, unlike her wartime rank on the home front, was restricted to what she could purchase on the battlefield of the supermarket and how she deployed her appliance arsenal to wage a war on dirt, germs, and inefficiency in the home.

8 What *Did* Happen to the Dreamworld?

Realities of the Postwar Commercial Fallout

You have a date with PLASTICS . . . Styron and other plastics produced by Dow promise new luxury, new comfort, new scope—to everyday life and to "dress-up" occasions. They'll be within reach of everybody's pocketbook, too. And that's Dow's aim in striving for better plastics and hundreds of other useful products of chemistry.[1]

Dow Chemical's ad from 1945 debuts Miss Postwar America at her assembly-line toilette, which conveniently descends upon her from the heavens on a conveyor belt (fig. 8.1). Underscoring the flawless perfection of plastics, Dow pairs its postwar product with advertising's fittest female type: the streamlined, Aryan blonde. Both the product and the woman are Dow's conception of the ultimate hygienic solution. In this reconversion narrative, Miss Postwar America seems to ready herself for a romantic rendezvous with Prince Charming: Dow plastics. According to Dow, its postwar "date" is affordable, but not cheap. Offering "new luxury, new comfort," its character is "better," "useful," and new in "scope"—far above the ordinary suitor. But we've heard this same line from other postwar Prince Charmings before. The plastics industry, in courting Miss Postwar America's dollars, made all sorts of promises about everlasting beauty and easier living

8.1. Dow Chemical advertisement for Styron, Courtesy Post Street Archives, Dow Chemical Corporation.

after the war, as Dow does here. From the critics' standpoint, however, Miss Postwar America's date stood her up.

Were the wartime promises nothing but a misleading lie? Commercial propagandists, even after victory, continued to claim that the "miracles" extracted from war's destruction had arrived and were busy revolutionizing American life, escorting it to higher levels of cleanliness, perfection, and leisure—despite criticisms suggesting that the female consumer had been jilted at the postwar altar. Perhaps attempting to ignite prosperity by encouraging consumer spending, advertisers after the war claimed that the long-anticipated shopping orgy had begun. Following this trend in its 1946 ad, Texaco tries to boost confidence in its manufacturing clients by depicting the postwar market as an ocean of frenzied buyers, flooding stores with an unprecedented deluge of dollars (fig. 8.2). Bolstering its clientele, Texaco claims that the postwar commercial fallout, which it refers to as the "counter attack," could be easily met head-on by American industry, which had proven its superior ability to outproduce its enemies in war: "No one questions America's pent-up, product-hungry eagerness to buy. Nor can we question U.S. Industry's ability, in view of its colossal war record, to meet these peace-time demands."[2] Once again, "industry" in this context means management—not labor. For it is among the managerial elite, the readers of *Fortune,* that Texaco is trying to inspire confidence. But why would a group of heroes with a "colossal war record" need help stiffening their backbones when it came to facing the postwar future? The answer lies in the ad's picture, which perhaps unwittingly depicts the fulfillment of a nightmare, not a dream.

If we examine the picture closely, what's being suggested is actually quite a frightening dilemma: an ocean of hungry consumers hits a store counter like a tidal wave. Of course, the artist has given this mob the veneer of middle-class respectability: the men wear suits, ties, and fedoras, while the women sport tidy little hats and kid gloves. But some act more animalistic than middle class despite the character type their clothing initially suggests. A few men and women climb boldly, and rather rudely, over the heads of those closest to the counter. The clerks in this picture seem to take the mob in stride. And why not? Were the long lines of disgruntled *wartime* consumers, irritated by rationing and shortages, any worse than this postwar "counter attack"? Besides, it's not the clerks who are shaking in their boots. It's those corporations who made all sorts of unsubstantiated innuendos about revolutionary miracle products. The signs of trouble in this ad are *behind* the counter. Above the clerks' heads, we see a wringer washing machine and a manual push-mower, two products anyone would have assumed had been rendered completely obsolete by the miraculous inventions spun from the assembly lines of war. Their old-fashioned technology, still for sale in April 1946, makes us question the "newness" of the refrigerator and stove also on the shelf. Are these prewar models, too? What's going to happen, we wonder, when this mob gets close enough to the sales counter to find out the goods aren't as "postwar" as promised?

Wartime ads posed pretty pictures of the war as a catalyst for universalizing middle-class comforts, conveniences, and efficiency. Yet in the eyes of some commentators, the forecasts never materialized into concrete reality, and although

Counter attack!

No one questions America's pent-up, product-hungry eagerness to buy. Nor can we question U. S. Industry's ability, in view of its colossal war record, to meet these peace-time demands.

Texaco too can exceed its own pre-war output of quality lubricants for your peacetime production . . .

ONE PURCHASE AGREEMENT will serve for all your plants, wherever located, in the 48 states . . .

INSURING you the benefits of uniform-ity of products and so — uniformity of performance . . .

PLUS a convenient source of supply for lubricants and fuels from *more than 2300 Texaco wholesale supply points* . . .

PLUS the services of skilled *Texaco Lubrication Engineers*—to cooperate in increasing output, reducing costs.

'PHONE the nearest of Texaco's more than 2300 wholesale supply points or write to The Texas Company, National Sales Division, 135 East 42nd Street, New York 17, N. Y.

The Texas Company

—in all 48 States

8.2. Texaco advertisement, *Fortune,* April 1946, 12. Reproduced with permission of Chevron Corporation.

expectations for a "better America" remained after the war, disappointments over utopia's slow arrival were many. One skeptic expressed his disgust for the discrepancies in a 1947 *Fortune* article aptly titled "What Happened to the Dreamworld?" If a "better America" had evolved from the chaotic destruction of war, he asks, where was it? "What Happened to the Dreamworld? . . . To That Thermoplastic, Aerodynamic, Supersonic, Electronic, Gadgetonic World the Admen Promised During the War? . . . The implication was that effort, pain, and death were to be eliminated from this earth—or at least from the U.S.A. . . . The postwar dreamworld seems to hover in the same relative position between yesterday and tomorrow as it did in wartime."[3]

Here was the future, he scoffs, but where was this effortless hygienic world "in which stockings never ran" and "fabrics never had to be washed"? Women were not the only beneficiaries of this new world, his rant suggests, where the "man of the house was to commute to his office in a modest four-place helicopter."[4] Apparently, in the future everyone would have managerial status: all men marched off to white-collar jobs, while all women sported elite roles as glamorous housewives, overseers of leisure and perfection. This anonymous critic's bluster continues as he questions the mythic properties ascribed to the postwar house—the war's "revolutionary" answer to a world beset with chronic filth, poverty, ill will, and ill health. Virtually every labor-saving and hygienic claim made by advertisers during the war is succinctly disparaged in this critic's sarcastic poke at wartime speculations: "The American, in the postwar was going to live in a house built of glass, plastic, and maybe a slab or two of steel or aluminum. . . . [This house] was bought in a department store, delivered in a van, and erected in a few hours. It was radiant-heated, this house: it stayed warm in sub-zero winter with the windows wide open, and in the summer, by the switch of a button, it was cooled with equal effectiveness."[5]

The *Fortune* naysayer sees no evidence that the war manifested a bridge to social and material betterment, and his perturbed tone indicates to us the inherent irony behind the wartime claims. Postwar visions, his criticism implies, suggested the wild misconception that liberating the world from fascism would automatically free it from the tyranny of inefficiency, inconvenience, and discomfort, as well as such enemies as germs, dust, termites, and grime: "[The imagined postwar house] was a fluorescent-lighted domicile that was soundproof, dustproof, termiteproof, and germproof (by ultraviolet lamps). . . . Its interior could be thoroughly cleansed with a damp cloth. . . . It had a kitchen equipped with automatic dishwasher, automatic laundry, and ultra-short-wave diathermic cooking controls."[6] Forecasters and propagandists had slated all household pathologies for extinction, allowing America's hygienic evolution to flow effortlessly into domestic perfection and leisure. But were they wrong?

This author's caustic remarks articulate the insightful realization that "world of tomorrow" prophesies represented romantic escapes from global, national, and social uncertainties. In wartime America, the quest for victory became tied with the evolutionary leap into a "better America," which involved the struggle to shore up the status quo—in both the corporate arena and the middle-class home. Implicit in the "world of tomorrow" theme was a germ-free, dust-free, stain-free world of a well-plumbed future that upheld a moral authority against the tyrannical regimes of wasteful drudgery, poverty, poor housing, and social decay. Affordable effortlessness and automatic control stood as symbols of democracy's supposed conquest over the "fascism" of unhygienic savagery. The American middle-class standard of living had been positioned as a beacon of order and hygiene, a light in the harbor drawing the lost ships of an inefficient war-torn world to the magical shores of the techno-corporate order, where a parade of experts anticipated every need with antiseptic science and convenient technology.

A noticeable schism separates the sarcasm apparent in the *Fortune* critic's rant from the enthusiastic forecasts discussed in part 2. Such a polarity suggests that the truth lies somewhere in the middle, raising the question, were *any* of the wartime forecasts realistic? Did *any* forecasts come to pass at all? Specific realities of the postwar commercial fallout, examined in the next sections, are disappointing by comparison with the utopian visions painted in wartime ads. The desire for betterment on all fronts (commercial, social, political) clashed with fears that compelled many Americans to reach for what they were accustomed to in the past. But, nonetheless, the changing nature of global politics gave the postwar commercial fallout an unexpected twist, and the war by itself, without its advertising gimmicks, gave many Americans a glimpse of social uplift for which they would continue to struggle despite the return of prewar conservative anxieties and sentiments.

Prewar Models Masked in Postwar Rhetoric

"The inventiveness that won a war is the greatest promise of better living in peace."[7] It would seem from postwar platitudes, like those expressed in this line from a 1946 Huff-Duff ad, that the "world of tomorrow" was certainly on its way, if it hadn't already arrived. But according to a Consumer's Union report made later that year, "business as usual" outweighed the "revolutions" for sale in the postwar market. Arthur Kallet, director of the Consumer's Union, lays out the bald facts for us in his *New Republic* article "How Good Are Postwar Goods?" From his perspective, "postwar" meant only a production date, not a genuine or significant product improvement. The "postwar" label, he warns, was merely slick advertising, so let the buyer beware:

> During the war, industry diverted many millions of dollars of excess profits to the task of telling consumers what marvelous electrical and mechanical products were in store for them when peace came. [After one year of peace] many of the promised goods have passed through the laboratories of Consumer's Union. [And we have found that] the expensive promises have not been kept, [and] with few exceptions the new products are "postwar" by virtue only of the date of their manufacture, not of improved materials or design.[8]

MAYTAG'S MAKING WASHERS AGAIN!

But please don't expect to get one right away. Remember, 6,000,000 women are waiting to buy new washers and our production is limited. Remember, too, that *a Maytag is worth waiting for!*

After all these strenuous years of war production, we're now getting back into our stride making the handsome new Post-War Maytags we promised you, the finest we've ever built.

However, be assured we are bending every effort to get these new Maytags into your dealer's hands as fast as possible.

Even so, you're probably going to have to wait. In the meantime, to make sure you get your new Maytag the very minute it is available, see your Maytag dealer at once.*

The handsome New Maytag "Post-War" models give you:

1. Maytag's gyrafoam action—gentle, effective—saves clothes, saves time.

2. Maytag's damp drier—safe, speedy, and fingertip controlled.

3. Maytag's sediment zone—traps dirt—clothes wash cleaner.

4. Maytag's one-piece square cast aluminum tub—big capacity, long life.

5. New quality, efficiency, ruggedness.

Plus many important new-day improvements.

* If you don't know your Maytag dealer, write the Maytag Company, Newton, Iowa.

8.3. Maytag advertisement, *Life,* 1 October 1945, 125. Courtesy of Maytag.

Postwar progress was just a return to prewar models, despite the hype, as Kallet points out: "Tests of washing machines . . . again show no revolutionary developments."[9] A Maytag ad from October 1945 unwittingly supports the Consumer's Union findings (fig. 8.3). Maytag boasts of its "handsome" postwar model with "gyrafoam action . . . damp drier . . . fingertip [control] . . . sediment zone [which] traps dirt . . . [and] new quality, efficiency [and] ruggedness."[10] But the washer pictured in the ad—the supposed postwar prototype—is simply a prewar wringer model, similar to the one pictured in the 1946 Texaco ad. Such superfluous descriptors, impressive as they seemed, were tacked onto prewar models like fancy packaging and used to excite consumers about products they could have bought just after Pearl Harbor.

The disgruntled author of "What Happened to the Dreamworld?" echoes Kallet's sober assessment. Much of what was heralded as war-born "miracles," he asserts, had actually been around before the war. But these "miracle" products' mystique had intensified as a result of their manufacturers' exaggerated wartime contributions. The only "new" product whose technology was developed as a result of the war and was thus entitled to the label "postwar product" was the humble ball-bearing ink pen:

> The unvarnished truth is that there is practically no consumer product of any kind on today's market, or on the production line of any manufacturer, that can claim clear title to a postwar birthright. A lot that is touted as such is actually prewar—synthetic fibers, for example, out of which we are now getting new uses. But a thorough search for genuine postwar creations in the consumer-goods field yields only the ball-bearing pen. . . . So far as is known, the principle was not present in any pen marketed before the war.[11]

Reading between the lines of postwar criticisms, we see that corporate leaders sought to implement a successful reconversion through frugal means. Miss Postwar America's Prince Charming was actually a very chintzy date. Although the hype may have looked expensive in print, the reality of reconversion was skimpy by comparison. Shortly after Japan's surrender in August 1945, the *Baltimore Afro-American* put the grim reality of reconversion into perspective that crossed racial and class lines. The government's reconversion announcements were as full of hype as the forecasts promoted in wartime ads. Business had the green light from Washington to switch production to peace. But no one had the raw materials at hand to fill the backlog of consumer needs. And even if a substitute material were used, such as plastics or wood, no manufacturer was going to be able to retool its assembly lines from making bombers one day to autos or refrigerators the next. Product distribution channels were as much tied up in war production as had been the factories and raw materials. Despite the return to "normalcy" expected after victory earlier that month, the reality was that "normal" was still a long way off. Postwar shopping was going to be rationed for the meantime, much as it had been during the war:

> Because the War Production Board has lifted certain limits on the manufacture of civilian goods, we hear a lot of talk these days about new electric refrigerators, autos, electric irons, et cetera. Some of the announcements read as if these goods are about to pop on the market any day. . . . Giving business the go-ahead sign without providing the steel with which to do it may bring us refrigerators in wood and plastics and autos in light metals, but even these won't be forthcoming tomorrow. Even when the larger consumer durables begin to appear there will be only a trickle and in most cases they will reach the market on a rationed basis.[12]

Columnist J. Saunders Redding, writing in the *Baltimore Afro-American* in 1946, voiced consumers' concerns that industry was going "Nowhere Fast." The public had revolted against the overblown claims, as Raymond Loewy had anticipated in 1943. It was indeed a consumers' war and the shopping "mob's" restlessness had reached its peak, as Texaco had feared. Brand loyalty and advertising appeals made no difference "in this fight": "What the public wants is to see the cars and refrigerators and washing machines rolling off the assembly line again. They no longer care very much who gets licked in this fight. They no longer read the ads which both sides fill whole pages of newspapers."[13]

According to the conservative business argument, if postwar attention could be focused on producing 1942 models instead of retooling for radically new 1946 designs, then the manufacturing of familiar products could offset a postwar depression by putting returning soldiers to work in private industry immediately. With jobs secured, and a postwar depression minimized or averted, the public's confidence in the economy would grow. Under these stabilized conditions, consumers would be more likely to unfreeze war bond savings in an economy that *looked* promising—even if the 1946 products failed to live up to the wartime predictions. A quick and easy return to prewar civilian production would jump-start postwar prosperity, and business could derail any government plans for "fixing" the postwar economy with public work projects fueled by tax dollars, as during the Depression. Following this logic, the conservative business establishment poured its industrial investment into the last models designed before U.S. involvement in the war. "Miracle" products and "revolutionary" improvements would be put on hold indefinitely.

What about prefabricated housing? Did prefabrication fulfill *any* of the "house of tomorrow" claims? Housing reformers and forecasters had been right to speculate that the lessons of war applied to peacetime construction would launch the prefab industry into the mainstream. But many predictors had not anticipated the political fallout resulting from the return to a peacetime economy. The anonymous *Fortune* critic echoed the architectural establishment's conservative estimates on prefab housing, and added that it wasn't simply industrial limitations that stalled plans for the "house of tomorrow." Rather, impediments arising from *outside* the prefab industry would create roadblocks inhibiting fulfillment of the forecasters' inventive dreams:

> Prefabricated housing on a sizable scale is still ten or twenty years away from making a real impact on American living. At first it seemed that the war had definitely and finally released prefabricated housing from its imprisonment in the dreamworld. Between Pearl Harbor and Hiroshima almost 120,000 such houses came off the U.S. assembly lines. . . . Strong forces—political, economic, and emotional . . . obstruct the progress of industrialized housing in this country.[14]

One could argue, however, that the Levittown houses and other similar postwar suburban developments democratized home ownership for the white working class.[15] Abraham Levitt and his sons, William and Alfred, had launched their construction business in 1929, focusing on the upper middle class. Throughout the 1930s, they built for this elite market, pricing their homes between $9,100 and $18,500.[16] Levitt and Sons did not begin to specialize in the quickly constructed, low-cost housing for which they became famous until 1941 when the company received its first wartime contract, which required building 1,600 defense worker houses in Norfolk, Virginia. Later this amount was increased to 2,350, and the speed with which they were forced to work taught them the expeditious value of preassembled, standardized parts and building houses on an assembly-line basis. William Levitt's experience as a Navy Seabee (the naval construction crew corps) between 1943 and 1945 would also prove useful for the accelerated construction methods the Levitt company adopted after the war.[17] Architectural historian Kenneth Jackson in his aptly titled 1985 book *Crabgrass Frontier* attributes the unprecedented pace of their construction (which at its peak allowed the Levitts to erect about thirty houses in one day) to new power hand tools and construction crews specialized in performing only one task—Taylor style. The Levitts' company was successful largely because it made its own concrete, grew its own timber, cut the lumber itself, and hired less expensive nonunion labor—aspects that wartime

predictors did not exactly take into account in their forecasts of the prefab industry. Whenever possible, each part of a Levitt house was preassembled before it
reached the site. A 1947/48 photograph of an emerging Levittown on Long Island, New York, visually attests to this scientifically managed process. Cape Cod
cottages fill a raw horizon like boxes systematically moving down an assembly line
(fig. 8.4). And as with any mass-produced good, they all look the same.

Although prefab houses such as the Levitts' were not as fully automated as
wartime forecasters predicted, the postwar "revolution" in housing was more the
result of a "revolution" in bureaucracy than any "miracle" materials, gadgets, or
production techniques. Granted, an assembly-line style of production lowered
housing costs (just as all postwar speculators claimed). The Levitts' Cape Cod
houses initially cost $6,990, then $7,990. Ranch houses sold for $9,500. Given the
median American income of the early postwar years, these prices were certainly
affordable. The average family income in 1947 was approximately $3,000, a 20 per-
cent increase over the average family income of 1944. One out of every five American families was above this average, earning approximately $5,000 per year.[18]
Certainly, having the cost of the house in proportion to average incomes was a
revolutionary factor. But the Levitts' simplified purchasing process is what provided

8.4. "1947–1948 Cape Cods, Levittown, Long Island, New York." Photograph. Courtesy
Levittown Public Library.

the easy evolution into a higher standard of living.[19] Perhaps the postwar "revolution," then, can be found in the enhancement of consumer purchasing power by dismantling some of the barriers to *owning* a new home and its modern amenities. Levittown housing and other suburban tract housing developments were not only a boost up the social ladder for many Americans but also the first home for families who had been doubling up with relatives in single-family shelters or apartments for years.[20] The nonexistent *private* housing starts during the war had exacerbated a residential shortage begun before the Depression. In 1947, six million families were sharing domiciles with their relatives, while an additional five hundred thousand were living in defense housing, such as Quonset Huts, reconverted to temporary, peacetime shelter.[21] And although the first Levittown mechanical amenities were 1942 models, most buyers of the Levittown dream had never owned their own washing machines before. At least a portion of Roosevelt's "third of a nation" was finding itself better housed.

The hygienic revolution in postwar housing, however, was not limited to owning modern conveniences, such as a washing machine or electric stove, for the first time. Through prefabrication, many working-class families could afford the social artifacts of middle-class status. Despite the emphasis on providing inexpensive versions of elite social trappings, Levittown houses, and the other suburban developments that followed the Levitts' lead, were actually divested of many traditional artifices of aristocratic wealth; formal parlors, halls, grand staircases, and porches were replaced with open-plan interiors, attached garages, and informal patios. But the pretentious ornamentation and historical references that did remain, such as fireplaces and clapboards, were mass-produced and resurrected from the past in modern construction materials.[22] (We can see in figure 8.4 chimneys poking through the slanted roofs and shutters on the street-side façades.) Although the Levitts' period-style models, such as the Cape Cod (a takeoff on the old New England saltbox type) were a far cry from the "scientific" Dymaxion house, they incorporated modern radiant-heated concrete slabs, double-glazed sliding windows, aluminum frame doors, and outdoor patios— progressive features that many wartime forecasters had ascribed to the postwar house.[23] Mass-produced Cape Cod cottages and ranch-style houses were set alongside curving streets, as we see in figure 8.4—another artificial gesture meant to evoke upper-class garden communities and essentially transform farm fields dotted with mass-produced tract houses into veritable, albeit cheap and diminutive, English estates.[24]

Affordable single-family houses on suburban plots were perceived as the tangible results of the war's seemingly magical ability to democratize hygienic propriety through technical innovation and increased levels of mass production.[25] But what circumstances made it easier for some Americans to actualize this vision than others? Wartime forecasts illustrated in white middle-class women's and business magazines pictured scenarios that were a far cry from the substandard living conditions in which many poor urban and rural Americans resided, especially nonwhite minorities. What realities did African American consumers face after the war, and what relationship did they have to the postwar commercial fallout?

The Myth of Democratized Progress

In this new year of 1946 America has suddenly awakened to find that the housing problem has no color or complexion. The housing headache that has been the Negro's up to now has become everybody's headache. . . . And because it's white Americans, and not blacks, who are looking [for housing] scowling government brain trusters and breast-beating politicians are excited.[26]

The promise that wartime production would democratize progress was held out to all in theory but not in practice, as this 1946 editorial from *Ebony* attests. Launched shortly after victory, this new national black magazine boldly revealed the hypocrisy behind wartime narratives of progress and stated what no mainstream publication dared utter but often implied: not all Americans were invited to share in the "world of tomorrow." In one of its first issues, *Ebony* argued that America's perennial housing shortage only received adequate attention when it became "white." The author of this *Ebony* editorial denounced the status quo agenda inherent in visions of suburban postwar progress: "Huddled in tenements, shacks and kitchenettes, jammed into ghettos and slums, the Negro has been living in hand-out homes."[27] From *Ebony*'s standpoint, the average black family's standard of living had advanced little since Gunnar Myrdal's study of "the Negro problem" was published in 1944, when he wrote: "The economic situation of the Negroes in America is pathological. Except for a small minority enjoying upper or middle-class status, the masses of American Negroes . . . are destitute."[28] It would seem that the war's "great expectations" in production had done little to improve life for the majority of black Americans.

Ebony succinctly reveals the discrepancy inherent in the black exclusion from postwar progress. Black Americans, *Ebony* argues, likewise participated in the war effort, an oblique reference to the Double V objective. Despite their equal contribution and sacrifice, the editors assert, they were still subjected to substandard housing because of racial discrimination: "Are these men and women perpetually to live in homes without plumbing, in a nation which judges other nations by their plumbing? Or is this [Roosevelt's] third of the nation, which gave its blood and its sons to defend democracy, to get a taste of that democracy here at home?"[29]

The black consumer's absence from the mainstream "world of tomorrow" raises questions about the racial prerogative of progress at this time. African Americans were initially assumed to be ancillary to the war effort. Black women in defense plants were the last hired and the first fired, and they received less pay; and black men in the military were generally relegated to segregated domestic service corps.[30] Barred from higher-paying jobs and thus better economic opportunities, most black Americans found themselves deliberately blocked from entering the white "world of tomorrow." An editorial published in the *Pittsburgh Courier* shortly after victory concurred with this outlook: "As was anticipated, the color line has entered the reconversion picture. As war industry ends and peace-time production starts up, reports come from many parts of the country that certain employers are asking for only 'white employees' from the U.S. Employment Service."[31] Horace R. Cayton, a columnist for the *Pittsburgh Courier,* likewise summed up blacks' disappointing postwar prospects: "We were needed once, now it's back to the kitchen."[32]

Modern houses, suburban plots, bank loans, and domestic amenities were placed beyond blacks' reach either through discriminatory practices or, in some cases, lack of purchasing power. *Ebony* argued that the efforts to defend the nation against the Axis could easily convert to combating poverty and substandard housing. Wartime production could have democratized progress for all, as the ads and forecasters had predicted, but the black postwar reality fell far short of the vision: "If America could mobilize overnight to arm itself against the Japanese enemy, it can today with four years of experience in speedy construction do as much to arm our returning heroes against the rigors of reconversion."[33]

Ebony's polemics were not limited to editorials exposing racial discrimination in housing and the substandard conditions that many black Americans were forced to tolerate.[34] By highlighting episodes in black achievement and progress, *Ebony* silently articulated the contradictions embedded in the mechanism of American democracy—one could argue, an equally polemic view.[35] In 1945 the magazine published a photograph of a hygienic streamlined kitchen in the Hollywood home of African American entertainer Eddie Anderson, known as the servant "Rochester" on the Jack Benny radio show.[36] The photo portrayed two African American women working in the kitchen, which was not exactly news, but this kitchen *belonged* to one of them, Mrs. Eddie Anderson, completely overturning racist truisms about the black woman's "natural" and only role in the middle- or upper-class home as the maid.[37] Here, she is not only middle or upper class herself, but also the mistress. Blacks too enjoyed and desired the hygienic comforts and conveniences of modern civilization. *Ebony*'s earlier description of inequity and denied progress contrasts with this photo-spread. In the Andersons' household, with all the modern amenities, he is the master and she is the mistress: an ironic image of black hygienic propriety ignored by the mainstream view.

Marketing research data on African Americans put blacks universally in the light of postwar abundance, functioning as affirmative barometers of black progress, whether their wartime employment gains were permanent or temporary. Specializing in the black postwar market, David J. Sullivan published surveys of African American demographics and offered advice to the techno-corporate order on courting black customers. One of the few African American market researchers at the time, Sullivan showed white readers of *Sales Management* in 1945 that blacks' expenditures on durables such as housing and automobiles had increased enormously over the last two decades, despite economic depression and war.[38] In 1920, blacks spent $647,744,800 on housing compared with $1,718,430,000 in 1943. Automobile purchases in 1920 accounted for only $30,554,000 but climbed to $144,060,000 in 1943. Sullivan forecast that African American incomes would rise to $10,500,000,000 in 1944.[39] Sullivan's market research was intended to seduce the managerial elite with visions of additional profit venues gained through convincing the mainstream to advertise specifically to blacks. By presenting his white counterparts with the economic progress made by his race during the war, he used his market data to imply that ignoring this source of postwar profits was an irrational managerial oversight:

> The effective buying income of the Negro market in 1942 exceeded nearly two and one-half times the total American exports to South America. . . . Its 1943 gross national income reached an all-time high of $10,290,000,000, far greater than Canada's 1943 total of $8,800,000,000. . . . It is expected that Negroes will maintain substantially a large part of the gains they have made in employment, due to the war. . . . Sales are waiting for the manufacturer who will investigate the Negro Market, and plan sales and advertising campaigns to reach this expanding market . . . who yearly are increasing in both population and buying power.[40]

Like the Negro Market ad from *Advertising & Selling* (see fig. 4.13), Sullivan points not merely to an untapped consumer reservoir but to an intentionally ignored one, and he asks why business should shun a source of revenue simply because it flows from the pockets of customers with a different skin color. Sullivan's advocacy of African Americans *as consumers* also exposes capitalism's less-than-democratic nature. To Sullivan, money was green—not black or white—and this was an extension of the Double V message that he, and many other blacks, articulated during the war. Black dollars saved in war bonds would not simply be spent on "skin whiteners, hair straighteners, and patent medicines," low-cost fast-moving consumer goods (FMCGs) customarily advertised in the black press.[41]

The black-owned advertising and marketing firm Interstate United Newspapers carried Sullivan's work into the postwar years and furthered the Double V commitment by acting as "intermediary between black newspapers and potential corporate advertisers."[42] Interstate, led by sales manager William G. Black, secured advertising contracts from big businesses such as "Seagrams, Pabst, Coca Cola, Pepsi Cola, the Nehi Corporation, Ford, Buick, Chrysler, Best Foods, American Sugar Refineries, and Safeway."[43] Interstate conducted a nationwide survey in 1945/46 with the Research Company of America to compile data on African Americans' brand preferences and how blacks spent their incomes.[44] Even accounting for inflation, the figures show us a staggering increase above Sullivan's 1943 findings: "$750 million for housing; $350 million for home furnishings . . . between $150 and $200 million for automobiles and related accessories."[45] Other studies, such as one conducted in 1947 by *Kiplinger Magazine,* provided statistics on aggregate black incomes in the billions and revealed, through survey data, the extent to which African American consumers exhibited shopping patterns similar to whites.[46] Reporting on *Kiplinger*'s findings in 1947, the *Management Review* summarized the disparity between the concept of black purchasing power and corporate America's racist marketing practices. The *Kiplinger* data revealed that blacks were "just as reliable a risk as anyone with similar income."[47] So why were they not regular customers of corporate America? The *Management Review* and

Kiplinger, institutions of the white business press, openly acknowledged the "fiction of equality" that black activists, journalists, and columnists had expressed during the war: "blacks were unwelcome in many public places."[48] The findings thus implied that black billions were not being significantly channeled into corporate coffers because of prejudicial assumptions.

Corporate America did not change its or white America's attitudes toward blacks overnight, but it certainly went to great pains to conduct scientifically managed studies of the African American consumer's income and buying habits. In the postwar years, this attempt to decipher (if not include) the African American consumer manifested itself through the practice of hiring Negro Market specialists (also black) in the marketing departments of major corporations.[49] Although stereotypes persisted in postwar media and discrimination against blacks continued to flourish in areas of housing, employment, and education, corporate America increasingly acknowledged blacks as consumers in its marketing investigations and attempts to understand blacks through Negro Market insiders.[50] It is difficult to grasp the specific motives behind the new postwar marketing strategy, how accurate any of these studies were, what systematic methodology was employed (if any), and how reflective their demographic samples were of a large and diverse population. Nevertheless, social change ironically evolved more consistently under the aegis of the techno-corporate order in the name of commercial profits than it did through government legislation in the name of democracy.

Although some corporations may have included blacks in their plans for conquering postwar markets, none made a habit of advertising the "world of tomorrow" in the African American press. Nor did any major corporations depict African Americans in advertising narratives of democratized progress—despite the fact that of all Americans, they would have profited the most. A perusal of black newspapers with a national readership, such as the *Baltimore Afro-American,* the *Pittsburgh Courier,* and Harlem's *People's Voice,* shows no national advertising of major durables such as automobiles, kitchen appliances, or homes matching the scope and scale of such advertising found in newspapers and magazines geared toward a white audience. There were, surprisingly, few ads for war bonds, and the war bond messages that did appear did not include heavily illustrated visions of postwar consumer bounty as they did in the white press.

Nevertheless, black Americans saw an empowering potential in the techno-corporate order's narrow view of commercialized democracy that mainstream business had promoted so ruthlessly to white consumers during the war. By aligning democratic freedoms with consumerism, blacks conceptualized their race as an economic aggregate that agitated for equality and full citizenship through purchasing power.[51] Excluded from the image of progress, blacks leveraged capitalism's contradictory and self-serving assumption that consumerism and free enterprise represented the ultimate expression of American liberty. The luxury car, especially the Cadillac brand, was a ubiquitous postwar symbol of African Americans asserting their identity, presence, and voice through purchasing power. Because their discretionary incomes were historically ignored and unvalued, such an extravagant purchase of a luxury automobile was a visible gesture of defiance. Black connoisseurs of the Cadillac took charge of the car's image and their own, claiming their right to American citizenship through consumer choice. A 1946 *Ebony* editorial called the Cadillac a "weapon in the war for racial equality" and summarized its symbolic role among black purchasers: "[A] Cadillac is an instrument of aggression, a solid and substantial symbol for many a Negro that he is as good as any white man. To be able to buy the most expensive car made in America is as graphic demonstration of that equality as can be found."[52]

Unlike the mainstream media, journalists writing for the black press assumed without question that African Americans *were* consumers of the "world of tomorrow." A 1945 editorial quoted earlier from the *Baltimore Afro-American* warrants a partial repeating here: "*Afro* readers should not raise false hopes of getting any of these products [such as refrigerators and autos] soon because of the steel bottleneck. . . . Even when the larger consumer durables begin to appear there will be only a trickle and in most cases they will reach the market on a rationed basis."[53] The editorial's advice to its readership is not couched in terms of any racial issue but instead speaks to them of a colorless *consumer* issue, an inconvenience they would be sharing (for once) with white Americans. The *Pittsburgh Courier* columnist Marjorie McKenzie likewise considered the consumer role of blacks when she boldly argued in 1945 that allowing discrimination to herd blacks back into a low-skilled, low-paying postwar future would threaten the country's economic stability. Equal employment opportunity for McKenzie was a commonsense law of economics of which white America, with all its expert managers, did not seem cognizant: "If one large segment of the war labor force is forced back to prewar levels of under employment, the first step in a downward spiral of limited consumer power, overproduction, and ultimate depression is taken."[54]

War bond savings definitely made a difference in black economic status. Specific documentation on the scope of their investment in war bonds does not exist, but the Treasury Department's head of the Inter-Racial Section, William Pickens, estimated sales of $300,000,000.[55] Buying into the war bond savings plan gave black consumers a way to be seen as more than just purchasers of low-cost, racially specific grooming products, along with cigarettes, soda, and alcohol—FMCGs that did not require credit or a substantial disposable income. The war bond savings plan allowed blacks to gain greater purchasing power for products that were not traditionally advertised to their market: major consumer durables, those comforts and conveniences of modern civilization. The ownership of such middle-class amenities would elevate their standard of living and put them on a more equal social footing with whites. Democracy on the consumer front would give their race political leverage.

Valuing blacks as consumers meant that the African American market required educational and job opportunities like those automatically accorded to whites. Corporate growth was, of course, contingent on increases in consumer income. But here is where the most unfortunate disparities of the postwar years can be found. Although big business began to more seriously court black dollars and hire Negro Market specialists during the 1950s, blacks continued to face discriminatory obstacles that kept them from acquiring an equal education and access to higher-skilled and higher-paying occupations.[56] The Reverend A. Clayton Powell, Sr., summed up the Negro Market paradox with aplomb: "You cannot expect the colored man to feel and act like an American citizen if you keep him in the concentration camp of segregation."[57]

What was the economic reality for African Americans during and immediately after the war? Robert C. Weaver, writing in 1950, attributed "wider occupational and industrial distribution, longer hours of work, and an expanded volume of employment" to the "higher earnings for Negroes." To illustrate the rise in African American income on account of the war, Weaver turned to Chicago as a case study for comparing the war years to 1935, when "over two-thirds of all nonwhites in Chicago were either on relief or earned less than $1,000 annually and only 4.2 per cent had earnings of $2,000 or more a year."[58] Deriving his data from the Chicago Housing Authority, Weaver compared the 1935 results with the 1945 earnings of black families living outside public housing: "Only an eighth of the residents earned less than $1,000 a year; 30 per cent received from $1,000 to $2,000 annually; 29 per cent reported between $2,000 and $3,000, and 27.5 per cent had over $3,000 per year. Even when consideration is given to the rise in prices . . . from 1935 to 1945, comparison of these earnings . . . indicates that the war appreciably improved the economic status of Negroes in the city."[59]

Having acquired skills and status in industry, African Americans were not content to take menial, low-paying positions after the war. Their insistence on moving up into the "world of tomorrow," instead of back to its margins, as one journalist for the *Baltimore Afro-American* tells us in 1945, came, for some, at a heavy cost: "Despite the prospect of large numbers of skilled peacetime jobs, reports are current that some U.S. Employment Service interviewers are referring former colored skilled war workers to unskilled peacetime jobs at low pay. When they refuse the jobs, the interviewers cut off their unemployment benefits by declaring them [the laid-off workers] ineligible."[60]

Defense contracts helped stimulate industrial growth during the postwar years, as did America's new role as a global leader; both affected the domestic economy, thus touching African American workers and consumers. With the lift in the economy, nonwhite incomes continued to rise after the war (in 1948, the average nonwhite income was $1,614, which increased to $2,338 in 1953).[61] But any downturn in the economy was felt more keenly by blacks, and during the recessions of 1953–55 and 1957–60, African Americans seemed to lose some of the economic ground they had gained during World War II. At the close of the Korean War (1953), unemployment levels in the black community rose from 4.5 percent to 9.9 percent in one year. The second recession of these so-called boom years for white Americans saw black unemployment increase to 12.6 percent in 1958. Income data for employed African Americans also revealed regression. In 1947, blacks made up 17.7 percent of all American families with incomes below $3,000. In 1960, this percentage for blacks had increased to 20.8 percent.[62] Elton Rayack, writing in 1961, saw the income differentials between blacks and whites narrow on account of the World War II need for full employment. But when the severe wartime labor shortages were filled after 1948, the trajectory of African American occupational advances "slowed down considerably and, in fact, contributed to a slight decline in the Negro's relative position since 1950."[63]

The Double V objective to democratize the "world of tomorrow" remained a struggle for decades into the future, a disappointing reality presaged by black columnist George Schulyer shortly after victory: "I can see no evidence whatever that American Negroes have won anything fundamental, except a sharpened sense of dilemma. They are still second-class citizens, although, admittedly they have had much job experience."[64] This lack of economic and social fulfillment for blacks is particularly evident in view of the postwar policies enforced by the Federal Housing Administration (FHA), which helped institutionalize racist practices in the postwar housing industry by using existing resources to enhance suburbs, which, not coincidentally, were closed off to black families.[65]

Although housing entrepreneurs, such as the Levitts, showed how the lessons of war could lead to low-cost "luxuries" in peacetime, the great dream of solving social ailments through affordable housing and universalizing middle-class standards remained largely unrealizable. Postwar resources and plans poured into suburbia, transforming old farm fields into tract housing developments, ignoring the needs and aspirations of urban (especially black) communities. The FHA and even nonfederal housing organizations (such as real estate associations) helped reinforce racial segregation because of the perceived need for maintaining "social harmony," accomplished, of course, by closing minority access to all-white housing developments on the outskirts of the city.[66] This attitude was supported by the loan-granting and federal funding policies themselves. Federal housing programs favored detached, single-family housing starts, which, according to building entrepreneurs, were more easily and profitably executed in cheap, empty farm fields rather than in inner cities, where space was expensive and new housing required the removal of old slums. Consequently, federal dollars for road, school, sewer, and highways, as well as business investments, followed the white middle- and working-class families migrating to the suburbs.[67] The inner city, which was losing a substantial chunk of its tax base and was ineligible for FHA new housing government-insured loans, sank into worse decline.[68] Government intervention made it more profitable for contractors, banks, and investors to build large, monotonous developments in the suburbs than to rebuild urban neighborhoods.

The Housing Act of 1949 did manage to encourage contractors to invest in urban redevelopment projects. As a result, the federal government promised to cover two-thirds of the cost of overhauling run-down and dilapidated inner-city neighborhoods. However, welfare of this type provided greater assistance to the techno-corporate order than to the urban poor. Moreover, the act favored large, single-family, residential developments, most of which were built in suburbs, not in the inner cities. Thus, the 1949 Housing Act, and the 1954 Urban Renewal Act, did not necessarily benefit the poor and correct their substandard housing situation. The acts allowed contractors and municipalities the opportunity to clear slums and erect luxury apartments and office buildings instead of quality, low-cost housing. Urban minorities, who possessed little to no power to agitate against the demands of wealthy contractors, were evicted from their homes (or rather slums) and channeled into the controlled communities of high-rise housing projects. Such segregated dwellings made room for highways that would rush hygienic suburban commuters into city business districts and speed them past the dirty problems of the inner-city poor—a streamlining model reminiscent of Norman Bel Geddes's and GM's 1939 Futurama (see fig. 2.4).

Through legislation, the federal government actually helped shape white consumers' access to postwar progress more than did the war-proved "miracle" products and "revolution" in prefabricated housing.[69] Attempting to alleviate the housing stress, the federal government offered to underwrite billions of dollars' worth of mortgage insurance through the FHA. Consequently, this form of federal support help spur the postwar suburban housing boom, which began to take off as soon as servicemen returned from overseas and started taking advantage of the government's special endorsement of GI home loans, which was part of the Servicemen's Readjustment Act of 1944. As a result, single-family housing starts jumped from 114,000 in 1944 to 937,000 in 1946 and from 1,183,000 in 1948 to 1,692,000 in 1950.[70] Progress was democratized for certain members of the white working class as a result of government policies and at the expense of the inner city.[71] The real estate lobby, like the federal government, influenced access and distribution of postwar progress. In one telling example, realtors adamantly opposed reconverting temporary wartime defense housing for use in peacetime, which affected the options for postwar housing. The realtors' agenda contributed to the preference for new housing starts in the suburbs, which would feature conventionally styled, single-family houses.[72]

Another twist in the course of black postwar progress derived from the cold war's political fallout. The civil rights leader Malcolm X is credited with saying, "Stalin kept up the pressure," meaning that the cold war multiplied military needs. America's role as superpower compelled the armed forces to desegregate in order to utilize all draftable manpower.[73] Horace R. Cayton, reporting an unnamed author's sobering forecast, published a kindred observation in 1945: "[T]he basic change in race relations will arise out of the sheer need for manpower. . . . America will need her black population for future wars."[74] By joining an integrated military, an institution that had blocked their full participation in the war effort, African Americans found the educational and vocational opportunities that had not been readily accessible to them in civilian society.

A Postwar Dreamworld Eclipsed by Cold War Realities

What geopolitical factors shaped the way in which wartime promises developed (or rather mutated) in the postwar world?[75] After the Soviets exploded their first atomic bomb in September 1949, brinkmanship and containment fueled both national arrogance and technological progress. The continual threat of nuclear war and the spread of Communism directed attention and resources toward military and cultural rivalry. Instead of channeling military ordnance and production into the "good" that had been expected to evolve from war, concentrating on military progress during a cold peace absorbed the resources that *could* have universalized the "world of tomorrow" and elevated all members of American society equally, not merely to higher hygienic standards but also to a higher sense of social responsibility. The cold war's nuclear weapons, rocket technology, and intensified mistrust of Soviet Communism—also by-products of World War II—contributed to an adjustment in the American concept of progress and altered the circumstances under which the wartime vision of the "world of tomorrow" could evolve and exist. Despite the desire for a "better America," the postwar political world failed to live up to the wartime dream.

When the reality of global politics shifted, a new cold war version of the "house of tomorrow" emerged. In response to atomic age threats, New York industrial designers Jacques Martial and Robert C. Scull devised two versions of their "Atom Bomb House" (fig. 8.5). Combining earlier domestic fantasies with atomic age realities, the designers incorporated the bomb shelter idiom of civil defense into the new "house of tomorrow's" design. In Martial and Skull's plan, the conventional picket fence is abandoned for a concrete slab that encircles the dwelling like a rampart, suggesting that fortification will be the new sales gimmick for the cold war's "shelter of tomorrow." Ironically, the slanted bulwark is well suited to the modernist, streamlined styling of the Atom Bomb House. The bulwark's functionalist appearance lends not only some protection from an atomic blast but also privacy in an expanding postwar suburbia. With its flat roof,

8.5. Jacques Martial and Robert C. Scull, "Atom Bomb House," *Architects' Journal,* 28 February 1946, 176. One of two versions. Courtesy Avery Architectural and Fine Arts Library, Columbia University and *Architects' Journal,* London.

cement walls, and lack of rustic features, we wonder if the FHA would have found such antinuclear shelter practical to mortgage. If such a unique appearance failed to convince FHA experts on the merits of this design, Martial and Skull itemized how the house's defensive form followed its emergency shelter function:

> [In the Atom Bomb House] the inner walls are lined with a layer of compound of asbestos and lead to prevent the harmful effects of heat and the gamma ray. . . . All openings can be shut tight by concrete shutters of the venetian blind type. The sunken opening around the home is used for a driveway to the sunken garage. . . . Below this level is an air-tight cellar which has another compartment for emergencies. It includes sleeping quarters, wash-room and toilet.[76]

Unlike cities such as London, Dresden, and Tokyo, U.S. cities and their homes had remained untouched by the ravages of aerial bombing during World War II. But after the long-awaited peace arrived, international harmony quickly evaporated and the tables turned. The postwar's "suburban refuge" became the cold war's front line. Civil defense literature pictured the American single-family home as the new battleground of modern push-button warfare. The 1951 manual *This Is Civil Defense* gave civilians the hard facts of the postwar era—a frightening vision none of the forecasters had anticipated: "Your own back yard may be tomorrow's front line. . . . If the bombs from enemy planes ever fell on your city, they would not fall on a plant, or an organization, or a system of government. They would fall on you and your family and friends."[77] No wonder Martial and Skull's Atom Bomb House was designed in concrete and lead!

Ralph Lapp's 1955 article in *Science Digest* opens with a doomsday scenario (fig. 8.6) that aptly illustrates the dire warning we read in *This Is Civil Defense*. Lapp attempts to instruct civilians on "how to be safe from atomic dust," but the picture does not inspire confidence in his message. The former postwar dream house is blasted with cold war realities. Here, the conventional nuclear family huddles in the basement of a suburban ranch-style house, seeking futile shelter from a "world of tomorrow" gone wrong. Ultimately, in the case of the cold war, the middle-class mandate for single-family home ownership could do little to save anyone.

Postwar American consumers were increasingly deluged by news of contaminating fallout too microscopic to see and menacing atomic machines too complex for the average person to grasp.[78] Much like wartime commercial propagandists, managerial experts from the federal civil defense program offered the key to coping with the uncertainties and demands of the new age.[79] How-to manuals provided checklists for survival, encouraging families to practice a routine that they would deploy when the ubiquitous air raid signals sounded. Civil defense instruction was intended to assure civilians that a nuclear Armageddon could be survived—as long as they practiced and followed the experts' directions. The 1956 edition of *Home Protection Exercises: A Family Action Program* provided a step-by-step drill for civilians to follow: "The eight home-protection exercises described

8.6. Ralph E. Lapp, "How to be safe from ATOMIC DUST," *Science Digest,* May 1955, 73.

in this booklet are the foundation for a home defense action program. . . . Keep practicing until you can conscientiously score the family performance as 'excellent.' Then review and refresh your preparations and practice at least once every 3 months."[80]

Civil defense literature assigned home protection duties according to conventional male and female roles. The cover of *Home Protection Exercises* shows each family member dutifully carrying out "women's work" or a "man's job" as a prescribed civil defense chore—identifying gender distinctions according to traditionally ascribed types or traits. Despite technological progress, it seemed that biology continued to determine domestic destiny. Mother carries home the groceries to stockpile, Father holds a ladder and fire extinguisher, Junior carries a radio, flashlight, and shovel, Grandma sweeps, and Sister reads a nursing manual. The lack of order in the cold war era was dealt with through the futile pretenses at militarizing the conventional family unit and sheltering its values from the destructive potential of nuclear war.

Civil defense drills, such as those described in *Home Protection Exercises,* were geared toward sustaining social order by regimenting domestic life and by training women to deploy their household skills and products in the battle to survive a nuclear assault: "Civil defense . . . makes the best use of your own special ability and skill in an emergency."[81] Federal planners assumed that American women would be working at home when the Russians launched their nuclear assault. *This Is Civil Defense* informs us that typical domesticity was peculiarly fitted to efficiently executing community preparedness: "Women, and especially housewives, play an important part in the [neighborhood] warden service. Most women are at their home posts day and night. Usually they know their own neighborhoods better than men can ever know them." The cold war housewife's "natural" domestic and consumer abilities were enlisted to prepare her household and suburban neighborhood for defense against the likelihood of a nuclear attack. The authors of *This Is Civil Defense* assumed that middle-class housewives had an innate affinity for cleanliness and proper health, which would easily transfer into suitable community contributions they could make after a nuclear war: "Women are especially urged to interest themselves in the health service as part of the civil defense program. Even if your only skill is the ability to wash laboratory glassware or mop floors, the health service will have a place for you."[82]

The civil defense program was designed to conform to the hygienic contours of the middle-class domestic paradigm. Civil defense experts encouraged the public to follow the Federal Civil Defense Administration's (FCDA) exacting rules, which were structured in the familiar rhetoric of scientific housekeeping. The mobilization of the American household, especially in suburbia, was described as another routine household chore, and nuclear fallout was just high-tech household dust, easily eliminated with modern household conveniences that, presumably, any "normal" (i.e., middle-class) family would have on hand. The 1955 manual *What You Should Know About Radioactive Fallout* told civilians: "You can also use a vacuum cleaner to pick up contaminated dust."[83] Civil defense planners recommended drinking from the home's hot-water heater if no other clean source of liquid was available, thus converting a conventional household appliance into part of the family's "survival kit" for a nuclear attack. And middle-class nutritional standards were integrated into civil defense routines, thereby tagging civil defense as the "norm." *Home Protection Exercises* encouraged mothers to stockpile "A Well-Balanced Emergency Supply of Food" and provided a shopping list for the shelter, which included groceries that were convenient and quick to prepare in an emergency: "Instantaneous drinks, Canned meat and fish, Baby food, Raisins and chocolate, Packaged cereals and dried foods."[84]

Thanks to decades of hygienic reform propaganda, civil defense planners capitalized on America's heightened insecurity about contagion, defectiveness, and disease. The stigma of poor health or genetic pathology was easily converted into a cold war crusade to avoid contamination during an attack from the ultimate menace of mutation: nuclear fallout. Civil defense literature stressed the importance of cleanliness and purity, with instructions that involved adherence to strict pollution taboos that the American public had already been taught to rigidly obey. *Home Protection Exercises* gives an insightful picture into the purity/pollution issues of the postwar nuclear age. Plans for the future were punctuated with ultimate destruction and contagion instead of optimum hygienic order, as had been the case during World War II:

> Even a cellophane wrapper may protect food from [radioactive] contamination if the wrapper itself remains unbroken. . . . After an atomic attack, wash or wipe clean any food or water container before opening it, . . . Make some temporary toilet provisions for members of your family. . . . A covered pail, a large cooking vessel, or a small kitchen garbage can with

a foot-operated lid can be put to bathroom use in an emergency. . . . Gather your family together and discuss the dangers of dirt and disease which can bring illness or death following a disaster. . . . Make sure you know what you are going to do about household sanitation if an emergency occurs, and see that you have on hand the supplies you would need to protect your family health.[85]

Domesticity turned civil defense, it was believed, would ensure a stable home life for workers in munitions plants, an intention revealed in *This Is Civil Defense*. If productivity could remain disciplined amid the bombs and chaos of a *third* world war, then (ironically) American freedom and democracy stood a fighting chance. Civil defense drills and rules would take on a managerial function during a nuclear war: "One of the chief aims of civil defense is to help you to stay at work no matter what may come. Unless all of us kept at our jobs in the face of attack, the enemy would win the war. . . . Your aim would be to keep working and to give our armed forces the things they need to beat the enemy."[86] Such statements reveal that civil defense literature was intended to instill an internal policing agent inside all civilians from factory workers to housewives. Repeated drills and psychological preparedness would ensure that home front drones would fulfill their duties no matter how much nuclear chaos and contamination engulfed them.

A cold war mentality infiltrated and redefined the conventional concept of "home" in the postwar era through more ways than civil defense propaganda. Just as the nation and politicians were polemically engaged with the Soviets, so too were suburban neighbors engaged in rivalry with each other over the amount of progress and leisure they could consume.[87] Indeed, individualism and conspicuous consumption had eclipsed thrift and collectivism as wartime business leaders had hoped. This trend was epitomized in the consumer "race" to personally stockpile the commercial accoutrements that lent the appearance of being comfortably middle class.[88] Domestic cold warriors and their shopping skills were not only valued as armaments of middle-class civilian defense but also prized as symbolic testimonies to the moral authority of capitalism and consumption as a way of life.[89] Similarly, containment abroad was echoed in the containment of traditional gender and race roles in the secluded suburban household, where the family unit sought stability and comfort away from the chaos of the city, geopolitics, and society as a whole.[90] Consequently, global disharmony and the threat of violence dominated visions of domestic progress during the postwar era. Universal order and domestic peace were still promised through low-cost rational housing, antiseptic housework, and democratized hygienic propriety, just as these concepts had been promoted in postwar visions during World War II.

9 The Cold War's Commercial Fallout

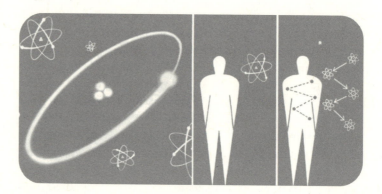

When the classic work on the history of women comes to be written, the biggest force for change in their lives will turn out to have been war.[1]

A 1959 *Business Week* ad by the Controls Company of America (fig. 9.1) appears to confirm Max Lerner's ironic deduction published in 1945. Lerner, a liberal columnist, was largely referring to ways in which wartime mobilization had chipped away at the psychological boundaries dictating women's socially ascribed roles both in and out of the home. But in light of the cold war, his remark could have easily applied to the growing intimacy between defense production and domestic labor-saving devices—those comforts and conveniences of modern civilization. That relationship is illustrated by the Controls Company ad, in which the firm's push-button technology makes a dual contribution to advancing American standards of living by simultaneously propelling the arms race and eliminating domestic drudgery. The ad is fairly straightforward in this regard. A rocket ascending from its launch-pad is paired with a porthole view into 1950s American middle-class domesticity. The Controls Company tells us that its push buttons resonate with the needs of both the defense lab and the middle-class home: "*to a scientist*—missile and aviation controls that help launch a rocket to its target . . . *to a housewife*—comfort and

Controls Company of America
(*who are we?*)

to a scientist — missile and aviation controls that help launch a rocket to its target

to a housewife — comfort and appliance controls that make her life far easier

how can we work for you?

When it's countdown time for a rocket or missile, chances are it's a precision push-button switch by Controls Company of America that triggers the final send-off. And both before and after launching, myriad indicator lights (also by CC) flash the vital data that guides it unerringly to its goal.

Closer to home, controls we make put automation into a wide variety of appliances — for heating, air conditioning, refrigeration, laundry and cooking.

Launching rockets or manufacturing household appliances may not be your line. However, creating controls for these and hundreds of other products is the primary concern of Controls Company of America. Yes, CC very likely has a "controlling" interest in your product — only CC offers the total engineering necessary to control all factors . . . to perfectly mate a system to the product it controls. Write today for further facts on this most comprehensive control service.

This is our line

 Time Control    Flow Control   Temperature Control   Motion Control

If you're looking for a better way to control time, flow, temperature or motion, our creative engineering service may help you find it. We can supply single controls or complete, integrated systems.

Creative Controls for Industry

 CONTROLS COMPANY OF AMERICA

EXECUTIVE OFFICES: SCHILLER PARK, ILLINOIS

 HEATING AND AIR CONDITIONING CONTROLS DIV. MILWAUKEE, WIS.   APPLIANCE AND AUTOMOTIVE CONTROLS DIV. SCHILLER PARK, ILL.   REDMOND COMPANY, INC. OWOSSO, MICHIGAN   MILWAUKEE VALVE COMPANY MILWAUKEE, WIS.   HETHERINGTON, INC., FOLCROFT, PENN. • LAKE CITY, INC., CRYSTAL LAKE, ILL. CONTROLS COMPANY OF AMERICA (CANADA) LTD., COOKSVILLE, ONTARIO, CANADA • INTERNATIONAL DIVISION, SCHILLER PARK, ILL., U.S.A. • CONTROLS AG, ZUG, SWITZERLAND • CONTROLS MAATSCHAPPIJ EUROPA N.V., NIJMEGEN, HOLLAND • CONTROLS COMPANY OF AMERICA (ARGENTINA) SRL, BUENOS AIRES.

9.1. Controls Company advertisement, *Business Week*, 26 September 1959, 51.

appliance controls that make her life far easier." The glamorous woman in the ad looks vacantly out at the viewer; she seems either unconcerned about or ignorant of her interconnectedness with defense technology. Her dark hair is beauty-parlor set, she is bejeweled and manicured, and her face is made up like a movie star's. Those Liz Taylor looks are hardly an appearance we would associate with housework, but we have seen visual codes like these before in ads for domestic labor-saving devices.

Yet what differs from ads already examined is that this ideal housewife leisurely reads as she does her laundry. What a concept! Reading while washing *and* drying one's clothes would not have been possible for the average American in the 1940s, and in 1959, it certainly was not all that common. Given the similar domestic scenarios that we have seen, it is safe to assume that she is not reading the repair manual for the washer/dryer set in the background—the very reason she is able to lounge around her home all dolled up with her favorite book. To realize how revolutionary this simple picture is, we must remember that wringer models such as Maytag's (see fig. 8.3), even if they had electric components, lacked an agitator and required the arduous chore of hefting wet clothes up to the washing machine's wringer and passing each piece—by hand—through the rollers to squeeze out excess water. Moreover, the "dryer" that preceded the one in the Controls Company ad consisted of an old-fashioned clothesline, clothespins, good weather, and a lot of bending and stooping. None of this work became entirely automatic *and* affordable until the mid-1950s, and it was not until later in the decade that prices for these appliances aligned with the average consumer's budget.[2] The washer/dryer set in the ad, far in the background, seems insignificant in comparison to the woman, but it would be wrong to make this assumption by default because the set, too, is another lucky recipient of cold war push-button technology.[3] Finally, a fully automated washer/dryer set has relegated the wringer type and clothesline to obsolescence—thanks to the defense research and development that became an integral part of the techno-corporate order during the cold war. According to advertisements like this one, the innovations that changed the nature of war were also responsible for ushering in the long-awaited hygienic revolution.

In the years following World War II, commercial propagandists continued to extol the material progress extracted from industrial mobilization and reconversion. Like mobilization narratives that told how Machine Age progress could easily catapult the Americans to victory, cold war narratives credited the war with launching the United States on an unstoppable evolutionary ascent. A *Changing Times* article from 1961 recounts how an anticipated postwar depression was foiled by a "second industrial revolution" made possible by wartime production:

> September 1946 . . . A war-born depression was dead ahead and with it serious crisis for the nation. . . . Well, it didn't happen. Reconversion didn't bring ruin. Employment didn't drop. Instead, the nation was launched on its greatest period of growth, discovery, production, prosperity, and social and geographic upheaval. Rare was the man with the acumen to see that by 1960 the nation would have gone almost as far as in the entire 169 years that preceded 1945. . . . We breached an industrial frontier after

World War II, with breakthroughs in electronics, metallurgy, petrochemistry, plastics, [and] molecular physics . . . [which were] put to work for the civilian economy. . . . This second industrial revolution is not over.[4]

Despite its critics, the promised postwar world optimistically proliferated across the pages of magazines, depicting glamorous, antiseptic lives more fantastically efficient, convenient, and comfortable than ever before imagined—thanks to manufacturers who had ingeniously transferred their war-related industries to the civilian market. The defense-theme advertising and narratives about domesticity revolutionized by war found a welcome haven in the global complexities, political uncertainties, and ideological contradictions of the cold war years. The wartime version of the "world of tomorrow" segued seamlessly into a culture beset with brinkmanship, atomic bombs, and containment policies. Optimum domestic freedoms, modeled on human-engineering precepts, were not at odds with the restriction of liberties implicit in McCarthyism and the civil defense program. The postwar hygienic revolution thrived in a defense-dependent economy that eventually subsumed civilian life in a permanent cycle of mobilization and reconversion. A 1948 article in *Business Week* tells us how government funding during World War II backed the rise of this cycle—a strain of commercial fallout dubbed the "military-industrial complex":[5]

> The military need for new offensive and defensive weapons resulted in a flood of new materials, new products, new techniques. Now most of these are being turned to peacetime use. . . . Industry has been able to capitalize on the huge federal sums spent to insure adequate weapons for victory. . . . With war, too, industry got the research benefit of government money, [and] was drawn into many new fields that in peace would have been economically unsound.[6]

Industries geared for the civilian market competed for a piece of the financial spoils from the United States' cold war rivalry with the Soviets.[7] As *Business Week* claimed in 1957, the armed forces were the new "Leading Patron of the Sciences":

> The Defense Dept. accounts for about one-third of the nation's total outlay for research and development and, some say, fully half of all basic research in the U.S. Government spending in these fields has already jumped from an average $245-million a year during World War II to $1.5-billion this year [1957]. And it's going higher. The military-supported research program is to meet the needs of highly complex weapons systems and worldwide defense, but it also helps industry too.[8]

Defense *was* the economic plan of the cold war years, as the advertising agency J. Walter Thompson explains: "It is within our ability to provide for BOTH defense AND better living. . . . We can have $40 billion [in government spending] for defense and increase our standard of living too."[9] The democratization of postwar progress and the rise in the American standard of living was fueled by funding from defense contracts. But consumers who enjoyed this "better America" were expected to reciprocate. Consumption provided a tax base on which to build the military-industrial complex and feed the arms race, as the J. Walter Thompson Company also informs us: "Today [1951], selling has a double responsibility. Not only will increased selling stimulate greater production, but it will also provide the increased earnings necessary to finance strong defense."[10]

Free enterprise ideologues tied justifications for greater and greater military expenditures to the necessities of economic growth and the democratization of progress both at home and abroad. Industrial productivity, it was argued, created prosperity. Widespread abundance, fostered by individual enterprise rather than collectivist effort, was the *proper* cure for curbing all forms of socialism, from the liberal agenda to Communism.[11] Communist threats overseas had heightened the imagined dangers of the liberal agenda at home, thus further solidifying the arguments in favor of an economy and a country dependent on big military budgets.[12] Higher standards of living and available employment became locked into a pattern of arms betterment and military procurement, thus resulting in an American Way inseparable from a perpetual wartime economy. The New Deal social welfare state was twisted into politically sanctioned welfare for the techno-corporate order so that free enterprise would be protected from the collectivist approaches preached by liberals, unions, and Communists lurking in every dark corner of the world.[13]

Postwar economic ascendancy thus depended on an economy *and* a national identity permanently geared for defense.[14] Convair's 1959 *Time* advertisement illustrates how national identity was intricately tied to each state's contribution to cold war defense: "The B-58 . . . is a product of Convair and more than 4,700 participating suppliers and subcontractors. . . . In this, the American Way [of business and defense cooperation] Convair . . . has taken leadership—for nationwide employment, for prosperity, and for peace."[15] In the ad a huge B-58, "America's first supersonic bomber," soars out of a series of packing crates overlapped with the shape of the continental United States. Each packing crate is stenciled with the name of a participating state, visually indicating the scope and depth of the commercial fallout from just the B-58. This economic interdependency demonstrates how the rhetoric of capitalism, militarism, and cold war ideology complemented each other to the point where their overlap made them nearly interchangeable. An Armco Steel ad from 1958 asserts this connection and adds superpowered domesticity to the mix. In the ad an intercontinental ballistic missile soars alongside a stainless steel place setting (fig. 9.2). A fork, knife, and spoon are aimed in the same direction as the ICBM, suggesting that Armco utensils and weaponry share a similar power, if not also an identical political, economic, and military objective. This interchange between commerce and domesticity with defense, and between capitalist tenets and cold war rationales, was the hallmark of the American Way and the postwar's prevailing signifier of a proper American identity.

This new composite identity—where domesticity, progress, and the cold war meshed—was reinforced in announcements of new "miracle" products developed from defense-related initiatives that cascaded from business journals and popular

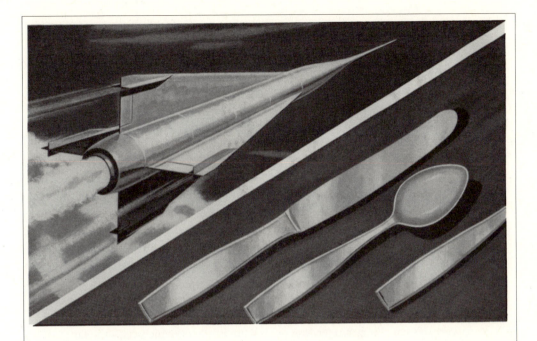

Armco markets range from rockets to tableware

They're both made of Armco Stainless Steel —but not the *same kind of* stainless steel. The missile is jacketed in a revolutionary new steel that keeps air friction from destroying it. The tableware is made of a stainless steel that holds a soft, lustrous finish.

Each of these products has its own pattern of demand. Yet, they are only two of thousands of uses for *one* family of Armco products.

Other Armco product-families have equally broad markets: zinc- and aluminum-coated steels, special electrical steels, and steel products such as drainage structures and steel buildings.

This broad group of products helps level the hills and valleys of tonnage demand. It keeps Armco sales more evenly distributed throughout the year.

Plant locations near big industrial areas are also strong assets. Armco's major steel producing plants are located near the hub of a heavily concentrated complex of defense plants, automobile stamping plants, appliance plants, and general sheet metal fabrication shops.

This diversification of plants and products . . . and a growing list of new steels . . . is adding momentum to Armco's sound and steady growth, both at home and throughout the rest of the free world.

ARMCO STEEL

ARMCO STEEL CORPORATION, MIDDLETOWN, OHIO

SHEFFIELD DIVISION · ARMCO DRAINAGE & METAL PRODUCTS, INC. · THE ARMCO INTERNATIONAL CORPORATION

9.2. Armco Steel advertisement, Courtesy A. K. Steel. N. W. Ayer Advertising Agency Records, National Museum of American History, Behring Archives Center, Smithsonian Institution. (Series 2, Folder 1, Box 43.)

science, women's, and general-circulation magazines, bombarding consumers of the late 1940s and 1950s with a seemingly never-ending flow of war-proved progress. Just as we saw in World War II, the "battle-tested" theme promised to increase the sales potential of any household product whose superiority was proven by its active role or inception in the arms race. Ads and articles that fell into this genre tended to suggest that military needs were not that far a leap from the civilian demands for higher standards of perfection and efficiency.

Revlon followed this promotional trend in its 1955 advertisement for hand lotion where it announced its own hygienic revolution, a "War-proved Healing Agent," glyoxyl diureide.[16] Which "war" Revlon is referring to—Korea, World War II, or the ongoing arms race—we can't be sure. But it seems that this "war-proved healing agent" has had a particular effect on the American ideal female. Similar to the Controls Company's glamorous vixen (see fig. 9.1), the model in Revlon's ad is a slick femme fatale who utterly eschews housework. She seems, instead, to have captured a polar bear rug, on which she lies, staring provocatively out at the reader. The ad is composed of a close-up view of this victorious woman and the head of the bear, its long fangs stretching from its mouth as if frozen in an eternal, primal roar. This once fierce bear is certainly in the grip of this dangerous woman's icy clutches. Her long, manicured fingers, which echo the fangs of the bear, curl seductively around the fur of its white head. Surely, these powerful yet feminine hands were enhanced by glyoxyl diureide (a substance so scientifically remote that the ad's copywriter provided a pronunciation key for the ingredient). Given the year of this ad, 1955, the bear from the North Pole might be a symbolic, and not too complimentary, reference to Communist Russia. Whatever the bear's intended symbolism, it would be difficult to imagine this femme fatale pushing a vacuum cleaner across its back. (It is a rug, after all.) Nevertheless, she dominates the beast with another weapon. Female sexuality here is superpowered by a product initially developed for war, glyoxyl diureide, Revlon's "war-proved healing agent." Interestingly, it is female sexual prowess, instead of manly management or science, that is the victor here.[17] Obviously, the perfect postwar world had arrived— for both the female consumer *and* the armed forces.

The introduction of civilian labor-saving devices and "miracle" products became contingent on the scientific and technological developments pursued within the growing military-industrial complex. A *Business Week* article on Westinghouse, makers of household electrical appliances, tells us how the company sought to reinforce its niche in the domestic market by signing up for cold war service: "Back in 1957 Westinghouse Electric Corp. decided to go seriously into the defense business. . . . The company didn't really have much choice. Electrical manufacturing is an industry firmly based on research, and in the U.S. these days much of the most advanced research is involved with defense. . . . If it weren't deep into advanced study and development, it probably couldn't keep pace with the best technology in its field."[18]

Westinghouse showcased its new cold war "product" in a 1959 *Time* ad with the headline "New from Westinghouse," mimicking the company's standard announcements for new household wonders.[19] But in this case, "New from Westinghouse" was an atomic reactor in a navy submarine—instead of the latest dishwasher or garbage disposal. As if to emphasize the mystique of its association with U.S. military technology and to flex some corporate muscle, a nuclear-powered submarine containing the latest Westinghouse "appliance" is shown rising ominously on an ocean horizon.

Enlisting "new and improved" sciences and technologies in cold war civilian products promised to accelerate the trajectory of higher standards of living and also propel the United States safely ahead of its Communist rival, the Soviets. Corningware provides a fitting example of this quest with its discovery that channeled missile technology into the middle-class home. Its announcement of the "world's newest cook-and-serve ware made of an astounding new missile material" reveals how 1950s domesticity evolved naturally along with advances in the cold war (fig. 9.3).[20] In Corningware's case, the techno-corporate order takes credit for revolutionizing mealtime and simultaneously closing the missile gap with Pyroceram, a "miracle" material applicable to both "missile nose cones and smartly styled percolators."[21] "Rocketing into your daily life!" opens Corningware's 1959 full-page *Life* magazine ad for Pyroceram; a documentary-style photograph of a phallic rocket at the top contrasts with a close-up view of pink, feminine domesticity below. Could two pictures be any more different—an intimate, family table setting versus the lone rocket, heading into unknown space? And yet Corningware, like other advertisers, suggests that the two are, if not identical, certainly on the same evolutionary path because in the "daily life" of the cold war, defense and middle-class norms share a symbiotic mission in the United States' fight against Communism.

Worth noting, too, is that Corningware emphasizes Pyroceram's durability: "it can't crack from heat or cold." It seems that safety and reliability are essential assets in a future filled with uncertainties—for both the lone rocket and the American family. Despite the promises of better living with new "miracle" products, perpetual preparedness in a defense-oriented economy was sometimes unsettling—to say the least.[22] An emphasis on the overlapped military/civilian domestic markets reveals as much about American insecurities at this time as it does about the country's new superpower status. Advertising narratives attempted to downplay the threats that mushroomed along with America's postwar prosperity. Another Armco steel advertisement, for example, inadvertently exposes the paradoxical threat and promise of cold war science and technology. This ad from 1956 stresses how cold war defense translates into "better living," as well as an improved level of national security. Ironically, it was the cold war creating the threats that advertisers reinterpreted as catalysts for material abundance and revolutionary standards of living.

The 1956 Armco ad consists of four photographs laid out in a grid. One displays the interior of an Armco foundry, representing manufacturing expansion in the present; below that, another assembly line–type picture shows a nurse pushing a cartload of ten newborns who will need "more steel in their future." From babies, the ad progresses to a picture of a steely fighter pilot who stands ready with his jet on an air force tarmac; the pilot and jet represent "Greater security for America." The last quadrant depicts a middle-class streamlined kitchen bedecked with porcelain-enameled appliances representing "Better living for America's families."

Rocketing into your daily life!

WORLD'S NEWEST COOK-AND-SERVE WARE

CORNING ✳ WARE

made of an astounding new missile material, Pyroceram®

–for all its beauty, it can't crack from heat or cold

9.3. Corningware Pyroceram advertisement, *Life,* 28 September 1959, 84–85. Courtesy World Kitchen, Inc./AKA/Corningware.

The managerial father in this better America wears a white shirt and tie—he's just back from the office—and the children play on a hygienic linoleum floor. Despite Armco's inclusion of the latest domestic technologies, the trim, pretty mother wears an (ostensibly obsolete) apron. Armco's snapshots of cold war life suggest that steel strengthens middle-class domestic values as it upholds "America's first line of defense."[23] In this sense, Armco associates the strength of its steel with military might and links these icons of durability to the promise of "better living." In a defense-run economy fueled by cold war rivalries, the boundaries between middle-class suburbia and missile launchpads or defense-funded laboratories have evidently collapsed.[24]

The techno-corporate order capitalized on the institutionalization of the arms race and updated the obsessions of scientific housekeeping with the rhetoric of militarism and defense technology.[25] Cold war tales of germ purges, dirt annihilation, and stain elimination echoed earlier hygienic reform precepts that valued human-engineered perfection, but in the 1950s, cleanliness and efficiency had a superpowered twist. In Hotpoint's 1959 ad campaign for its new washing machine, the exacting standards of scientific housekeeping are made congruent with the cold war's superpowered domesticity. In the ad, housework and hygiene are defined in the visual rhetoric of warfare (fig. 9.4). With her finger hovering over a control panel, a housewife stands poised to launch her laundry with the mere push of a button—a scenario recalling the authority vested in the U.S. president to launch a retaliatory attack on the Soviets from the Oval Office. As if to further reinforce the extent of this woman's newfound automatic power, a regiment of filthy clothes lies prone at attention, awaiting her command. She's no longer just the manager but the supreme commander over a machine that will handle the hard work involved in cleaning the family laundry.

In response to potential attacks on middle-class hygiene by enemy inconvenience, waste, imperfections, and filth, cold war consumer products were imbued with militaristic powers, actually surpassing the perfectionism of scientific housekeeping. Although domestic narratives from the 1910s through World War II had adapted the rhetoric and techniques of scientific management, cold war domestic discourse echoed the contents of news headlines about civil defense initiatives, the Communist menace, and the new technologies fueling the arms race.[26] A host of words borrowed from the realms of the military, defense, espionage, and the atomic age, such as "enemy," "war," "fight," "weapon," "rocket," "battle," and "bomb," were ascribed to the advanced features of products ranging from cleansers and deodorants to brassieres and Buicks. Aligning with this marketing trend, Wizard Spray Deodorizer and Air Sanitizer announced that "science declares war on germs in the home." Equipped with "germ-fighting TD-4," which "vaporizes in the air," this new miracle formula was dubbed "science's modern household weapon against many of the dangerous, airborne germs."[27] Also jumping on the militarized bandwagon, Formfit lingerie claimed to perfect the female body by adapting cold war spy techniques for its latest brassiere: "Undercover Strategy begins with 'New Romance' by Formfit."[28] Jet and rocket technologies provided another series of associations with cold war military muscle and were somehow adapted

9.4. Hotpoint advertisement, *American Home*, December 1959, back cover. Used with permission of General Electric.

to perfect every detail of civilian life. The 1958 GM Cadillac was upgraded with a "new 'Sound Barrier' Body" (fig. 9.5).[29] GM's ad in *Better Homes and Gardens* shows a chassis zipping through the air past a blurred background, its wheels tucked up like a supersonic jet in flight. To underscore the aeronautic connotations, GM has added aerodynamic tail fins and taillights that recall the shape of jet or rocket engines. Amazingly, jet and rocket technologies could be found throughout the cold war household. Nescafe announced how "New Jet Process Explodes Pure Coffee into Tiny Gems of Nescafe," while Kelvinator promised

This unusual picture shows the Fleetwood Body by Fisher in the 1958 Cadillac Sixty-Two Coupe

"Room" with a view —
THE NEW "SOUND BARRIER" BODY BY FISHER

Your ears *hear* the difference—your eyes *see* the difference in a new "Sound Barrier" Body by Fisher.

Sound waves are *sealed out*, glass "waves" are *straightened out*. In every Fisher Body, Safety Plate glass is used in every window, front, rear *and* side. Driver and passengers enjoy a clear, ripple-free view.

That is just one of the extras you get in every Fisher Body. There are others: Life-Span Build—lacquer instead of paint—"Custom-Furnished" interiors.

The new "Sound Barrier" Body is another Fisher Body exclusive — the latest in 50 years of "firsts."

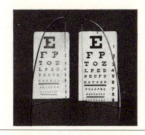

A **MARKED** DIFFERENCE. On the left, an eye chart seen through "wavy" safety window glass. On the right, the same chart seen through the laminated Safety Plate glass of a Fisher Body. On every Fisher Body window, the word "PLATE" spells better visibility, less eye fatigue.

9.5. GM advertisement, *Better Homes and Gardens,* July 1958, 94. Courtesy General Motors Corporation.

that its new electric range could deploy the latest military device for modern cooking: a "new high-speed Rocket unit."[30] Coleman offered to rescue the cold war housewife from inconveniences that assailed her family's hygienic propriety with its "Jet Recovery!" system, an automatic water heater: "Jet Recovery means water that's really hot for tub or shower. No more waiting . . . Jet Recovery means hot water aplenty whenever you want it for sparkling clean dishes. Jet Recovery means *always enough* hot water to take care of the biggest wash."[31] Language borrowed from the space race was also employed as a means to superpower domestic hygiene and increase standards of effortlessness along with efficiency. Hoover's new vacuum cleaner, the "Constellation," was designed in the spherical shape of a space satellite. Equipped with a "telescoping wand," it allowed the housewife to easily reach dust hiding in unseen places, while its "airlift" feature promised to propel the machine forward on its own "airstream," an automatic feature that took "the pulling and tugging out of cleaning."[32]

A brief look at the titles of some advice articles and product announcements reveals the extent to which cold war language infiltrated domestic discourse: "My 30 Day's War," "The Detergents Strike Back," "This Kitchen Took Cover," "The Germ's Last Stand?" and "How to Win the Chore War," in which two housewives (one equipped with a rifle, the other a slingshot) take aim at their domestic enemies: cobwebs, garbage, outmoded appliances, and dirty footprints.[33] Inefficiency and vilified dirt threatened the course of cold war domestic progress, just as untrained civilians or Communist bombs endangered the home that was not safeguarded by civil defense. But any domestic product rhetorically linked with America's status as a military leader was bound to win the consumer's attention, if not actually perform better than (the few) commercial goods lacking cold war–inspired features.

Civil defense literature had depicted the home as the field of battle in the cold war's atomic age, claiming that efficient home protection, family preparation, and fallout spring cleaning fulfilled the recipe for survival in a nuclear attack. Similarly, defense motifs in magazine advertisements only created the illusion of domestic power. Nonetheless, defense technologies were celebrated as the ultimate hygienic solution for achieving a more "rational" and "peaceful" world—and home.[34]

Atomic rhetoric and symbols abounded in cold war narratives of progress. Allan Fisher's 1958 article "You and the Obedient Atom" is typical of visionary tales about harnessing the atom as a hygienic servant of the civilian population. Fisher tells us how a never-ending supply of atomic power was the way to achieve a better, cleaner, faster, more efficient "world of tomorrow." He writes, "Abundant energy released from the hearts of atoms promises a vastly different and better tomorrow for all mankind."[35] Belief in the peaceful atom was not merely a sales gimmick—it also enhanced the fantasy of national security and repressed social panic over a potential nuclear war. Not only did civil defense planners want to curtail mass hysteria and pathological anxiety about a Soviet atomic attack, but those corporations with financial interests in the nuclear energy program also felt it necessary to curb public fears about building nuclear reactors near civilian suburban communities. As a result, atomic information literature of this era tended to adopt a patronizing tone whether it spoke to children or adults.[36]

Icons of the friendly atom or congenial mushroom cloud were intended to dampen fears of nuclear Armageddon and to train youngsters and parents alike to trust the nuclear authorities without question. The children's activity booklet for "Atomic Frontier Days" offered an image of tamed atomic power, which assumed that something so useful in the advance of progress could not possibly be hazardous, too (fig. 9.6).[37] An atomic blast on a western desert is rendered like a sunset in an Albert Bierstadt painting, evoking the romantic mythology of the American pioneer spirit. The theme, "A New Light on the Old Frontier," aligns atomic science with Senator Thomas Hart Benton's quest for American Manifest Destiny, masking the destructive side of technological progress, to which the Old West fell victim in the late nineteenth century.[38] Whether intended for adults or youngsters, cartoons and elementary explanations seemed to turn nuclear hazards into child's play. The destructive potential of nuclear power, for example, is overlooked for its leisure potential in a logo for Dow Chemical's new magnesium bowling pin. The logo is dominated by an exploding mushroom cloud that has blown up a series of bowling pins, thus representing a "strike." In this respect, fun in the cold war means having a blast with an atomic bomb.[39]

Containing atomic power in the form of the domestic atom neutralized its role as a military weapon of mass destruction and reinforced its image as an instrument of progress that coincided with the policies of civil defense. In "You and the Obedient Atom," Allan Fisher also tells us how drafting the atom for household use would ensure the cold war housewife a friendly germ-fighting, labor-saving device. Food bombarded with gamma rays "Stay[s] Germ-Free as Others Rot," he states; "changes in taste are scarcely noticeable; gamma radiation does not

9.6. *Atomic Frontier Days* (Richland, Wash.: Richland Junior Chamber of Commerce, 1948), front cover. Courtesy of Hagley Museum and Library, Wilmington, Delaware.

linger."[40] According to articles such as Fisher's, atomic energy could infuse domestic technologies with an unprecedented "new and improved" strength—certainly granting them more power than any improvements that earlier scientific housekeeping literature could have suggested. Packaging atomic power in the guise of domestic progress promised to advance the cause of female freedom and ultimate home efficiency. Vicks VapoRub offered mothers the comfort of "atom tracer tests" in the battle against the common cold (fig. 9.7). Here we see the elliptical rings of the atomic symbol, ubiquitous throughout 1950s advertising and product design. In this guise as a germ killer, the atomic symbol underscores how nuclear radioactivity offered the pinnacle of hygienic solutions.[41]

Besides the military-industrial complex, what other forms of commercial fallout were generated by the war? The techno-corporate order and the advertising industry emerged victorious after V-J Day, when the last of the Axis powers surrendered. Their efforts to halt the New Deal's expansion had worked,[42] and they graduated from their war accomplishments with a renewed respect from the public due to their seemingly selfless, yet self-promoted, promises to manufacture a "better America." Although New Deal collectivism had been shelved, businessmen recognized a more serious threat to the American Way in the form of Communist influences at home. Business leaders sought to counter Communist and socialist leanings by educating Americans on their country's economic system. This massive corporate-sponsored propaganda effort was justified by the widespread belief among the managerial elite that "too few people know . . . what makes America tick."[43] The American Way first needed to be understood by the average citizen in the hope that cementing capitalist doctrine at home would help spread its adaptation overseas. Leaders of the techno-corporate order devised "A Program of Economic Education for all the People . . . An Aggressive answer to all the forces trying to undermine America."[44] The political ramifications behind wartime advertising evolved into the cold war business community's attempts to wipe out any opposition and to human-engineer a "proper" belief in the higher standards of living offered by the capitalist system of free enterprise.

The National Association of Manufacturers (NAM) never demobilized after the war despite the techno-corporate order's postwar political gains. The NAM, like other business groups of the period, sought to solidify the political shift toward a more conservative climate in America. It helped sponsor economic education programs for the public infused with patriotic accolades championing the American Way. Much of its public education propaganda was intended to curb union power and further reduce the (weakened) liberal agenda within American politics by associating unions and liberals with the Communist menace, thereby erasing as much dissent from the American Way doctrine as possible.[45] Another approach to this end was to reposition the profit system and persuade the average worker that he was getting his fair share of the postwar commercial fallout: "When people think *you're* making *too much,* they think *they're* getting too little—they are easily persuaded that there is something seriously wrong with our business system." Presenting the profit facts would obviously encourage the public to keep its patriotic faith in free enterprise. The 1948 booklet *Telling the Profit Story—In Your Town!*

from the laboratories of atomic medicine comes new proof of a more effective way to relieve distress of colds...

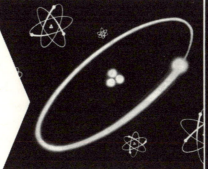

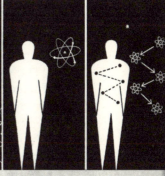

This is a peaceful atom working for human health. Its job is to trace how medicines act in the body—where they go, how fast, what they do.

Scientists used this atom in animal laboratory tests on many colds medications—found Vicks VapoRub acts faster, works hours longer!

ATOM TRACER TESTS PROVE.. **VICKS VAPORUB**
acts faster, longer than aspirin or any cold tablet
... WITHOUT INTERNAL DOSING

When your child has a cold, rub VapoRub over the area of lungs and heart—throat—back and neck where cold tension is. *Acts instantly.*

VapoRub penetrates while medicated vapors relieve head, throat, cough, bronchial congestion. Works as long as 10 hours! Your child feels good again fast.

While aspirin and cold tablets are still in your stomach...Vicks VapoRub is already treating nose, throat, bronchial area—keeps bringing relief hours after those tablets have stopped working.

Now—from the laboratories of atomic medicine comes *new proof* of a more effective way you and your family can get relief from miseries of colds.

For scientists have used atom tracer tests to check the action of colds medications—and found that Vicks VapoRub acts faster and longer than aspirin or any cold tablets.

No other type of colds medication treats all 3 cold areas — nose, throat, chest — all at once — for hours — with every breath—without internal dosing.

So it's no wonder that more mothers

rely on Vicks VapoRub than any other medication. Why don't you turn to VapoRub, too? Enjoy the fast relief—the peace of mind—VapoRub can bring.

Vicks VapoRub and Asian Flu

Whether caused by a cold or Asian Flu... VapoRub relieves nose stuffiness, coughs, local bronchial congestion – **for symptoms aspirin does not help.** If fever, call your doctor.

"Vicks" and "VapoRub" are registered trademarks of the Vick Chemical Co., Greensboro, N. C.

9.7. Vicks VapoRub advertisement, *Ladies' Home Journal,* January 1958, 6. © The Procter & Gamble Company. Used by Permission.

offered NAM members a "kit of advertisements" for doing just that. The kit consisted of sample ads intended for local plant-town newspapers or house organs. NAM members had only to plunk their name and address in the allotted space and repeat the message: "when industry profits—everybody profits."[46]

The War Advertising Council shed its uniform in the reconversion process and donned a peacetime persona, the Advertising Council (AC). But cold war tensions compelled the AC, like the NAM, to keep its former defensive edge in the struggle to help human-engineer a capitalist rhetoric that justified America's defense economy and superpower status. Though more moderate than those of the NAM, the AC's campaigns were typical of the techno-corporate order's public education programs during the cold war years, which, similar to many World War II–era ads, depicted consumerism as a patriotic embrace of American democracy and an irrefutable rejection of Communism or other collectivist leanings (fig. 9.8). In its advertising samples and media guidelines for the "Miracle of America" campaign, which it disseminated to retailers, the Ad Council illustrated the American evolution of progress from 1900 to 1950 through a lineage of ever-advancing consumer products. Old-fashioned household tools and antiquated modes of transportation are transformed into modern conveniences in the promotional, as they cascade "down the corridors of time"[47]—symbolized by "1900" rendered in an old-fashioned font—toward the present—1950. The modern sans-serif typography used for "1950" underscores the chasm between the old and the new, the outmoded past and the high-tech future. Streamlined refrigerators, sinks, and stoves win significance as markers of a benevolent capitalism that can only produce better things that create an even better America.

The superpowered domesticity that emerged on the pages of postwar magazines complemented the technological superiority of a superpowered nation, which had been catapulted from the depths of economic depression to the status of global authority thanks to a few short years of war. Advertising narratives of postwar utopian dreams-come-true implied that the free enterprise system had survived the federal impositions and collectivist/liberal leanings of the war years and was ready to battle the oppressive tides of Communism sweeping over Asia and Eastern Europe. As suggested in the Ad Council's example, the new postwar domesticity not only was considered a symbol of Allied victory and wartime industrial achievements but also was celebrated as an icon of capitalism and a metaphor for the moral authority of the American Way. *House Beautiful* editor Elizabeth Gordon provides a pertinent example of how postwar domesticity was positioned as synchronistic with the precepts of free enterprise and democracy. What her article implies is that the archetypal postwar American household is able to thwart the totalitarian pathogens of liberalism or Communism primarily because the new superpowered domesticity had its roots in the middle-class normative mold, that is, single-family home ownership: "The modern American house . . . stands on its own piece of land for which it was designed. . . . It inspires democratic living by encouraging a personal life. It offers the physical structure for individual growth, so that the son of a tailor might become president of a college, or a haberdasher, [or] president of the United States."[48]

9.8. Advertising Council, "A 'Mid-Century' Retail Advertising Campaign by Retailers—for Retailers: The Miracle of America Thrives on Progress." Advertising Council Archives at the University of Illinois, Series 13/2/207: Advertising Council Historical File, Folder #482, The Miracle of America, c. 1950. Courtesy of the Advertising Council Archives and National Retail Federation.

Writing in magazines targeted to middle-class housewives, McCarthy-like style experts such as Gordon claimed that the merits of democracy and free enterprise could be seen in the aesthetics of the American residential abode, which, according to *House Beautiful* in June 1951, was "unpretentious to the point of plainness."[49] Following the tradition of scientific housekeeping and hygienic reform narratives, such style authorities "typed" domestic architecture through a superficial adaptation of physiognomy and euthenics rhetoric, as if a house's exterior "skin" was a measure of the owner's character and political outlook. Taste was not merely an aesthetic expression but "a documentation of everything you believe in."[50] Any house lacking in the hygienic traits of the "democratic look" certainly called into question the ideological health and social value of those residing within it.

These red-baiting style police explained how readers could discern the political leanings of neighbors through decoding the language of their taste. In a *House Beautiful* article from 1952, we learn that "[A] freely-operating taste can bring serenity without dogma, unity without sterility. . . . The architectural forms are powerful without being oppressive."[51] The "correct" taste, built into the house's appearance, would point to the "proper" embrace of the American Way and a belief in the "right" economic system: capitalism. According to Gordon, an inherently American dwelling had no modernist affectations from the International Style (see fig. 6.6), an aesthetic whose boxy forms and grids were supposedly a reflection of human-engineered societies, rather than open ones—such as the United States— which naturally produced only individualism and freedom. As if to further malign the un-American ideology she imagines lurking in modernist architecture, Gordon stigmatizes the International Style with not only connotations of Communist thinking but also rotten stench: "[Contrary to the style of American homes,] Le Corbusier's International Style has an odour of dictatorship. . . . The International Style school of design, if successful, will end in imposing a design for living that we associate with totalitarianism."[52]

If the look of the house bespoke the loyalties of those within it, what specific features did the archetypal American house possess? *House Beautiful* in May 1951 provided lengthy lists of attributes, but what is most noticeable is that the features of the American house type are mostly facets of meritorious habits rather than aesthetic details. Such a house was recognizable by (1) a blend of period-style furniture and decor in a single room because "Americans resent being told they must or must not do something"; (2) large windows and open plans that led to patios, features that were the result of "our great surge of progress in controlling all hazards of climate"; and (3) rooms with "flexibility of character" for all occasions and activities "because a living room that is truly American Style is made of easy-to-maintain materials. . . . It is designed primarily for use. . . . It invites relaxed and easy informal manners" typical of modern Americans. It was a style that "[put] people first" and was influenced by the Constitution because "our values about the rights of people could not help but affect design."[53] In the following month's issue, *House Beautiful* continued with its accolades for genuine American domestic architecture when it distinguished the proper housing type as possessing "obvious traditions as wood siding and a pitched roof" but was "utterly free of prescribed dogma . . . uncluttered by idle ornament and businesslike in the sense that it did the job it was supposed to do."[54] Ironically, this last trait, which earmarked the American Style, was an exercise in functionalism and the basis of modernism's hygienic "form follows function" tenet, the very aesthetic doctrine against which Gordon, also of *House Beautiful,* inveighed.

Given the fear of absolute annihilation (whether from nuclear bombs or Communist ideology), it is not surprising that differences between capitalism and Communism were described in the postwar years with a human-engineering tone and lexicon echoing the hygienic conceit of scientific housekeeping. David Lawrence, in his 1952 *U.S. News & World Report* article "The Moral Strength of Capitalism," explained the Communist aversion to capitalism as if the American Way were to the East a contagion that could sicken and weaken its economic antithesis: "The Communists look upon Capitalism as their real adversary. For the germs of infection are now regarded as so potent that everyone inside the Communist empire must be immunized against any facts concerning the successes of Capitalism."[55] Usually, an assertion of American superiority included condemnation of the Communists through the deployment of genetic determinist truisms to stress the inborn inferiority of the Russians. Communists were generally described in rather uncomplimentary terms, like pathogens needing a strong dose of capitalist hygiene: "The women of Russia wear men's clothes, are as dirty, grimy and as hard as men. As a result of the forced labor activities of women in the USSR, the family life has been almost completely abolished."[56]

The postwar American household, enhanced by automatic appliances and a housewife burdened with leisure, was hailed as a trophy of progress in the crusade against Communism and its perceived socialist threat. As with the archetypal middle-class home, excessive consumerism and higher standards of living also evolved into measuring rods of political hygiene, indicating an ideology free of collectivist pathologies or Communist contagion. The purchases that went *inside* the house were thus just as telling of the residents' character as the home's exterior style was. The ability to shop for a greater array of amenities was a testament not only to the industrial achievements of World War II but also to the superlative strength of American capitalism, which catapulted blue-collar workers into the hygienic strata of the middle class. David Lawrence, in "The Moral Strength of Capitalism," recognized this achievement: "Capitalism today has brought America the highest wage level and the highest standard of living that any nation has ever enjoyed in all history."[57] *Better Homes and Gardens* reaffirmed this popular concept in an article by former Soviet scientist Vladimir Niska, who asserted that the American Way naturally democratized progress. Superpowered domesticity was not simply for the rich: "America's brand of People's Capitalism gives us standards beyond anything the Communists have produced under a 30-year string of 5-Year Plans."[58]

Shipping the doctrine of consumerism overseas was considered an enlightened method of challenging the strength of Soviet Communism in other Eastern European and Asian countries.[59] The federal government found advertising to be a suitable tool for battling the demons of Communism sprouting in war-torn nations around the world. An article in a 1951 State Department bulletin entitled

"The American Idea: Package It for Export" explained how the federal government acknowledged the American Way as a psychological weapon in the cold war and viewed advertising as a vehicle for transmitting appropriate capitalist precepts. The techno-corporate order, operating under the rubric of foreign policy, was encouraged to tempt Iron Curtain subjects to revolt against their lack of "freedoms," that is, their paucity of consumer choice under a totalitarian Communist regime:

> Your [U.S.] Government recognizes that, in order to achieve the objectives of its foreign policy throughout the world, it must have the cooperation of private enterprise and private organizations whose daily relationships with people in foreign lands contribute to the building of international good will. In this great struggle, the interests of American Government and American business abroad are synonymous. . . . Companies selling products overseas can also sell America and our concept of freedom.[60]

Continuing its new cold war mission, the AC distributed how-to guidelines to foreign investors and American businessmen operating overseas, instructing them on ways to sell the U.S. capitalist ethic abroad. Just as its wartime counterpart had done, the AC taught the business community to weave positive and informative messages about the benefits of free enterprise into ad copy and artwork destined for a foreign market. The AC and the Department of State published a brochure in 1948 designed to educate American managers trading or manufacturing in foreign nations about ways to wield advertising like cold war projectiles: "Advertising can sell freedom. . . . This newest weapon of democracy can help fight for freedom wherever freedom is being attacked. . . . The overseas advertising of American business can play a vital role in saving other nations from succumbing to the police-state system and thereby save America and the American way of life."[61]

Trade fairs and commercial exhibitions held abroad supported the propaganda pitch about the American Way. Domestic consumer products, especially labor-saving devices, were drafted into the business community's arsenal against Communism, just as postwar visions had been enlisted to derail the collectivist tendencies and regulatory government of the New Deal during World War II. In commercial displays exported to the Eastern Bloc, such as those that appeared at the U.S. Exhibition held in Moscow (see introduction), American competition with the Communists was demonstrated with a tempting display of consumer goods, rather than a patriotic parade of military strength:

> Once inside the U.S. dome, the Poles [at the 1957 Poznan fair] were confronted with an outlay of consumer goods as inviting as a mirage in Wonderland—the output of 323 different manufacturers. There were hi-fi radios, sewing machines with pretty demonstrators . . . [a] jukebox blaring . . . rock "n" roll, washers, driers, electric ranges . . . Out in the back of the model house was a home workshop stuffed with power tools.[62]

In this respect, the United States projected its moral and technological super-powered status through dioramas of its prosperity: model houses and automatic appliances, which were touted as the benign by-products of its military-industrial complex and the hygienic spoils of its World War II victory over fascism. Like the wartime "world of tomorrow" motif, the cold war's militarized home front theme became a useful tool for spreading the gospel of capitalism's superiority and the symbol of its success: revolutionized domesticity and democratized progress. The American housewife's role as commander in chief of consumption and her stock-pile of automatic gadgets were emphasized at these overseas fairs because they framed cold war rivalries in terms of a standard-of-living race, a "survival-of-the-fittest" contest between Communism and the American Way. It was as if the trade fairs were instructing Eastern Bloc subjects that they too possessed the inherent consumer right to freely choose among competing brands. In the case of the trade fairs, however, the two competitors were Communism and capitalism, and "consumer freedoms" boiled down to the choice between the two ideologies. The trade fair exhibits implicitly argued that the immediate "choice" was to rebel against the one political "brand" for the other. This marketing ploy apparently was not missed by the foreign audience:

> A few hard-line Polish Communists dismissed the display . . . as mere vulgar American ostentation. . . . But Mr. and Mrs. Poland . . . had no complaints beyond the wish for more. Even the appalling blare of the American music seemed to cheer them. "Where we've been for so long," said one [visitor], "a choice of such music as that could mean freedom."[63]

Putting the Cold War in Focus

Toward the close of World War II, policymakers and businessmen argued that offsetting a postwar depression meant American businesses needed to fish for profits overseas. Simply granting consumer status to minorities, such as African Americans, would not net enough profit and prosperity. Tapping into the ignored Negro Market represented only part of "the dual effort to solidify the national market and expand into international markets," as historian Dwight Brooks explains.[64] During the war, government had acted as the primary customer, but could average postwar citizens consume as much as the government had in order to keep production levels just as elevated, if not higher, after victory? A cluster of authorities in government, industry, and academia, as historian William Appleman Williams tells us, thought not. Foreign markets, according to this line of thinking, were essential to postwar prosperity *and* safeguarding the techno-corporate order's brand of democracy. Expansion into foreign markets would also help keep the Russians in check. It was in this context that foreign policy became not only more militarized but also more commercial. Those who opposed such an "imperial outlook," or those moderates who thought that the United States need not "police the entire globe" through commerce, were in the minority and their policy recommendations failed to take root.[65] A postwar economic and political expansion beyond U.S. borders required arousing popular sentiment around a common enemy through psychological persuasions. A committed American public was necessary to motivate high levels of production and militarism, as well as acceptance of their "related costs"—as had been the case during World War II. The postwar American public was thus rallied around a new crisis with threats that lurked inside and outside U.S. borders and had a reach that menaced not only the American Way but especially the private contours of family life. Leaders in business and government "adroitly deployed" their commercial and political agenda "behind the banner of anti-communism."[66] Basically, the bottom line of the cold war was that heightened insecurities were manufactured to support the profit margins of the techno-corporate order. Democratizing higher standards of living for average Americans, or peoples of other nations, was simply residual fallout.

Mobilization for World War II forced U.S. business and government leaders to take a thorough accounting of the country's resources in manpower, raw materials, industrial equipment, distribution lines, and infrastructure. This intense examination represented an incredible shift in focus. That is, leaders looked for evidence of America's *wealth* at a time when an economic depression had certainly augmented the nation's *poverty*. Armed with that knowledge of actual and potential abundance in the midst of scarcity, these leaders set out to "rid the world of fascism," "make it safe for democracy," and "liberate freedom-loving peoples," to borrow some popular phrases of the time. With all the productivity and creativity at hand and with all the new investment made in training, equipment, and infrastructure during the war, definitely there could have been a postwar revolution where genuine democratic empowerment, rather than a commercial illusion of it, could have been built, enhanced, and sustained.

Perhaps wartime plans for the "world of tomorrow" did not evolve into the market exactly or as quickly as promised. But what did emerge was a spotlight on the technological mystique of modern warfare, which became an enduring trait of the American Way. Commercial propaganda of the early 1940s had shown how modern comforts and conveniences had not only helped win a global war but had been improved and revolutionized by industry's participation in defense production. The effort to sanitize war by integrating war-tested technologies into domesticity was not just a passing footnote in American history. Cold war narratives of progress masked the dire realities and threats of ultimate destruction by concentrating on the defense industry's sales potential in the civilian market. The commercial propaganda of World War II thus established a militarized home front theme that never entirely disappeared after victory because the specter of war was never fully eclipsed again by a commitment to real, enduring peace.

Afterword

The "Better America" Today

Did the attempt to create a "better America" wind up making the country worse? In the years since 1959, the United States has seen a rapid increase in the production of electronic marvels for the home and workplace but far slower advances in achieving the much-touted ambition of democratizing progress to manifest an egalitarian society. It seems that America's postwar role as a global leader, and the military might developed to support that position, did not produce the desired hygienic remedies to solve America's social ills.[1] According to Joel Andreas, who cites figures derived from the Center for Defense Information, $15 trillion has gone toward supporting the U.S. military since 1948.[2] Despite the postwar visions of a better America born from "the crucible of war,"[3] this $15 trillion expenditure appears to have had the opposite effect. From the cold war's inception to the post–cold war era's "new world order,"[4] war and military intervention have failed to offset unemployment, build affordable housing, or democratize a middle-class standard of living for all Americans—expectations that were encouraged during World War II and the early cold war years. It is ironic that the country's public education system and public infrastructure and services (to name just a few casualties) have steadily deteriorated since the United States became a global power.[5] The high cost of defense and preparedness since 1948 most definitely did not close the gap between the rich and the poor. As reported by the *New York Times* in 2004, "A dollar invested in a weapons system, many economists argue, does not have the multiplier effect of a dollar invested in automated machinery installed in factories to make trucks and computers, which in turn become tools for additional product."[6]

Interestingly, the U.S. economy experienced tremendous growth during the 1990s, also a period when military budgets were forced to go on a diet due to the collapse of Communism. September 11, 2001, reversed these two trends and provided a way to fill the "evil enemy" vacuum created when the Soviets were no longer seen as a national threat. An antiterrorist crusade replaced the cold war's anti-Communist quest.[7] The post-9/11 fixation on terrorism is accompanied by enormous leaps in federal expenditures for domestic security, from $21 billion in 2001 to $41 billion in 2004. Since October 2004, the feds alone have spent nearly $100 billion on security, while state and local governments, following the feds' lead, have spent more than $7 billion.[8]

Although September 11 destabilized employment and financial security for many average Americans, it acted as a fiscal boost for those companies that produced defense technologies and security systems.[9] Businesses support this emerging "homeland security–industrial complex," wishing to protect investments and avoid damaging liabilities ranging from theft of electronic data to a terrorist attack on company property.[10] Multinational companies operating in countries pockmarked with insurrection, and where hostility toward the United States is common, find it especially necessary to protect their employees and facilities from outside violence. Rather than pulling out of danger zones, such companies gravitate to the security services offered by privatized military firms (PMFs) because "high political-risk areas are among the last frontiers of market expansion." Such "unenticing places" ironically make the "best business opportunities."[11] The privatized military industry, which is the engine behind the "homeland security–industrial complex," has an estimated "annual market revenue in the range of $100 billion." P. W. Singer, author of *Corporate Warriors,* tells us that this figure will "at least double" by 2010.[12] It is not only U.S. *companies* that engage PMF services, but also foreign governments—and the U.S. government, too.

The important role public relations firms play in maintaining the U.S. imperialist stronghold was recognized by the postwar Advertising Council during the early years of the cold war. The Rendon Group, for example, a former elections campaign publicity consulting firm, "now specializes in assisting U.S. military operations." During (and after) Operation Desert Storm (1990–91), the firm manufactured negative publicity about Saddam Hussein. Contracted by the CIA, the Rendon Group "spent more than $23 million producing videos and comic books ridiculing Saddam, a traveling photo exhibit of Iraqi atrocities, and two separate radio programs that broadcast messages from Kuwait into Iraq, mocking the regime and calling on Iraqi army officers to defect."[13] September 11 boosted the firm's revenues when it received a $397,000 contract from the Pentagon "to handle PR aspects of the U.S. military strikes in Afghanistan" for four months.[14] Likewise, the media relations company Benador Associates received more business due to 9/11 and the Bush administration's push for a major retaliatory strike. Benador was responsible for booking Middle East and terrorist experts on television and placing their op-ed articles in leading newspapers. High-profile clients of Benador Associates "vocally supported war with Iraq."[15] Calculating the flow of information in the media was intended to shape "the public debate over U.S. Middle East policy."[16]

Although many corporate elites and security experts, as well as the military, are much better off financially since World War II, more and more average middle-class Americans living under the "new world order" find themselves *less* well off than their parents who grew up during the Great Depression and World War II. Their incomes drained each year by the demanding costs of progress (high taxes, high rents, exorbitant health insurance for those who can get it, inflated medical costs, and cyclical unemployment), the "new" middle class relies on an army of credit cards to fend off another terrorist: poverty.[17] Granted, the lives of these average Americans have been revolutionized by the miracle of the Internet, thanks to military partnering with university laboratories.[18] The greater comforts and conveniences of modern civilization abound. But average Americans have also seen their health, safety, and liberty jeopardized even as they have indirectly reaped the rewards of the fallout from massive military and security spending. Since World War II, the "$15 trillion" military price tag has included a generous outlay for developing weapons of mass destruction (WMD), especially nuclear weapons—a stockpile that could effortlessly wipe out humanity. Radioactive waste generated by the nuclear weapons plants leaks poisonous toxins into air, soil, lakes, and rivers, often near middle-class suburbs not unlike those developed by the Levitts.[19] It could be argued that this huge environmental hazard, ironically the result of "defending" democracy, has imperiled American lives. Despite its flaws and hypocrisy, the "better America" rhetoric of World War II surely did not mean human-engineering the ultimate destruction of the world.

It could also be argued that some aspects of the federal reaction to 9/11 are not dissimilar to McCarthyism and the inclination toward cultural homogenization found in some examples of wartime commercial propaganda. A familiar less-than-democratic tenor echoes in the federal mechanism behind the post–cold war era's "war on terrorism." The Office of Homeland Security and the Patriot Act created in the emotional wake of 9/11 are protections that also infringe on American liberties at home and threaten undemocratic invasions on personal privacy.[20]

But are corporate elites and political leaders completely to blame for the imbalance of power in the post–cold war "new world order"? Who allows them their power? Who voted for this new order that has contributed to such an awful mess? One could argue that wars and a "$15 trillion" military shopping spree did not induce a more conscious American citizenry, either.[21] Certainly, the utopian concept of a "better America," even in retrospect, appears harmless and well intentioned. Yet America's World War II victory ultimately gave rise to an illusory paradise that today is anything but utopian. This dichotomy should prompt us to consider whether it is time for a reality check about the dystopian side of war-born progress that we have, since the 1940s, been so effectively trained to ignore.

NOTES

Introduction

1. "Encounter," *Newsweek,* 3 August 1959, 17.

2. The international trade fairs of this period are discussed in more detail in chapter 9.

3. The term "symbol management" was borrowed from a statement by Burton Bigelow, a Republican National Committee publicist, writing in the April 1938 *Public Opinion Quarterly* about the failure of some antiquated business leaders to adapt their oratory skills to radio. He accused them of being "unskilled in the more subtle aspects of symbol management." I have used this term throughout the book and applied it to the management of wartime publicity, advertising, and public opinion. Found in William L. Bird, Jr., *"Better Living": Advertising, Media, and the New Vocabulary of Business Leadership, 1935–1955* (Evanston, Ill.: Northwestern University Press, 1999), 15.

4. Robert Haddow explains that there were three kitchens exhibited at the fair. The "debate" actually was an ongoing dialogue throughout Nixon and Khrushchev's tour of the fair—in front of reporters—as the two leaders passed by various American household amenities. Haddow says scholars still wonder "whether or not the kitchen debate was a carefully planned media event or just a fortuitous accident (for Nixon)." Haddow, *Pavilions of Plenty: Exhibiting American Culture Abroad in the 1950s* (Washington, D.C.: Smithsonian Institution Press, 1997), 212–17. For another examination of the "kitchen debate" in the context of American cold war gender values, see Elaine Tyler May, *Homeward Bound: American Families in the Cold War* (New York: HarperCollins/Basic Books, 1987), 18–19.

5. For details on the type of consumer products at the fair, see "What the Russians Will See," *Look,* 21 July 1959, 52–54; Cynthia Kellogg, "American Home in Moscow," *New York Times Magazine,* 5 July 1959, 24–25. For more on Nixon's visit, see "The Net Gain," *Newsweek,* 17 August 1959, 100; "Afterthoughts on Nixon and the Exhibition," *New Republic,* 21 September 1959, 6–7; "Nixon Talks about Russia" and "Into the Red Shadowland," *Newsweek,* 27 July 1959, 39–42; "The Vice President in Russia: A Barnstorming Masterpiece," *Life,* 10 August 1959, 22–35; "The New Diplomacy," *Time,* 3 August 1959, 11–16; "When Nixon Took On Khrushchev" and "Setting Russia Straight on Facts about the U.S.," *U.S. News & World Report,* 3 August 1959, 36–39, 70–72; Richard M. Nixon, "Russia as I Saw It," *National Geographic,* December 1959, 715–50; "That Famous Debate in Close-Up Pictures," *Life,* 3 August 1959, 26–28, 31. For Nixon's public addresses upon arrival in Moscow and for the opening of the fair, see "Vice President Nixon Opens American Exhibition at Moscow," *United States State Department Bulletin,* 17 August 1959, 227–36; "What Freedom Means to Us," *Vital Speeches of the Day,* 15 August 1959, 677–82.

6. The "American Way" was a vague yet nostalgic term for corporate capitalism, private ownership, and the perceived unrestricted democracy associated with the American free enterprise system. It also was linked to the dream of owning a detached, single-family house as well as having the liberty and opportunity to ascend

from "rags to riches." The American Way concept is addressed at greater length in chapter 2.

7. Many thanks to Thomas Henthorn for his insights in this area.

8. The "democratization" process by way of economic access to consumer goods and technological progress is further explained in chapter 2.

9. David Hounshell, *From the American System to Mass Production, 1800–1932: The Development of Manufacturing Technology in the United States* (Baltimore: Johns Hopkins University Press, 1984), 307–8; Roland Marchand, *Advertising the American Dream: Making Way for Modernity, 1920–1940* (Berkeley: University of California Press, 1985), 2.

10. "What Nixon Learned in Russia," *U.S. News & World Report,* 10 August 1959, 39. See Elaine Tyler May's *Homeward Bound* for a similar interpretation and discussion of this quote (19).

11. The Russians were judged through the lens of postwar American standards of living and middle-class gender roles. For example, "Domestic pigs run loose in [the Russian town of] Kazhegi. . . . 'Foods' in display windows of shops are actually cardboard." "They Let Us Talk to the Russians," *Ladies' Home Journal,* June 1955, 51.

12. See Robert MacDougall, "Red, Brown, and Yellow Perils: Images of the American Enemy in the 1940s and 1950s," *Journal of Popular Culture* 32 (Spring 1999): 59–75, which provides an excellent context for the prevailing racial and ethnic attitudes during the World War II and early cold war years, and how they shaped popular images of the Japanese, Germans, and Russians. MacDougall describes how the Russians were seen as racially/ethnically inferior.

13. See Susan E. Reid, "The Khrushchev Kitchen, OR Rockets for Housewives: Domesticating the Scientific-Technological Revolution," unpublished paper delivered at the AAASS conference in Pittsburgh, Penn., 2002. Reid is a specialist on Russian culture at the University of Sheffield, UK, and examines the cultural significance of kitchens during the cold war from the Soviet perspective. Reid, as I do, asserts that the kitchen's cultural meanings should be far from the cultural territory of war, but in the 1940s and 1950s, such was not the case.

14. Vance Packard, *The Hidden Persuaders* (New York: Van Rees, 1957), 123.

15. Ballaster et al. in a study of women's magazines refer to the promotional/marketing edge of some magazine editorials as "advertorials." Rose Ballaster, Margaret Beetham, Elizabeth Frazer, and Sandra Hebron, *Women's Worlds: Ideology, Femininity, and the Woman's Magazine* (London: Macmillan, 1991), 116.

16. Egmont Arens and Roy Sheldon, *Consumer Engineering: A New Technique for Prosperity* (New York: Harper & Brothers, 1932), 18–19.

17. See, for example, Lawrence R. Samuel, *Pledging Allegiance: American Identity and the Bond Drive of World War II* (Washington, D.C.: Smithsonian Institution Press, 1997). Lawrence receives more attention later as his study involves the advertising and marketing of war bonds to consumers and thus is somewhat different from the other World War II home front studies. See also Meg Jacobs, "'How About Some Meat?' The Office of Price Administration, Consumption Politics, and State Building from the Bottom Up, 1941–1946," *Journal of American History* 84, no. 3 (1997): 910–41; Amy Bentley, *Eating for Victory: Food Rationing and the Politics of Domesticity* (Chicago and Urbana: University of Illinois Press, 1998); Robert E. Weems, *Desegregating the Dollar: African American Consumerism in the Twentieth Century* (New York: New York University Press, 1998). Although Weems's study spans the century, its treatment of

blacks as consumers and a target market during World War II is substantial and invaluable to a history of advertising produced during this era, as is Dwight Ernest Brooks, "Consumer Markets and Consumer Magazines: Black America and the Culture of Consumption, 1920–1960" (Ph.D. diss., University of Iowa, 1991). Meg Jacobs's "'Democracy's Third Estate:' New Deal Politics and the Construction of a 'Consuming Public,'" *International Labor and Working-Class History* 55 (Spring 1999): 27–51, focuses more attention on the 1930s, but links the politics of the New Deal's consumer culture to the 1940s. Lizabeth Cohen, in *A Consumers' Republic: The Politics of Mass Consumption in Postwar America* (New York: Alfred A. Knopf/Borzoi Books, 2003), gives significant attention to the Depression and war years, though her book's title suggests otherwise. The exhibition catalogue *Produce & Conserve, Share & Play Square: The Grocer & the Consumer on the Home-Front Battlefield during World War II,* edited by Barbara McLean Ward (Portsmouth, N.H.: Strawbery Banke Museum; Hanover, N.H.: University Press of New England, 1994), covers day-to-day issues of consumption, rationing, price controls, and shortages during the war. With articles by Ward, Roland Marchand, and other scholars, the catalogue's array of illustrative material brings into focus how war reshaped the contours of American consumerism for the duration. For examples of wartime consumer issues and imagery in England, see Pat Kirkham, "Beauty and Duty: Keeping Up the (Home) Front," in P. Kirkham and D. Thoms, eds., *War Culture: Social Change and Changing Experience in World War Two Britain,* 13–28 (London: Lawrence & Wishart, 1995).

18. For more extensive, but certainly not exhaustive, studies that include dimensions of wartime advertising, see Jordan Braverman, *To Hasten the Homecoming: How Americans Fought World War II Through the Media* (Lanham, Md.: Madison Books, 1996). Braverman's book has a significant section on advertising and war information, but it is not limited to a study of just print media and also includes wartime posters. Chapters in the collection *Visions of War* have similar coverage; see James Rodger Alexander, "The Art of Making War: The Political Poster in Global Conflict," and Sue Hart, "Madison Avenue Goes to War: Patriotism in Advertising during World War II," in M. Paul Holsinger and Marry Anne Schofield, eds., *Visions of War: World War II in Popular Literature and Culture,* 96–113, 114–26 (Bowling Green, Ohio: Bowling Green State University Popular Press, 1992). Two less recent but equally significant studies that examine home front issues as reflected in examples of wartime advertising and posters include Robert B. Westbrook, "Fighting for the American Family: Private Interests and Political Obligation in World War II," in Richard Wightman Fox and T. J. Jackson Lears, eds., *The Power of Culture: Critical Essays in American History,* 195–221 (Chicago: University of Chicago Press, 1993); and Mark H. Leff, "The Politics of Sacrifice on the American Home Front in World War II," *Journal of American History* 77, no. 4 (1991): 1296–1318. Andrew Shanken's dissertation straddles the history of wartime advertising and architecture: "From Total War to Total Living: American Architecture and the Culture of Planning, 1939–194X" (Ph.D. diss., Princeton University, 1999). Jackson Lears in *Fables of Abundance: A Cultural History of Advertising in America* (New York: HarperCollins/Basic Books, 1994) has a particularly apt section on the wartime ad industry and corporate America's advertising agenda. He briefly shows how a "better world" idiom became part of the postwar institutional advertising strategy (246–56).

Other articles on wartime advertising that focus on a particular ad, topic, or media issue include Richard Tansey, Michael R. Hyman, and Gene Brown, "Ethical Judgments about Wartime Ads Depicting Combat," *Journal of Advertising* 21, no. 3 (1992): 57–74; Michael R. Hyman and Richard Tansey, "Ethical Codes and the Advocacy Advertisements of World War II," *International Journal of Advertising* 12 (1993): 351–66; Charles Lewis and John Neville, "Images of Rosie: A Content Analysis of Women Workers in American Magazine Advertising, 1940–1946," *Journalism & Mass Communication Quarterly* 72, no. 1 (1995): 216–27; Charles Pinzon and Bruce Swain, "The Kid in Upper 4," *Journalism History* 28, no. 3 (2002): 112–20. Pinzon and Swain examine the history and development of a popular wartime ad produced for the New Haven Railroad. MacDougall's "Red, Brown, and Yellow Perils" largely analyzes descriptions of wording from film, literature, music, and the popular press. Although he doesn't cover consumerism or advertising, his work is relevant to a full picture of popular conceptualizations of the "enemy" that appeared in wartime advertising.

The main sources on advertising and World War II to which scholars have consistently turned include Frank Fox, *Madison Avenue Goes to War: The Strange Military Career of American Advertising, 1941–1945* (Provo, Utah: Brigham Young University, 1975). Scholars have tended to reiterate Fox's version of the advertising industry's role during the war. Utilizing articles published in advertising trade magazines (mostly *Printer's Ink*), Fox provides an excellent study of the issues plaguing the wartime ad industry. Fox also reveals the animosity between the ad industry and the New Deal administration and how ad men attempted to make a role for themselves in, and eventually take over, the government wartime propaganda machine, though this isn't the central issue of his book. The second most popular source for wartime advertising among scholars is John Morton Blum, *V Was for Victory: Politics and American Culture during World War II* (New York: Harcourt Brace Jovanovich, 1976). Blum's study is not limited to advertising and is considerably useful, though not footnoted. For an overview of the War Advertising Council (WAC) and its cold war role, see Robert Griffith, "The Selling of America: The Advertising Council and American Politics, 1942–1960," *Business History Review* 57 (Autumn 1983): 388–412. Griffith's is the third most popular study. The German publisher Taschen has compiled a fantastic collection of American ads from the 1940s and 1950s. Though no commentary or critique accompanies these ads, the series contains hundreds of full-color, full-page illustrations. Jim Heimann, ed., *All-American Ads 40s* and *All-American Ads 50s* (Cologne: Taschen, 2001).

For studies on the government side of wartime communications, see Allan M. Winkler, *The Politics of Propaganda: The Office of War Information, 1942–1945* (New Haven, Conn.: Yale University Press, 1978); David Lloyd Jones, "The U.S. Office of War Information and American Public Opinion during World War II, 1939–1945" (Ph.D. diss., State University of New York, Binghamton, 1976); Richard W. Steele, "Preparing the Public for War: Efforts to Establish a National Propaganda Agency, 1940–1941," *American Historical Review* 75, no. 6 (1970): 1640–53.

General overviews of the World War II home front include some insightful assessments and descriptions of advertising, posters, and other propaganda artifacts and campaigns, some in more depth than others. See, for example, Paul Fussell, *Wartime: Understanding and Behavior in the Second World War* (New York and Oxford: Oxford University Press, 1989); Martin Folly, *The United States and World War II: The Awakening Giant* (Edinburgh: Edinburgh University Press, 2002); Allan M. Winkler, *Home Front U.S.A.: America during World War II* (Arlington Heights, Ill.: Harlan

Davidson, 1986); John W. Jeffries, *Wartime America: The World War II Home Front* (Chicago: Ivan R. Dee, 1996); Ross Gregory, *America 1941: A Nation at the Crossroads* (New York: Macmillan/Free Press, 1989); Richard Lingeman, *Don't You Know There's a War On? The American Home Front, 1941–1945* (Toronto: Longmans Canada, 1970). See also various articles that discuss issues of war and advertising, including mine, in the three-volume *Encyclopedia of Advertising*, edited by John McDonough of the Museum of Broadcast Communications, Karen Egolf of *Advertising Age*, and Jacqueline V. Reid of the Hartman Center for Sales, Advertising, and Marketing History, Duke University (New York: Taylor & Francis Group/Fitzroy Dearborn, 2003).

Wartime posters have garnered much attention as pop culture or artistic artifacts. Some advertising has been included in these compilations. See, for example, William L. Bird, Jr., and Harry R. Rubenstein, *Design for Victory: World War II Posters and the American Home Front* (New York: Princeton Architectural Press, 1998); Zbynek Zeman, *Selling the War: Art and Propaganda in World War II* (New York: Exeter Books, 1978). Picture books on wartime ads, posters, and other visual culture include Robert Heide and John Gilman, *Home Front America: Popular Culture of the World War II Era* (San Francisco: Chronicle Books, 1995); Stan Cohen, *V for Victory: America's Home Front during World War II* (Missoula, Mont.: Pictorial Histories, 1991); Sylvia Whitman, *V Is for Victory: The American Home Front during World War II* (Minneapolis: Lerner, 1993). Whitman's is a young adult book. Some American wartime posters are included in Wendy Kaplan, ed., *Designing Modernity: The Arts of Reform and Persuasion, 1885–1945* (New York: Thames & Hudson; Miami Beach, Fla.: The Wolfsonian, 1995). Essays in this book largely focus on art and design of the interwar years and include Germany and Italy.

19. The architecture of the World War II era has begun to receive more attention lately, but one study stands out. The National Building Museum's exhibition catalogue emphasizes the direct impact of World War II on architecture and product design from 1943 to 1950: Donald Albrecht, ed., *World War II and the American Dream: How Wartime Building Changed a Nation* (Washington, D.C.: National Building Museum; Cambridge, Mass.: MIT Press, 1995). In "Enlisting Modernism," his essay for this catalogue, Peter Reed examines the role of modernist architects in wartime and their defense building projects for both U.S. civilian and military use. Reed also highlights the attempts of modernist architects and designers to apply their war-won knowledge in defense housing and design problems to solving the postwar housing shortage. Reed's main thesis is to show that the wartime experience of modernist architects helped popularize the International Style as a postwar building type for identifying corporate and government culture, although its application for household design remained on the fringe. Robert Friedel's catalogue essay, "Scarcity and Promise: Materials and American Domestic Culture during World War II," shows how wartime shortages in resources and building materials prompted product developments in plastics, plywood, and new construction techniques. Friedel covers several cases in which a given modern designer or architect was called upon to solve a design or materials problem, and he also shows how such wartime developments were perceived as "miracles" able to usher in a postwar consumer utopia.

For histories of suburban housing that give an overview of World War II's impact on postwar suburban development, see Gwendolyn Wright, *Building the Dream: A Social History of Housing in America* (Cambridge, Mass.: MIT Press, 1981); Kenneth T.

Jackson, *Crabgrass Frontier: The Suburbanization of the United States* (New York: Oxford University Press, 1985); Marc Silver and Martin Melkonian, eds., *Contested Terrain: Power, Politics, and Participation in Suburbia* (Westport, Conn.: Greenwood, 1993); Rosalyn Baxandall and Elizabeth Ewen, *Picture Windows: How the Suburbs Happened* (New York: Basic Books, 2000); Dolores Hayden, *Building Suburbia: Green Fields and Urban Growth, 1820–2000* (New York: Vintage, 2004). Lizabeth Cohen in *A Consumers' Republic* also covers a great deal of ground on postwar suburbia and issues of wartime housing. Shanken's "From Total War to Total Living" is a study of World War II architecture. It largely examines this topic through advertising illustrations, especially ones looking to the postwar era. Of all these studies, Shanken's work comes closest to mine because he focuses on the housing styles as well as the marketing strategies and the ads' implied messages.

Designers' participation in World War II has been generally overlooked, but this trend is changing as scholars of design history look more at this industry as "consumer engineering," as opposed to "decorative art." For examples of this trend, see Pat Kirkham, *Charles and Ray Eames: Designers of the Twentieth Century* (Cambridge, Mass.: MIT Press, 1995). Jeffery Meikle's *American Plastic: A Cultural History* (New Brunswick, N.J.: Rutgers University Press, 1995) is another example of the new attention given to the design projects and proposals created during the war years, although Meikle's book is more focused on the industrial development of plastics and their public perception. Arthur J. Pulos, in *American Design Adventure, 1940–1975* (Cambridge, Mass.: MIT Press, 1988), provides an insightful look at certain designers' activities for the war effort and their postwar plans, but design is not examined in the larger context of World War II politics, business, and advertising. See also Brooke Kamin Rapaport and Kevin L. Stayton, *Vital Forms: American Art and Design in the Atomic Age, 1940–1960* (New York: Harry N. Abrams; Brooklyn, N.Y.: The Brooklyn Museum, 2002).

20. Bruce Catton, *The Warlords of Washington* (New York: Harcourt, Brace, 1948), 80, 189.

21. On advertising's attempts to muster its forces and find a legitimate role for itself in a wartime economy, see "Ad Men's Arsenal," *Business Week,* 11 October 1941, 14; James Webb Young, "How Advertising Can Meet Today's Critical Challenges," *Advertising & Selling,* December 1941, 102, 104, 106, 108. For a New Deal administrator's perspective, see Leon Henderson, "Advertising's Crisis Is Everybody's Crisis," *Advertising & Selling,* December 1941, 100. Lears covers the WAC in brief in *Fables of Abundance,* 247–49.

22. On the ad industry's fall from grace in the 1930s, see Lears, *Fables of Abundance,* 233–47. On salesmen's fall from grace during the same period, see Walter A. Friedman, *Birth of a Salesman: The Transformation of Selling in America* (Cambridge, Mass.: Harvard University Press, 2004), 228–31.

23. "Design for Socialization," *Business Week,* 23 January 1943, 79.

24. WAC advertising guidelines tried to ensure consistent war information. See *A War Message in Every Ad* (n.p.: Magazine Marketing Service and WAC), n.d.; *War Theme Digest: A Quick Reference Guide to Home Front Information Campaigns Requiring Advertising Support* (1944; reprint, n.p.: WAC, 1945); *The Word Is Mightier Than the Sword* (n.p.: WAC, n.d.); *How Industry Can Help the Government's Information Program on Woman Power* (n.p.: WAC, Office of War Information, and War Manpower

Commission, 1944). All sources found in the Advertising Council archives, New York City (hereafter cited as AC archives).

25. Sydney Weinberg, "What to Tell America: The Writers' Quarrel in the Office of War Information," *Journal of American History* 60 (June 1968): 81; Blum, *V Was for Victory*, 39; Fox, *Madison Avenue*, 53; Lears, *Fables of Abundance*, 248–49; "Advertising in Wartime," *New Republic*, 21 February 1944, 235–36.

26. On the myth that a laissez-faire market is entirely free of any government action, see Cass R. Sunstein, *The Second Bill of Rights: FDR's Unfinished Revolution and Why We Need It More Than Ever* (New York: Basic Books, 2004), 17–34. Sunstein focuses largely on this myth in the political and business climates of the 1930s.

27. Claude C. Hopkins, *My Life in Advertising & Scientific Advertising, Two Works by Claude C. Hopkins* (1966; reprint, Chicago: NTC Business Books, 1998), 179. Hopkins's *My Life in Advertising* was written in 1927 and first serialized in *Advertising & Selling*. *Scientific Advertising* was first published in 1923 by the Lord & Thomas ad agency and later reprinted by Alfred Politz.

28. A vast amount of scholarly attention has covered the rise of advertising and its relationship to an expanding consumer lifestyle during this time. Dwight Brooks provides a helpful comparative survey of this literature published up to 1991 in "Consumer Markets and Consumer Magazines," 10–26.

29. Robert Weibe, *The Search for Order, 1877–1920* (New York: Hill & Wang, 1967), 165–76; Samuel Haber, *Efficiency and Uplift: Scientific Management in the Progressive Era, 1890–1920* (1964; reprint, Chicago: University of Chicago Press, Midway Reprint, 1973), 51–66.

30. Alan Brinkley, *The End of Reform: New Deal Liberalism in Recession and War* (1995; New York: Vintage Books/Random House, 1996), 9–10. Brinkley asserts that the Roosevelt administration was to a certain degree unlike its predecessor reform agents of the early twentieth century because it "rarely challenged, and indeed did much to buttress, the power of bosses and machines." Nevertheless, although certain political machines may have remained in place during the Progressive Era, no authority—political, corporate, or otherwise—was immune to the human-engineering ethos that enveloped the country.

31. Martha Banta, *Taylored Lives: Narrative Productions in the Age of Taylor, Veblen, and Ford* (Chicago: University of Chicago Press, 1993), 15; Brinkley, *End of Reform*, 4. The concept that a politician's constituency was a mass of consumers expanded dramatically during the 1930s under the New Deal. See Lizabeth Cohen, *A Consumers' Republic*, 21–24, 54–55.

32. On Roosevelt's battles with the Supreme Court and the constitutionality of his reform measures, see Sunstein, *Second Bill of Rights*, 54–57.

33. Ibid., 44. "Security" involved not only secure employment but also access to adequate education and a decent standard of living (ibid., 11).

34. Ibid., 54. On the practice of intimidating or firing union members, see William Serrin, *The Company and the Union: The "Civilized Relationship" of the General Motors Corporation and the United Automobile Workers* (1970; reprint, New York: Vintage Books/Random House, 1974).

35. Jordan Schwarz, *The New Dealers: Power Politics in the Age of Roosevelt* (New York: Alfred A. Knopf, 1993), 309–10. For more on Roosevelt's relationship with the business community, see Steve Fraser and Gary Gerstle, *The Rise and Fall of the New*

Deal Order (Princeton, N.J.: Princeton University Press, 1989); and Ronald C. Tobey, *Technology as Freedom: The New Deal and the Electrical Modernization of the American Home* (Berkeley: University of California Press, 1996), 92–177.

36. Scholars continue to make these distinctions today. On "defense period" defined, see Jeffries, *Wartime America,* 19; Brian Waddell, "Economic Mobilization for World War II and the Transformation of the U.S. State," *Politics & Society* 22, no. 2 (1994): 167.

37. See, for example, "In War, Prepare for Peace," *Business Week,* 9 September 1939, 60.

38. "Positioning" is a marketing term used today to describe how marketing professionals shape consumers' perceptions about a given product, brand name, corporation, or service. See Al Ries and Jack Trout, *Positioning: The Battle for Your Mind* (New York: McGraw-Hill, 1981; reprint, New York: Warner Books, 1993). The word "positioning" aptly describes how wartime "consumer engineers" used persuasive media to shape the public's conception of the war and the conversion/reconversion processes.

39. Shanken touched on this issue in his introduction to "From Total War to Total Living." Though his take on the issue was brief, perhaps we can look forward to its further development in his book in progress, titled *194X: American Architecture and Culture in the 1940s.* There are four excellent studies that incorporate chapters on business hostilities toward the New Deal and how they were manifested in wartime campaigns and agendas to capture public opinion: Richard S. Tedlow, *Keeping the Corporate Image: Public Relations and Business, 1900–1950* (Greenwich, Conn.: JAI, 1979); Stuart Ewen, *PR! A Social History of Spin* (New York: HarperCollins/Basic Books, 1996); Roland Marchand, *Creating the Corporate Soul: The Rise of Public Relations and Corporate Imagery in American Big Business* (Berkeley: University of California Press, 1998); and Bird, *"Better Living."* Although these books do not entirely focus on World War II, they are significant because they trace the historical development and consequences of the animosity of the National Association of Manufacturers (NAM), the business community, and other business organizations toward the New Deal.

40. See Samuel, *Pledging Allegiance.* Samuel shows how Henry Morgenthau, secretary of the treasury, infused war bond promotions with New Deal rhetoric and social vision. Morgenthau's sales pitch placed bonds in the context of empowering the average (or even below-average) consumer.

41. Gunnar Myrdal, *An American Dilemma: The Negro Problem and Modern Democracy* (New York: Harper & Row, 1944; reprint, New Brunswick, N.J.: Transaction, 2002), 576. Trained in the law, Myrdal was a Swedish political economist. During the late 1930s, he was commissioned by the Carnegie Corporation of New York to perform a study of the "Negro problem," out of which his 1944 book developed. Roosevelt's reform agenda in terms of expanding consumer purchasing power is discussed at greater length in chapter 2.

42. Shanken's dissertation, "From Total War to Total Living," overlaps in part with my study in terms of recognizing the racial, ethnic, and political biases embedded in certain postwar planning narratives. Shanken's focus in this regard is on the architectural community. Though he examines advertising of the postwar house, no study to date has examined in depth the social hygiene and human engineering rhetoric and symbols found in advertising fictions of the postwar world.

43. See Mary Douglas, *Purity and Danger: An Analysis of Concept of Pollution and Taboo* (1966; reprint, London: Routledge Classics, 2002), on social conventions aris-

ing from categories of the clean and unclean. On the social construction of offensiveness in waste and odor (among other related conceptualizations), see Dominique Laporte, *History of Shit,* trans. Nadia Benabid and Rodolphe el-Khoury (1978; reprint, Cambridge, Mass.: MIT Press, 1993). For histories of evolving standards of cleanliness and attitudes toward hygiene, see Vincent Vinikas, *Soft Soap, Hard Sell: American Hygiene in the Age of Advertisement* (Ames: University of Iowa Press, 1992); Suellen Hoy, *Chasing Dirt: The American Pursuit of Cleanliness* (New York: Oxford University Press, 1995); Margaret Horsfield, *Biting the Dust: The Joys of Housework* (New York: St. Martin's, 1998); Susan Strasser, *Waste and Want: A Social History of Trash* (New York: Henry Holt, 1999); Juliann Sivulka, *Stronger Than Dirt: A Cultural History of Advertising Personal Hygiene in America, 1875 to 1940* (Amherst, N.Y.: Humanity Books, 2001); Beth Sutton-Ramspeck, *Raising the Dust: The Literary Housekeeping of Mary Ward, Sarah Grand, and Charlotte Perkins Gilman* (Athens: Ohio University Press, 2004).

For related sources with an emphasis on household technology, see Dolores Hayden, *The Grand Domestic Revolution: A History of Feminist Designs for American Homes, Neighborhoods, and Cities* (Cambridge, Mass.: MIT Press, 1981); Susan Strasser, *Never Done: A History of American Housework* (New York: Pantheon Books, 1982); Ruth Schwartz Cowan, *More Work for Mother: The Ironies of Household Technology from the Open Hearth to the Microwave* (New York: HarperCollins/Basic Books, 1983); Donald MacKenzie and Judy Wajcman, eds., *The Social Shaping of Technology: How the Refrigerator Got Its Hum* (Philadelphia: Milton Keynes/Open University Press, 1985); Christina Hardyment, *From Mangle to Microwave: The Mechanization of Household Work* (Cambridge, Mass: Polity, 1988); Ellen Lupton and J. Abbott Miller, *The Bathroom, the Kitchen, and the Aesthetics of Waste: A Process of Elimination* (Cambridge, Mass.: MIT List Visual Arts Center, 1992); Ellen Lupton, *Mechanical Brides: Women and Machines from Home to Office* (New York: Cooper-Hewitt National Museum of Design; Princeton, N.J.: Princeton Architectural Press, 1993).

44. Christina Cogdell examines the term "human engineering" in light of its use by eugenic reformers and designers who worked in the streamlined style. See *Eugenic Design: Streamlining America in the 1930s* (Philadelphia: University of Pennsylvania Press, 2004). Marouf Hasian and Steven Selden show the extent to which a eugenics lexicon and way of thinking permeated American class, gender, social, and racial paradigms from early childhood through adulthood, especially in the decades surrounding World War I. Thus, adults during World War II, the men and women whose cultural legacy we examine herein, would have been heavily inculcated with a human engineering mentality (which included eugenics and scientific management) while children. See Hasian, *The Rhetoric of Eugenics in Anglo-American Thought* (Athens: University of Georgia Press, 1996); Selden, *Inheriting Shame: The Story of Eugenics and Racism in America* (New York: Columbia University, Teachers College, 1999). See also Donald K. Pickens, *Eugenics and the Progressives* (Nashville, Tenn.: Vanderbilt University Press, 1968). On the development of scientific management and the spread of the Progressive Era's "efficiency craze," see Samuel Haber, *Efficiency and Uplift;* Banta, *Taylored Lives;* Weibe, *The Search for Order.*

45. On the development and scope of an American social Darwinist paradigm before the war, see Richard Hofstadter, *Social Darwinism in American Thought* (Philadelphia: University of Pennsylvania Press, 1944; Boston: Beacon, 1966). On the relationship between social Darwinism and eugenics, see Mike Hawkins, *Social Darwinism in*

European and American Thought, 1860–1945: Nature as Model and Nature as Threat (1997; reprint, Cambridge: Cambridge University Press, 1998). For histories of the scientific study of human difference and typing based on pseudo-scientific methods, see Stephen Jay Gould, *The Mismeasure of Man* (New York: W. W. Norton, 1981), which covers social Darwinism, evolutionary thought, eugenics, and phrenology; and Nancy Leys Stepan, "Race and Gender: The Role of Analogy in Science," in David Theo Goldberg, ed., *Anatomy of Racism*, 38–57 (Minneapolis: University of Minnesota Press, 1990). Martha Banta covers typing of female offenders in *Imaging American Women: Idea and Ideals in Cultural History* (New York: Columbia University Press, 1987), 136–38. Kerry Soper (Brigham Young University) supplied me with his unpublished essay that examined the influence of "types" established by eugenicists, physiognomists, and criminologists (guided by pseudo-sciences) on the cartoon series *Dick Tracy*. See "Gunning Down the Criminal Rates: Popularized Eugenic Theory in Chester Gould's Comic Strip, *Dick Tracy*, 1931–1940" (unpublished manuscript, in the author's possession, n.d.).

46. On manifestations of a human engineering mentality, see Alan M. Kraut, *Silent Travelers: Germs, Genes, and the "Immigrant Menace"* (Baltimore: Johns Hopkins University Press, 1994); Nancy Tomes, *The Gospel of Germs: Men, Women, and the Microbe in American Life* (Cambridge, Mass.: Harvard University Press, 1998); Mary Donahue, "Design and the Industrial Arts in America, 1894–1940: An Inquiry into Fashion Design and Art and Industry" (Ph.D. diss., City University of New York, 2001). Donahue's work examines the overlay of eugenics and fashion ideals. Martha Banta analyzes the rhetoric of scientific management in early twentieth-century literature, advertising, and other modes of commercial propaganda in *Taylored Lives*. Eugenic discourse is examined in tandem with imagery explaining "types" in Banta's *Imaging American Women*. Christina Cogdell focuses on the eugenic matrix of streamlined design in "The Futurama Recontextualized: Norman Bel Geddes's Eugenic 'World of Tomorrow,'" *American Quarterly* 52 (June 2000): 193–245; "Products or Bodies? Streamline Design and Eugenics as Applied Biology," *Design Issues* 19 (Winter 2003): 36–53; and her book *Eugenic Design*. My critique of the power dynamics behind the human engineering logic found in much wartime advertising has been shaped by Michel Foucault's approach to examining history and society, especially his *Discipline and Punish: The Birth of the Prison*, trans. Alan Sheridan (New York: Vintage Books/Random House, 1979).

47. The historian Roland Marchand reiterates this observation, noting that "advertising artists . . . were in the business of trading upon stereotypes, not of overturning them." See "Suspended in Time: Mom-and-Pop Groceries, Chain Stores, and National Advertising during the World War II Interlude," in Ward, *Produce & Conserve*, 117–39, quotation on 126.

48. For an example of Rosie the Riveter merchandise, see http://www.giftapolis .com/roripr.html, an online store for pop culture characters. The "We Can Do It" Rosie icon comes packaged in a variety of configurations, such as light switch plates, "tin tote" lunchboxes, nightlights, air fresheners, gift wrap, wall clocks, coasters, action figures, magnets, and so on. Norman Rockwell's depiction of Rosie the Riveter is also available.

49. See Maureen Honey, *Creating Rosie the Riveter: Class, Gender, and Propaganda during World War II* (Amherst: University of Massachusetts Press, 1984). Honey

gives a lengthy account on the work of the OWI and Magazine Bureau, which sought to encourage women's participation in the war effort through popular fiction. Although the main focus of her book covers wartime literary narratives, she provides an excellent comparison of middle- versus working-class wartime messages. She does look briefly into the role of the WAC and its commercial messages targeted to middle-class women during the war. Her brief examination of wartime advertising imagery is insightful. Leila J. Rupp, in *Mobilizing Women for War: German and American Propaganda* (Princeton, N.J.: Princeton University Press, 1978), also provides an informative overview of propaganda targeted to women during World War II. What is most useful about Rupp and Honey's work for the context of my study is their examination of the organization behind the wartime propaganda machine, which in other studies of wartime women is not emphasized.

50. Regarding stereotyped images of African Americans as domestic servants in advertising imagery, see Marilyn Kern-Foxworth, *Aunt Jemima, Uncle Ben, and Rastus: Blacks in Advertising, Yesterday, Today, and Tomorrow* (Westport, Conn.: Greenwood, 1994); M. M. Manring, *Slave in a Box: The Strange Career of Aunt Jemima* (Charlottesville: University Press of Virginia, 1998).

51. One of the hurdles to writing a parallel history of this sort involves identifying and locating women's and consumer magazines geared for a black audience. See Noliwe M. Rooks, *Ladies' Pages: African American Women's Magazines and the Culture That Made Them* (New Brunswick, N.J.: Rutgers University Press, 2004). Rooks describes in her book's introduction how rare "it is . . . to find a list of libraries in possession of the materials. One is more likely to find . . . notes or asides saying that the magazines themselves are either lost, missing, or of such minor importance that their absence is negligible" (3). Dwight Brooks in "Consumer Markets and Consumer Magazines" confirms this "scant corpus on Black magazines" (82).

Rooks's focus is on magazines—not newspapers—which is a major contribution since, as one can read in her bibliography, there are histories of African American newspapers, especially those printed by abolitionists during the nineteenth century. Rooks indicates that "between 1891 and 1950 there were eight African American women's magazines published for a variety of purposes" (4). Though she says later scholars may discover publications she was unable to find, only one of the magazines she cites was in print during the war years, *Aframerican Woman's Journal* (1935–54). However, Rooks does not indicate if any copies are still available or where. Nor does she discuss the content of this magazine while it was in print. This may be an example of a magazine, as she said, noted as once existing but neglected by libraries and archives.

Certainly, black magazines existed during the war, as Maureen Honey's collection of wartime essays, fiction, and poetry attests. See *Bitter Fruit: African American Women in World War II* (Columbia: University of Missouri Press, 1999). But I could not uncover wartime African American *equivalents* to magazines like *Life* or *Ladies' Home Journal* or *Better Homes and Gardens*. Thus, I relied on black newspapers as a way to integrate the African American consumer experience and perspective of the war years. Lizabeth Cohen in *A Consumers' Republic* provides an excellent model for integrating black consumers' experience into a history of American consumer culture, whether or not parallel marketing materials and messages targeted to white consumers can be found in African American media. Many thanks to Thomas Henthorn for helping me explain this issue.

52. See Weems, *Desegregating the Dollar.* Weems is noted as a pioneer in the historical study of African Americans as consumers and how advertisers have geared appeals
to the black consumer. The relative newness of this area of scholarship also made it
difficult to pursue a parallel history between progress as depicted in the white mainstream press and the black press during the mid-twentieth century. Dwight Brooks's
"Consumer Markets and Consumer Magazines," which is cited in Weems, is an earlier,
and quite possibly the first, scholarly study of African Americans as consumers. He examines not only the absence of African Americans from the mainstream promises of
consumer culture, but also the Eurocentric focus of scholarly research in this area.
Brooks is especially relevant to my book since he examines advertising in black magazines. Also building on Brooks's work is Rooks's *Ladies' Pages.*

On issues of race and wartime labor, see Neil A. Wynn, *The Afro-American and the
Second World War* (1975; reprint, New York: Holmes & Meier, 1993); Karen Ander-
son, "Last Hired, First Fired: Black Women Workers during World War II," *Journal of
American History* 69, no. 1 (1982): 82–97; Honey, *Bitter Fruit;* Sally M. Miller and
Daniel A. Cornford, eds., *American Labor in the Era of World War II* (Westport,
Conn.: Praeger, 1995). On other wartime media issues and African Americans, see
Patrick Washburn, *A Question of Sedition: The Federal Government's Investigation of the
Black Press during World War II* (New York: Oxford University Press, 1986); Clayton
Koppes and Gregory Black, "Blacks, Loyalty, and Motion-Picture Propaganda in
World War II," *Journal of American History* 73 (1986): 383–406.

53. Examinations of gender and the early cold war years have been important for
my study because I reveal how the image of wartime progress, which linked domesticity with the culture of war, became an important symbol of U.S. superiority in its technological rivalry with the Soviet Union. Susan Hartmann's *The Home Front and Beyond:
American Women in the 1940s* (Boston: Twayne, 1982) is one of the rare exceptions in
the body of World War II scholarship that not only states but also documents how the
wartime experience shaped gender attitudes in the postwar years. Also exceptionally
useful for this area of scholarship is Elaine Tyler May's *Homeward Bound,* which is a
comprehensive study of gender issues of the postwar and early cold war years. May's
book sheds light on the domestic, class, and consumer roles of women in the cold war
as American society emerged from World War II, but she does not give a great deal of
attention to the commercial imagery and products that reinforced the traditional gender roles she explores. Another study of 1950s cold war culture, although it makes a
significant contribution, also does not focus specifically on the commercial imagery of
the era: Lary May, ed., *Recasting America: Culture and Politics in the Age of Cold War*
(Chicago: University of Chicago Press, 1989). The essays in this anthology cover several 1950s issues and cultural forms, from painting to jazz, suburbia, gender, corporate
culture, and the Red Scare in Hollywood.

54. Homeland Investing advertising brochure, Houston, Texas (no address, no
date, but received in the mail in spring 2003).

55. We will cover recent amounts spent on defense and security in the afterword.

Part 1

1. President Franklin D. Roosevelt, "The Preservation of American Independence,"
Vital Speeches of the Day, 15 January 1941, 194, 197 (my emphasis). Roosevelt's message

was originally a radio speech delivered from Washington, D.C., on 29 December 1940. The United States had not officially entered the war at the time of the speech, but was gearing up production in order to supply weapons, matériel, food, and other services to its allies. In March 1941 Congress passed the Lend-Lease Act, a means by which the United States could commit to the British cause without violating U.S. neutrality. The act was extended to include China and Russia later that year, and it aided thirty-eight nations deemed vital to American interests by the war's end.

2. See the introduction for explanation of "defense" versus "war" periods.

3. *War Facts: A Handbook for Speakers on War Production* (n.p.: Office of Emergency Management, n.d.), 81, 82, available at New York Public Library. *American Home* magazine presented a complementary set of facts about industry's reorganization for wartime production. See "Another Kind of National Defense," *American Home,* April 1942, 10, 14–17. The Office of Emergency Management (OEM) was eventually merged into the Office of War Information (OWI).

4. *Nation at War: Shaping Victory on the Home Front* (n.p.: Reprinted from *Compton's Picture Encyclopedia,* n.d.), 12n, available at New York Public Library.

Chapter 1

1. Tedlow, *Keeping the Corporate Image,* 81.

2. Jeffries, *Wartime America,* 16. Jeffries also indicates that federal civilian employment "quadrupled, from some 950,000 in 1939 to 3.8 million in 1945." Expenditure increases were equally staggering, from just under "$9 billion to over $98 billion." After the war, "government did not revert to its prewar dimensions." According to George Lipsitz in *A Rainbow at Midnight: Labor and Culture in the 1940s* (Urbana and Chicago: University of Illinois Press, 1994), factories with "government-administered contracts . . . automatically made workers in war industries members of unions" (21). Surely, this would have seemed to business leaders like government meddling in management's affairs.

3. Waddell, "Economic Mobilization," 174. Original quote from R. Elberton Smith, *Army and Economic Mobilization* (Washington, D.C.: U.S. Department of the Army, 1959), 456–57.

4. James Olson, *Saving Capitalism: The Reconstruction Finance Corporation and the New Deal, 1933–1940* (Princeton, N.J.: Princeton University Press, 1988), 84.

5. Ibid., 103. Roosevelt tended to "chart a conservative middle ground" with his reforms (84). Despite his "middle ground" stance, the NRA was found unconstitutional by the Supreme Court in 1935. On the NRA from the standpoint of consumerism, see Jacobs, "'Democracy's Third Estate,'" 35–44.

6. Roland Stromberg, "American Business and the Approach of War, 1935–1941," *Journal of Economic History* 13, no. 1 (1953): 63, 74. "Regimentation" was a loaded word often used by businessmen during the war to refer to the New Deal, new government regulations for business, and the federal government's expansiveness.

7. The debate over private versus state-controlled industry is referred to in greater detail in chapter 5. Olson in *Saving Capitalism* discusses how the federal government financed and then owned a synthetic rubber industry, for example, under the aegis of the Reconstruction Finance Corporation (RFC), an entity initiated by President Hoover but retained as a New Deal agent of state capitalism: "By 1945 RFC investment

in synthetic rubber had reached $677 million and the government was managing fifty-one plants producing 760,000 tons of synthetic rubber a year" (218).

8. Waddell, "Economic Mobilization," 185, in reference to a remark made by Nelson Lichtenstein in *Labor's War at Home: The CIO in World War II* (New York: Cambridge University Press, 1982), 39; Joe R. Feagin and Kelly Riddell, "The State, Capitalism, and World War II: The U.S. Case," *Armed Forces & Society* 17, no. 1 (1990): 59, 60. Donald M. Nelson in his *The Arsenal of Democracy: The Story of American War Production* (New York: Harcourt, Brace, 1946) details the logistical dilemmas behind government financing of expanding existing production facilities (105–7). Nelson was War Production Board (WPB) chairman.

9. Jeffries, *Wartime America,* 20.

10. William O'Neill, *A Democracy at War: America's Fight at Home and Abroad in World War II* (New York: Free Press/Macmillan, 1993), 20; Lizabeth Cohen, *A Consumers' Republic,* 62–64.

11. Jeffries, *Wartime America,* 20. Incentives were eventually devised, such as government subsidies, low-cost loans, and tax write-offs, for those businesses that invested in defense production facilities. Essentially, the federal government built new plants from scratch with the Defense Plant Corporation and then leased the facilities at low rates to private corporations.

12. Ibid., 19; Feagin and Riddell, "State, Capitalism," 53–55, 57, 60. See also David Brody, "The New Deal in World War II," in John Braeman, Robert Bremner, and David Brody, eds., *The New Deal: The National Level,* 1:267–309 (Columbus: Ohio State University Press, 1975). Donald Nelson in *Arsenal of Democracy* explains the various rates of compensation for dollar-a-year men, from zero to small daily fees for consultation (329–30).

13. The NDAC was succeeded by the Office of Production Management (OPM), headed by William Knudsen and labor leader Sidney Hillman, the associate director. The secretary of the navy was Frank Knox, a newspaper magnate and a bank director from Chicago. The secretary of war was Henry Stimson, who had been a Wall Street corporate lawyer in civilian life. Both served on Knudsen's policy council of the OPM. See Feagin and Riddell, "State, Capitalism," 60. Feagin and Riddell also list the names and titles of the corporate executives who occupied the top eleven positions on the WPB during 1943, the most crucial year of war production. They also give the names and titles of those executives "at the helm of the armed services" (62–64). Feagin and Riddell suggest that even loading wartime decision-making posts with corporate brass did not deter conflicts, because tensions existed between "different groups of capitalists" (65).

14. Howell John Harris, *The Right to Manage: Industrial Relations Policies of American Business in the 1940s* (Madison: University of Wisconsin Press, 1982), 41–43. Harris indicates that "America acquired a planned war economy in which business power was safe, and in which the largest corporations' interests and opinions counted most." With their leverage in place, business "used that freedom to begin to dismantle the New Deal" (42).

15. Waddell, "Economic Mobilization," 164 (my emphasis).

16. Paul A. C. Koistinen, *Planning for War, Pursuing Peace: The Political Economy of American Warfare, 1920–1939* (Lawrence: University Press of Kansas, 1998), 73, 93, 202. One of the business organizations with which the military had an established interwar

preparedness relationship was the NAM, whose anti–New Deal rhetoric we shall explore in greater detail in chapter 5. The military saw the NAM as "probably the most powerful industrial organization of its kind in the world" (91, originally quoted by Koistinen from an Office of the Assistant Secretary of War memorandum dated mid-1923).

17. Jeffries, *Wartime America,* 21–22. Nelson had been the chief merchandising executive for Sears, Roebuck prior to the war.

18. Koistinen, *Planning for War,* 205. Mobilization was "gradual" and "haphazard." Koistinen blames "the lack of an integrated supply system and inadequate coordination between the army and navy" as "the principle source of difficulty" (206).

19. See Donald Nelson, *Arsenal of Democracy;* Catton, *Warlords of Washington.* Catton served in the Information Division of the Office for Emergency Management. See also Roger Beaumont, "Quantum Increase: The Military Industrial Complex in the Second World War," in Benjamin Franklin Cooling, ed., *War, Business, and American Society: Historical Perspective on the Military-Industrial Complex* (Port Washington, N.Y.: Kennikat Press/National University Publications, 1977), 127.

20. O'Neill, *Democracy at War,* 20.

21. Folly, *United States,* 34, 39.

22. Beaumont, "Quantum Increase," 122–23.

23. Donald Nelson, *Arsenal of Democracy,* 42.

24. Ibid., 34.

25. Ibid., 33–34.

26. Jeffries, *Wartime America,* 23. Labor agitation during the war was stigmatized as "unpatriotic." For labor gains and losses during the war, see Harris, *The Right to Manage;* George Q. Flynn, *The Mess in Washington: Manpower Mobilization in World War II* (Westport, Conn.: Greenwood, 1979).

27. Honey in *Bitter Fruit* includes wartime essays from African American publications about the discriminatory practices in hiring blacks into wartime military or nursing service and defense factory work (35–37, 91–97, 100–107, 112–14, 117–25). Discrimination against black soldiers drafted to defend American democracy was also widely discussed in the African American press, as Honey's collection reveals (127–254). The military went so far as to segregate blood as well as medical treatment by drafting black nurses to attend to soldiers of their own race. Such gross paradoxes, along with other wartime pressures, sparked several race riots during the war. Honey cites "242 violent clashes in forty-seven cities throughout 1943" (129). Lipsitz in *A Rainbow at Midnight* indicates that the "largest strike wave in history" occurred both during and after the war (20). Both white women and men organized strikes to protest integrating blacks into war plants, but white resistance was divided by gender. On racially oriented "hate strikes" during the war, see ibid., 69–92. Men feared losing their monopolies in the factory hierarchy and their higher pay, while white women were inclined to maintain "social distance" from blacks, especially black women (ibid., 50). This attitude is significant in light of the many middle-class women who entered factories for work and the numbers of black women who did as well. According to Lipsitz, before the war only 6 percent of black women held factory jobs. The majority of African American women, 60 percent, were domestics. By 1946, the statistics had shifted with 18.6 percent of black women in manufacturing while 48 percent worked in a domestic capacity (ibid., 49). Sally Miller and Daniel Cornford (*American Labor,*

2–3) indicate that African American employment tripled between 1942 and 1945. In manufacturing, their numbers rose by 150 percent, up to 1.25 million in 1944.

28. Neil Wynn shows that as the United States prepared for defense, the unemployment rates among white workers began to drop "from 17.7 percent to 13 percent," but this was not the case for blacks, whose unemployment rate "remained static at 22 percent" (*The Afro-American,* 40). On strikes during World War II due to hiring blacks, see ibid., 50–54.

29. The black press was filled with stories of African Americans who were either denied work or, when they got it, felt compelled to overcompensate and prove their worth in order to hang onto the opportunities. Many blacks in such positions felt that providing a stellar example of the black work ethic would dispel stereotypes and open up more job opportunities for their race. See "Skilled Workers Get Chance, Prove Worth at $1,276,000 Defense Housing Project at Sparrows Point," *Baltimore Afro-American,* 4 April 1942, 20; "Noise of Riveting Machines Drowns Out Bells of Christmas as Women War Workers Continue to Produce Fighting Planes," *Pittsburgh Courier,* 2 January 1943, 11. This article is interesting for its photo spread of black "Rosie the Riveters." On "passing" in order to acquire defense industry jobs, see "Race Relations in Jersey War Plants: Colored Girl Passing for White, Jewish Girl Who Passes, and Colored Workers Talk for AFRO," *Baltimore Afro-American,* 13 March 1943, 6. The expansion of manufacturing during the war drew large numbers of African Americans to industrial cities of the North and West. African Americans found it harder than white workers to settle in these areas of explosive population growth where housing was limited. African Americans were equally discriminated against in government-sponsored housing built for defense workers in towns where new shipyards and factories had been constructed for the war effort. Wartime strains and struggles were also exacerbated in the black community because African Americans were relegated to overcrowded segregated sectors. See Delores Nason McBroome, "Catalyst for Change: Wartime Housing and African Americans in California's East Bay," in Miller and Cornford, *American Labor,* 186–99; "Ku Kluxers Start Riot in Detroit: Heads Are Cracked When Whites Defy President Roosevelt's Housing Order," *Baltimore Afro-American,* 7 March 1942, 2; "Three Whites Held in No. Philly Riot," *Baltimore Afro-American,* 18 April 1942, 14. This last story is also about white protests against blacks moving into an all-white neighborhood.

30. Wynn, *The Afro-American,* 50.

31. "CIO Anti-Discrimination Group Issues Report," *Pittsburgh Courier,* 16 January 1945, 1. On unions and black laborers' obstacles during the war, see Wynn, *The Afro-American,* 51–54. Unions were not always supportive of black labor.

32. "CIO Anti-Discrimination Group Issues Report," 1. See also "Will Our Military Policy Change?" *Pittsburgh Courier,* 1 June 1945, 6; "Fighting the War the Axis Way," *Baltimore Afro-American,* 18 April 1942, 4. In this editorial cartoon, a black sailor, sitting on the porch of the U.S. Navy's headquarters, is told by a white butler, "Mr. Knox says you can come in now but you will have to go around to the back door." On discrimination in hiring blacks as nurses, see "Wanna Be a Red Cross Nurse? Read This First," *People's Voice,* 4 April 1942, 8. The *Baltimore Afro-American* ran a cartoon on 13 March 1943 (4) with the headline: "WANTED At Once 30,000 Nurses *White* Only." In the cartoon, Uncle Sam, hauling a torpedo on his back, says to a black Liberty figure, "I'm going to win this war." She replies, "You could do it quicker if you used everybody."

33. "War Race Prejudice Like Blunder at Pearl Harbor," *Baltimore Afro-American*, 11 April 1942, 5. Another astute observer articulated the paradox of the war's purpose this way: "'[A] long period of social neglect and discrimination has raised serious questions in the minds of millions of dark-skinned Americans regarding the quality of the democracy which they are now in the act of defending.' . . . Dissatisfaction and resentment among Negroes over the defense program [included] exclusion from employment and training in defense industry, unsatisfactory provision for defense housing, limiting chance for participation in civilian programs, and the exclusion or segregation practices in the armed services." From "National Urban League's 1941 Report Sees Negroes Tensed," *People's Voice*, 4 April 1942, 35.

34. A "March on Washington," consisting of thousands of African Americans, had been organized by black leaders and was threatened until Roosevelt issued Executive Order 8802 on 25 June 1941, "commanding an end to discrimination in defense industries." See Wynn, *The Afro-American*, 45.

35. The term "total war," like "all-out war," means that every aspect of the economy, including all resources and all manpower, were harnessed to the war effort.

36. *Pittsburgh Courier*, 9 January 1943, 19.

37. Myrdal, *American Dilemma*, 576.

38. Marjorie McKenzie, "Supreme Court's Okay of Removal of Japanese Can Affect Negro Rights," *Pittsburgh Courier*, 6 January 1945, 6.

39. "Barring Japs in California May Be Boon," *People's Voice*, 21 February 1942, 24. Upon reading this article, I am not sure whether the author is being sarcastic with this polemic.

40. Neil Wynn states that though rationing was an imposition, in the United States it never became a "great hardship." Wynn details the various goods that were controlled and the shortages experienced by consumers of all backgrounds (*The Afro-American*, 13).

41. Donald Nelson, *Arsenal of Democracy*, 37–38.

42. Daniel J. Opler of New York University provides an interesting account of wartime consumerism from the vantage point of department store workers. See "For All White Collar Workers: The Possibilities of Radicalism in New York City's Department Store Unions, 1934–1953" (unpublished manuscript in author's possession, 2004).

43. "Uncle Sam's Housekeeping Job," *Journal of Home Economics*, September 1942, 421–24.

44. O'Neill, *Democracy at War*, 248–49. On wartime consumerism, see also Lizabeth Cohen, *A Consumers' Republic*, 62–110; Bentley, *Eating for Victory;* Leff, "The Politics of Sacrifice"; and Carolyn F. Ware, *The Consumer Goes to War: A Guide to Victory on the Home Front* (New York: Funk & Wagnalls, 1942).

45. "They Don't Shirk the *Mean Jobs*—Do You?" *Baltimore Afro-American*, 2 June 1945, 16. From an ad approved by the War Food Administration (WFA) and the Office of Price Administration (OPA). On shortages, regulations, rationing, and scrap and fat salvage campaigns, see Strasser, *Waste and Want*, 227–63. Strasser discusses the ad campaigns instructing—and motivating—the American public to recycle their waste products for use in manufacturing military ordnance. Her study covers the bureaucratic and political contradictions that led to public confusion over the campaigns and mismanagement of salvaged scrap. She argues that the "scrap drives had more utility as propaganda than as a means of collecting strategic materials" (262). Strasser's chapter

also provides a very real and unglamorized look at everyday inconveniences and struggles faced by home front consumers. Ward's *Produce & Conserve* covers the messages, imagery, and bureaucratic means used to promote conservation, rationing, salvaging, price controls, substitutions, and so on. See especially Ward's article, "A Fair Share at a Fair Price: Rationing, Resource Management, and Price Controls during World War II," 79–103. Ward outlines the four different rationing programs, what they covered, and their limitations. She covers how the scarcity of priorities, especially metals and paper, put a strain on manufacturers of containers and processed foods. Such businesses were induced to create alternative boxes, cartons, cans, jars, wrappers, and so forth, that conserved materials and reduced waste. The catalogue illustrates many wartime examples of the substitute or rationed packaging that consumers saw on store shelves. Ward explains how rationing systems and price controls demanded extra administrative work for grocers, retailers, packagers, and distributors. Marchand's "Suspended in Time" examines wartime consumerism from the perspective of the grocer.

46. Ward, "A Fair Share," in *Produce & Conserve*, 84. Though the declarations were conducted on an "honor system," consumers still had to register to receive their ration books in order to shop for daily food and supplies.

47. Jeffries, *Wartime America,* 29.

48. Ibid., 29–30. War production, which had absorbed the Depression's great masses of jobless and underemployed, had also produced a higher yield of consumers by raising wage levels and thus altering the consumption habits of low-income families. This issue is covered in chapter 3. For more on the improved standard of living for the rural poor and working class who acquired defense jobs, see Hartmann, *Home Front and Beyond,* 309–10, 322–23; Margaret Crawford, "Daily Life on the Home Front," in Albrecht, *World War II,* 105, where she says that for many war workers, migrating from the South and from rural areas, government-sponsored housing near shipyards and war plants, although flawed, "was the best they had ever had." Even though the wartime diet, regulated by rationing, kept a cap on the amount civilians could consume, government control of inflation kept the cost of rationed food products down. As a result, low-income families, especially in the rural South, were able to afford a better diet. Not only were they introduced to higher nutritional standards than before, but they also enjoyed the luxury of commercially canned and frozen convenience foods. See "War Changes Buying Habits," *Science Digest,* February 1945, 34.

49. Robert Beaumont contends that the country's isolationist leanings created a "strong political resistance to involvement [that] prevented the formation of a formal effective war-production system until well after Pearl Harbor" ("Quantum Increase," 118).

50. We need to remember that wartime propaganda was largely shaped by business leaders. Given their presence in virtually every sector of wartime mobilization, production, and public information, a managerial voice and human engineering ethos tends to surface in all types of war information.

51. Robert and Helen Lynd's investigation sheds an intimate light on the lifestyle changes experienced by a sampling of "average America" during the rise of the Machine Age. See Robert S. Lynd and Helen Merrell Lynd, *Middletown: A Study in Contemporary American Culture* (New York: Harcourt, Brace, 1929). For a similar study conducted between 1939 and 1941, see James West, *Plainville, U.S.A.* (New York: Columbia University Press, 1945). On the 1920s understanding of modern "civilization," including the cult of expertism, see Warren I. Susman, "Culture and Civilization: The

Nineteen-Twenties," in *Culture as History: The Transformation of American Society in the Twentieth Century,* 105–21 (New York: Pantheon Books, 1984).

52. Such was the message deftly implied in many of the advertising "tableaux" and "parables" from the Machine Age. See a wide array of examples illustrated in Marchand's *Advertising the American Dream.* On the concept of "progress" in advertising and mass marketing strategies, see Pamela Walker Laird, *Advertising Progress: American Business and the Rise of Consumer Marketing* (Baltimore: Johns Hopkins University Press, 2001). Walter Friedman in *Birth of a Salesman* attributes, in large part, the rise in national brands and the shift to a consumption lifestyle to a critical court decision of 1876. Prior to this year, manufacturers and dealers in one state could not legally send salesmen into another state to sell goods without paying costly regional licensing fees. The U.S. Supreme Court case *Welton v. Missouri* "found that interstate commerce should be 'free and untrammeled.'" Friedman stresses how the "decision was pivotal for American commerce, because it prevented the balkanization of American domestic trade" (96).

Chapter 2

1. Lewis Mumford, *Technics and Civilization: A History of the Machine and Its Effects upon Civilization* (New York: Harcourt, Brace, 1934), 365.

2. We shall return to the use of the word "industry" in this context because in most cases of commercial propaganda, it was an idiom for the managerial elite. In Roosevelt's case, that meaning is slightly ambiguous as the speech he gave would have been directed to a national audience, "the people." But in mobilizing the public mind, as we shall see, it was managerial authority that needed a cheerleader.

3. On the rags-to-riches mythology and the belief in consumption and accumulation as tools of social uplift, see Simon J. Bronner, "Reading Consumer Culture," in Simon J. Bronner, ed., *Consuming Visions: Accumulation and Display of Goods in America, 1880–1920,* 16–24 (Winterthur, Del.: The Henry Francis du Pont Winterthur Museum; New York: W. W. Norton, 1989).

4. Alan Trachtenberg, *The Incorporation of America: Culture and Society in the Gilded Age* (New York: Hill & Wang, 1982), 42.

5. For a critique of the concept of progress in historical perspective, see Christopher Lasch, *The True and Only Heaven: Progress and Its Critics* (New York: W. W. Norton, 1991).

6. On critiques of the assembly line, see Terry Smith, *Making the Modern: Industry, Art, and Design in America* (Chicago: University of Chicago Press, 1993), 16–18, 52. Smith also provides an excellent overview of Taylorist principles and Henry Ford's own interpretation of scientific management (18–56).

7. Edward A. Filene, *Successful Living in This Machine Age* (New York: Simon & Schuster, 1932), 1. Quoted in Hounshell, *American System,* 307.

8. On Taylor and Taylorism, see Banta, *Taylored Lives;* Samuel Haber, *Efficiency and Uplift;* Daniel Nelson, *Frederick W. Taylor and the Rise of Scientific Management* (Madison: University of Wisconsin Press, 1980); Robert Kanigel, *The One Best Way: Frederick Winslow Taylor and the Enigma of Efficiency* (New York: Viking, 1997).

9. Samuel Haber, *Efficiency and Uplift,* 30. Howell John Harris examines scientific management through the human engineering side of systematic personnel management (*The Right to Manage,* 160–63).

10. Frederick Winslow Taylor, *The Principles of Scientific Management* (1911; reprint, Norcross, Ga.: Institute of Industrial Engineers, Engineering and Management Press, 1998), 16.

11. Ibid., 65.

12. Ibid., 62.

13. Ibid., 3. Taylor believed in a "friendly cooperation" between labor and management. "Sharing equally in every day's burden," Taylor's management-labor interchange was intended to increase the productivity of both parties, resulting in higher wages and the dissemination of prosperity (ibid., 17).

14. Ibid., 16. Speeding up assembly lines, in Taylor's eyes, had a civilizing effect upon laborers because "a steady drinker would find it almost impossible to keep up with the pace which was set, so that they were practically all sober. . . . They all lived better than they had before" (ibid., 59–60).

15. For more on the rise of corporate culture and mass merchandizing from the nineteenth century to the 1920s, see Friedman, *Birth of a Salesman;* Laird, *Advertising Progress;* William Leach, *Land of Desire: Merchants, Power, and the Rise of a New American Culture* (New York: Random House/Vintage Books, 1993); Lears, *Fables of Abundance;* and Stuart Ewen, *Captains of Consciousness: Advertising and the Social Roots of the Consumer Culture* (New York: McGraw-Hill, 1976). For a look at this era through the lives of industrialist Henry Ford, ad man Bruce Barton, and sports star Babe Ruth, see Warren I. Susman, "Culture Heroes: Ford, Barton, Ruth," in *Culture as History,* 122–49. (Ruth is included as a barometer of the era's fascination with measurable abilities as well as the way mass communication systems mass merchandized the cult of celebrity personality.) On the industrial transformations of management, production, distribution, transportation, and communications, see Alfred D. Chandler, Jr., *The Visible Hand: The Managerial Revolution in American Business* (Cambridge, Mass.: Harvard University Press/Belknap Press, 1977); Thomas McCraw, *Creating Modern Capitalism: How Entrepreneurs, Companies, and Countries Triumphed in Three Industrial Revolutions* (Cambridge, Mass.: Harvard University Press, 1998). On the history of this transformation from the angle of sales and marketing professionals, see Friedman, *Birth of a Salesman.* Though written as a critique of the postwar business class, C. Wright Mills's *White Collar: The American Middle Classes* (New York: Oxford University Press, 1951) provides an insightful survey of the historical development of the managerial and bureaucratic elite. For a more recent study on the rise of managerial organization and bureaucratic conceit, see Oliver Zunz, *Making America Corporate, 1870–1920* (Chicago: University of Chicago Press, 1990).

16. Trachtenberg, *Incorporation of America,* 84–85.

17. Ibid., 79.

18. Samuel Haber's *Efficiency and Uplift* provides an astute survey of scientific management's viruslike spread.

19. For a study of Progressive Era attitudes, concerns, and reform strategies, see Ellen Fitzpatrick, *Endless Crusade: Women Social Scientists and Progressive Reform* (New York: Oxford University Press, 1990). Fitzpatrick focuses on four notable female reformers, Sophonisba Breckinridge, Edith Abbott, Katharine Bement Davis, and Frances Kellor, and their impact on social policy and change. On rural Progressivism, see David B. Danbom, *The Resisted Revolution: Urban America and the Industrialization of Agriculture, 1900–1930* (Ames: Iowa State University Press, 1979). Danbom cov-

ers how urbanites attempted to modernize rural America and make country life efficient through administering scientific management approaches to agricultural production. The book details the hardships and lack of sanitary amenities that characterized rural life at this time. For a book that focuses on women's writing and the attention to "cleaning up" society and the home during the late-Victorian era and the opening of the Progressive movement, see Sutton-Ramspeck, *Raising the Dust.*

20. The quote is by a Columbia University professor of political economy, Richmond Mayo-Smith, and is extracted from his *Emigration and Immigration: A Study in Social Science* (New York: Scribner's, 1890), 133. Quoted in Kraut, *Silent Travelers,* 109. Though the quote was specific to Italian immigrants in New York's tenements, such sentiments were widely assumed about other immigrant ethnicities.

21. Kraut in *Silent Travelers* covers this issue, as does Tomes in *The Gospel of Germs.* For more on the institutionalization of middle-class values linking righteousness and cleanliness in city immigrant services and private social reform movements, see Elizabeth Fee and Steven H. Corey, *Garbage! The History and Politics of Trash in New York City* (New York: New York Public Library, 1994), 22. On the role of Taylorism and scientific management in Progressive social reform movements, including housekeeping, see Samuel Haber, *Efficiency and Uplift,* 54–65. On late nineteenth-century ideals of cleanliness and morality, see "Cleanliness and Godliness: The Tyranny of Housework," in Harvey Green, *The Light of the Home: An Intimate View of the Lives of Women in Victorian America,* 59–92 (New York: Pantheon Books; Rochester, N.Y.: The Margaret Woodbury Strong Museum, 1983). Turn-of-the-century associations between trash and class hierarchy are covered in Strasser, *Waste and Want,* 136–40. Strasser's book examines a range of examples revealing social attitudes toward trash, health, cleanliness, and filth, especially during the rise of mass merchandising and mass consumerism. Her study provides insights into the new twentieth-century equation in which "comfort and morality united with science" (ibid., 174). For examinations of the Progressives' notion of housing and environment as a moral barometer for society, see Kenneth Jackson, *Crabgrass Frontier,* 174–75; Wright, *Building the Dream,* 156–57; Hayden, *The Grand Domestic Revolution,* 162–74.

22. On Progressive ideology and social control (especially in the context of consumerism and mass communications), see Ewen, *PR!* 39–145. Although Ewen emphasizes the history of the concept of the public mind and mass persuasion, he also shows how certain Progressive Era ideals did not necessarily die out after World War I but instead underwent various transformations during the 1920s and 1930s. On the Progressive crusade to help the poor and minorities achieve "the middle-class Protestant norm," see Stephanie Coontz, *The Way We Never Were: American Families and the Nostalgia Trap* (New York: HarperCollins/Basic Books, 1992), 133–37. Coontz does address the humanitarian reforms established by the Progressives, but their social progress was deliberately guided by a human-engineering undercurrent bent on reconstructing society in the image of the "native-born" white middle class while expanding "the tools for monitoring, regulating, and fine-tuning [immigrant] home life" (ibid., 134).

23. Quoted from William R. Taylor, "The Evolution of Public Spaces in New York City: The Commercial Showcase of America," in Bronner, *Consuming Visions,* 299.

24. For an overview of nineteenth- and early twentieth-century values concerning the interrelationship of health, hygiene, and morality, see "The Temple of Virtue: Health in Body and Mind," in Green, *Light of the Home,* 112–43.

25. Edward Alsworth Ross, *The Old World in the New, The Significance of Past and Present Immigration to the American People* (New York: Century, 1914), 113. Quoted in Kraut, *Silent Travelers,* 109.

26. Woods Hutchinson, *Community Hygiene* (Boston: Houghton Mifflin, 1929), 320. This 1929 copy was a "new edition—revised and enlarged," but the earlier work's date was not provided. Available at Old Mill Village Museum Collection, New Milford, Pennsylvania.

27. Mary Pattison, *The Business of Home Management: The Principles of Domestic Engineering* (New York: Robert M. McBride, 1915), 1; quoted in Samuel Haber, *Efficiency and Uplift,* 62. See also Hayden, *The Grand Domestic Revolution,* 153. On hygiene and soap as "Americanizing agents" wielded by Progressive reformers in immigrant neighborhoods and public schools attended by the children of immigrants, see Sivulka, *Stronger Than Dirt,* 109–15.

28. Banta, *Taylored Lives,* 235–40, 282–83.

29. Banta lists popular books from the interwar years with titles such as *The Man-Building Process* and *Human Engineering* that "applied the language" of the machine and engineering to "human activities" (ibid., 286). The practice was thus not limited to the Progressive Era.

30. Sivulka, *Stronger Than Dirt,* 109, 111, 113.

31. For more on advertising's role as proselytizer for the era's popular hygienic gospel, see Vinikas, *Soft Soap, Hard Sell.* Sivulka in *Stronger Than Dirt* examines this and three other Cleanliness Institute ads from 1928 and 1930 (229–43).

32. Sivulka in *Stronger Than Dirt* indicates that the Cleanliness Institute was "established to teach the public the importance of keeping clean" and was formed in 1927 by "the big soapmakers—Lever Brothers, Palmolive, Procter & Gamble, Colgate, Kirk, and Swift—along with other members of the Association of Soap and Detergent Manufacturers" (229).

33. "There's CHARACTER—in SOAP & WATER," *Ladies' Home Journal,* April 1928, 223. Reprinted in Wright, *Building the Dream,* 211.

34. *Ladies' Home Journal,* April 1928, 223. Original emphasis.

35. Ewen in *Captains of Consciousness* analyzes how the U.S. immigrant population was "educated" about the perceived inadequacies of their "dirty alienness" through advertising imagery that encouraged self-conscious introspection about how one's bodily smells, manners, and habits were publicly judged. Ewen shows how advertising played a decisive role in molding and homogenizing behaviors in order to solve problems of perceived inadequacies by relying on mass-produced consumer products.

36. Louis-Ferdinand Céline, *Journey to the End of Night* (1932; New York: Penguin, 1966), 195–97. Quoted in Terry Smith, *Making the Modern,* 16–17.

37. On Henry Ford's factory in this regard, see Terry Smith, *Making the Modern,* 47–55. Automobile workers were routinely laid off during the several weeks it took to retool a factory each year for a new model car—the result of planned obsolescence, a major aspect of the consumer engineering approach that was a child of the new Machine Age. See Serrin, *The Company and the Union,* 172.

38. Mumford, *Technics and Civilization,* 374.

39. Friedman in *Birth of a Salesman* indicates that in addition to the heavier criticism and scrutiny of big business after the 1929 crash, the Depression damaged the prestige enjoyed by the corporate elite as public confidence in corporate leadership

evaporated (228, 231). Friedman chronicles some of the business strategies for training salesmen during this challenging era (232–48).

40. Jeffery Meikle, *Twentieth-Century Limited: Industrial Design in America, 1925–1939* (Philadelphia: Temple University Press, 1979), 160.

41. George E. Mowry, *The Urban Nation* (1965; reprint, New York: Hill & Wang, 1968), 16–17, 69–72; Carroll Pursell, *The Machine in America: A Social History of Technology* (Baltimore: Johns Hopkins University Press, 1995), 251–69.

42. Arens and Sheldon, *Consumer Engineering*, 19.

43. James Howard Kunstler in *The Geography of Nowhere: The Rise and Decline of America's Man-Made Landscape* (New York: Simon & Schuster, 1993) places the blame for the Depression's far-reaching effects on America's overaccommodation of the automobile. The motor car industry, he claims, was so intensely integrated into the economy that when it faltered and declined during the Depression, it took numerous industries (and jobs) with it. Part of the problem was a "market saturation" reached during the 1920s in automobile ownership, road building, and suburban development (93–96).

44. Harris, *The Right to Manage*, 19. Harris's book provides an in-depth look at the reactions of big business to the challenges posed by industrial unions of the late 1930s and 1940s. On consumer discontent and consumer-directed reform initiatives during the 1930s, see Lizabeth Cohen, *A Consumers' Republic*, 24–61.

45. See Donald Nelson, *Arsenal of Democracy*, 69–70, regarding public opinion polls and the emotional climate during the defense period. Nelson covers the popular desire for America to stay out of the escalating European conflict. Nelson's account indicates that public leanings toward isolation and opposition to involvement impeded Congress in its implementation of legislation for defense mobilization. Koistinen confirms this in *Planning for War*, 211.

46. Hounshell, *American System*, 330. Original quote from Mumford, *Technics and Civilization*, 94. Mumford in the original passage asserts that war is the health of the state too.

47. Anne Trotter, "Development of the Merchants-of-Death Theory," in Cooling, *War, Business, and American Society*, (93–94).

48. Ibid., 100–102; Koistinen, *Planning for War*, 209–11, 254–58. Koistinen's earlier publication *The Military-Industrial Complex: A Historical Perspective* (New York: Praeger, 1980) covers the same material, but in a more abridged form. See also Stuart D. Brandes, *Warhogs: A History of War Profits in America* (Lexington: University Press of Kentucky, 1997); and H. C. Engelbrecht and F. C. Hanighen, *Merchants of Death: A Study of the International Armament Industry* (New York: Dodd, Mead, 1934).

49. Donald Nelson, *Arsenal of Democracy*, 31–32.

50. Hounshell, *American System*, 307.

51. Sunstein, *Second Bill of Rights*, 38. Sunstein indicates that this quote was from a Chicago newspaper but does not provide the original source. Sunstein quotes other similar observations, government reports, and newspaper stories from the era and lists a series of telling statistics that further document the layers of social and economic collapse during the Depression (36–69).

52. Quoted from a report given to Congress by investigator Carey McWilliams about a 1939 California migrant farmers' housing federal survey, which tabulated American squalid standards of living. United States Congress, *Hearings, 1941, House*

Select Committee to Investigate the Interstate Migration of Destitute Citizens (Washington, D.C., 1941), 2543–44. Quoted in James Gregory, *American Exodus: The Dust Bowl Migration and Okie Culture in California* (New York and Oxford: Oxford University Press, 1989), 401–2.

53. The "one-third" statistic was made public in Roosevelt's second inaugural address: "A Changed Moral Climate in America," *Vital Speeches of the Day,* 1 February 1937, 227. See also: "It is not particularly heartening to learn that the now-famous 'one-third of the nation,' which among other tragedies is 'ill-housed,' is just the most conservative sort of an estimate." From "40% of the Nation Is Ill-Housed, Federal Health Survey Ups the President's Ratio," *Architectural Forum,* June 1938, 34. On the New Deal and the government's attempts at housing programs during the 1930s, see Baxandall and Ewen, *Picture Windows,* 51–66.

54. Roosevelt's New Deal administration struggled to engineer a constitutionally sound policy for expanding the economy and increasing consumer purchasing power. In 1935, the Supreme Court found the New Deal's National Industrial Recovery Act unconstitutional. During Roosevelt's first term, the economy had grown at an annual rate of 10 percent. Nevertheless, this climb still left 14 percent of the workforce unemployed because the 1929 crash had set production back so low that any increase, even a spry 10 percent growth, failed to lead the country out of economic depression and eradicate the vestiges of abject poverty and social decline. In 1937, a recession set the economy back again and raised the already high unemployment rate to 19 percent. Even government-sponsored work relief projects only benefited 40 percent of the unemployed. Throughout the rest of the 1930s the unemployment rate would remain above 10 percent, until 1941, when the United States began mobilizing for defense production. See Anthony J. Badger, *The New Deal: The Depression Years, 1933–1940* (New York: Hill & Wang, 1989), 66–67, 299–300.

55. See Carl Fleischhauer and Beverly W. Brannan, *Documenting America, 1935–1943* (Berkeley: University of California Press, 1988); Ewen, *PR!* 233–336. The Photographic Section of the RA and FSA operated under the direction of Roy Stryker between 1935 and 1943. Dorothea Lange was a member of the Photographic Section. Her work illustrated here was photographed under the aegis of this government agency. See Ewen, *PR!* 275–76, for a discussion of how the avoidance of color in the publication of the RA/FSA photos purposely clashed with the commercialized, chromatic view of advertised American prosperity. The stark, black-and-white imagery of the RA/FSA photos underscored the disparity between commerce and the lives that progress had left behind. The RA/FSA photos presented an image of America not previously publicized and not readily introduced to the middle class. Consequently, these images challenged a conventional way of understanding not only the poor but also the paradox of industrial progress. On the role of mass media during the 1930s, see Susman, "The Culture of the Thirties," in *Culture as History,* 159–60. Susman explains how the photograph and the newsreel brought the perils of the Depression years into vivid perspective on a universal scale. Susman also discusses the "sociological and psychological triumph" of the New Deal by way of Roosevelt's agile exploitation of symbols.

56. Fleischhauer and Brannan in *Documenting America* show photographs taken by Arthur Rothstein of an FSA-operated migratory labor camp in California. The agency ran several western camps for migrants from Oklahoma and Arkansas. Although the shelters were small, temporary structures, the camps were intended to provide an arena

for building a permanent community. Rothstein's images include photos of organized recreation, cooperative store meetings, laundry facilities, and health care. Significantly, however, none of the photos from this particular series show any evidence of social isolation or economic despair, as do Dorothea Lange's infamous 1930s icon, "Migrant Mother," and the image of a migrant woman with her children shown in figure 2.3. These two images, in contrast to the Rothstein photos of the FSA camps, would have been used as visual arguments in support of the federal government's intervention in the country's economic and social woes. See also Terry Smith, *Making the Modern,* 286–328. Smith covers examples of the RA/FSA photographing "beneficiaries of modernity rather than its victims" (325).

57. For more on the New Deal's intent to expand consumer purchasing power, see Lizabeth Cohen, *A Consumers' Republic;* Jacobs, "'Democracy's Third Estate'"; Tobey, *Technology as Freedom;* Shelley Nickles, "'Preserving Women': Refrigerator Design as Social Process in the 1930s," *Technology and Culture* 43, no. 4 (2002): 693–727; Shelley Nickles, "Object Lessons: Household Appliance Design and the American Middle Class, 1920–1960" (Ph.D. diss., University of Virginia, 1999). On the New Deal and rural electrification, see Katherine Jellison, *Entitled to Power: Farm Women and Technology, 1913–1963* (Chapel Hill: University of North Carolina Press, 1993), 67–105.

58. Despite certain mishaps and inconsistencies within New Deal reform attempts (including the NRA), Roosevelt inaugurated his ideal to democratize modern progress through massive public works projects like the Tennessee Valley Authority.

59. Tobey, *Technology as Freedom,* 95.

60. Jacobs, "'Democracy's Third Estate,'" 27. This is issue is also raised in Marchand, *Advertising the American Dream.*

61. Tedlow, *Keeping the Corporate Image,* 81. Original quote from *Economic Forum* (Winter 1936), insert following 324. BBDO stood for Batten Barton Durstine and Osborn. Barton was a "staunch Republican" and vocal enemy of the New Deal. He was a congressman from 1937 to 1940, when he unsuccessfully ran for the Senate and then returned to BBDO. See John McDonough, "BBDO Worldwide, Inc.," in *Encyclopedia of Advertising,* 150.

62. The NAM stepped in for business with their own propaganda machine—a series of billboards and advertisements promoting the American Way. See Ewen, *PR!* 304–21, 323. For the NAM's anti–New Deal campaign along with others launched by the "entrepreneurial right" in the 1930s, see Bird, "Better Living."

63. Ewen, *PR!* 324; Robert Rydell, *World of Fairs: The Century-of-Progress Expositions* (Chicago: University of Chicago Press, 1993), 115–36.

64. "The New York World's Fair offer[s] an ideal opportunity for business to seek a way out of the dire straits into which it has been precipitated in the last few years. Other fairs have been chiefly concerned with selling products; this one will be chiefly concerned with selling ideas. . . . The New York World's Fair of 1939 is going to be the greatest single public relations program in industrial history." From Bernard Lichtenberg, "Business Backs New York World Fair to Meet the New Deal Propaganda," *Public Opinion Quarterly* 2 (April 1938): 314–15. Quoted in Ewen, *PR!* 325.

65. For more on how the New York World's Fair was planned as a blueprint for building the ultimate American Way of life, which would be predicated on corporate visions and consumer products, see Marchand, *Creating the Corporate Soul,* 249–311; Joseph P. Cusker, "The World of Tomorrow: Science, Culture, and Community at the

New York World's Fair," in Helen A. Harrison, ed., *Dawn of a New Day: The New York World's Fair, 1939/40*, 13–15 (New York: New York University Press and the Queens Museum, 1980). According to Cusker, domestic utopia was used as a way to demonstrate the benevolent side of the Machine Age and counter some of the anti-automation sentiments of organized labor. Warren Susman, "The People's Fair: Cultural Contradictions of a Consumer Society," in *Dawn of a New Day*, 22, explains that certain corporate exhibits were intended to show how a given company or industry had recently raised standards of living, which pointed to the possibility of higher standards for more consumers in the future. See Francis V. O'Connor, "The Usable Future: The Role of Fantasy in the Promotion of a Consumer Society for Art," in *Dawn of a New Day*, 57, for how visions of technology were intended to imply that it could raise standards for all and how the New York fair as a whole was meant to project this idea. See Gerald Wendt, *Science for the World of Tomorrow* (New York: W. W. Norton, 1939), 41–42, 151–52, for the official fair planners' rationalization as to why mechanization was advancing at the expense of human labor and how that would ultimately facilitate progress. In his book, Wendt, who was the director of the Department of Science for the fair, glorifies the mechanization process that, as he explains it, puts labor temporarily out of work. Ewen in *PR!* (322–36), building on Susman's argument in *Dawn of a New Day*, says that the New York World's Fair planners (who included designer Walter Dorwin Teague) publicized their project as a "People's Fair" and thus capitalized on the New Deal's social and egalitarian symbolism, which also permeated the latter's RA/FSA publicity. Consequently, fair planners tried to downplay the disparity and tensions between corporate hegemony and a New Deal liberal/collectivist leaning by using the democratic rhetoric of New Deal propaganda in order to resuscitate the public's faith in corporate authority and store-bought technology. The fair planners' pastiche of the New Deal agenda and liberal concerns is also exemplified by the inclusion of social commentator Lewis Mumford, who wrote the script for the film "The City," shown at the Science and Education Building. See Richard Wurts, *The New York World's Fair 1939/1940* (New York: Dover, 1977), 89. Not unlike the business community, Roosevelt also saw the fair as a way to mold public understanding about the New Deal and its plan for the future, which relied on the cooperation between business and government. For the Chicago 1933 and New York 1939 fairs, Roosevelt hoped to find support for his New Deal programs by, ironically, riding the wave of consumer enthusiasm stimulated by the business community at the fairs. See Rydell, *World of Fairs*, 118, 146–56.

66. Apparently, the fair's corporate planners were not immune to the human-engineering impulse of the time, as their concept of "betterment" suggests in this contemporary article: "We believe that the program of the Fair must have an *underlying social objective*. It must demonstrate the *betterment* of our future American life. *It must stress the vastly increased opportunity and the already developed mechanical means which this twentieth century has brought to the masses for better living and accompanying happiness*." From John Deventer, "Jobs in the World of Tomorrow and . . . A Job for the 'World of Tomorrow,'" *Iron Age*, 9 February 1939, n.p. Quoted in Ewen, *PR!* 325 (my emphasis). On Machine Age aesthetics and mass production, see Terry Smith, *Making the Modern;* Ray Batchelor, *Henry Ford: Mass Production, Modernism, and Design* (Manchester, UK: Manchester University Press, 1994); Christopher Crouch, *Modernism in Art, Design & Architecture* (New York: St. Martin's, 1999).

67. Norman Bel Geddes, *Magic Motorways* (New York: Random House, 1940). See also "City of 1960," *Architectural Forum,* July 1937, 57–62. Other corporate displays included the U.S. Steel pavilion, National Cash Register's giant cash register, and Underwood's larger-than-life typewriter.

68. Harris, *The Right to Manage,* 23–24, 28–31; Serrin, *The Company and the Union,* 115–17. Serrin details the threatening conditions and brutality to which many auto union members and organizers were subjected during the 1930s.

69. For an examination of the influence of eugenic rhetoric and symbols on the era's top industrial designers, such as Bel Geddes, see Cogdell, "The Futurama Recontextualized," "Products or Bodies?" and *Eugenic Design.*

70. Descriptions and analyses of streamlining in terms of design and social hygiene are discussed in chapter 4.

Chapter 3

1. "What Can We Do Starting Now . . ." Untitled, National Industrial Information Committee (NIIC) typescript, NAM #1411, NIIC Box 843, Advertising 1943 Folder, p. 13, National Association of Manufacturers Collection, Hagley Museum and Library (hereafter cited as NAM/Hagley). The NIIC was the NAM's public relations arm. The NAM's campaign to reshape public opinion in favor of big business and mass production was also tied to their motive to undermine the New Deal, as discussed in depth in chapter 5.

2. We will see this catchphrase, American industry, again in NAM propaganda. Its meaning in terms of the managerial elite's prowess and virility (not labor's) is discussed in chapter 5.

3. Some liberals went so far as to claim that capitalism was obsolete, but the basic universal belief shared by most liberals was that capitalism was flawed and that government should be responsible for fixing it. See Brinkley, *End of Reform,* 5–6.

4. Government-sponsored public housing projects, such as the suburban garden communities called the Greenbelt Town Program, provide a case in point. Kenneth Jackson in *Crabgrass Frontier* says that the Greenbelt Town planned for New Jersey "never even made it off the drawing board" because the resistance was so strong. The three Greenbelts that were constructed, Greenbelt, Maryland, Greenhills, Ohio, and Greendale, Wisconsin, were undermined "by excessive construction costs and never served as models for future metropolitan development." The program was part of the Resettlement Administration, which "was scrapped by Congress in 1938" (195). We will cover more on attitudes toward public housing in chapter 6.

5. For histories of big business in Washington, D.C., during the war, see Donald Nelson, *Arsenal of Democracy,* and Catton, *Warlords of Washington.*

6. Mobilization narratives were infused with similar confidence-building themes, but their focus on postwar consumption and abundance assumed that the public's faith in industry had been won. See subsequent chapters on postwar commercial propaganda.

7. *Ladies' Home Journal,* July 1944, 74. See also "You've got beauty, brains, breeding but you haven't a Proctor toaster," in *Ladies' Home Journal,* April 1944, 135, and the Smith-Corona typewriter ad in *Time,* 15 September 1941, 42–43: from homework to war, "it was all in the day's work." Some companies with brands still available worked

overtime to retain customers during the war by offering consumers promotional items related to new wartime realities. The makers of Lysol, the disinfectant, gave away a free "Victory Cook Book" with every Lysol purchase. This was not just any cookbook; it explained "how to eat well, live well, plan balanced meals under food rationing" (*Ladies' Home Journal,* June 1943, 123). It is truly amazing how creative advertisers and ad makers were in developing mobilization announcements. The ads referred to throughout this book are only a small sampling, by comparison, of the variety of approaches, topics, and categories found in wartime print media.

8. Mobilization *and* reconversion narratives included tie-ins with explanations or inducements for scrap drives, recycling, rationing, recruiting women for factory jobs, and buying government war bonds. We shall see examples of these in this and subsequent chapters.

9. For stereotyping of the Japanese and Germans during World War II, see Mac-Dougall, "Red, Brown, and Yellow Perils," 59–76.

10. Francis R. Dieuaide, *Civilian Health in Wartime* (Cambridge, Mass.: Harvard University Press, 1942), 292–93. Dieuaide did not indicate that the Japanese's derailment from "the line of progress" was a temporary cultural setback, like the German's. For depictions of the German and Japanese enemy "type" in wartime propaganda posters, see Braverman, *To Hasten the Homecoming,* illustration plates at 98–99 and 194–95; Fussell, *Wartime,* 115–28.

11. In a *Ladies' Home Journal* ad of January 1943 (13), for example, caricatures of Italy's dictator, Benito Mussolini, Germany's Adolf Hitler, and Japan's prime minister, Hideko Tojo, are shown as ridiculous, technologically backward, and enfeebled compared to the United States, typified by an Uncle Sam mascot. See also the November 1942 ad in *Ladies' Home Journal* for Blackstone washing machines where the three Axis leaders are shown as grotesque cartoons. The copy reads, "Kill 3 Birds with 1 Bond" (87). Thanks to Dennis Henthorn for finding these examples.

12. Strasser describes a similar ad sponsored by an Allis-Chalmers dealer of Clinton, Missouri. In the ad an Uncle Sam type disposes of an Asian man into a trash barrel filled with empty cans. The copy reads, "let's Junk the Jap" (*Waste and Want,* 243).

13. See Banta, *Imaging American Women,* on nineteenth-century physiognomy.

14. The idea of the enemy's intent to "infect" the "health" of the nation during the war can also be found in Dieuaide, *Civilian Health in Wartime:* "The aim of our enemies is to destroy our health, but through health we shall defeat them" (preface, n.p.).

15. For more on U.S. isolationism and its standing military of the 1930s, see Michael S. Sherry, *In the Shadow of War: The United States Since the 1930s* (New Haven, Conn.: Yale University Press, 1995), 15–63. Earl A. Molander contends that there existed a popularly held belief toward the end of World War II that the Japanese and German military expansions of the 1930s had been galvanized by a sinister military-industrial complex. See his "Historical Antecedents of Military-Industrial Criticism," *Military Affairs* 40, no. 2 (1976): 59.

16. Donald Nelson, *Arsenal of Democracy,* 28, 34–35, 51, 54.

17. *War Facts,* 46.

18. The OEM was initiated in 1940 by Roosevelt. It was set up in the White House to serve "as a sort of incubator and umbrella for mobilization agencies." See Jeffries, *Wartime America,* 19.

19. This is dealt with in chapter 5.

20. Lears comments on the deployment of the managerial idiom during the war by advertising spokesmen. See *Fables of Abundance,* 247.

21. *Fortune,* September 1943, 74.

22. Ibid.

23. On devising the image of the corporation as paternal benefactor, see Marchand, *Creating the Corporate Soul.*

24. *Ladies' Home Journal,* September 1943, 151. This ad also appeared in *Good Housekeeping,* October 1943.

25. In addition to adapting their V-8 engines to the M-5 tank, Cadillac built engines for the P-38 bomber. See the ad "Cadillac: Craftsmanship is still our stock in trade," in Albrecht, *World War II,* 230.

26. *Woman's Home Companion,* September 1943, 101. Lastex is a trademark for a type of yarn possessing an elastic core. The core is wrapped with cotton, silk, nylon, or rayon threads.

27. See chapter 4 for more on the streamlined woman. Streamlining as an efficiency aesthetic is examined later in this chapter.

28. On the development of the beauty industry in the United States, see Philip Scranton, ed., *Beauty and Business: Commerce, Gender, and Culture in Modern America* (New York: Routledge, 2001).

29. We shall examine the myth of freedom gained through labor-saving devices in chapter 7. For an overview of leisure, femininity, and consumer themes in women's magazines, see Ballaster et al., *Women's Worlds.*

30. For example, Hinds hand lotion used the image of the streamlined kitchen and streamlined woman in a 1943 ad (which also included a message about recruiting women into factories). A slim, attractive, blonde housewife (in frilly apron and high-heeled shoes) stands at a white, streamlined sink and explains how she is able to maintain her femininity with the use of Hinds lotion despite "Fighting the War in the Kitchen Sink!" From *Woman's Home Companion,* November 1943, 121.

31. Samuel Haber, *Efficiency and Uplift,* 62.

32. Strasser, *Waste and Want,* 181–87, 197–99; Christine Frederick, *The New Housekeeping: Efficiency Studies in Home Management* (Garden City, N.Y.: Doubleday, 1913).

33. See Hayden, *The Grand Domestic Revolution,* 280–86; Lupton and Miller, *The Bathroom,* 41–63; Adrian Forty, *Objects of Desire: Design and Society Since 1705* (London: Thames & Hudson, 1986), 156–81.

34. *Business Week,* 17 April 1943, 65.

35. On World War II pinups, see Maria-Elena Buszek, "War Goddess: The Varga Girls, World War II, and Feminism," *n.paradoxa* 6 (March 1998), http://web.ukon-line.co.uk/n.paradoxa/.

36. *Ladies' Home Journal,* June 1943, 105.

37. Ibid.

38. On disciplining the body in modern, machine culture, see Carolyn Thomas de la Peña, *The Body Electric: How Strange Machines Built the Modern American* (New York: New York University Press, 2003); Mark Seltzer, *Bodies and Machines* (New York: Routledge, 1992); Anson Rabinbach, *The Human Motor: Energy, Fatigue, and the Origins of Modernity* (New York: HarperCollins/Basic Books, 1990). Rabinbach's book covers this phenomenon in nineteenth-century European culture, but its emphasis on

the human motor metaphor is appropriate for a study of the mechanized body in U.S. twentieth-century society, too.

39. Wartime media are replete with a variety of ads where "women's work" was, as Mary Drake McFeely put it, "part of meeting the challenge of war." From McFeely, "The War in the Kitchen," in Ward, *Produce & Conserve,* 106. Several wartime ads made direct parallels between the front line and conducting efficient housework and home-making on the home front (see note 49 below for examples). Campaigns for salvaging cans and fats—the refuse of cooking—especially made such appeals that equated housework with important war work.

40. For another advertising example where implied eugenic truisms attempted to highlight Japanese inferiority, see "Mrs. Parker's cooking utensils are making it hot for the Japs." In this ad for Revere Copper and Brass, an attractive white housewife stands before a battleground scene with her Revere pot held out for the viewer as if it were a rifle. The ad suggests that a mere pot from an American middle-class kitchen is so superior that it can foil the Japanese enemy. *Business Week,* 10 October 1942, 39.

41. For intimate glimpses into domesticity during the war, see McFeely, "The War in the Kitchen," 104–16. McFeely discusses wartime trends in nutrition education, meal preparation (altered by shortages), and the return of the home to a site of production (as opposed to consumption), including self-sufficient activities such as gardening and canning. Working women generally had to do "double duty." Their employment in factories did not preclude them from domestic and family obligations. Though this was not new in the 1940s (and is still common today), the war's obstacles to convenience, as noted above, did not make "double duty" any easier. See Lipsitz, *A Rainbow at Midnight,* 50–51.

42. *Ladies' Home Journal,* May 1943, 10. For another Hoover ad with a similar sentiment, see "I'm not ashamed of my calloused hands," *House Beautiful,* March 1943, 75. On prewar ads that stressed leisure in housework, see Marchand, *Advertising the American Dream,* 171–79.

43. *American Magazine,* April 1945, front cover.

44. Neet advertisement, *True Story,* September 1942, 110.

45. Helen Channing, "Beauty Up!" *True Story,* July 1942, 97. See also "Beauty—an Aid to Morale!" *Independent Woman,* January 1942, 25. Middle-class magazines also emphasized women's duty to their looks in wartime. See, for example, "Fragrance of Victory," an ad sponsored by exclusive perfumer Solon Palmer in *Ladies' Home Journal,* December 1943, 142.

46. *Women in the War . . . For the Final Push to Victory* (n.p.: Office of War Information with U.S. Army, U.S. Navy, U.S. Marine Corps, U.S. Coast Guard, and War Advertising Council, 1944), 4, 5, 6. Available at AC archives.

47. *United States Marine Corps Women's Reserve* (n.p., n.d.), 16, 21. From War Contributions 1941–45, Box 1, J. Walter Thompson Collection, Hartman Center, Duke University, Raleigh, North Carolina (hereafter cited as JWT/Duke). On British women and femininity during the war, see Kirkham, "Beauty and Duty."

48. Lipsitz, *A Rainbow at Midnight,* 49.

49. In addition to appeals to take on a "man's job" in a munitions factory, women were encouraged to turn their actual households into arsenals of domesticity. Just as the Production Soldier was asked to think about war work in terms of housework, the Victory Homemaker was required to consider her chores as a military priority.

Domestic efficiency at home was depicted as playing a vital role in winning the war, and as a result, women were encouraged to focus more energy and attention on household management because it, too, was a crucial ingredient for expediting victory. See "Our Kitchen at War," *American Home,* September 1944, 92–93; "Double Shifts on the Home Front," *Ladies' Home Journal,* April 1941, 108; "Join the Millions Cooperating for Victory" and "Maintenance—The Most Powerful Weapon on the Home Front!" *American Home,* May 1942, 6, 7, 8–9; "Simply, Smartly, Adapt Your Home to Wartime Living," *House & Garden,* October 1942, 56–57; Webb Waldron, "Yankee Kitchens Go on the Production Line," *Better Homes and Gardens,* June 1943, 17, 64–66.

Such concepts were especially prevalent in advertising found in women's magazines. See "This Battle Station is Closer to the Fighting Front than You May Think!" pertaining to Youngstown pressed steel kitchens in *Ladies' Home Journal,* April 1943, 160. Regarding the homemaker as a "soldier of food," see "The Army Behind the Armies—the 'Food Front'" from a Chef Boyardee ad in *Ladies' Home Journal,* May 1943, 145. Also from Chef Boyardee, see "Woman's Place in the War . . . building the Builders of Victory," in *Ladies' Home Journal,* April 1943, 155. On kitchen pantry and cupboard shelves as sites of victory, see the Royledge Shelving company's ad, "Your Victory Shelf!" in *Ladies' Home Journal,* November 1943, 164. Oftentimes food itself was likewise empowered, such as in the grapefruit juice ad "It's the Commando of Fruit!" in *Ladies' Home Journal,* March 1944, 135. See also the National Dairy Products Corporation advertisment pictured in figure 1.1.

50. U.S. Department of Labor, Women's Bureau, *What Job Is Mine on the Victory Line* (Washington, D.C.: Government Printing Office, April 1943), 2–5. AC Archives. The booklet details more examples of the correlation between the tasks of modern domesticity and femininity and those in war plants.

See also Laurence Hammond, "Kitchen Lore Speeds War Production," *Independent Woman,* December 1943, 362; *America at War Needs Women at Work: A Plan Book Published by the Information Services of the War Manpower Commission for Use in Recruiting Women in Critical War Areas for War Factories and Necessary Civilian Services* (n.p.: War Advertising Council, 1943). JWT/Duke. Leila Rupp in *Mobilizing Women for War* (142) asserts that recruitment campaigns carried out by the OWI, the WAC, and the War Manpower Commission (WMC) largely ignored working-class homemakers who were compelled for financial reasons to acquire work in war production facilities. Her argument is that presumably these women needed no convincing to work in factories, but middle-class women, who usually did not hold down a full-time job (especially in dirty, blue-collar facilities) while also running the home, *did* need gentle persuasion. On women, work, and wartime roles, see Karen Anderson, *Wartime Women: Sex Roles, Family Relations, and the Status of Women during World War II* (Westport, Conn.: Greenwood, 1981); Ruth Milkman, *Gender at Work: The Dynamics of Job Discrimination by Sex during World War II* (Urbana: University of Illinois Press, 1987); "'A Call to Farms': 'Tractorettes' Go to War," in Jellison, *Entitled to Power,* 131–48; Lipsitz, *A Rainbow at Midnight,* 45–65.

51. In other literature, war work was touted as having improved women's skills as homemakers. See Gretta Palmer, "They Learned About Women," *Reader's Digest,* September 1944, 105–7; Dorothy Canfield Fisher, "From the Lathe to the Hearth," *New York Times Magazine,* 5 December 1943, 6, 46.

Part 2

1. "What Happened to the Dreamworld?" *Fortune,* February 1947, 93.

2. "The Impact of War on Advertising," *Advertising & Selling,* March 1942, 21. Thirty-two articles appeared in a series under this title from January 1942 to July 1944. For the initial debate on advertising's attempt to establish a legitimate role for itself in war, see "The Impact of Defense on Advertising," *Advertising & Selling,* December 1941, 19–30.

3. Advertisement for buying advertising space in *Woman's Home Companion, Advertising & Selling,* February 1944, 15.

4. For an example of how the business community utilized its "selfless" role in the war for its own propagandistic ends, see Donald Wilhelm, "Business Rushes to Government's Aid in Preparedness Crisis," *Printer's Ink,* 16 August 1940, 11–14. In the article, Wilhelm claims that business was doing a superlative job with expediting the defense mobilization process—much better, by comparison, than during World War I.

Chapter 4

1. Franklin Delano Roosevelt, "Post-War Goals: America's Ability to Produce," *Vital Speeches of the Day,* 15 January 1943, 194, 197 (my emphasis). The speech was the president's Annual Message to Congress, Washington, D.C., 7 January 1943. The Four Freedoms were first articulated in a speech Roosevelt delivered to the 77th Congress on 6 January 1941: "Message to Congress: The State of the Union," *Vital Speeches of the Day,* 15 January 1941, 197–200. The Four Freedoms included (1) "freedom of speech and expression—everywhere in the world"; (2) "freedom of every person to worship God in his own way—everywhere in the world"; (3) "freedom from want, which, translated into world terms, means economic understandings which will secure to every nation a healthy peacetime life for its inhabitants—everywhere in the world"; (4) "freedom from fear, which, translated into world terms, means a world-wide reduction of armaments to such a point and in such a thorough fashion that no nation will be in a position to commit an act of physical aggression against any neighbor—anywhere in the world."

2. Walter Dorwin Teague, "Planning the World of Tomorrow," *Popular Mechanics,* December 1940, 808–9 (my emphasis).

3. For additional narratives of war mobilization, see Albert W. Atwood, "The Miracle of War Production," *National Geographic,* December 1942, 693–715; Burnham Finney, "The Miracle of American Production," *American Mercury,* September 1943, 279–85; "Glamour Goes to War," *Saturday Evening Post,* 29 November 1941, 18–19, 56, 58; "Yes, Even the Kitchen Sink," *American Home,* March 1945, 142; "The Consumer's War," *Fortune,* August 1941, 94–95, 116, 118; "Join the Millions Cooperating for Victory," *American Home,* May 1942, 6–7.

4. Jeffries, *Wartime America,* 26, 44. Jeffries indicates that he adjusted these figures relative to inflation at the time. In "constant dollars," he says, in order to "correct for wartime inflation," the GNP increased to approximately $150 billion in 1944—which would be a two-thirds growth over the 1939 GNP of $91 billion. I rely on Jeffries's research extensively over other sources because of his attempt to synthesize, decon-

struct, and recontextualize common misconceptions of wartime production and economic mobilization.

5. Ibid., 44–45. Jeffries also demythologizes common beliefs about wartime "miracles" by arguing that although wartime production may have been plentiful, it was certainly not infallible. Apparently, America's ordnance was sometimes lacking in quality compared to the equipment used by the Germans and Japanese. Americans outproduced the Axis powers, working about five times the hours of the Japanese and approximately twice the hours of their German counterparts (ibid., 45, 47.) Jeffries also provides some individual examples of production failures or inadequacies.

6. Ibid., 43.

7. Tessie Agan, *The House: A Text for a College Course on the House* (Chicago: J. B. Lippincott, 1939), 9. Agan footnotes the following text for her statistics: Marice Leven, Harold G. Moulton, and Clark Warburton, *America's Capacity to Consume* (Washington, D.C.: Brookings Institution, 1934), 87. Agan's is a superb example of the hygienic conceit found in domestic science literature.

8. C. W. Stuart, "New Possibilities of Electric Home Equipment," in Paul Zucker, ed., *New Architecture and City Planning: A Symposium* (New York: Philosophical Library, 1944), 243.

9. Kenneth K. Stowell (editor in chief), "Higher Standards of Living," *Architectural Record,* November 1942, 31. From the magazine's "Design for Democracy" section. Other business leaders recognized the same trend: "[C]ountless men and women in America, England and in the British Dominions, are for the first time in their lives enjoying the opportunity to work and to save. To put it broadly, war alone has thus far accomplished full employment." Henry Kaiser, "The American Way: Pessimism for Post War Era Assailed," *Vital Speeches of the Day,* 1 December 1942, 119. A similar assessment of low-income Americans' increase in job opportunities and standards of living can be found in *Peacetime Plans of Industrial Companies* (n.p.: NAM, April 1943), 11. NAM #1411, Box 860, Series III, Postwar Publications Folder 1942–43, NAM/Hagley.

10. By 1943, the military grew to a force of nine million, and employment of civilians in defense plants was approximately six million. Unemployment dropped to 1 percent during 1944. Correcting for inflation, Jeffries asserts that the national income increased by approximately 85 percent between 1939 and 1944. Consumer savings increased from $3 billion in 1939 to $37 billion in 1944—the equivalent of $27 billion in 1939 (Jeffries, *Wartime America,* 48–49). Tables on personal income gains during the war years appear on 62–63, where Jeffries asserts that although many Americans (including businesses) prospered as a result of the war, there were others who, by comparison, did not see any improvement over their previous experience. Poor Americans were still poor during the war—even if they had jobs. The lowest 20 percent "still earned on average well under $1,000 per year in 1944" (ibid., 63).

11. Ibid., 44. Economic growth, according to Jeffries, was "comparable in rate" to what (mostly middle-class) Americans had experienced between 1921 and 1924/25 (ibid., 46).

12. Walter Dorwin Teague, "Industry Plans for the Future," *Advertising & Selling,* February 1943, 110, 156. For more on the expanding consumer market, see "War Changes Buying Habits": "The varying effects of rationing, shortages, substitutions, taxes, and shifts in income have cut down consumption by previous high-income groups and have increased and broadened consumption by people in the previous

low-income classes" (33). Consumers "from every income group" were awaiting their chance to acquire new goods. See Arnold E. Baragar, "Postwar Equipment," *Journal of Home Economics,* January 1946, 11.

13. Walter Dorwin Teague, "Design for Peace," *Studio International,* April 1943, 154–55.

14. "War Changes Buying Habits," 33. See also J. D. Ratcliff, "Your Home Tomorrow," *Woman's Home Companion,* July 1943, 34.

15. "War Changes Buying Habits," 33. Leo Rich also touched on this issue in "The Public Expects Progress," *Advertising & Selling,* July 1944, 36, 150–52.

16. For an expression of these sentiments during the war, see Norman V. Carlisle and Frank B. Latham, *Miracles Ahead! Better Living in the Postwar World* (New York: Macmillan, 1944), 1, 5; S. Ward Seeley, "Planning Now for the Business of Peace," *Advertising & Selling,* January 1943, 44, 46; Gordon Simmons, "Postwar Daydreams," *Advertising & Selling,* June 1944, 27–28, 148, 150, 152; Parker James, "Products for Postwar: New and Substitute Materials That Will Be Advertised After the War," *Advertising & Selling,* March 1943, 13–15, 78. See also the promotional booklet created by the ad agency J. Walter Thompson for prospective and current clients: *A Primer for Postwar Prosperity* (New York: J. Walter Thompson, 1945), 3. Box 9, Company Publications 1937–1946, JWT/Duke; John Perry, "New Products for Postwar America? The Challenge to Engineers and Business Men," *Harper's Magazine,* February 1943, 330–31; "Industry Learns from Defense," *Scientific American,* January 1942, 16.

17. James, "Products for Postwar," 14. For an early assessment of reconversion, consumer products, and the postwar economy, see "The United States in a New World— III: The Domestic Economy, Appendix, Technology and Postwar Life," *Fortune* supp., December 1942, 19–20. On further postwar speculations, see "Science Speeds Victory," *Science News Letter,* 23 December 1944, 405; Waldemar Kaemffert, "War Brings Peace-Time Gains," *Science Digest,* July 1942, 15–18; "Ingenious New World," *Newsweek,* 28 May 1945, 70; "Post-War Promises," *Science News Letter,* 10 July 1943, 26. The new products, materials, and production processes that formed the "miracle" of wartime reconversion narratives had been "discovered" before the conflict but had not been developed until the war, when they were rushed into production for military use.

18. "I'm Fed Up!" *Better Homes and Gardens,* July 1944, 22–23.

19. John Sasso, "Are You Learning the Language of Tomorrow?" *House Beautiful,* March 1943, 21.

20. Carlisle and Latham, *Miracles Ahead!* 115. Carlisle and Latham's book is quoted often because it so succinctly articulates the reconversion arguments and corporate platitudes about postwar progress. Why it does so is significant for this study because the predictions in *Miracles Ahead!* were, according to the authors, based on a synthesis of contemporary advertisements, articles, and booklets published by corporations, architects, and designers about their postwar forecasts and strategies. Consequently, Carlisle and Latham used many of the types of sources I also used for my study. There is no biography for Carlisle and Latham in *Miracles Ahead!* However, both were writers for *Scholastic* and both wrote on job opportunities available during the war and the postwar era. Carlisle also wrote on aviation, chemistry, and engineering for the duration of the war. For other contemporary predictions about the postwar house, see George Nelson and Henry Wright, *Tomorrow's House* (New York: Simon & Schuster, 1945); Zucker, *New Architecture.*

On household servants, see Shelby Cullom Davis, "Household Servants Are Gone Forever," *American Magazine,* March 1942, 32. Mrs. Davis laments the loss of servants to factory jobs. M. M. Manring, in *Slave in a Box* (80–89), looks at the role of servants as advertising icons for affluence. During the "industrial revolution of the middle-class home," advertisers either depicted servants to suggest the "elite life" accorded by a given product or stressed the unparalleled efficiency of their product by the domestic servant's absence.

21. Ratcliff, "Your Home Tomorrow," 34.

22. "Post-War Promises," 26.

23. Carlisle and Latham, *Miracles Ahead!* 169–70. Advertisers of synthetic textiles suggested that those synthetics proven on the battlefield would usher in a new world of durable, lasting beauty for the wardrobe of tomorrow. Velon used this argument in its ad published in *Modern Plastics,* September 1945, 53.

24. For more on the disparity between the claims made in plastics publicity and the material's uneven performance, see Meikle, *American Plastic,* 155, 165–66.

25. In an attempt to reverse consumer opinion, publicists for the plastics industry tried to refurbish plastics' tarnished public image. See "War Changes Buying Habits," 33.

26. For more on plastics' reconversion, see "The United States in a New World," 18.

27. Arthur C. Miller, "Necessity Creates Our Inventions: New Methods and Materials Dictated by Wartime Needs Prove Better Than the Old," *Popular Science,* December 1942, 64–68. See also "Bright Plastics Go to Bat for Metal in the Home," *Popular Mechanics,* June 1942, 16.

28. B. M. Sternberg, for example, provides examples of plastic adaptations, especially products earmarked for the personal hygiene industry, in "New Opportunities in Postwar Markets," *Modern Plastics,* April 1945, 103. For more on plastic uses in wartime and their sanitary features, see also "Plastics in Review," *Modern Plastics,* February 1944, 114–15.

29. Carl C. Austin, Jr., "War as a Proving Ground," *Modern Plastics,* October 1944, n.p. Reprint from Dow Chemical Corporation, Post Street Archives, Midland, Michigan (hereafter cited as Dow Archives). See also James, "Products for Postwar," for an example of the "stamina" rhetorical formula.

30. Refer to figures 4.7 and 4.8 for examples.

31. See, for example, the women in figures 3.5, 3.7, 4.8, and 6.14. Paul Fussell in his chapter on wartime typecasting observes that home front readers "could not help inferring that the war was designed primarily to defend and advance the interests of such tall, clean blonds" as those pictured in the aforementioned illustrations, so dominant was this type in advertising (*Wartime,* 127).

32. On the vamp type's development in popular culture from the 1920s to World War II, see Lois W. Banner, *American Beauty* (New York: Alfred A. Knopf, 1983), 278–83.

33. See also another Columbia Plastics ad, "Glamour . . . for sale," which depicts the perfect postwar world as a well-groomed goddess receiving the spoils of war from an outstretched hand. Published in *Modern Plastics,* May 1945, 23.

34. Tessie Agan in her 1939 textbook lists the hygienic merits of single-family home ownership; her discussion of this debate typifies the American obsession with avoiding urban defects (*The House,* 66–67). In order to offset the physical, moral, and mental decline caused by overcrowding, the single-family house fostered health through privacy, and when set on its own plot of land, not too close to others, it engendered

vitality through sunlight and fresh air that circulated around all four sides (ibid., 19–21).

35. On the Shirley Temple type in the spectrum of American ideals of femininity, see Banner, *American Beauty,* 282–83.

36. V. E. Yarsley and E. G. Couzens, "The Expanding Age of Plastics," *Science Digest,* December 1942, 57–59.

37. Ibid., 59–60. For various designers' visions of future products made of plastics, like Dave Chapman's electric typewriter and Donald Deskey's push-button telephone, see E. F. Lougee, "Plastics Post-War," *Art & Industry,* August 1944, 34–40.

38. Prior to the use of Saran Film for munitions packaging, guns were transported from U.S. factories to the front line in wads of grease, which required extra labor and time to clean up before the weaponry could be issued to soldiers in the field.

39. Carlisle and Latham, *Miracles Ahead!* 115–16.

40. The housewife who practiced scientific housekeeping faithfully, according to Tessie Agan, would barely have time to sleep, let alone relax. On page 254 of *The House* she charts the "average number of hours and the percentage of time spent on various homemaking activities." Women in "town and country families" spent 64 hours and 37 minutes per week on chores, which Agan breaks down into categories. Farm families spent 61 hours and 2 minutes on weekly domestic duties by comparison. Agan included "time spent per week [performed by] paid workers as well as time spent by family members," though she did not indicate the percentage of women who had paid domestics. Still, for a housewife with no paid help, especially during the war years, the workload of sixty hours per week spent just on the home is enormous. Despite the amount of time any woman would have directed toward housekeeping, leisure was an important, if impossible, goal of hygienic propriety.

41. Walter Adams, "Mystery Weapon Today—Your Servant Tomorrow," *Better Homes and Gardens,* August 1943, 21. A maintenance-free home would also manufacture its own clean air. The Precipitron was forecast to do just that by eliminating dust and soot. The Precipitron was the 1934 invention of Westinghouse employee Gaylord W. Penney, who installed and tested the device in his Pittsburgh home. See Carlisle and Latham, *Miracles Ahead!* 30–31.

42. Walter Adams, "Mystery Weapon Today," 21.

43. Carlisle and Latham, *Miracles Ahead!* 30, 131.

44. Mary Roche, "Awaiting the New Kitchen," *New York Times Magazine,* 14 October 1945, 34.

45. *Business Week,* 17 July 1943, 99.

46. For overviews of streamlining as a concept and an aesthetic device, see Claude Lichtenstein and Franz Engler, eds., *Streamlined: The Esthetics of Minimized Drag: A Metaphor for Progress* (Baden, Switzerland: Lars Müller, 1995); Lupton and Miller, *The Bathroom;* and the following works by Cogdell: "The Futurama Recontextualized," "Products or Bodies?" and *Eugenic Design.* Cogdell examines the style as a cultural manifestation of evolutionary beliefs and/or a eugenics mindset that pervaded not only American thought but also the theoretical underpinnings within the industrial design fields. For emphasis on the streamlined style as a Machine Age aesthetic, see J. Stewart Johnson, *American Modern, 1925–1940: Design for a New Age* (New York: Harry N. Abrams and the American Federation of Arts, 2000); Richard Guy Wilson et al., *The Machine Age in America, 1918–1941* (New York: Harry N. Abrams; Brooklyn,

N.Y.: The Brooklyn Museum, 1986); Meikle, *Twentieth Century Limited*. On modernism, functionalism, and the Machine Age, see Harvey Green, "The Promise and Peril of High Technology," in Janet Kardon, ed., *Craft in the Machine Age, 1920–1945*, 36–45 (New York: Harry N. Abrams and the American Craft Museum, 1996); Martin Eidelberg, ed., *Design, 1935–1965: What Modern Was* (New York: Harry N. Abrams; Montreal: Le Musée des Arts Décoratifs de Montréal, 1991). African Americans also contributed to the look, feel, and sound of Machine Age aesthetics. Joel Dinerstein argues that jazz, swing, and popular dance styles of the era were black adaptations of machine sounds, tempos, and movements. See *Swinging the Machine: Modernity, Technology, and African American Culture between the World Wars* (Amherst, Mass.: University of Massachusetts Press, 2003). Terry Smith's *Making the Modern* covers the development of modernism as it related to the rise of America's industrial, assembly-line culture. Smith discusses streamlining, the machine aesthetic, and functionalism in the context of images of industrial progress during the rise of mass manufacturing and mass consumption.

47. Cooper-Bessemer was a manufacturing concern that compressed synthetic rubber for various military needs.

48. *Business Week,* 16 September 1944, 93.

49. On commercial beauty ideals, see Vicki Howard, "'At the Curve Exchange': Postwar Beauty Culture and Working Women at Maidenform," in Scranton, *Beauty and Business,* 195–216. Various references to commercialized beauty can be found in chapters throughout Scranton's book. On the "look" of the average consumer, see Nickles, "Object Lessons." On the ideal type, see Donahue, "Design and the Industrial Arts"; Banta, *Imaging American Women;* Maxine Leeds Craig, *Ain't I a Beauty Queen? Black Women, Beauty, and the Politics of Race* (New York: Oxford University Press, 2002).

50. For example, designer Henry Dreyfuss and aircraft manufacturer Consolidated Vultee attempted to capitalize on wartime production experience with the postwar Convair Car. See Albrecht, *World War II,* xxxix. See also J. Gordon Lippincott, "As the Crow Flies," *Modern Plastics,* April 1945, 98–99; and "Is the 'Whirligig' for You?" *Nation's Business,* April 1947, 49.

51. The dream of personal aviation in suburbia was not new to wartime visionaries. William Lescase, George Keck, and Buckminster Fuller, for example, had all conceived of houses with hangars or rooftop heliports prior to the war. See Joseph Corn and Brian Horrigan, *Yesterday's Tomorrows: Past Visions of the American Future* (1984; reprint, Washington, D.C.: Smithsonian Institution; Baltimore: Johns Hopkins University Press, 1986).

52. World War II scientists (and their corporate sponsors) were bestowed with a Hollywood aura, evoking connotations of science-fiction wizardry, rather than derided as "merchants of death," as DuPont had been in the 1930s for its role in World War I. For more on this issue, see Meikle, *American Plastic,* 133–35.

53. *Fortune,* December 1943, 104. The business trade press expressed its great expectations for unbridled female spending in several ads encouraging manufacturers and designers to start focusing their wartime attention on satisfying Mrs. Postwar Middle-class Consumer. Consequently, many ads with this message depicted female figures as shopping queens and businessmen as their subjects.

54. Ratcliff, "Your Home Tomorrow," 34.

55. Brooks in "Consumer Markets and Consumer Magazines" documents the evolution of how African Americans were perceived, interpreted, constructed, and courted as consumers in the white business press from the 1920s through the 1960s. He indicates that this trend gained considerable strength and legitimacy during the 1940s and 1950s (105, 108). For additional coverage on consumer-producer-advertiser relations as they pertained to blacks and corporate America, see Weems, *Desegregating the Dollar;* and Lizabeth Cohen, *A Consumers' Republic.*

56. According to Brooks, *Sales Management* magazine raised business awareness of the black consumer market's financial gains during the war ("Consumer Markets and Consumer Magazines," 107), but it appears that much more attention was given to African Americans as a viable market segment toward the end of the war and shortly after. Brooks also covers a major 1945 research study that surveyed black consumers, which was ultimately published in 1947 and discussed at length in advertising trade journals such as *Printer's Ink* (ibid., 109). This issue is discussed at greater length in the context of postwar planning in chapter 8.

57. As a mobilization example, see the H. K. Ferguson Company ad in *Time,* 15 September 1941, 77, which features the African American cook, Suzie, dressed like the stereotypical Aunt Jemima figure.

58. *Advertising & Selling,* February 1944, 126. A U.S. Bureau of the Census table in Elton Rayack's 1961 study indicated that in 1939, African American men's income on average totaled $460 per year compared to $1,112 for white males. Rayack's table shows that although the gap between white and black incomes remained fairly wide, by 1947 the differential was narrowing with a significant increase for blacks. African American males increased their median wage to $1,279, while white males averaged $2,357. (Rayack did not indicate if inflation was taken into account in these figures.) See "Discrimination and the Occupational Progress of Negroes," *Review of Economics and Statistics* 43, no. 2 (1961): 211.

59. For an overview of theories and "sciences" of racial typing, including the "pure" racial type, see Cogdell, *Eugenic Design,* 192–200. On advertising in the black press, black beauty standards, and the pressures to fit the white normative mold, see Brooks's coverage of the prewar and postwar years in "Consumer Markets and Consumer Magazines," 95–98, 179–80, 184; Sivulka, *Stronger Than Dirt,* 251–90. Rooks also deals with black beauty and fashion paradoxes in the African American women's magazines of the prewar years in *Ladies' Pages,* especially on 47–88. See also Rooks's earlier work on black beauty issues, *Hair Raising: Beauty, Culture, and African American Women* (New Brunswick, N.J.: Rutgers University Press, 1996).

60. *People's Voice,* 21 February 1942, 8. It was largely presumed by white audiences that African Americans' sexuality was of a "primitive" nature: open, overt, and excessive. On the stereotyped sexuality of black women and its roots in slavery, see Rooks, *Ladies' Pages,* 25–46, 120–23.

61. *Baltimore Afro-American,* 4 November 1944, 2; 10 March 1945, 3, 7.

62. *Pittsburgh Courier,* 16 January 1943, 2.

63. Ibid., 30 September 1944, 11.

64. *Baltimore Afro-American,* 11 November 1944, 13; 10 March 1945, 12.

65. *Pittsburgh Courier,* 11 August 1945, 2; 25 August 1945, 4. On Sweet Georgia Brown advertising messages, see Sivulka, *Stronger Than Dirt,* 288–90.

66. The zoot suit, also referred to as a "drape shape," was an oversized article of male clothing popular among black and Hispanic youths during the 1930s and into the war years. It consisted of an oversized fedora hat, extravagantly padded shoulders (from which extra fabric would "drape"), and baggy trousers tapered sharply at the ankles. The inordinate amount of wool cloth it took to create the exaggerated appearance was forbidden by the WPB during the war years due to rationing measures. Young black men had been wearing the zoot suit for several years as a way to snub the conventions of middle-class white society and as an emblem of pride in their racial identity. The zoot suit was also associated with urban youth delinquency and the subversive sexual rawness of jazz nightlife. During the war, it was worn as a way to flaunt wartime restrictions, because rationing was considered an expression of patriotic duty. The zoot suit thus stood as a political statement in protest against a war waged to preserve freedoms that were consistently denied to African Americans and their families at home. Racial tensions due to the disparity of equal opportunity and treatment during the war erupted in one particular urban riot dubbed the Zoot Suit Riots, which involved Los Angeles Hispanic youths in 1943. See Stuart Cosgrove, "The Zoot-Suit and Style Warfare," *History Workshop Journal* 18 (Autumn 1984): 77–91.

67. African American advice literature at the turn of the century recognized white America's insistence on the interrelationship between moral purity, character, and middle-class respectability. Such literature, written by middle-class black women, sought to teach other African Americans how to adapt inwardly and outwardly to the respectability norms established by whites. Such adaptations of propriety were not perceived as markers of subordination but rather as signifiers of racial equality. See Rooks, *Ladies' Pages,* 98–100.

68. Roi Ottley, *New World A-Coming: Inside Black America* (Boston: Houghton Mifflin, 1943), 280.

69. Ibid., 280–81.

70. Brooks, "Consumer Markets and Consumer Magazines," 80–81. According to Brooks's coverage of the World War II era (which is scant by comparison to his examination of the prewar and postwar years), it seems that corporate America's wartime focus on the Negro Market emerged in articles limited to business trade publications, rather than through magazine or newspaper advertisements that mirrored the ones targeted to white consumers. The rise in black consumer marketing research and the black Negro Market expert are covered in chapter 8. These trends, though noticeable during the war, really took off around 1945 and after.

71. Mary Alice Sentman and Patrick S. Washburn, "How Excess Profits Tax Brought Ads to Black Newspapers in World War II," *Journalism Quarterly* 64 (1987): 769–74.

72. Ottley, *New World A-Coming,* 343. See Rayford Whittingham Logan's *The Negro and the Post-War World: A Primer* (Washington, D.C.: The Minorities Publishers, 1945) for another contemporary account of wartime African American experience and expectations for the postwar world.

73. This is not to say that the black press did not describe or depict African American women as homemakers (rather than domestic servants). Brooks discusses the domestic advice literature targeted to "black women as homemakers" before and after the war ("Consumer Markets and Consumer Magazines," 93–94, 185–87). For more

on the issue of black women, appropriate homemaking, and advice literature, see Rooks, *Ladies' Pages,* 89–112.

74. Brooks, "Consumer Markets and Consumer Magazines," 63–76. Brooks details how black activists and leaders in business established a tradition early in the twentieth century of using consumerism and capitalism as ways to attain full American citizenship, respect among whites, equality, and racial harmony. See also Lizabeth Cohen, *A Consumers' Republic,* 41–61.

75. Weems, *Desegregating the Dollar,* 7–30.

76. On the symbolic role of consumerism as an instrument for gaining equality and respectability in the black community, see Rooks, *Ladies' Pages,* 108–11. Rooks indicates that African American women's magazines years earlier had advocated the concept that "purchase and consumption of the proper products would lead to societal acceptance and racial uplift" (ibid., 108).

77. George E. Schuyler, "Views and Reviews," *Pittsburgh Courier,* 25 August 1945, 7.

Chapter 5

1. "Introductory Material to Ads Recommended by [Arthur] Kudner" (n.p., n.d.), 1, 2, 4, 5 (my emphasis), NAM #1411, NIIC Box 843, Advertising 1943 Folder, NAM/Hagley.

2. Stromberg details the business state of mind following World War I and outlines how the war was seen by businessmen as a catalyst for increasing New Deal powers (perhaps leading to a "war socialism"), giving leverage to those who would abolish or diminish free enterprise ("American Business," 63, 69).

3. Tedlow, *Keeping the Corporate Image,* 112. Tedlow asserts that although "business is not monolithic," there *does* exist a dominant business outlook known as "business sentiment." This "business sentiment," Tedlow writes, consists of "the opinions of those businessmen who have made use of public relations" (ibid., 111). Thus, those businesses or corporate leaders who publicized their opinions and solutions (perhaps in an attempt to change the minds of other businesses or the public) became the mouthpieces of the business community at large. Marchand's "Suspended in Time" examines the relationship between national chains and supermarkets (i.e., denizens of corporate America) and small-town grocers and corner urban shops as another example of the complexity of wartime business. Although big business's agenda overlapped often with the concerns of small business owners, Marchand points out that during the war, small and large companies were not exactly united in their efforts. Shortages and rationing gave large corporations the edge over small grocers, who were often overlooked by distributors in favor of the greater, usually nationally known enterprises. Ironically, as their leverage pressured small stores (in some cases, running them out of business), large corporations sought to "associate themselves as closely as possible with small business." In an effort to "counterattack" the New Deal, "many corporations turned . . . to 'Main Street' Norman Rockwell images" as illustrative of free enterprise and the "American Way" (ibid., 124–26).

See Philip H. Burch, Jr., "The NAM as an Interest Group," *Politics & Society* 4 (Fall 1973): 97–130, for a list of corporate members who led the NAM during the Depression and war years. Burch's research explains what was considered "big" business at the time and the extent to which these large-scale firms were involved in the NAM and shaped the ideological direction of its publicity campaigns. From "1933 to 1946 the active leadership of the NAM had been provided primarily by a very small group of big industrial firms" (ibid., 98). Executive committee members, for example, included "top officials" from large companies including American Cyanamid, Borden, Colgate-Palmolive-Peet, Curtis Publishing, DuPont, Eastman Kodak, Firestone, General Foods, General Mills, McCall Corp., Sears Roebuck & Co., Standard Oil, Sun Oil, Swift & Co., Universal Atlas Cement (an arm of U.S. Steel), and Weekly Publications (publisher of *Newsweek*). Burch details the "ideological orientation" of the NAM members who governed the organization by indicating which right-wing groups these members belonged to or which conservative causes they supported. Olson in *Saving Capitalism* reveals the extent of ideological diversity within the business community. He discusses the gamut of "recovery theories" prevalent during the Depression. Certainly, the business community, liberal leaders, and government officials offered varied approaches from the extremely conservative to the socialistic. Roosevelt was somewhere in the middle with his state capitalism and the "idea of cooperative planning between the federal government and the private sector" (84).

4. A. H. Sypher, "Post-War Problem No. 3," *Nation's Business,* July 1943, 38, 40 (last article in the series).

5. According to Brandes in *Warhogs,* by 1945 "the federal government owned 90 percent of the synthetic rubber, aircraft, and magnesium industries, and 55 percent of the aluminum business" (260).

6. Olson, *Saving Capitalism,* 219; Beaumont, "Quantum Increase," 122.

7. Olson, *Saving Capitalism,* 219. Major manufacturers that profited from "doing business with the government" included Aluminum Company of America, Anaconda Copper, Bendix Aviation, B. F. Goodrich, Chrysler, Curtis-Wright, Dow, DuPont, Ford, General Electric, General Motors, Goodyear, Packard, Republic Steel, Sperry, Standard Oil, Studebaker, Union Carbide, United Aircraft, and U.S. Steel. Olson astutely asserts that "state capitalism proved to be a windfall to corporate America." He writes of the various "companies" the New Deal devised to handle mobilization: the Rubber Reserve Company, for example, was formed to eliminate American dependency on rubber supplies from areas of the Pacific that were under Japanese control. The agency grew to become the country's "sole importer of crude rubber" and eventually "launched a government-owned synthetic rubber industry," operating fifty-one plants. Similar "companies" were formed as well: the Metals Reserve Company, the United States Commercial Company (which bought raw materials from neutral countries), the Defense Supplies Corporation, the Smaller War Plants Corporation, the Petroleum Reserve Company, and the War Damage Corporation, which gave assistance to insurance companies "in underwriting business property against enemy attack." The Defense Homes Corporation made loans for the construction of housing intended for defense plant workers. Such entities were an outgrowth of the recovery efforts that had culminated in the RFC (initiated under Hoover but retained by Roosevelt) and New Deal state capitalism developed during the Depression (ibid., 217–18).

8. Brandes, *Warhogs,* 259; Beaumont, "Quantum Increase," 131.

9. Brandes, *Warhogs,* 260. Brandes aptly refers to this section in his book as "The New Deal Subsidizes Corporate America."

10. Sypher, "Postwar Problem No. 3," 38, 40.

11. As mentioned in chapter 1, corporate leaders also thought that regulations through military fiat were better than any imposed by the government. According to Waddell in "Economic Mobilization," military controls in the area of economic mobilization were perceived by the wartime business community as less invasive than the New Deal's interventions because "military stewardship of mobilization heralded a turn *away* from the expanding state autonomy of the late New Deal" (166). Business leaders feared an expanded New Deal in the form of a "civilian-state authority" during and after the war. Waddell asserts that this federal entity was perceived as possibly allowing government and nonbusiness civilian leaders too much "control over business decisions" in the short and long runs (ibid., 166–67).

12. A. H. Sypher, "Post-War Problem No. 1," *Nation's Business,* May 1943, 21–22, 58 (first article in the series).

13. Brinkley, *End of Reform,* 260–64. The concept of full employment, in terms of the "right to a useful and remunerative job," can also be found in Roosevelt's "Second Bill of Rights," which was articulated in his famous "Four Freedoms" speech (11 January 1944). See Sunstein, *Second Bill of Rights,* 9–16.

14. Schuyler, "Views and Reviews," 1 September 1945, 7.

15. Roger William Riis, "Industry's Plan for Prosperity," *Advertising & Selling,* May 1943, 15, 16. Harris in *The Right to Manage* covers business groups in the 1940s who organized to handle unionization pressures and/or to counter the New Deal reforms. Harris discusses the NAM and the CED in this context (105–15, 118–25, 181–84).

16. Robert Collins, "American Corporatism: The Committee for Economic Development, 1942–1964," *Historian* 44 (February 1982): 153. Collins adds that the goals of the CED were focused on helping "businessmen plan for the reconversion to peacetime conditions and to determine . . . how high employment might be achieved" (ibid.).

17. Ibid., 155.

18. On the NAM anti–New Deal campaigns of the 1930s, see Marchand, *Creating the Corporate Soul,* 202–48; Burch, "The NAM as an Interest Group"; Ewen, *PR!* 215–336; "The National Association of Manufacturers and Public Relations during the New Deal," in Tedlow, *Keeping the Corporate Image;* Stromberg, "American Business." As the NAM launched its ideological mobilization of business, it simultaneously "pledged its knowledge and its resources to the task of national defense" in a *New York Times* ad on 23 June 1940 (ibid., 72). Though such a stance demonstrated that big business (including the NAM) was a willing participant in mobilization, corporate cooperation did not mean that the NAM would relinquish its anti–New Deal/pro–free enterprise agendas, which it had initiated in the 1930s. See also "Creative Discontent" in Bird, *"Better Living,"* 144–81. This chapter in Bird's study explores business organizations' campaigns, including that of the NAM, that "educated" the wartime public and labor on the business version of postwar America. This chapter also discusses the PR battle between corporate leaders and labor largely by examining media produced by labor organizations. Bird's focus in his study is on institutional films. See also "Little Towns and Big Corporations: The Wartime Imagery of a Nation United," in Marchand, *Creating the Corporate Soul,* 312–56, for corporate identity building, free enterprise messages, and wartime publicity. Marchand also covers the hostilities and fears that big business harbored toward the New Deal and how such animosity and anxiety surfaced in wartime commercial propaganda.

19. "'A Better America' Is Banner of Industry's Postwar Program," *Newsweek,* 20 December 1943, 50 (my emphasis).

20. See Marchand, *Creating the Corporate Soul,* 323–24, on corporate leaders' "rhetorical ploys" during the war, including usage of "regimentation" as a "code word for the New Deal."

21. "What Can We Do Starting Now. . . ," 1, 10. NAM/Hagley (my emphasis). (Document hereafter cited as "What Can We Do Starting Now . . . .") The full context of this presentation, and to whom it was specifically given, is unclear from the existing document. However, the basic NAM message is echoed throughout other published NAM/NIIC literature and advertising copy. Whenever I quote from this presentation, I will provide references to published NAM/NIIC sources where the intentions articulated in this 1943 presentation were carried out, including messages in ads from a 1944 nationwide newspaper campaign designed by Kenyon & Eckhardt for the NAM.

22. "What Can We Do Starting Now . . . ," 51B. The "inherent pioneer spirit" of America was also used to deploy NAM messages in newspapers. One example from the Kenyon & Eckhardt 1944 newspaper ad campaign was illustrated with a buckskin-clad mountain man. His wrinkled face, long hair, and chest-length beard referenced an indefatigable strength and inventive ethos—traits that he had passed on to his Machine Age progeny. See "Great, Great Grandpa Would Laugh Himself Sick!" NAM #1411, Series III, NIIC Box 848, Oversize Records, Subject Files, "Advertising," 1944, ad proofs produced by Kenyon & Eckhardt for the NIIC, NAM/Hagley.

23. James S. Adams, *Working Together for Postwar America* (New York: National Association of Manufacturers, 1943), 6. NAM #1411, Series III, Subject Files, NIIC Box 843, Folder: Campaign Promotion 1944, NAM/Hagley.

24. Ibid., 5–8. The concept that American progress and high standards of living are due to industrial management and *not* government is also expressed in the Kenyon & Eckhardt series of 1944 newspaper ads titled "How Americans Can Earn More, Buy More, Have More": "To assure post-war prosperity, Americans must be able to buy the output of an expanding industrial capacity. To make this possible, ever better values must be offered. . . . How You Can Help . . . By insisting on legislation that is 'good for jobs.' . . . Business operation under established laws instead of unpredictable 'directives.'" From "How Americans Can Earn More, Buy More, Have More," NAM #1411, Series III, NIIC Box 848, Oversize Records, Subject Files, "Advertising," 1944, Ad proofs produced by Kenyon & Eckhardt for the NIIC, NAM/Hagley. Though it has the same title as a Kenyon & Eckhardt ad cited later, this one has an insertion with slightly different copy.

25. The quote begins with the statement: "If we have thoroughly sound policy and speedy policy by government on [postwar reconversion]—and if we get our contract termination money quickly—it will help restore confidence on the part of the people who have pent-up purchasing power." From Second War Congress of American Industry, *Jobs in Peacetime: A Panel Discussion* (New York: NAM, 8 December 1944), 6, 7, 17. Stapled into "Conference on the Subject: 'What Can Industry Contribute to a Better America After the War,'" NAM #1411, Series III, NIIC Box 843, NAM/Hagley.

26. See Bird, *"Better Living,"* 146–47, on GM's 1942 publicity campaign that countered the United Auto Workers' (UAW) wartime claims heralding labor as the primary contributor to victory. GM countered with its emphasis on the corporation as responsible for victory. Its wartime slogan (as a counterresponse to the UAW's assertions)

was "Victory Is Our Business." The word "our" didn't necessary include or refer to labor, as the PR campaign was created for the sake of management.

27. James S. Adams, *Working Together for Postwar America,* 12. The Association of National Advertisers corroborated Adams's statement when it claimed that mobilization had shifted public opinion in favor of business: "Today business management has a tremendous backlog of public good will and appreciation which stems primarily from its war production achievements. . . . Thus, management finds itself today with a public much more inclined to recognize the achievements of business and to accept the leadership of business than was true as recently as two years ago." From *What the Public Thinks About You* (New York: Association of National Advertisers, 1944), 6, 7, 8. NAM #1411, NIIC Box 843, Advertising Subject File, NAM/Hagley.

28. Waddell in "Economic Mobilization" indicates that corporate leaders were able to "enhance" their "leverage" due to wartime mobilization, which required their managerial expertise in organizing resources and the industrial infrastructure. Thus, wartime necessities, as well as Roosevelt's eventual deferment to corporate expertise, helped restructure big business's reputation and increased its ability to influence the postwar economic reconversion to the benefit of the business community.

29. "What Can We Do Starting Now . . . ," 51C, 51E, 52. "The men who can get things done" is another reference to managerial superiority. Kenyon Research Corporation provides another example of management as superman: "A receptive audience awaits the plans of any group for solving the post-war unemployment problem. It is a time for management to step in and instill in the public confidence that industry is honestly trying and can solve this problem." From *Digest of Findings of Public Opinion Polls on the Subject of Post-war Problems and Planning* (New York: Kenyon Research Corporation, 1944), 6. NAM #1411, NIIC, Box 843, NAM/Hagley. A similar sentiment was expressed in an NAM ad from the defense period. Intended for management, it read: "Nearly 57% of the public believes that all or most large business is synonymous with monopoly. About 30% of our citizens have no idea what or who have done the most good for the country in the last ten years. . . . With the democratic system under attack on all sides [meaning from the federal government, too], if a democratic nation is to survive, *more than ever before* its citizens must have a clear understanding of the basic economic principles upon which that democracy has prospered" (original emphasis). From "In America Today It's the 'Don't Knows' Who Count," promotional flyer, NAM #1411, Series III, Subject Files, NIIC Box 848, Oversized Records: "Miscellaneous NIIC Material, 1938–1940," NAM/Hagley.

30. Ironically, some manufacturers had dragged their heels about mobilization because of their resentment of government controls. Industrial mobilization did *not* proceed as smoothly and voluntarily as the business propaganda suggested. On reluctance to convert, see Tedlow, *Keeping the Corporate Image,* 114; Beaumont, "Quantum Increase," 118. An initial isolationism among business leaders, which had a great deal to do with their mistrust of government influence in a war economy, was glossed over in propaganda detailing mobilization. See Stromberg's "American Business" for more on this isolationism.

31. *Business Week,* 29 July 1944, 47.

32. "What Can We Do Starting Now . . . ," 38I, 73, 79, 80, 85. See also "Introductory Material to Ads Recommended by [Arthur] Kudner." Very similar wording can be found in the booklet *An Advertising Program for the N.A.M.* (New York, Chicago,

Montreal, and Hollywood: Kenyon & Eckhardt, n.d.). NAM #1411, NIIC Box 843, Advertising 1943 Folder, NAM/Hagley. This booklet was produced for the NAM by the ad agency who developed their 1944 nationwide newspaper campaign, "How Americans Can Earn More, Buy More, Have More." Pages 3 and 6 of the booklet read: "What Should the Advertising Sell? . . . (1) We must show the public a road to the future that is more attractive because it is filled with more promise than anything our collectivist rivals can provide, and (2) We must convince them that business has a tangible policy for the realization of that future. . . . Americans turned to Government in the thirties out of fear, and out of the defeatist belief that we had reached the end of expansion. If we can only sell them *another feeling* about the future it will do as much as anything to change the course of our affairs."

The concept that business had the better deal for postwar America is articulated in the following ads produced for the NAM: "To make possible [a better future], a group of many business organizations representing more than 50,000 separate enterprises, has adopted and published a blueprint for the future. It is called, *A Platform for a Better America.*' In this plain-spoken document, business has pledged itself unreservedly to the principles of *greater earnings for more people* and *more for their money in better, lower-priced goods.* It proposes to accomplish these objectives through full and free competition, properly regulated, under law [i.e., no New Deal plans like the NRA] to prevent any kind of monopoly. But to make this possible also requires *your* assistance. . . . You, by encouraging wise legislation . . . see to it that business is regulated by law rather than by government 'directive,' so it can lay its plans with certainty of seeing them through" (original emphasis). From "So You Think He's Ready for the Old Folks' Home!" NAM #1411, Series III, NIIC Box 848, Oversize Records, NAM/Hagley.

See also the following Arthur Kunder, Inc., ad, which was geared for newspaper circulation in 1944: "Right now, American business is heart and soul behind the nation's war effort. But it has a program which it believes will make fullest use of America's commercial and industrial strength—for the common benefit of the whole nation in a postwar world. . . . But . . . it will take cooperation—and the government can help industry do its job if it will take such steps as these: *Clear the way for national harmony and progress* through government policies which recognize that only free [i.e., unregulated] men have futures worth working for . . . *Clear the way for postwar jobs* by . . . prompt reconversion [and] disposal of government-owned plants and surplus . . . *Clear the way for postwar buying* by freeing the American public from needless red tape and restrictions as soon as the war is won . . . It is a freedom to shape, by our own hard efforts, the kind of bright life that has been so freely and glibly *promised*—but never has been, and never can be, handed to us by any force [i.e., such as government] outside ourselves" (original emphasis). From "Does Business Have a Program for a Better Postwar America?" NAM #1411, Series III, NIIC Box 848, Oversize Records, NAM/Hagley.

33. "How Americans Can Earn More, Buy More, Have More," NAM #1411, Series III, NIIC Box 848, Oversize Records, Subject Files, "Advertising," 1944, ad proofs produced by Kenyon & Eckhardt for the NIIC, NAM/Hagley (original emphasis). The booklet is in box 842 of this collection. The Kenyon & Eckhardt newspaper ads for the NIIC were generally text heavy, with no illustrations, and their large scale suggests that they were most likely printed full-page. The copy varies slightly from ad to

ad in the campaign. For another NAM booklet intended for the public's edification, see Ryllis and Omar Goslin, *Primer for Americans* (New York: NAM, 1940). This publication was targeted to American women. NAM #1411, Series III, NIIC Box 846, NAM/Hagley.

34. NIIC, *A Time for Action: The Job That Industry Must Do Now* (New York: NAM, 1944), n.p. NAM #1411, Series III, Box 842, NAM/Hagley (emphasis in original). A similar booklet by the NIIC also sought support for "the N.A.M.'s Public Information Program" from "all business, all non-industrial groups, and patriotic citizens." See NIIC, *Vigilance Today for a Free Enterprise Tomorrow* (New York: NAM, n.d.). NAM #1411, Series III, Box 846, NAM/Hagley.

35. "Re-Selling the American Way to America," promotional flyer, NAM #1411, Series III, Subject Files, NIIC Box 848, Oversized Records: "Miscellaneous NIIC Material, 1938–1940," NAM/Hagley.

36. James S. Adams, *Working Together for Postwar America,* 14. Adams's speech was published in the aforementioned booklet for the 1943 annual meeting of the National Association of Insurance Agents in Pittsburgh, Pennsylvania. The booklet has an NAM copyright. Selling the system of free enterprise was also part of the NAM public relations strategy during the Depression. See Tedlow, *Keeping the Corporate Image,* 72. Using advertising to communicate the business postwar agenda and plans in order to sway public opinion is also described in "Stop Shouting 'Free Enterprise' Unless You Give the Term Meaning: A Constructive Suggestion for 'Institutional' Advertisers," *Printer's Ink* (ca. 1940). John Orr Young, Public Relations Counsel, writes, "The opportunity that businessmen want in postwar America, however, lends itself to advertising that reaches the felt needs and concrete aspirations of the American people." From NAM #1411, Series III, Subject Files, NIIC Box 848, Oversized Records: "Miscellaneous NIIC Material, 1938–1940," NAM/Hagley.

37. "'A Better America' Is Banner of Industry's Postwar Program," 50.

38. *American Home,* May 1942, 27. The copy also refers to the wartime use of Armco Steel as a product proving ground. Framing the purpose of the war as a fight for a better America defined by democratizing higher standards of living was also articulated in NAM ads intended for newspapers. "Maybe it did take a brutal war to shake us out of our bad dream of the thirties. But America . . . is on the march again. Will we slip back when the war is over? Not unless we think that poverty and backwardness and lack of full opportunity for all aren't every bit as worthy of our blood and our steel as the Japs and Nazis. The re-birth of our . . . incredibly increased productivity, can give us a life of abundance such as no people on earth . . . has ever seen." From "So You Think He's Ready for the Old Folks' Home!" Some of this copy can be found almost verbatim in other NAM newspaper ads from 1944.

39. Beaumont states that "war-bond drives were designed not to buy war matériel but to soak up surplus earnings which could generate inflation" ("Quantum Increase," 129). He thus provides another example of the ulterior motives behind war bond advertising.

40. Walter Adams, "Mystery Weapon Today," 21, 65, 67.

41. Strasser in *Waste and Want* looks briefly at war bond messages, especially in light of scrap salvage campaigns (231). Westbrook in "Fighting for the American Family" briefly covers the issue of war bonds and the commercial incentives for which Americans were supposedly fighting—at least according to the ads (213–15).

42. Samuel in *Pledging Allegiance* explains how government and business played roles in shaping public expectations that abundance would result from America's participation (and sacrifice) in the war. Samuel stresses that a consensus emerged during the war in which "personal aspirations, nationalism, and consumerism" were fused together and that the ideology behind the Treasury's marketing of war bonds "effectively translated New Deal populism into wartime capitalism and served as a tangible articulation of pluralistic democracy" (xiv, 15).

43. Jacobs in "'Democracy's Third Estate'" asserts that consumers' purchasing power became greatly politicized during the war—even more so than it had been during the Depression within New Deal discourse, policies, and programs.

44. Samuel, *Pledging Allegiance*, 31.

45. Ibid., xvii, 13.

46. Ibid., 14.

47. Wynn, *The Afro-American*, 40–43, 48–56.

48. See Samuel, *Pledging Allegiance*, 136–38; and Honey, *Bitter Fruit*, 257–59. Honey's anthology includes several articles, poems, and pieces of fiction that dealt with blacks' double fight and the ironies persistent in the wartime mandate to make, in the words of a popular slogan, "the world safe for democracy" (see 259–314).

49. Mary McLeod Bethune, "Along the Battlefronts," *People's Voice*, 14 February 1942, 14.

50. Ibid., 14.

51. "Does Business Have a Program for a Better Postwar America?" NAM #1411, Series III, NIIC Box 848, Oversize Records, NAM/Hagley.

52. "Guts," NAM #1411, Series III, NIIC Box 848, Oversize Records, Subject Files, "Advertising," 1944, ad proofs produced by Kenyon & Eckhardt for the NIIC, NAM/Hagley.

53. For more on the New Deal's participation in structuring support of the war effort as an impetus toward higher standards of living, see Jacobs, "'How About Some Meat?'" which states, "Much government propaganda during World War II actually fueled popular expectations that abundance was not only a reward for winning the war but the essence of American life itself" (910). Though a powerful and relevant observation, Jacobs does not distinguish the extent to which leaders from business actually controlled and disseminated wartime propaganda that came from government bureaus. Although Roosevelt and Morgenthau indeed promoted the war in this way, one cannot tell from Jacobs's statement if she is referring to a propaganda strategy that was strictly governmental or one also influenced by business. Due to the significant role the WAC played in coordinating government wartime information and business public relations needs, it is sometimes difficult to segregate government propaganda from that of business. For examples of government and business's wartime wedding and the frictions that surfaced in their union, see Catton, *Warlords of Washington*. Leff in "The Politics of Sacrifice" explores the "privatizing of the wartime propaganda apparatus" as it pertained to the symbolism of wartime sacrifice (1318). The principle, ownership, and responsibility of sacrifice infused wartime discourse from government policymaking to private advertising.

54. *Better Homes and Gardens*, June 1943, 16.

55. *Life*, 12 October 1942, 9. For more on the Hotpoint war bond campaign and how advertisers tied the war effort to an incentive plan for postwar consumer purchases

(especially in terms of domestic products), see the article by the manager of the advertising division of General Electric, H. E. Warren, "Take a Kitchen—and Wrap It Well," *Advertising & Selling,* July 1945, 58, 60, 94, 96, 98. The reader will no doubt note that the Hotpoint ad invites consumers to write to General Electric (GE) for a "home planning file" in which women were encouraged to save "ideas for your new home." For more on this wartime promotional strategy, see Shanken, "From Total War to Total Living." For another example of the streamlined kitchen in war bond advertising, see the Congoleum-Nairn ad in *Ladies' Home Journal,* October 1944, 172. The Universal company provided consumers with a checklist of incentives for purchasing more war bonds: "Check here for the Universal appliances you've dreamed of owning." Consumers were encouraged to send away for a planning kit called "U plan for V day," which referred not only to the end of the war but also to a consumer's victory (*Ladies' Home Journal,* February 1944, 111).

56. Note that the house features a very traditional style with shutters and a chimney.

57. *Better Homes and Gardens,* June 1943, 3.

58. *American Home,* May 1943, 3. See also the GE advertisement "That dream home on BOND STREET will come true," *Collier's,* 6 March 1943, 43, which is very similar to GE's "U.S. Victory Highway 1." War bond ads illustrated the "house of tomorrow" in conventional middle-class architectural clichés, such as pitched roofs, chimneys, and dormer windows, as if to suggest that the war would lead to security and continuity in the controlled environment of a well-manicured suburbia. I will elaborate on this issue and also explore the human-engineering rhetoric and symbols within such advertisements in chapter 8.

59. See chapters 6 and 7 for more on social evolution metaphors in "world of tomorrow" narratives pertaining to the postwar house and kitchen.

60. Throughout this chapter and others, we will see how the term "better" was a highly loaded adjective in wartime discourse about the postwar world.

61. See especially "African Americans and World War II Bonds," in Samuel, *Pledging Allegiance,* 127–86.

62. "The Convenient Accused," *Pittsburgh Courier,* 9 January 1945, 1. See the lower left corner of figure 6.9, which has a "buy war bonds" appeal with the American Revolutionary War minuteman figure as illustrated by the *Pittsburgh Courier.* For more on the messages voiced by African American journalists and columnists during the war, see Washburn, *A Question of Sedition.*

63. James S. Adams, *Working Together for Postwar America,* 5–8, 11–12. The NAM newspaper ads stress labor's cooperation with management. One ad in particular insisted that business would uphold its end of the prosperity bargain if the public would take steps to "*Clear the way for sound labor relations* by the development of a labor policy recognizing that labor and management each have responsibilities to be met as well as rights to be enjoyed—and that they are natural allies rather than natural enemies" (original emphasis). From "Does Business Have a Program for a Better Postwar America?" Similar wording and concepts are found in the NAM ad "Let's Work for Industrial Peace," NAM #1411, Series III, NIIC Box 862, NAM/Hagley. The NAM's "Soldiers of Production" rallies also highlighted labor/management cooperation. The NAM produced brochures to assist manufacturers in staging "employee morale drives" where an NIIC spokesperson would deliver a keynote address. See *Soldiers of Production,* NAM #1411, Series III, NIIC Box 846, NAM/Hagley.

64. "Conference on the Subject: 'What Can Industry Contribute,'" n.p. James Adams, in his 1943 speech, made a similar remark: "What [things do] the American people want in the postwar world? . . . They include productive jobs for all, higher standards of living, economic security, economic opportunity, and individual freedom. And full production is the only method of attaining them. . . . Higher standards of living come only from production. . . . Consumers must have an incentive to buy. New products and better products must be developed. Advertising must be used extensively to stimulate public desire for them." James S. Adams, *Working Together for Postwar America,* 5–8, 11–12.

65. NAM ad campaigns especially stressed that the public needed to earn its prosperity and freedom. "Brave men and women have fought and died to win American rights for me. But these rights truly belong to me only if I earn them." From "Eight American Rights and Eight American Duties," NAM #1411, Series III, NIIC Box 848, Oversize Records, NAM/Hagley. A note at the bottom of this ad reads, "Reprinted by the NIIC from a leaflet used in a large American city's school system, by permission of Board of School Commissioners—1943." The "earning" concept was also defined as the public's proactive pursuit of postwar prosperity. Freedom was not defined as "freedom from responsibility." See the NIIC publication from the "You and Industry" series: *The Freedom We Defend* (1941; New York: NAM, 1943), NAM #1411, Series III, NIIC Box 846, NAM/Hagley. This thirty-five-plus-page booklet, intended for the "average" American, included a table comparing "the type of services you receive in America compared with what you would have if you lived in a totalitarian state" (n.p.). Much of the list under "Totalitarian State" echoed the current wartime rationing and regulations.

66. See Ewen, *PR!* 288–336.

67. *Digest of Findings,* 6, 10, 21, 25. For more on the issue of convincing the public to unfreeze its war bond savings to help stimulate postwar progress, see Leo Cherne, "We *Can* Buy Postwar Prosperity," *Science Digest,* February 1945, 1–5. The NIIC's guide for advertisers showed how this plan would be devised: "ALTERNATIVE APPROACHES TO ADVERTISING SERIES . . . Copy to develop idea that during the war, the consumers' purchases of War Bonds bought guns. But in peace, they provide employment. . . . So every purchase the housewife makes helps build a job for someone." From NIIC, "Alternative Approaches to Advertising Series," 2 December 1943, NAM #1411, NIIC Box 843, Advertising 1943 Folder, NAM/Hagley. The NIIC elaborated on this concept again in *What the Public Thinks About You,* where it blatantly stated: "We have made Americans want more and better things—enough so that they work harder and more intelligently in order to buy those things about which we have so persuasively told them. This acts like a steady dosage of vitamins in stimulating ambition and activity in our economy. . . . Our real progress in using advertising to promote doctrines and ideas through informative messages has had its greatest impetus since Pearl Harbor" (1).

68. For more on the issue of consumption fostering postwar prosperity and jobs, see Mordecai Ezekiel, "The Road to Postwar Prosperity," *Science Digest,* September 1943, 37–42. Robert Higgs in "Wartime Prosperity? A Reassessment of the U.S. Economy in the 1940s," *Journal of Economic History* 52 (March 1992): 41–60, argues that full, steady employment and full production in wartime did not by themselves lead to recovery from the Depression. Nor did these high levels of employment and production

alone create an economic boom after victory. A wartime economy is a "command economy" in which supply and demand are all predicated on the needs of the military, the ultimate consumer. Despite jobs, escalating production, and war bond sales, the wartime economy was not real prosperity, regardless of widespread belief to the contrary both during and long after the war. Higgs highlights the significance of "the build up of financial wealth" by investors and the public as contributing to the postwar economic boom—but even the creation of wealth did not alone pull the United States out of the Depression. Rather, Higgs asserts that it was the psychological catalyst of optimism—a "transformation of expectations"—that was largely responsible for postwar prosperity. Due to the necessities of wartime production, people perceived the "possibility of genuine economic recovery," which eventually came to fruition (ibid., 58).

69. Interestingly, critics of the techno-corporate order saw through business's postwar vision schemes: "This dream of utilizing the scientific advances made under the stress of war to streamline and cushion the American home is not merely for the favored few. Industry has in mind the mass market. . . . All [business] asks from the government is freedom from excessive regulation and taxation. . . . Business, big and little, now wants to show what it can do in the interest of the common good. . . . For with many American business leaders rugged individualism has been replaced by a new sense of social responsibility." "Post-war Life of Riley?" *Commonweal,* 10 September 1943, 506–8.

70. Stromberg argues that business underwent an ideological shift in which an initial isolationist attitude toward the war waned when business leaders' "fear of wartime controls gradually dissipated." Stromberg emphasizes, "It could be argued . . . that once businessmen were at the helm of the defense commission, their attitude toward government control underwent a remarkable change" ("American Business," 74, 75). This shift is attributed to the idea that democracy and free enterprise were at greater risk from tyrannical threats abroad than from those at home. I would argue that this may have been the case for some individuals or may have occurred at varying degrees throughout the business community, but, as the documents quoted herein attest, it was not true for conservative business leaders on the whole. I would assert that the "chief irony" of the war (as Stromberg puts it) was that business actually profited symbolically and financially from a mobilization it initially resisted and from an administration it considered its "inveterate enemy" (ibid., 78). I would caution against considering business as monolithic in its thinking, even in terms of intervention versus isolation. For example, Catton reveals that businessmen did not possess a monopoly on isolationism. Some anti–New Dealers were for intervention while others were not. The same split occurred among liberals (*Warlords of Washington,* 16–17).

71. Antonin Heythum, "Industrial Design in Wartime," *Architect & Engineer,* September 1940, 24.

72. Industrial design, like advertising, also promoted itself as a purveyor of progress and a stimulant of the desire for ever higher standards of living. Although nineteenth-century industrially produced objects for sale had been "designed," the concept and process of "styling" (changing the appearance of mass-produced goods for the purpose of stimulating consumption) had not been widely adopted and put into practice by the business community until the 1920s—at about the same time when advertising began relying on psychological manipulation to perpetuate consumer dissatisfaction

and thereby increase sales. Although "styling" had connotations of surface decoration, industrial designers emphasized that they put a high priority on adapting appearance to functional utility, and thus many times they lauded their efforts as "efficiency engineering" or "rational planning." For more on the history of how the business community commercialized art and wedded it to the corporate rhetoric of mass production, see Ewen, *Captains of Consciousness,* 61–67. For more on the intersection between art, industry, and business prior to World War II, see Michele H. Bogart, *Artists, Advertising, and the Borders of Art* (Chicago: University of Chicago Press, 1995); Terry Smith, *Making the Modern;* Rydell, *World of Fairs.*

73. Furniture designer Don Wallance received a commission with the Office of the Quartermaster General's Research and Development Branch, for which he designed "army equipment ranging from portable tent shelters to funerary caskettes [*sic*]." His close observation of efficient army life led to the development of standardized furniture for the army in the postwar years, which he later tried to convert to civilian use. See "Planning for the Furniture Requirements of the Army," 1947, Don Wallance Collection, Box 4 (Projects Furniture, U.S. Army), Cooper-Hewitt Museum, National Museum of Design, Smithsonian Institution, New York. Hans Knoll, whose company's minimalist furniture designs became the hallmark of a corporate efficiency aesthetic after the war, recruited Florence Schust, his future wife and business partner, to design an office for Henry Stimson, secretary of war. See Eric Larrabee and Massimo Vignelli, *Knoll Design* (New York: Harry N. Abrams, 1981), 19. Raymond Spilman, between 1942 and 1946, designed a waterproof flashlight, portable field telephone, and signal flash gun for the U.S. Army Signal Corps. See Box 5, Armed Forces Equipment Folder, Spilman Collection, Syracuse University. See also "Defense Called Spur to Industrial Design," *New York Times,* 4 October 1941, 28. A staff of jewelers in Norman Bel Geddes's design office created miniature replicas of battle scenes for news photographers. See Bel Geddes, *War Maneuver Models Created for Life Magazine* (New York: Museum of Modern Art, 1944). Henry Dreyfuss "was connected with the development of radar equipment, automatic plotting devices, and world globes . . . used by Roosevelt, Churchill, Stalin, and the Chiefs of Staff." He acted as consultant with "Army Ordnance, the Office of Strategic Services, the Red Cross, and other government agencies." See Dreyfuss, *A Record of Industrial Designs, 1929 through 1946* (New York: n.p., 1946). Russell Wright created nesting dishware for the navy out of plastics. See "Reducing Breakage in the Navy," *Modern Plastics,* November 1942, 80–81, 122.

74. Kirkham, *Charles and Ray Eames,* 212–14. The Eameses' wartime design team included Harry Bertoia, Herbert Matter, and architect Gregory Ain. See also Peter S. Reed, "Enlisting Modernism," and Robert Friedel, "Scarcity and Promise: Materials and American Domestic Culture during World War II," in Albrecht, *World War II,* 2–41, 42–89; John Neuhart, Marilyn Neuhart, and Ralph Caplan, *Connections: The Work of Charles and Ray Eames* (Los Angeles: Frederick S. Wight Art Gallery, University of California, 1976), 23. See also "Furniture's War," *Business Week,* 13 June 1942, 62.

75. Heythum, "Industrial Design in Wartime," 23.

76. Teague, "Industry Plans for the Future," 109–10, 156, 158.

77. Raymond Loewy, "Selling Through Design," *Art & Industry,* February 1942, 37, 38.

78. Teague, "Design for Peace," 156.

79. Definitely, designers worked with the government during the war. And certainly, we cannot consider the design profession to be monolithic in its thinking and

approach. But as noted in the introduction and in chapter 1, although disagreements abounded between the New Deal administration and the business community, of which designers were members, antagonism toward Roosevelt or the New Deal did not stop businessmen from participating in wartime production.

80. Rich, "The Public Expects Progress," 36, 150–51. Rich was a Teague associate. Parker James also spoke of the "NEED FOR PLANNING" during the war, not after: "Industry's postwar future depends on intelligent planning right now, and those companies with no plans at all should lose no time in carving their niche in the postwar pattern" ("Products for Postwar," 15). The same argument in terms of design and how it would "revive our trade" after the war can be found in "The Future of Industrial Design," *Art & Industry,* August 1943, 33–35. Donald Dailey, of the design firm Harold Van Doren and Associates, encouraged business to adapt for new postwar consumer markets. According to his industry's (somewhat biased) advice, changing the appearance of a prewar product would prove the big factor in cashing in on the postwar market. See Dailey, "What Will the Postwar Consumer Want?" *Advertising & Selling,* June 1943, 54, 56. For a glowing report of the necessity of the industrial designer as a business asset, and how the war supposedly increased the awareness of his value, see "The Industrial Design Consultant," *Art & Industry,* March 1944, 69, 78–79.

81. Rich, "The Public Expects Progress," 152.

82. Teague, "Industry Plans for the Future," 109–10, 156, 158.

83. In looking through various designers' client files from collections at Syracuse University, Cooper-Hewitt Museum of Design, and University of Texas, Austin (which holds Norman Bel Geddes's papers), there are references to many projects that designers worked on during the war that were not geared for military ordnance, suggesting that designers' pronouncements about planning for the postwar economy during the war must have been readily heeded.

84. According to Tedlow, belief in the rightness and potential of corporate autocracy was never lost "even in the Depression's darkest days" (*Keeping the Corporate Image,* 62).

Chapter 6

1. Carlisle and Latham, *Miracles Ahead!* 29.

2. The political response to the media's portrayal of shantytowns and Hoovervilles burgeoned into the New Deal's housing legislation, which included the inception of the Federal Housing Administration (FHA) and the Public Works Administration's Housing Division. For more on the New Deal and housing in the 1930s, see Kenneth Jackson, *Crabgrass Frontier,* 193–230; Wright, *Building the Dream,* 220–29; Joseph Arnold, *The New Deal in the Suburbs: A History of the Greenbelt Program, 1935–1954* (Columbus: Ohio State University Press, 1971).

3. "The House We Live In," *Ebony,* January 1946, 20. According to *Ebony,* statistics were retained from the U.S. Housing Census of 1940, reported in 1941.

4. For more on the wartime housing dilemma, see "Building for Defense . . . Headway and Headaches," and Edith Elmer Wood, "Building for Defense . . . Emergency Housing Proposals," *Architectural Forum,* April 1941, 10, 12, 14, 18, 98, 102, 106. For more on the anticipated postwar housing crisis, see "Construction Potentials: Postwar Prospects and Problems, a Basis for Action," *Architectural Record,* December 1943, 1–32.

5. Thanks to David Vis for the wording "built-in better living," a takeoff on "better living built in" as found in figure 5.7.

6. Lupton and Miller, *The Bathroom,* 41–47; Hayden in *The Grand Domestic Revolution* covers the history of domestic science and rational household planning from the nineteenth to the early twentieth centuries.

7. This trend continued throughout the 1930s as well. Many articles published during the Depression about household modernization offered ways in which the family of moderate income could raise their house's "proper" efficiency level through economical, rational planning. From *American Home,* see "The Magic Kitchen," January 1938, 39, 58, and "Streamlined for $9.92!" March 1941, 123; see also "Trends in Sanitation," *Architectural Record,* November 1939, 66–73. The article shows pictures of the hazards experienced from lack of sanitary running water and waste disposal systems from the eighteenth to the twentieth centuries. Coupled with these images of unhygienic doom is the pinnacle of scientific achievement in bathroom and kitchen utility design, including Buckminster Fuller's machine-stamped bathroom unit, which is discussed in this chapter. On experiments and opinions about tackling the housing problem during the 1920s and 1930s, see Baxandall and Ewen, *Picture Windows,* 37–77.

8. Fuller had initially called his house the 4-D Utility Unit, referring to the fourth dimension. "Dymaxion," a more scientific-sounding title, was coined by publicists for Marshall Field's department store in Chicago, where a small model was first exhibited in April 1929.

9. Brian Horrigan, "The Home of Tomorrow," in Joseph J. Corn, ed., *Imagining Tomorrow: History, Technology and the American Future,* 139–41, 160 (Cambridge, Mass.: MIT Press, 1986). Fuller also devised a mobile, "trailer" version of his "scientific" house plan, which would ensure that maximum personal cleanliness and domestic efficiency could be transported anywhere. See "The Mechanical Wing," *Architectural Forum,* October 1940, 273, supp. 92.

10. On the state of these trends in 1939, see "Equipment for the Modern House," *Architectural Record,* November 1939, 77–81. The article discusses electrical heating panels, the mechanical core, built-ins, and trends toward utility unit prefabrication and standardization. Companies that sold kitchen equipment, flooring, and cabinetry sponsored experimental houses and kitchens at world's fairs, and they also held contests and public expositions to promote both their products and their rational planning services. On the Glass Container Association's experimental all-glass kitchen, see "All Clear," *House Beautiful,* October 1938, 68, 117; on the all-gas kitchen of the American Gas Association, and an all-electric one from GE, see "Kitchens of Today, Built for Tomorrow," *House & Garden,* August 1935, 22–23, 72; on the GE Architectural Competition, see "Houses with All the Comforts of Home," *Good Housekeeping,* September 1935, 84–85, 165. On magazine sponsorship of experimental reform kitchens and housing displays, see "The Institute Presents the Kitchen and Laundry at the Good Housekeeping–Stran-Steel House, A Century of Progress, Chicago," *Good Housekeeping,* August 1933, 88–89, 124. On the plan by the Good Housekeeping Institute for Gas Exhibits, see "Homewood Kitchen at the New York World's Fair," *Good Housekeeping,* July 1939, 138–39. "House Beautiful's Ivory Washable House at Rockefeller Home Center, New York," *House Beautiful,* November 1940, 59–62. On experimental reform kitchens and housing for African Americans, see discussions of the post–World War I campaign "Better Homes in America" in Brooks, "Consumer Markets and Consumer

Magazines," 44, 58–63. A broader discussion of this social reform movement (which largely encompassed white middle-class domesticity) can be found in Karen E. Altman, "Modernity, Gender, and Consumption: Public Discourses on Woman and the Home" (Ph.D. diss., University of Iowa, 1987). The "Better Homes in America" campaign, launched between 1921 and 1922 and ended in 1935, pulled together the (sometimes conflicting) "interests of government, academia, and the media" (Brooks, "Consumer Markets and Consumer Magazines," 58). See Kenneth Jackson, *Crabgrass Frontier,* where the commercial intentions behind the 1930s corporate-sponsored model house are briefly discussed (187). Companies such as GE in 1935 and *Ladies' Home Journal* sponsored "house of tomorrow" competitions, but the demonstration houses' main attractions were their array of gadgets, and their primary goal was to stimulate immediate sales, not to offer long-term solutions to democratizing higher standards of living by narrowing the progress gap between classes.

11. On prewar rational planning, built-in and flush-surface appliances and cabinetry, and the "scientific" kitchen, see Eleanor Raymond, "A Model Kitchen: Designed for the Woman Who Does Her Own Work," *House Beautiful,* June 1933, 269–71, 289. Eleanor Raymond was the architect of this kitchen. See also "What Is Happening to the Kitchen?" *Good Housekeeping,* January 1933, 84–85; "Kitchens in Logical Order," *Better Homes and Gardens,* October 1934, 18–19, 100. On the Brooklyn Union Gas Kitchen Compact built-in kitchen unit, see "Unit Kitchen," *Business Week,* 10 June 1933, 12–13. See also "Six Experts Design Our Ideal House," *House & Garden,* July 1935, 21–23, 64, 66, 69–70, 72; "Planning the Service Unit," *House & Garden,* April 1937, 56; "Now We Buy Kitchens by the Package," *American Home,* November 1936, 32, 100; "New Structural Materials for Your Kitchen," *American Home,* June 1938, 31–32, 54.

12. For a more detailed study covering marketing, advertising, and retailing modern design during the 1930s, see Kristina Wilson, ed., *Livable Modernism: Interior Decorating and Design during the Great Depression* (New Haven, Conn.: Yale University Press, 2004).

13. The cartoon was found in Wright, *Building the Dream,* 228, and was credited to Keith Temple.

14. Tessie Agan in her 1939 textbook asserted the common euthenics-inspired assumption that delinquency was a socially unhygienic trait because overcrowding and substandard housing did not just create physical risk but were also mentally and emotionally damaging: "Bad housing does not automatically or inevitably produce delinquents, [but] it is one of the major factors in warping the lives of the young and bringing them into conflict with society" (*The House,* 28).

15. "Delinquency's" nose is a bit obscured from the reader, but one can make out the protruding upturned hook at the end—a feature commonly ascribed to the Irish type that, although white, was deemed innately unable to adequately assimilate into America's Anglo-Saxon "nativist" society. See Banta, *Imaging American Women,* for nineteenth-century narratives of physiognomy and the Irish type.

16. Our slum protagonists have also been drawn in slouching positions. According to Agan, proper posture had hygienic value (*The House,* 261).

17. On euthenics, architecture, and urban planning in the decades before the war, see Cogdell, *Eugenic Design,* 160–74.

18. Agan, *The House,* 18.

19. Walter Dorwin Teague, "A Sane Prediction About the House You'll Live in After the War," *House Beautiful*, August 1943, 75. For predictions about an automatic postwar house, see Gilbert Rohde, "Gadgets for 194X," *Architectural Forum*, September 1942, 112–13; see also "Tomorrow's House—and Gadgetry," *Business Week*, 9 March 1946, 18, regarding Fritz B. Burns's house, which is covered in chapter 8. For other visions of how wartime experience would alter traditional furniture, appliance, and house design in the postwar future, see Carlisle and Latham, *Miracles Ahead!* 15–26, regarding Paul Nelson's plan for the postwar house as a shell fitted with prefabricated room units, which could be traded in like used cars; Elizabeth Coit's visions of the apartment house of the future, in which the efficiency of bedrooms would be maximized with built-in furniture, which would also eliminate a chore because dust would not collect under them; and Walter B. Sanders's apartment of the future, in which tenants would purchase standardized units of movable panels with a trade-in value and plug them into loft buildings consisting of just the rentable floor and ceiling space.

20. Teague, "A Sane Prediction," 58.

21. Ibid., 73, 75.

22. Stuart Ewen says that much wartime advertising (especially that which was influenced by the NAM agenda) spoke to the working class in order to raise their expectations for progress and possible entry into the middle class. Doing so, it was believed, would make them complacent and would quell labor discontent. Ewen, *PR!* 343–45.

23. "Industrializing Shelter: The Fuller House," *Architectural Record*, May 1946, 118–20, 134.

24. Ibid., 119–20, 134. Fuller's $6,500 price tag would not have included the price of the lot, and would have still been affordable to many average consumers possessing modest, but steadily rising, incomes after the war. Of course, for low-income families, $6,500 would have been out of the question. See "Construction Potentials," 31. Despite his attempts to capitalize on the mystique of wartime science and aircraft technology, Fuller's solution to the postwar housing crisis never really got off the ground, so to speak. The Wichita, Kansas, promotional model was the only Dymaxion to be built at full scale. See "What Has Become of Yesterday's Inventions?" *Business Week*, 8 March 1952, 88–89.

25. "Industrializing Shelter," 120, 134. Fuller's design reflected his sensitivity to household pests, inconveniences, and dust: "New floor coverings will curve slightly at the walls, to eliminate inaccessible dust collection." From "Dwelling Machines," *Architectural Record*, April 1945, 122.

26. Teague, "Design for Peace," 155 (my emphasis).

27. Ibid., 155–56.

28. Ibid., 156.

29. Ibid.

30. Carlisle and Latham, *Miracles Ahead!* 1, 5–6.

31. The terms "modernist," "modernism," and "modern" should not be read as a monolithic style, whether in painting, sculpture, architecture, commercial objects, or graphics. For an assessment of the variations in the aesthetic and a critique of its misinterpretation, see Rosemarie Haag Bletter, "The Myths of Modernism," in Janet Kardon, ed., *Craft in the Machine Age, 1920–1945,* 46–51 (New York: Harry N. Abrams and the American Craft Museum, 1996). A modernist design vocabulary was frequently used in prototypes but not necessarily in houses for a middle-class housing market.

See Rosemarie Bletter, "The World of Tomorrow: The Future with a Past," in *High Styles: Twentieth-Century American Design,* 86–90 (New York: Whitney Museum and Summit Books, 1985), for more on American responses to modernist architecture and the International Style. Regarding how structures built for world's fairs were for showmanship and were accepted for domestic consumption only by a small minority of home buyers, see Thomas Holden, "New Materials, New Construction Methods, New House Architecture," in Zucker, *New Architecture,* 140. The disparity between modernist austerity and middle-class consumer taste for period styles is covered by Kristina Wilson in *Livable Modernism.* Wilson writes that modernist-trained designers of the 1930s developed a compromise that would help make their functional Machine Age aesthetic appeal to the average middle-class consumer's taste and comfort. She dubs this "sympathetic model" "livable modernism" (ibid., 3–4). In magazines geared for average consumers, traditional-style postwar "houses of tomorrow" were more common than modernist fantasies. Naturally, one exception was the airport of tomorrow depicted in designer John Tjaarda's article "Your Home, Your Clothes, Your Car Tomorrow," in which teardrop cars possess detachable airplane wings (*American Magazine,* May 1943, 44–45). In certain cases, depictions of a modernist, flat-roofed suburbia were intended as parodies about the "miracles" forecast for postwar living. See David O. Woodbury, "Your Life Tomorrow," *Collier's,* 8 May 1943, 40.

32. On the historical roots and development of modernism's functionalist aversion to ornament and its practitioners' embrace of machine forms as inspiration for aesthetic standards, see Brent C. Bolin, *The Failure of Modern Architecture* (New York: Van Nostrand Reinhold, 1976), 14–59. Bolin's study reveals the irrational flaws behind modernism's rational dictates.

33. Whether Wright considered himself a "modernist" is not the point here, but the idioms of his style definitely had an influence on the modernist vocabulary of the twentieth century, including that of the International Style, to which he was adamantly opposed, as least publicly.

34. For an examination of the suburban house styles that did emerge after the war, see Tom Martinson, *American Dreamscape: The Pursuit of Happiness in Postwar Suburbia* (New York: Carroll & Graf, 2000).

35. Teague expressed these concepts into the 1950s. See "The Growth and Scope of Industrial Design in the U.S.," *Journal of the Royal Society of Arts* (July 1959): 640–51. Found in Cogdell, *Eugenic Design,* 165.

36. The California-style model, though somewhat marginalized in this depiction, would have been an acceptable "healthy house" solution found more often in upscale neighborhoods, especially in warm, sunny regions, rather than in standard middle-class suburbia. See figure 6.6 as an extreme example. The California style's appeal (to those in the minority) was its intention to promote health by bringing the outdoors inside. Holden describes this type of house and predicts its increase in the future ("New Materials," 146). For a historical perspective on California modernist houses of the prewar years, see Wendy Kaplan, "Building Utopia: Pioneer Modernism on the American West Coast," in Paul Greenhalgh, ed., *Modernism in Design,* 101–22 (London: Reaktion Books, 1990); Martinson, *American Dreamscape,* 158, 165.

37. Teague, "A Sane Prediction," 48. *Fortune* magazine confirmed this assumption about the future's mechanical service core in its 1942 postwar economic prediction "The United States in a New World," 20.

38. Holden, "New Materials," 140–41.

39. Holden says that builders apply old designs to new methods and materials in order to avoid having to sell innovations at the same time as trying to sell the house. They instead seek to "avoid the stigma of producing 'freak' houses" (ibid., 141). Robert L. Davison's article, "When Science Takes Over the Home," in Zucker, *New Architecture and City Planning,* also discusses the reputation and realities of prefab houses (151–52).

40. For a critique of the fears, myths, and logistic and economic problems raised by mass-producing houses after the assembly manner of Henry Ford, see Douglas Haskell, "Houses Like Fords," *Harper's,* February 1934, 286–98; "Housing and Prefabrication: Some Reasons Why the Factory Will Not Soon Supplant the Architect," *Pencil Points,* June 1936, 303–4, 306, 308, 310, 312; Lewis Mumford, "Mass-Production and the Modern House," *Architectural Record,* January 1930, 13–20.

41. In an *Architectural Record* issue (January 1934) highlighting prefabrication trends, several companies attempted to erase the stigma attached to prefabricated housing by displaying their houses in suburban settings. For example, the Buell System (the name of which evokes a detached, machinelike efficiency) is depicted in action. Trucks (which appear to have been custom designed to haul Buell houses) roll one by one in assembly-line fashion into a suburban setting, where they pass a Buell System already erected on its lot of manicured grass surrounded by shrubbery. The Buell System owners attempt to show how cheap, boxy, prefabricated houses could fill the desire for single-family home ownership and also fit snugly in a middle-class setting. The same prefabrication issue of *Architectural Record* featured Stran-Steel and *Good Housekeeping*'s "house of tomorrow," which had been exhibited at the 1933 Century of Progress fair. Like its contemporaries, Stran-Steel also attempted to downplay the unconventional nature of its house (which needed neither plaster nor water to be built) by trimming it with middle-class domestic idioms such as a bay window and a fireplace. Other Stran-Steel model houses were offered in more traditional period styles, such as the "English Gable Type Home," which it listed along with its "Contemporary Flat Roof Type" in a pamphlet made available at the fair (Bletter, "The World of Tomorrow," 91). Despite the fact that it appeared in the prefabrication issue, Stran-Steel stressed that its products were not mass-produced units; rather, its innovation was simply a redefinition of house construction.

42. "Demand for Better and Cheaper Homes," *Architect & Engineer,* May 1934, 32. The article consists of the highlights of the proceedings of the Home Building Conference. See also the prefabrication issue of *Architectural Record,* January 1934.

43. For examples of those prefabricators who managed to put some of their prefabrication into commercial practice, see, on American Houses, Inc., J. F. Higgins, "Introducing the Pre-Fabricated House," *House & Garden,* March 1935, 36–37, 76; on Schindler-Shelters, "News of Planning and Construction," *American Architect,* May 1935, 69; "New Demountable Cottages Developed by the Tennessee Valley Authority," *Pencil Points,* June 1941, 397, 400. In *Architectural Forum,* see "Sears Roebuck Boards the Prefabrication Band-Wagon with Plywood Houses," October 1935, 452; "Home Building Goes Indoors," May 1939, 374–76, supp. 36, 38; "A Product of General Houses," July 1932, 65–66, 69, 71–72; "House by the Celotex Corporation," October 1939, 285; Irving H. Bowman, "An Industrial Approach to Housing," July 1932, 73–75, 78–79. In *Architectural Record,* see "National Houses, Inc., Begins Production," July

1936, 71–73; "Plywood Prefabrication," February 1937, 42–44. In support of prefabrication and housing, see "The Standardized House," *Architectural Forum,* September 1938, 188–96. For a contemporary assessment of Howard Fisher and his General Houses, Inc., as well as Buckminster Fuller and their place in the 1930s prefabrication debate, see also "Housing VI: Solutions," *Fortune,* July 1932, 61, 69, 104–8. Further examples of the 1930s mass-produced "house of tomorrow" craze included Richard Neutra's "Diatom One + Two" (1933), William Van Allen's "steel-shell" house for National Homes, Inc. (1935), and Frank Lloyd Wright's "Usonian Houses" (1934), which were intended for his futuristic "Broadacre City." See Horrigan, "The Home of Tomorrow," 148–54.

44. Ross Gregory, *Modern America, 1914 to 1945* (New York: Facts on File, 1995), 124.

45. "Old Newspapers to New Houses," *Architectural Forum,* December 1940, 531.

46. For more details about the role of the prefabricated housing industry during World War II, see Albrecht, *World War II;* and Kevin Starr, "The Case Study Program and the Impending Future: Some Regional Considerations," and Dolores Hayden, "Modern Houses for the Millions: Architects' Dreams, Builders' Boats, Residents' Dilemmas," in Elizabeth A. T. Smith, ed., *Blueprints for Modern Living: History and Legacy of the Case Study Houses,* 131–44, 197–212 (Cambridge, Mass.: MIT Press, 1989).

47. "Building for Defense . . . Prefabrication Takes New Shape," *Architectural Forum,* April 1941, 20.

48. "Blown-Up House," *Popular Mechanics,* April 1945, 48. See also Buckminster Fuller's wartime version of his Dymaxion house, called the Deployment Unit, described in "Building for Defense . . . 1,000 Houses a Day at $1,200 Each," *Architectural Forum,* June 1941, 425. Fuller's unit, like Neff's concrete Bubble House, failed to sustain popularity with either the military or the public. Other architects were more successful. For Albert Kahn's factory designs see "Architects and Defense," *Pencil Points,* October 1941, 657–64; "Producer of Production Lines" and "Architecture for War Production: A Military Aircraft Plant in the East, by Albert Kahn," *Architectural Record,* June 1942, 39–52. For more examples of defense housing, see Albrecht, *World War II;* Elizabeth Smith, *Blueprints for Modern Living;* and "Saarinen's Studies for Defense Housing," Box 5, Folder 7, Saarinen Family Papers, Cranbrook Archives. Regarding the Haul-a-Way Home, see "Building for Defense . . . Prefabrication Takes New Shape," 20, 110. On the Willow Run Townsite near the Ford bomber plant in Michigan, see "Build Frontier Town to House Bomber Builders," *Hotel Monthly,* May 1943, 14–21. For Russell Wright's furniture design contributions to defense housing, see General Files, Box 3, Defense Housing Portfolio folders, Wright Collection, Syracuse University.

49. "Old Newspapers to New Houses," supp. 36.

50. Ibid., 531, 534.

51. Ibid., supp. 35–36. For more on Homasote during the war, see "Suitcase Houses for the Army," *Popular Science,* February 1944, 69.

52. *Business Week,* 11 April 1942, 79.

53. "Post-War Homes," *Architect & Engineer,* May 1943, 47. See also Henry S. Churchill, "War-Housing Remainders—Post-War Slums," in Zucker, *New Architecture and City Planning,* 308–10.

54. "Post-War Homes," 47.

55. Business certainly felt threatened by government-sponsored housing. On the private sector's overall belligerent attitude toward federally funded housing during the war and the initiatives the private sector launched to curb government's involvement in housing, see Baxandall and Ewen, *Picture Windows,* 80–82.

56. First designed in 1941 at the Quonset Point Naval Air Station in Rhode Island, the Quonset Hut offered an efficient, standardized, prefabricated, and demountable solution to the military's diverse ordnance needs. By 1946, 170,000 had been erected. Their adaptability to diverse climates added to their wartime popularity. From the standard Quonset Hut form, eighty-six different interior layouts could be devised. See Albrecht, *World War II,* xxx, 25, 27.

57. "The 8,000 Lb. House," *Architectural Forum,* April 1946, 129, 131, 132–36.

58. Teague, "A Sane Prediction," 73. See also Tjaarda, "Your Home," 44–45.

59. Illustrated in Albrecht, *World War II,* xxxix. Despite claims to the contrary, four to six thousand dollars for a house was not dirt cheap at the time.

60. Teague, "A Sane Prediction," 58. We will see this approach again in chapter 9 in relation to Communism during the 1950s.

61. "For us the living . . . better homes," *Time,* 15 September 1941, 31.

62. Teague also asserted this opinion in "A Sane Prediction," where he discussed how mass-produced, movable panel walls provided multiple design options and inexpensive "individual preferences" that were "far less" standardized than what was then seen "in speculator-built sections of our cities and suburbs today" (58, 73).

63. For more on the concept of modular units in prefab houses, see "The United States in a New World," 20.

64. "For us the living . . . better homes," 31.

65. Ibid. On Bel Geddes and eugenic-inspired design forms, see Cogdell, "The Futurama Recontextualized" and *Eugenic Design.* Both of Cogdell's publications cover in depth the designer's interests in evolutionary theory and eugenics and how such interests manifested themselves in Bel Geddes's work.

66. Agan, *The House,* 23–25.

Part 3

1. Miles L. Colean, "The Miracle House Myth," *House Beautiful,* December 1944, 78.

2. Eric Sevareid, "Super-Dupering the War: A Report on the Battle of the Adjectives," *Saturday Review of Literature,* 12 February 1944, 9.

3. W. B. B. Fergusson, "American Advertising at War," *Art & Industry,* December 1943, 181. Fergusson was managing director of Masius and Fergusson Ltd. See also Sypher, "Post-War Problem No. 1," 21.

4. Raymond Loewy, "What of the Promised Post-War World," *New York Times Magazine,* 26 September 1943, 14, 27.

5. Ibid.

6. Ibid.

7. Carl W. Sundberg, "The Realities of the Future," *Modern Plastics,* May 1945, 105, 106. Sundberg's firm was called Sundberg-Ferar, Industrial Designers.

8. Ibid.

9. Ibid.

Chapter 7

1. Teague, "A Sane Prediction," 48. Despite his indignation, Teague published a variety of his own predictions during the war.

2. We shall examine the famed L-O-F kitchen later in this chapter.

3. Mary Davis Gillies, *What Women Want in Their Kitchens of Tomorrow: A Report of the Kitchen of Tomorrow Contest* (New York: McCall Corporation, 1944), 30.

4. Mary Davis Gillies, *What Women Want in Their Living Rooms of Tomorrow: A Report of the Living Room of Tomorrow Contest* (New York: McCall Corporation, 1944), 26. *McCall's* also offered contests regarding the bedroom and dining room of tomorrow. Women entered these contests in order to win war bonds, which they could put toward the postwar house of their dreams. However, the data gained through the contest were ultimately intended for manufacturers of domestic products, furniture, and appliances. The *McCall's* surveys also included demographic statistics, indicating that the majority of the women entering the contest came from working-class backgrounds with husbands who worked in skilled labor vocations. For other wartime surveys and market research articles, see the articles by the director of Market Research & Promotion for the McCall Corporation, Arthur P. Hirose: "Attention Manufacturers! 115 Suggestions for Postwar Product and Home Improvements," *Advertising & Selling*, September 1943, 15–16, 77, 80; "What Postwar Products Do Women Want? A Check-List for Manufacturers of Foods and Cosmetics," *Advertising & Selling*, January 1944, 29–30, 106. See also Margaret H. Gammon, "The Consumer Viewpoint: What Women Want in Postwar Merchandise," *Advertising & Selling*, February 1944, 29, 124, 126, 128.

5. Colean, "Miracle House Myth," 78–79.

6. "Picks out just the families-about-to-build." F. W. Dodge Corporation advertisement, early 1930s. From http://historyproject.ucdavis.edu/imageapp.php?Major=AD&Minor=V&SlideNum=98.00. For historical background on the F. W. Dodge Corporation, see Andrew M. Shanken, "From the Gospel of Efficiency to Modernism: A History of Sweet's Catalogue, 1906–1947," *Design Issues* 21 (Spring 2005): 28–47.

7. Thomas S. Holden, "Postwar Realism vs. Romance," *Architectural Record*, April 1943, 60, 84. Holden was president of the F. W. Dodge Corporation. His chapter in Zucker's *New Architecture and City Planning* ("New Materials") takes a similar approach.

8. Ibid., 84.

9. Kenneth K. Stowell, "There's No Place Like Home," *Architectural Record*, December 1943, 41. Another *Architectural Record* editorial from this year echoed Stowell's assessment: "With almost surprising unanimity these experts agree that . . . radical innovations are not expected, and that the postwar house will, like the postwar automobile, be to all intents and purposes a 1942 model." From "Construction Potentials," 11. For an analysis of the practical and impractical postwar forecasts for postwar electric appliances, see C. W. Stuart, "New Possibilities of Electric Home Equipment," in Zucker, *New Architecture and City Planning*, 243–53. Stuart was from GE's Home Bureau.

10. Stowell, "There's No Place Like Home," 41.

11. The woman's attire is a bit hard to pinpoint. Her hat signals a prim and proper character, but it appears she is wearing men's overalls. One might presume this is a new

postwar fashion derived from women's greater participation in factory work during the war—another future trend that Dunn parodies. Indeed, in a picture accompanying this cartoon, which we shall examine shortly, Dunn depicts the housewife of tomorrow wearing factory overalls to vacuum her living room (see fig. 7.5).

12. "What People Say They Want: *House Beautiful*'s Postwar Primer for Manufacturers," *House Beautiful,* July 1944, 21–23.

13. Loewy, "What of the Promised Post-War World," 14, 27.

14. H. A. Smith, "Don't Promise the Public Too Much—Too Soon," *Advertising & Selling,* June 1944, 28.

15. Colean, "Miracle House Myth," 78–79. See also Lucius Beebe, "Horrors of Progress," *American Mercury,* January 1944, 95–96.

16. "What! A house with no kitchen!" *Saturday Evening Post,* 22 November 1941, 85. Advertisement sponsored by Revere Copper and Brass. For more on the scientifically planned postwar kitchen and the standardized housewife, see Mary Kelly Heiner, "Where Research Is Needed," *Journal of Home Economics,* January 1945, 10–11. Heiner's article includes diagrams with housewife motion studies. See also Helen E. McCullough, "The Kitchen of Tomorrow," *Journal of Home Economics,* January 1945, 8–10.

17. For another kitchen model that appears to follow the L-O-F format, see Peter Müller-Munk's plastic "kitchen of tomorrow" for Dow Chemical. In Müller-Munk's plan, cabinet and refrigerator doors would be made in easy-to-clean, see-through Dow plastic, as opposed to glass. See "Kitchen Prototype—Designed for Plastics," *Modern Plastics,* June 1945, 97–102; and "Kitchen Front," *Time,* 28 August 1944, 84, 86.

18. "Kitchens of Tomorrow May Look Like This," *Life,* 9 August 1943, 53. It is interesting to note that so modern a refrigerator is referred to as an "icebox."

19. Ibid.

20. Ibid.

21. "Dream House: Los Angeles Builder Gives Preview of All Things Americans May Someday Have in Their Homes," *Life,* 6 May 1946, 83–84. Also regarding Burns's automated house, see "Tomorrow's House—and Gadgetry." On Burns's military construction work, see Fritz Burns, "We're the Suicide Troops for the War Building Industry," *American Builder & Building Age,* December 1942. Found in Albrecht, *World War II,* 255.

22. "Dream House," 83–84.

23. Jean Austin, "Postbaloney," *American Home,* September 1944, 20–21.

24. Ibid.

25. Davis, "Household Servants Are Gone Forever," 89–90.

26. Marjorie McKenzie, "Pursuit of Democracy," *Pittsburgh Courier,* 8 September 1945, 7.

27. For an account of black women stereotyped as white "help" during World War II, see Honey, *Bitter Fruit,* 89–91.

28. Lipsitz in *A Rainbow at Midnight* indicates that high percentages of women wanted to remain in their wartime jobs. He cites a national survey documenting that "75 percent of all women workers (and 80 percent of those over the age of forty-five) wanted to continue their wartime employment" (49).

29. Whether Dunn was aware of this reference to Saturn as a state of melancholy is not certain, but the interpretation certainly fits the content of the picture. For more on Saturn's symbolism, see Raymond Klibansky, Erwin Panofsky, and Fritz Saxl, *Saturn*

and Melancholy: Studies in the History of Natural Philosophy, Religion, and Art (London: Nelson, 1964); Ken Perlow, "The Image of Melancholy and the Evolution of the Baroque Idiom" (1995/1997), http://vdgsa.org/hermes/image1.html.

30. "This New Era of Easy Upkeep," *House Beautiful,* October 1947, 122–24. This issue of *House Beautiful* also included Kenneth Young, "It Doesn't Look All Plastic, But It Is," 140–41; and Elizabeth Gordon, "What's Wrong with Plastics?" 166. The previous month also had its share of plastic propaganda. See Laura Tanner, "Not Only a New Look but a Look That Stays New," *House Beautiful,* September 1947, 162–63; Marion Gough, "What Do They Mean When They Say It's Plastic?" ibid., 142–43, 237–39.

31. "This New Era of Easy Upkeep," 122–24.

32. On the ways in which technology raises standards of living and concurrently places greater demands on women's time spent on housekeeping, see Cowan, *More Work for Mother;* Strasser, *Never Done.* On the hygienic principles of postwar plastics, see Alison J. Clarke, *Tupperware: The Promise of Plastic in 1950s America* (Washington, D.C.: Smithsonian Books, 2001).

33. For example, see the title of the 1942 Atwood article, "The Miracle of War Production."

Chapter 8

1. Dow Archives.

2. "Counter attack!" *Fortune,* April 1946, 12.

3. "What Happened to the Dreamworld?" 91.

4. Ibid.

5. Ibid.

6. Ibid.

7. "Now the secret of 'Huff-Duff' can be told," *Fortune,* April 1946, 54. Advertisement for a high-frequency radio direction finder.

8. Arthur Kallet, "How Good Are Postwar Goods?" *New Republic,* 4 November 1946, 582–84.

9. Ibid.

10. "Maytag's Making Washers Again!" *Life,* 1 October 1945, 125.

11. "What Happened to the Dreamworld?" 91.

12. "No Refrigerators, Autos Yet," *Baltimore Afro-American,* 25 August 1945, 4.

13. J. Saunders Redding, "A Second Look," *Baltimore Afro-American,* 2 February 1946, 4.

14. "What Happened to the Dreamworld?" 92. We will return to the economic and political fallout after the war in the following section and in chapter 9.

15. Baxandall and Ewen in *Picture Windows* cover Levitt's less-than-democratic controls for teaching the residents of his subdivisions "the ways of middle-class civility and manners." Levitt had rules for the "proper" ways in which residents should park their cars and the "proper" time to hang laundry outside to dry or to cut the lawn. Dissenters to his decrees, including his decision to change his Long Island suburb's name from Island Trees to Levittown, were tagged as "communist dupes." To Levitt's chagrin, he learned "that democratizing housing was great for sales but terrible for keeping people in their place" (144–45). However, according to Baxandall and Ewen,

he was most adept at keeping the suburbs white (175–76). This point is also raised by Lizabeth Cohen in *A Consumers' Republic,* who refers to Levitt and other such developers as "guardians of racial segregation" (217–19). It seems that the Levitts' postwar construction, including Levittowns in Pennsylvania and New Jersey, has become the focal point for examinations of suburbia. On postwar suburban development, other than the Levitts,' see Lizabeth Cohen, *A Consumers' Republic,* 197–200, which covers New Jersey; and Baxandall and Ewen, *Picture Windows,* 171–74, which looks at Freeport, Long Island.

16. The Depression rocked not only private housing starts but also values, which makes it difficult to assess a "true" average for the 1930s. For example, the value of a typical house fell from $5,000 in 1926 to $3,300 in 1932. See Kenneth Jackson, *Crabgrass Frontier,* 193.

17. Kenneth Jackson, *Crabgrass Frontier,* 234.

18. Department of Commerce, Bureau of the Census, *Current Population Reports: Consumer Income,* No. 5, Series P-60 (Washington, D.C., 7 February 1949), p. 1, http://www2.census.gov/prod2/popscan/P60–05.pdf.

19. The Levitts simplified the home-buying paperwork; they required no down payments and demanded no closing costs. An upscale Levitt house (in a more exclusive development) cost between $17,500 and $23,500. Kenneth Jackson indicates that between 1945 and 1960, most suburban tract houses cost "typically under $10,000" (*Crabgrass Frontier,* 234, 236, 371). Besides the Levitts, other prefabrication companies included Lustron, National Homes, and U.S. Steel. Lustron's prefab houses, with a price tag of $9,000, were more expensive than the Levitts' Cape Cod houses (Wright, *Building the Dream,* 245). Wright argues that the prefabrication business wasn't always a success and was not able to solve the postwar housing shortage overnight, contrary to what publicity surrounding prefabrication would have led the public to believe.

20. Kunstler, *Geography of Nowhere,* 105.

21. Kenneth Jackson, *Crabgrass Frontier,* 232–33; Wright, *Building the Dream,* 242.

22. The Case-Study House program, launched by *Arts & Architecture,* attempted to provide an "elite" aesthetic model for single-family suburban houses on which postwar suburban developers could draw their inspiration. (See Elizabeth Smith, *Blueprints for Modern Living,* for details.) Unfortunately for the Case-Study architects and other modernists, the FHA perceived the modern mass-produced, severe appearance of their buildings—flat roofs, steel frames, and plain, sometimes glass, façades—as a temporary fad and tended to reject loans for housing developments of this nature. Instead they favored contractors who mass-produced houses in period styles, such as Cape Cod cottages and Colonial revival models, which were perceived as safer investments. The basic suburban ranch-style model had been adapted from Frank Lloyd Wright's earlier Prairie-style houses, but, ironically, Wright's postwar housing proposals were rejected by the FHA. Nonetheless, builders of the typical middle-class ranch house borrowed Wright's Prairie-style idioms—low-pitched roof, deep eaves, and horizontal lines—but combined them with more conventional, period-style props (Wright, *Building the Dream,* 248–51). Even prefabricators whose mass-produced houses were adapted to an industrial aesthetic, such as Henry Dreyfuss's Vultee House (fabricated with aluminum walls), were not mass-marketed primarily because of revised mortgage-lending policies after the war (Albrecht, *World War II,* 29). The association between glass walls, flat roofs, steel frames, and European International Style designs also undermined

alternative modern aesthetics after the war because they were not perceived as "American" (Elizabeth Smith, *Blueprints for Modern Living*, 142, 207). This last issue is raised again briefly in chapter 9.

23. The majority of post–World War II houses also sported central heating, indoor plumbing, telephone connection, and automatic appliances sometimes built in (Kenneth Jackson, *Crabgrass Frontier*, 236, 240, 243). Wright, in *Building the Dream*, discusses the prefabrication techniques and materials adapted to tract house developments after the war (244, 253).

24. Levittown streets were all dubbed "lanes" and ascribed rustic names such as Harvest, Prairie, and Cobbler. Perhaps to underscore the civilization nature of suburbia, there was also a lane called Normal. See Baxandall and Ewen, *Picture Windows*, 143. Tom Martinson examines the popular Cape Cod, Colonial, and ranch styles of the postwar era and their architects in *American Dreamscape*.

25. For an insightful and detailed survey of America's suburban landscape development and its social and political history, see Hayden, *Building Suburbia*.

26. "The House We Live In," 20. See Brooks for a history of *Ebony*'s development and early years ("Consumer Markets and Consumer Magazines," 157–94).

27. "The House We Live In," 20.

28. Myrdal, *American Dilemma*, 205.

29. "The House We Live In," 20.

30. See Crawford, "Daily Life on the Home Front," 90–143; Anderson, "Last Hired, First Fired," 82–97; Honey, *Bitter Fruit*.

31. "A Permanent FEPC Needed," *Pittsburgh Courier*, 8 September 1945, 6.

32. Horace R. Cayton, "Paging the Liberals," *Pittsburgh Courier*, 8 September 1945, 7.

33. "The House We Live In," 20.

34. *Ebony* was following a long-established trend in the African American press, where inspiring stories of black achievement were juxtaposed with news articles and editorials concerning racial injustice in America. Rooks in *Ladies' Pages* covers the "biographical sketches" of notable black women in African American women's magazines (42–44, 52–55). Rooks explains that these narratives were in large part ways to subvert stereotypes and generalizations about blacks while also providing models of "ladyhood" in order to socially uplift other readers of their race.

35. Brooks in "Consumer Markets and Consumer Magazines" explains that *Ebony* offered "its readers a vision of America as it should be—with Blacks and whites enjoying the recognition and benefits of a prosperous society. Moreover, the races were pursuing the American dream together" (190). Rooks also covers *Ebony* in *Ladies' Pages* (130–34).

36. "Maymie and the Maid . . . in the Elegant Anderson Kitchen," *Ebony*, 16 November 1946, 16. Brooks refers to this editorial as well ("Consumer Markets and Consumer Magazines," 164). Brooks notes that *Ebony* advertisements of "insurance and appliances were among those that signified the home as the primary domain of women. . . . Implicit in these ads was a message that the home was incomplete for women if it did not contain the proper home appliances." Brooks refers to a Hoover vacuum cleaner ad in *Ebony* showing "Black women using the cleaner . . . and clothed in rather elegant dress" (ibid., 185–86). One could also argue that editorials like "Maymie and the Maid" also underscored this prevailing domestic construct for African American women.

37. On maid/mistress relations, see Judith Rollins, *Between Women: Domestics and Their Employers* (Philadelphia: Temple University Press, 1985).

38. Brooks covers the "advertiser discourse" on the African American consumer during the war, which, according to his study, began to express the need for statistics on "the exact size of the Black consumer market [which] had never been determined." Brooks cites a 1943 *Sales Management* article that lamented this dilemma but "estimated that the 1942 effective buying income [of blacks] was $4.8 million, equivalent to the total income of fourteen states" (David J. Sullivan, "Don't Do This—If You Want to Sell Your Products to Negroes!" *Sales Management* 52 (1 March 1943): 43, 48, 50; found in Brooks, "Consumer Markets and Consumer Magazines," 107.)

39. David J. Sullivan, "How Negroes Spent Their Incomes, 1920–1943," *Sales Management* 54 (15 June 1945): 106. Found in Weems, *Desegregating the Dollar,* 34, and Brooks, "Consumer Markets and Consumer Magazines," 107–8. Sullivan's article included a table of expenditures for the years 1920, 1929, 1935, 1941, and 1943. Categories of consumer goods included Household Furnishings, Fuel, Alcoholic Beverages, Medical, Transport, Personal Care, Recreation, Reading, Gifts/Contributions, Taxes, Food, Clothing, Drugs/Proprietaries, Tobacco, Education, and Savings. Lizabeth Cohen in *A Consumers' Republic* covers African Americans' experiences as consumers during the war; see especially 83–100.

40. David J. Sullivan, "The American Negro—An 'Export' Market at Home," *Printer's Ink,* 21 July 1944, 90, 94. Found in Weems, *Desegregating the Dollar,* 34.

41. Weems, *Desegregating the Dollar,* 35. See also Sentman and Washburn, "Excess Profits Tax."

42. Weems, *Desegregating the Dollar,* 35. Interstate was founded in 1940 and consisted of "a consortium of African American newspapers." The company originated from the ideas of Robert Vann, editor of the black paper the *Pittsburgh Courier.* Interstate replaced a white-owned establishment, W. B. Ziff, that had placed ads of national brands in black papers. Ziff abandoned this line of business, opening the niche for Interstate.

43. Weems, *Desegregating the Dollar,* 36.

44. Brooks also covers the Research Company of America study, which "was considered at that time to be one of the most comprehensive surveys of the Black consumer market." However, he dates the study as 1945 and says that "by 1946, all of the major trade journals were reporting the results" ("Consumer Markets and Consumer Magazines," 109–10). Weems (*Desegregating the Dollar*) dates the study as 1946. Given this discrepancy, I have provided the date of 1945/46.

45. Weems, *Desegregating the Dollar,* 37. The survey also included food, clothing, beverage, drug, toiletry, and tobacco purchases. Interstate's success gave rise to a competitor company in the black community, Associated Publishers, in 1944.

46. Brooks, "Consumer Markets and Consumer Magazines," 112–13.

47. "Fourteen Million Negro Customers," *Management Review* (June 1947), 336–38. Found in Brooks, "Consumer Markets and Consumer Magazines," 112–13.

48. Brooks, "Consumer Markets and Consumer Magazines," 113; "Fourteen Million Negro Customers," 337.

49. Weems gives a detailed account of this niche in books, newspapers, and radio (*Desegregating the Dollar,* 31–55). Brooks covers postwar corporate market research investigations of the African American market and the hiring of black Negro Market

experts and managers. He also examines campaigns by national advertisers such as Pepsi-Cola, and articles published in trade magazines, such as *Tide* and *Advertising Age,* which reported various summaries and findings of African American consumer market research data. His study also includes *postwar* sociological coverage of African Americans as consumers (Brooks, "Consumer Markets and Consumer Magazines," 117–30, 134–43).

50. Lizabeth Cohen in *A Consumers' Republic* examines the postwar segmentation trend and covers the challenges that Negro Market specialists faced in "convincing mainstream marketers to reach out to black consumers" (323–29, 331).

51. Weems sites William K. Bell as a dissenter from this trend. Bell's book *15 Million Negroes and 15 Billion Dollars* (New York: William K. Bell, 1958) emphasized that black progress meant keeping black dollars inside the community, not spreading them among the coffers of the white techno-corporate order (Weems, *Desegregating the Dollar,* 54).

52. "Why Negroes Buy Cadillacs," *Ebony,* September 1946, 34. Found in Brooks, "Consumer Markets and Consumer Magazines," 175.

53. "No Refrigerators, Autos Yet," 4.

54. McKenzie, "Pursuit of Democracy," 7.

55. According to Samuel in *Pledging Allegiance,* the federal government did not intentionally keep statistics on war bond purchases by race as a way of asserting the intention that bonds were an "equal opportunity" to support the war effort. Therefore, we can't know exactly how many war bonds African Americans purchased, but estimates of sales to blacks were made by Pickens (as noted) and at bond rallies: "Actual sales generated at rallies attended by the [Treasury Department's] Inter-Racial Section were estimated as $9,213,241 and $10,719,052 for 1943 and 1944" (Samuel, *Pledging Allegiance,* 186–87, 188).

56. A study by Gary S. Becker, *The Economics of Discrimination* (Chicago: University of Chicago Press, 1957), upheld that African American incomes had advanced little since 1910 and had been "stable," neither increasing substantially nor decreasing. It has been argued since Becker's book that blacks made substantial strides in their economic status relative to previous generations and relative to their white contemporaries. This economic uplift and the narrowing of the racial wage gap did not eradicate black poverty, however, as the following two studies attest: Rayack, "Discrimination and the Occupational Progress of Negroes"; James P. Smith and Finis R. Welch, "Black Economic Progress After Myrdal," *Journal of Economic Literature* 27, no. 2 (1989): 519–64. Rayack asserts in his conclusion that economic growth for blacks does not "reflect a significant reduction in discrimination" (214).

57. Rev. A. Clayton Powell, Sr., "We Cannot Live in U.S. Concentration Camps," *Baltimore Afro-American,* 29 September 1945, 5. The *Afro-American* published a series of excerpts from Powell's book *Riots and Ruins* (New York: Richard E. Smith, 1945).

58. Robert C. Weaver, "Negro Labor Since 1929," *Journal of Negro History* 35, no. 1 (1950): 30. Weaver, the first African American to serve in a presidential cabinet, held official roles in the 1930s with the New Deal agencies of the secretary of the interior and the Housing Authority. During World War II, he held offices that assisted in the mobilization of black labor. Weaver acted as secretary of housing and urban development from 1966 to 1968.

59. Ibid., 30.

60. "Mass Layoffs Follow Victory," *Baltimore Afro-American,* 25 August 1945, 2. Other editorials and articles in the black press highlighted unfair rehiring practices assisted by the government's Employment Services offices. (See McKenzie, "Pursuit of Democracy," 7.) The African Americans laid off from industrial jobs after victory and during reconversion were corralled toward more menial, low-skilled, and low-paying jobs, such as domestics and janitors. If such work were refused on the basis of having worked at higher pay and higher skill before, blacks' unemployment benefits were summarily cut off. The government Employment Services workers saw this as "refusing available work," which in their criteria made the disgruntled job seeker ineligible to receive unemployment benefits. The author of "Mass Layoffs Follow Victory" refers to a standard rule in state unemployment benefits compensation that still exists today. An unemployed American who receives unemployment insurance benefits—income—from the state may not refuse a job when it is offered. If a job offer is rejected, and a government official learns of this, the unemployed person becomes ineligible for further government assistance.

61. Wynn, *The Afro-American,* 123. On African Americans' World War II military experience from a socioeconomic interpretation, see John Modell, Marc Goulden, and Sigurdur Magnusson, "World War II in the Lives of Black Americans: Some Findings and Interpretation," *Journal of American History* 76, no. 3 (1989): 838–48.

62. Wynn, *The Afro-American,* 126. See also Marcus Alexis, "Assessing Fifty Years of African-American Economic Status, 1940–1990," *American Economic Review* 88, no. 2 (1998): 368–75; Richard B. Freeman, R. A. Gordon, Duran Bell, and Robert E. Hall, "Changes in the Labor Market for Black Americans, 1948–1972," *Brookings Papers on Economic Activity* no. 1 (1973): 67–131.

63. Rayack, "Discrimination," 214. In 1950, Weaver found these fears to have been quite sound: "All of [the Negro's wartime employment achievements do] not mean that job discrimination on account of color is a thing of the past. As a matter of fact, general advances toward equal employment opportunities for colored labor ceased with the end of the war effort and discrimination on the job front increased" ("Negro Labor Since 1929," 34–35). On the postwar experience of African Americans and their struggle to participate as full citizens, see Lizabeth Cohen, *A Consumers' Republic,* 164–91.

64. Schuyler, "Views and Reviews," 7.

65. Kunstler, *Geography of Nowhere,* 104. For more on inequality in postwar suburbia, see Lizabeth Cohen, *A Consumers' Republic,* 194–256.

66. Lizabeth Cohen in *A Consumers' Republic* (222) shows that white Americans' rate of home ownership remained substantially higher than that of African Americans after the war—despite war bond savings and government incentives to buy a new suburban home. In 1940, according to the government statistical reports she cites, 46 percent of white Americans owned homes compared to 24 percent of African Americans. Although later figures show an increase over the 1940 percentages, a significant gap is noticeable. In 1950, 57 percent of whites owned homes compared with 34.5 percent of African Americans, and in 1960, white home ownership rose to 64 percent, but for blacks the increase was comparatively negligible—38 percent, a less than 4 percent increase. There were rare exceptions, such as Thomas Romana, who, according to Baxandall and Ewen in *Picture Windows,* saw "minorities as an untapped market" and sought to develop suburban areas that were already segregated from white suburbia.

Romana developed Ronek Park on Long Island, which was intended to overlook race, creed, and color (178–79). Baxandall and Ewen refer to another black suburban development on Long Island, Bennington Park, which "had been built in the first decade of the [twentieth] century to house southern blacks who came to work as domestics in the wealthy South Shore estates" (172). Lizabeth Cohen in *A Consumers' Republic* refers to another liberal-minded developer, Joseph Eichler, who was the Levitts' West Coast rival (217–18). Baxandall and Ewen also cover Senator Joseph McCarthy's attempts in the 1940s to undermine any remaining New Deal social reforms in housing, fully stigmatize public housing, and thereby leverage more control over housing developments for private interests (89–105).

67. For more on the social and economic impact of urban-to-suburban migration, see Thomas C. Henthorn, "A Catholic Dilemma: Urban Flight in Northwest Flint, Michigan," *Michigan Historical Review* 31, no. 2 (Fall 2005): 1–42. Henthorn examines a Flint community and its anchoring institution and how both dealt with neighborhood succession from white to black.

68. Kenneth Jackson, *Crabgrass Frontier,* 244–45; Wright, *Building the Dream,* 232, 234, 236. Wright, like Jackson, outlines other discriminatory practices encouraged by the FHA and other federal housing programs, which institutionalized the ideal of the middle-class, suburban, single-family house at the exclusion of minority city dwellers. For more on this issue, see Andrew Weise, "Racial Cleansing in the Suburbs: Suburban Government, Urban Renewal, and Segregation on Long Island," in Silver and Melkonian, *Contested Terrain.* The thesis that federal aid and legislation favored the suburbs over the cities to the detriment of America's urban centers is also argued by William Issel in *Social Change in the United States, 1945–1983* (New York: Schocken Books, 1987), 88–94. Moreover, in an effort to capitalize on conditions and environments that would support their mass-produced housing businesses, Issel argues that large construction firms contributed to shaping the contours of postwar suburban development. Such firms were attracted to the expansive tracts of inexpensive land outside cities "where their mass production techniques could be most effective" (ibid., 89).

69. Coontz in *The Way We Never Were* states that the "1950s suburban family . . . was far more dependent on government handouts than any so-called 'underclass' in recent U.S. history. . . . [Postwar] suburbia was a creation of government policy and federal spending." Coontz provides examples of the ways in which the federal government gave Americans (especially lower- or new middle-class whites) access to postwar housing progress, including the Interstate Highway Act, which in 1956, she states, added 42,500 more miles to the 37,000-mile highway system, whose construction was launched in 1947. The main beneficiaries of these roadways were, she argues, the commuting suburbanites (Coontz, *The Way We Never Were,* 76–78).

70. Kenneth Jackson, *Crabgrass Frontier,* 232–33.

71. Lizabeth Cohen, *A Consumers' Republic,* 220–21.

72. Vance Packard in *The Status Seekers* (New York: David McKay, 1959) tells how some realtors intentionally interfered with social harmony and the black middle class's move to suburbia by stirring racial panic in order to stimulate sales of houses. Packard describes how realtors in a Queens, New York, neighborhood profited from the fears they stoked in white residents. One house sale to an affluent African American family, realtors insisted, meant that the "entire block was going Negro." Once the residents were persuaded that their houses' values were on the decline, the realtor would offer

immediate cash. Packard claims that "a panic sale of $10,000 in one year can bring [the realtors] $5,000,000 in fees" (ibid., 84–86).

73. Wynn, *The Afro-American,* 126. President Truman had ordered the desegregation of the military in 1948.

74. Horace R. Cayton, "Decline of Racism: Sheer Need of Manpower for Future Wars Will Lessen Race Conflict," *Pittsburgh Courier,* 1 September 1945, 7.

75. Portions of this section appear in my essay published in the following publication: "Commercial Fallout: The Image of Progress and the Feminine Consumer from World War II to the Atomic Age," in *The Writing on the Cloud: Conference Proceedings of "The Atomic Age Opens: American Culture Confronts the Atomic Bomb"* (Lanham, Md.: University Press of America, 1997).

76. "Atom Bomb House," *Architects' Journal,* 28 February 1946, 176.

77. Federal Civil Defense Administration (FCDA), *This Is Civil Defense* (Washington, D.C.: Government Printing Office, May 1951), 4, 10. Available at New York Public Library.

78. See Allen Smith, "Democracy and the Politics of Information: The St. Louis Committee for Nuclear Information," *Gateway Heritage* 17 (Summer 1996): 2–13. Smith shows before and after pictures of "Survival City," a model of a suburban neighborhood (with department-store mannequins and household appliances) built in 1955 in the Nevada desert, which was used to test the rate of destruction a modern postwar house and family could expect to experience in a nuclear holocaust. The "after" pictures of broken mannequins, shattered glass, and a destroyed middle-class neighborhood undermined civil defense planning because such images attested to the futility of finding a "safe" structural haven in the atomic age.

79. For a thorough study of the FCDA and its policies, see Guy Oakes, *The Imaginary War: Civil Defense and American Cold War Culture* (New York and Oxford: Oxford University Press, 1994). Because of the fear generated by the threat of atomic assaults on American soil, social chaos and panic in the civilian population were believed to be more lethal than the effects of the atom bomb.

80. FCDA, *Home Protection Exercises: A Family Action Program,* 2nd ed. (Washington, D.C.: Government Printing Office, 1956), 31. Available at New York Public Library.

81. FCDA, *This Is Civil Defense,* 10.

82. Ibid., 22, 25.

83. FCDA, *What You Should Know About Radioactive Fallout* (Washington, D.C.: Government Printing Office, 1955), 26. Available at New York Public Library.

84. FCDA, *Home Protection Exercises,* 10.

85. Ibid., 25. See also *What to Do NOW About Emergency Sanitation at Home: A Family Handbook,* rev. ed. (Washington, D.C.: Executive Office of the President, Office of Civil and Defense Mobilization, 1958). Available at New York Public Library.

86. FCDA, *This Is Civil Defense,* 4.

87. For contemporary commentary on suburbia of the 1950s, see John Keats, *The Crack in the Picture Window* (Boston: Houghton Mifflin, 1959). On suburbia and consumption, see Packard, *The Status Seekers,* especially his chapters "Snob Appeal = Today's Home Sweet Home" and "Choosing a Proper Address" (61–92).

88. The focus on individualism over collectivism is especially driven home in Kunstler's *Geography of Nowhere.* He defines what he sees as a wasteful and destructive

trajectory as a "fetish for extreme individualism" over "the common good" (105–8, 186, 275). Baxandall and Ewen in *Picture Windows* refer to this dichotomy as "two competing ideals, [the] commercial and communal, [which] would shape postwar housing politics and policies" (83). Kenneth Jackson in *Crabgrass Frontier* blames the loss of community and the "general withdrawal into self-pursuit and privatism" in suburbia to the rise of the automobile, air-conditioning, and indoor entertainments (such as phonographs and TV), and the decline of the wide front porch (272–81). Coontz in *The Way We Never Were* describes the seeds of rebellion against the 1950s norm of a patriotic loyalty to consumerism, individualism, and the American Way (37–38, 171–73).

89. On the ways in which commercial media promoted and encapsulated a consumer ideology during the postwar years, see Ewen, *Captains of Consciousness*, 207–14.

90. Elaine Tyler May's *Homeward Bound* covers these issues in depth. See especially her chapter "The Commodity Gap: Consumerism and the Modern Home" (162–82). William Chafe in *The Unfinished Journey: America Since World War II* (New York: Oxford University Press, 1986) concurs with the observation that postwar suburban living, especially in an era marked by a mix of affluence, fear, and suspicion, sparked a "profound irony." Americans who had sought refuge from the city "in order to find a private home of their own sometimes became enmeshed in a form of group living that crushed privacy and undermined individualism." Chafe's examination of postwar American life also includes an astute assessment of the "new culture of buying" that "took control" in postwar suburbia (ibid., 117–19, 120). Issel in *Social Change in the United States* provides a brief survey of observations and criticisms published during the 1950s concerning conformity and the social façades replicated by a mass-produced suburban lifestyle. Daniel Horowitz's *The Anxieties of Affluence: Critiques of American Consumer Culture, 1939–1979* (Amherst: University of Massachusetts Press, 2004) provides a more detailed coverage of dissenting voices who critiqued and challenged American consumerism during the postwar era. See also Loren Baritz, *The Good Life: The Meaning of Success for the American Middle Class* (New York: Harper & Row, 1982; repr. 1990), especially his chapter "Costs of the Dream" (166–224) on the problems that suburban living raised, the pressures to conform, and the distress that resulted.

Chapter 9

1. Max Lerner, *Public Journal* (New York, 1945), 19. Found in Eleanor Straub, "United States Government Policy Toward Civilian Women during World War II," *Prologue* 5 (Winter 1973): 240. Portions of this section have been adopted from my essay "Commercial Fallout."

2. On the history of automation in washing and drying machines, see Consumer Reports, *I'll Buy That! Fifty Small Wonders and Big Deals That Revolutionized the Lives of Consumers* (Mount Vernon, N.Y.: Consumer Reports Books, 1986), 232–36. Washers that could spin clothes dry by extracting "water through a separate basket rotating at high speed" in the washer's tub were introduced in 1926 by the Easy Washing Machine Company, but the innovation did not become popular due largely to its inability to clean as effectively as the standard wringer model. Finally in 1952, "streamlined, spin-dry automatic washers" began to catch up in sales with the wringer-style washers. Early dryers were considered more luxury than necessity and did not develop at the

same pace as washing machines. Maytag adapted electronics to dryers in the 1960s (ibid., 232, 234, 236).

3. The push button offered the aura of control to women compelled to strive for ever higher standards of household efficiency, cleanliness, and order in a world threatened by uncontrollable chaos and ultimate destruction. This theme characterized domestic advice in magazines throughout the 1950s. See "Everything's Under Control," *McCall's,* December 1958, 133; "Control Center: The Kitchen," *New York Times Magazine,* 27 March 1960, 78–79; "Command Post . . . For a Housewife," *Sunset,* September 1954, 70; "Automatic Housekeeping," *Look,* 14 May 1957, 84–86; regarding a Western Electric telephone advertisement, "Yours to Command," *Time,* 3 August 1959, 38; Hyman Goldberg, "Push-Button Future," *Cosmopolitan,* January 1958, 67; "Robots Are a Girl's Best Friend," *House & Garden,* April 1953, 122–23.

4. "The Fabulous Fifteen Years Ahead," *Changing Times,* January 1961, 7, 9, 10.

5. The term "military-industrial complex" is credited to President Dwight D. Eisenhower as spoken in his "Farewell Speech" given on 17 January 1961. For more on the historical development of the United States' cold war military-industrial complex, see Charles J. Hitch and Roland N. McKean, *The Economics of Defense in the Nuclear Age* (Cambridge, Mass.: Harvard University Press, 1960); Koistinen, *The Military-Industrial Complex;* Stuart W. Leslie, *The Cold War and American Science: The Military-Industrial-Academic Complex at MIT and Stanford* (New York: Columbia University Press, 1993). Sherry in *In the Shadow of War* traces the roots of American militarization and its role in U.S. politics, foreign policy, and the domestic economy. Mowry in *The Urban Nation* discusses the relationship between cold war defense and postwar prosperity (196–201). Lears in *Fables of Abundance* calls the collaboration between government and business to construct a "permanent war economy" a multiplication of "military Keynesianism" (247). For an account of how the military-industrial complex crafted consent for expanding its programs, see Hugh Gusterson, *People of the Bomb: Portraits of America's Nuclear Complex* (Minneapolis: University of Minnesota Press, 2004). For a similar critique, contemporary with early cold war military-industrial expansion, see C. Wright Mills's chapters "The Warlords" and "The Military Ascendancy" in *The Power Elite* (1956; reprint, New York: Oxford University Press, 1959), 171–224. Mills points to the Pentagon, built during World War II, as the "most dramatic symbol of the scale and shape of the new military [bureaucratic] edifice," calling it the "organized brain of the American means of violence" (ibid., 186).

6. "Reconverting War Research," *Business Week,* 10 January 1948, 56. Reconversion examples follow in the article.

7. Like manufacturers, industrial designers also sought defense contracts in the military-industrial complex. See, for example, Henry Dreyfuss's Nike missile launching platform and missile control console in his firm's public relations booklet, *Industrial Design: A Progress Report, 1929–1952* (New York: Henry Dreyfuss, 1952). Dreyfuss's handheld Geiger counter is illustrated in *Industrial Design: A Pictorial Accounting, 1929–1957* (New York: Henry Dreyfuss, 1957). See also Walter Dorwin Teague's plans for the U.S. Air Force Academy's Colorado Springs complex built in the late 1950s, available in the Teague Collection, Syracuse University.

8. "Defense Dept.: Leading Patron of the Sciences," *Business Week,* 12 January 1957, 96. Could U.S. research, development, and production have contributed solely to the postwar commercial fallout? Or did the Americans have some assistance from the

technology and scientists they scavenged from the Germans as the Nazi regime collapsed in 1945? This theory came to my mind while reading Nick Cook's *The Hunt for Zero Point: Inside the Classified World of Antigravity Technology* (New York: Random House, Broadway Books, 2001). Cook's emphasis is on evidence that points to the Germans' work on antigravity technologies during World War II and the Allies' "tech-plunder" that was later obfuscated in the United States by military authorities. I wondered if remnants of this tech-plunder made it into American corporate-sponsored laboratories and if any of it resulted in the postwar commercial fallout as illustrated by the examples in this chapter.

9. *Marketing in a Defense Economy* (New York: J. Walter Thompson, 1951), 14, 15. Box #11, Company Publications 1951–54, JWT/Duke.

10. Ibid., 11, 14, 15.

11. This was the thrust of the "Miracle of America" propaganda campaign, discussed later in this chapter. See, for example, "The Better We Produce/The Better We Live," from Advertising Council, *The 1950 Campaign to Explain the American Economic System* (n.p., 1950), front page. "Miracle of America" folder 486A, Ad Council archives, New York City.

12. On the techno-corporate order's post–World War II campaigns to fight Communism, unionism, and liberalism with American Way ideology, see Elizabeth Fones-Wolf, *Selling Free Enterprise: The Business Assault on Labor and Liberalism, 1945–60* (Urbana: University of Illinois Press, 1994); Bird in *"Better Living"* also deals with this issue after the war.

13. For more on this issue, see "War Profits and Cold War Culture," in Brandes, *Warhogs*, 269–76. On the role of postwar foreign aid and assistance programs, such as those that encouraged foreign purchases of U.S. military hardware, see David W. Eakins, "Business Planners and America's Postwar Expansion," in David Horowitz, ed., *Corporations and the Cold War*, 160, 167–69 (New York and London: Monthly Review Press/Bertrand Russell Peace Foundation, 1969). Eakins discusses how the postwar "world market would—with government help—support the needed American economic growth" (168). See below for more on this issue.

14. C. Wright Mills observed this equation in his 1956 book *The Power Elite*, where he wrote: "Professional economists usually consider military institutions as parasitic upon the means of production. Now, however, such institutions have come to shape much of the economic life of the United States" (222). For another contemporary observation, see Robert L. Heilbroner, *The Future as History* (1959; reprint, New York: Harper & Brothers, 1960), 66–67. Heilbroner writes of the economic and political impact of the U.S. military's powerful hold on the high-tech.

15. *Time*, 10 August 1959, back cover.

16. The legal department at Revlon denied permission to reproduce this advertisement because it did not agree with my description. For interested researchers, this ad can be found in folder 1955 DIII Revlon (1 of 2), 1955 Box 1, J. Walter Thompson Competitive Ads, JWT/Duke.

17. On discourse employing sexual norms and pathologies and their representation in cold war ideology, see Geoffrey Smith, "National Security and Personal Isolation: Sex, Gender, and Disease in the Cold-War United States," *International History Review* 14, no. 2 (1992): 221–440. On sexual and global politics, see Emily S. Rosenberg, "'Foreign Affairs' After World War II: Connecting Sexual and International Politics," *Diplomatic History* 18 (1994): 59–70.

18. "How to Build Defense Business," *Business Week*, 10 October 1959, 95. For more on this issue, see "The Biggest Most Baffled Business," *Business Week*, 10 October 1959, 71–72, 77–78, 83–84, 88, 90.

19. *Time*, 20 July 1959, 41.

20. *Life*, 28 September 1959, 84–85.

21. *Business Week*, 28 November 1959, 16.

22. See, for example, "Paradise or Doomsday?" *Woman's Home Companion*, May 1948, 32–33, 74–75; Howard Whitman, "What We're Afraid Of," *Collier's*, 20 March 1948, 13, 40, 42, 43; Paul O'Neil, "U.S. Change of Mind," *Life*, 3 March 1958, 91, 92, 94, 96, 98, 100. O'Neil's article is on American public opinions and anxieties concerning the country's rivalry with the Soviets.

23. Armco advertisement from Series 2, Box 42, Folder 3, N. W. Ayer Collection, National Museum of American History, Archives Center, Smithsonian Institution.

24. Other examples that show how the domestic and military markets overlapped or were naturally symbiotic include an AC Sparkplug advertisement, "Missile by Martin, Rocket by Olds," *Life*, 28 April 1958, 115; Waste King advertisement, "Waste King . . . [from] Food Waste Disposers for the Home [to] Technical Products for Military and Industry," *Life*, 23 November 1959, 171; U.S. Rubber/U.S. Royal Tires advertisement, "From jet age research . . . safer tires for you," *Life*, 30 September 1957, 16; Philco Corporation advertisement, "Reconnaissance television moves GHQ directly over any target zone," *Business Week*, 8 September 1956, 65; Bell Telephone advertisement, "Where do guided missiles get their 'Brains?'" *Fortune*, August 1959, 202; Ford Motor Company advertisement for weapons, atomic missile range systems, computer and space technology operations, "Ford Motor Company announces a new division—Aeronutronic specializing in products for the space age," *Time*, 13 July 1959, 60–61; General Electric Silicones advertisement, "GE Chemical Progress . . . New furniture polishes a shining example of how G-E silicones improve products . . . G-E chemical facilities help speed defense production," Box 61, Folder GE 1951 Trade Magazines, Darcy, Masius, Benton, and Bowles Collection, Hartman Center, Duke University. See also the following articles about specific product reconversion after World War II. On using ultraviolet radiation to detect microbes: "'Black Light' Examines Kitchen Pots and Pans," *Science Digest*, October 1950, 95; "Microwave Cooking," *Good Housekeeping*, May 1957, 263–64; "Washing with Sound Waves," *Popular Science*, October 1946, 74. See also the following from the Dow Archives: "New Saran Film Makes Its Debut," *Brinewell* (Dow Chemical house organ), 1 April 1947, 1; "New Peacetime Uses Discovered for Styrofoam," *Brinewell*, 24 June 1947, 2. Regarding wartime housing reconversion, see "Quonsets Converted to Peace," *Popular Mechanics*, April 1947, 114; "Home Is a Quonset," *Woman's Home Companion*, December 1946, 64–65; advertisement for plywood reconversion by Atlas Panels and Doors, "Some facts about . . . the RAF 'Mosquito' Fighter-Bomber," *American Home*, April 1952, 149.

25. Many advertisers emphasized the "double-duty features" of their appliances, a tactic left over from World War II–era advertising and magazine articles directed toward women performing double roles on the home front. See, for example, Amana refrigerator advertisement, "For double duty in your kitchen," Box 22 1956, Folder 1956 H211 Refrigerator & Freezer, number 2 of 3, Competitive Ads, JWT/Duke. Both the postwar supermarket, with its wide array of goods, and the enlarged storing capacity of new refrigerators and freezers encouraged the cold war housewife to "stockpile"

groceries in her suburban outpost. (Credit goes to Dennis Henthorn for this insight.) Many of these types of ads echoed the civil defense planners' advice and the imagery in civil defense literature, which suggested that consumers store up a large supply of canned goods, bottled water, and tranquilizers in the event of nuclear attack while they were at home. See Crosley refrigerator/freezer combo advertisement, "Crosley 'Fresh and Frozen Food Centers' specially designed for Supermarket Shoppers . . . Stock up on months of frozen meals, store away bushels of fresh things," Box 22 1956, Folder 1956 H211 Refrigerator & Freezer, number 2 of 3, Competitive Ads, JWT/Duke.

26. Cold war magazines, perhaps unwittingly, juxtaposed news stories and photographs documenting the elements of destruction with utopian advertising on the facing pages.

27. Wizard Deodorizer advertisement, Box 20 1958, Folder H240 1958, Deodorizers, Competitive Ads, JWT/Duke.

28. *Life,* 17 March 1958, 188.

29. *Better Homes and Gardens,* July 1958, 94.

30. Nescafe advertisement, *Life,* 17 May 1954, 135; Kelvinator Electric Range advertisement, *McCall's,* July 1950, inside front cover.

31. *American Home,* July 1951, 102.

32. For other examples of space-race rhetoric, see Philco range advertisement, "New Starflight Styled Philco," Box 22 1956 Folder H212 Electric 1 of 2; Necchi sewing machine advertisement, "Own a super automatic Necchi supernova ultra . . . with triple impulse action," Box 3 1959 Folder H215 misc. Sewing Machines; Stiffel lamp advertisement, "New space age flavor in this lamppole designed for the year 2000 by Stiffel," Box 2 1959 Folder H150 Lamps; TV remote control advertisement, "Motorola Golden Satellite [with] Tube Sentry," Box 25 1957 Folder H310 Motorola 2 of 2. All ads are from Competitive Ads, JWT/Duke.

33. Regarding selling a house: "My 30 Day's War," *House Beautiful,* June 1952, 18, 76; on the invasion of synthetic suds: "The Detergents Strike Back," *Fortune,* June 1956, 102; on remodeling a home: "This Kitchen Took Cover," *American Home,* March 1954, 80, 82; "The Germ's Last Stand?" *Newsweek,* 24 November 1958, 99–100; "How to Win the Chore War," *House & Garden,* April 1953, 118–19. As was true of narratives about the assault on germs, articles about cures for the common cold utilized the language of the arms race. See John D. Hillary, "Cold War on the Common Cold," *Science Digest,* February 1954, 10–14; "Cold War Strategy," *Newsweek,* 24 December 1951, 62; "Common Cold War," *Newsweek,* 10 November 1947, 47.

34. For another example of this tendency, see a 1952 Reynolds Aluminum advertisement in which a banal kitchen product plays a serious role. The ad depicts boxes of Reynolds Wrap, which have been upgraded with aircraft wings and jet engines, speeding toward victory in Korea. "Light, Strong Links in the Chain of Command," *Business Week,* 23 February 1952, inside front cover.

35. Allan C. Fisher, Jr., "You and the Obedient Atom," *National Geographic,* September 1958, 303–53. For more on the disparities between what the civil defense planners knew about the unsurvivability of an atomic attack and what they told the public, see Oakes, *The Imaginary War.*

36. Following this line of corporate reasoning, Consolidated Edison, the electric power company for New York City, produced a series of booklets attempting to educate the public on the safety of nuclear energy and its domestic uses. See *Atomic*

Energy—How?; Atomic Energy—Why?; Atomic Energy Power at Indian Point; Atomic Power and Safety (New York: Consolidated Edison, 1956). Available at New York Public Library. See also "Atomic Energy in Action" (no date), a public relations exhibition regarding the peaceful uses of the atom, held in the Union Carbide building in Manhattan. Energy Folder #1, Atomic Energy, Warshaw Collection, National Museum of American History, Archives Center, Smithsonian Institution. For Union Carbide and Carbon Corporation's publicity book on its "atomic energy activities . . . in its own plants and laboratories [and those] it operates for the Government," see *The Atom in Our Hands* (1955). Call number PAM, Hagley Museum and Library. For General Electric and Westinghouse's role in domesticating the atom, see, for example, "The Atom: Power by GE," *Newsweek,* 26 October 1953, 82, 85; "Industry's Progress Toward Harnessing the Atom," *Newsweek,* 13 April 1953, 88–90. The latter includes other companies' involvement in the atomic energy program. For more on the atomic power industry's history, see Daniel Ford, *The Cult of the Atom: The Secret Papers of the Atomic Energy Commission* (New York: Simon & Schuster, 1982); Philip L. Cantelon, Richard G. Hewlett, and Robert C. Williams, eds., *The American Atom: A Documentary History of Nuclear Policies from the Discovery of Fission to the Present* (1984; reprint, Philadelphia: University of Pennsylvania Press, 1991).

37. The family event "Atomic Frontier Days" was a public relations device to educate the public, especially children, about the benefits of domesticated nuclear energy.

38. For another children's book on atomic energy, see Heinz Haber, *The Walt Disney Story of Our Friend the Atom* (New York: Simon & Schuster, 1956). The Disney book emphasizes the mystique of scientific authority by using the allegorical figure of a genie for atomic power. There was also a film by Disney of the same title. See also Maxwell Leigh Eidinoff and Hyman Ruchlis, *Atomics for the Millions* (New York: McGraw-Hill/ Whittlesey House, 1947). The book credits Maurice Sendak for its cartoon illustrations.

39. *Magnesium Progress,* January 1963, front cover. Dow Archives. Allan M. Winkler in *Life Under a Cloud: American Anxiety About the Atom* (New York: Oxford University Press, 1993) covers attitudes reflecting the coexistence of the threat and euphoric promise of a nuclear future in his chapter "The Peaceful Atom." Winkler also provides descriptions of the cultural manifestations of atomic rhetoric in school curricula and popular songs. For more analyses of atomic age cultural responses to the bomb and atomic energy, see Margot A. Henriksen, *Dr. Strangelove's America: Society and Culture in the Atomic Age* (Berkeley: University of California Press, 1997); Alan Nadel, *Containment Culture: American Narratives, Postmodernism, and the Atomic Age* (Durham, N.C.: Duke University Press, 1995); Jayne Loader, *Public Shelter* (Waxahachie, TX: EJL Productions, 1995), CD-ROM. This CD-ROM is a collection of industrial/educational film clips, music, pictures, and documents concerning the atomic age. The CD-ROM is an offshoot of the research gathered for Loader's documentary film *The Atomic Café* created with Pierce Rafferty and Kevin Rafferty (n.p.: Archives Project, 1982).

40. Allan Fisher, "You and the Obedient Atom," 311. For more on atomic power as an industrial tool or household technology, see Robert E. Wilson, "Atoms in the Homes: How Soon?" *U.S. News & World Report,* 17 December 1954, 116–18; Darrell Huff, "Atomic Rays Keep Food Fresh," *Popular Science,* April 1956, 102–5, 248; "Atomic Miracles We Will See," *Look,* 25 August 1953, 27; "What the Atom Will Do for You," *Changing Times,* August 1957, 43; "Atomic Energy Progress," *Scientific American* March 1955, 50. On the transition of atomic energy into a regulated civilian utility, see

"Domestic Atom Puts on Mufti," *Business Week,* 13 October 1956, 30–31. ("Mufti" are civilian clothes worn by a soldier usually appearing in military garb.) Even parodies of atomic "worlds of tomorrow" focused on the benign side of atomic energy. See Lewis Nordyke, "Atoms in the Home," *New York Times Magazine,* 14 October 1945, 46. For examples that skirted the edge of parody but turned to the civilian atom's benign traits, see "Atomic Progress: As Bombs Pile Up, Nuclear Energy Finds New, Creative Applications," *Life,* 1 January 1951, 22–33.

41. For more on atomic-assisted cooking, see the publicity still for "Atomburgers," cooked on a range powered by "America's first operational nuclear-power plant" in 1955, illustrated in Thomas Hine, *Populuxe* (New York: Alfred A. Knopf, 1986), 134. Hine provides several other examples of atomic symbols used in advertising, signage, packaging, and product design of the era. For other examples of 1950s product, packaging, and architectural examples sporting outer space, atomic, rocket, scientific, and other decorative motifs, see Richard Horn, *Fifties Style* (New York: Friendman/Fairfax, 1993); Gideon Bosker, Michele Mancini, and John Gramstad, *Fabulous Fabrics of the 50s* (San Francisco: Chronicle Books, 1992); Lesley Jackson, *The New Look: Design in the Fifties* (New York: Thames & Hudson; Manchester: Manchester City Art Galleries, 1991); Alan Hess, *Googie: Fifties Coffee Shop Architecture* (San Francisco: Chronicle Books, 1985) and *Googie Redux: Ultramodern Roadside Architecture* (San Francisco: Chronicle Books, 2004).

42. Fones-Wolf, *Selling Free Enterprise,* 10, 22–29, 33–35; Robert Griffith, "Forging America's Postwar Order: Domestic Politics and Political Economy in the Age of Truman," in Michael Lacey, ed., *The Truman Presidency,* 58–63 (1989; reprint, Cambridge: Cambridge University Press and Woodrow Wilson International Center for Scholars, 1990); Brinkley, *End of Reform,* 259–71.

43. Advertising Council et al., *1950 Campaign.*

44. *A Campaign to Explain the American Economic System* (n.p.: Advertising Council, 1948), front cover.

45. Fones-Wolf, *Selling Free Enterprise,* 32–44. For more on the corporate public education programs of the immediate postwar years, including those of the NAM, see Bird, *"Better Living,"* 173–205.

46. *Telling the Profit Story—In Your Town!* (New York: NAM, 1948), n.p. (original emphasis). NAM #1411, Series III, 204/205, NAM/Hagley.

47. Advertising Council, "A 'Mid-Century' Retail Advertising Campaign by Retailers—for Retailers: The Miracle of America Thrives on Progress" (n.p., 1950). AC archives.

48. Elizabeth Gordon, "Does Design Have Social Significance?" *House Beautiful,* October 1953, 230. The "haberdasher" refers to President Truman. See also Karla Parker, "The Image of America Begins in the Home," *PTA Magazine,* June 1961, 2–3.

49. "A House That Says Made in America," *House Beautiful,* June 1951, 103.

50. Ibid.

51. "The Power of Free Taste," *House Beautiful,* October 1952, 192–94. The house was considered "American" because it had "two traditional elements—[a] stone chimney and [an interior] lily pond" but used in a "novel way." One had to be wary of tradition because, in one family's experience, it had "tyrannized their first home." Their second, built in 1952, had been "liberated" by "free taste."

52. Gordon, "Does Design Have Social Significance?" 315. See also "Defining the American Way of Life Executed in the New American Style," *House Beautiful,* May

1951, 107, where the author states, "This [home] symbolizes what the average American now has, or can reasonably expect to achieve by his own endeavors under the American democratic system." Ironically, the AC's "Miracle of America" campaign illustration in figure 9.8 has a picture of a flat-roofed modernist house squarely in the middle of the ad. According to style experts such as Gordon, such a house indicated Communist leanings, so what is it doing in an ad campaign that sought to flush socialism from the United States? We need to remember that the modernist flat-roofed style was applied as a visual code for "progress" in promotional material (as we saw in chapter 6) and was not meant to be indicative of the archetypal American middle-class norm.

53. "Defining the American Way of Life," 107–35. The issue also consisted of a "Pace-Setter" house, which was intended to "be a yardstick against which to measure your own mode of living. . . . For the house was designed to be a symbol of the accepted practices of good living current in . . . 1951."

54. "A House That Says Made in America," 103.

55. David Lawrence, "The Moral Strength of Capitalism," *U.S. News & World Report,* 11 January 1952, 72.

56. Gene Birkeland, "The Organization Mother," *American Mercury,* June 1960, 140–41. See also Martin O'Neil, "Shabby Showcase: In Red-weary Leipzig, U.S. Auto Show Is Hit of Fair," *Life,* 25 September 1959, 18, 21–24. See also the quote from "What Nixon Learned in Russia," cited in the foreword.

57. David Lawrence, "The Moral Strength of Capitalism," *U.S. News & World Report,* 11 January 1952, 72.

58. Vladimir Niska, "Why the Russians Fear 'People's Capitalism,'" *Better Homes and Gardens,* September 1957, 66. See page 67 for a comparison chart between Soviet and American standards of living. The chart shows how much more the Soviet must labor than his American counterpart to buy the simplest necessities, such as soap. "People's Capitalism" was also the name for another AC/government campaign to direct Americans' political consciousness during the 1950s. The reference to "People's Capitalism" in the Niska article was most likely in response to AC campaign literature directed to retailers, manufacturers, and the press on how to seamlessly incorporate lessons on free enterprise into articles and ad copy. See, for example, "Sell your merchandise while you sell 'The American Way' with this dramatic program of Economic Education. . . ." From Advertising Council, "A Powerful Retail Merchandising and Public Relations Program" (n.p., n.d.). Folder 460, AC archives. On the democratization of progress, see also "Worker Loses His Class Identity," *Business Week,* 11 July 1959, 90–92, 96, 98. The article explains how the working-class standard of living increased after the war by emphasizing the middle-class amenities enjoyed by the housewives and families of blue-collar workers, including single-family home ownership.

59. "Traveling Salesmen for Two Ways of Life: Eisenhower and Khrushchev are crisscrossing the world—and often each other's tracks—in pursuit of goodwill," *New York Times Magazine,* 13 March 1960, 22. Communists were also maligned in the U.S. media by showing what failures they were at advertising—the assumed stalwart institution of the American Way. See, for example, "Advertising, Russian Style: Soviets Use Capitalistic Campaign to Help Their Controlled Economy," *Life,* 2 May 1949, 59–60, 62; "Buy Red or You May Drop Dead," *Life,* 22 June 1962, 27. For more on the

propaganda war between U.S. business interests and the Soviets, see "Reds Can't Admit That Communism Is Harder to Sell," *Saturday Evening Post*, 26 July 1952, 10.

60. John M. Begg, "The American Idea: Package It For Export," *United States State Department Bulletin*, 12 March 1951, 409–10. Begg was director of the Private Enterprise Corporation's International Information and Educational Exchange Program. For more on the AC after World War II, see John Vianney McGinnis, "The Advertising Council and the Cold War" (Ph.D. diss., Syracuse University, 1991).

61. *Advertising: A New Weapon in the World-Wide Fight for Freedom: A Guide for American Business Firms Advertising in Foreign Countries* (n.p.: Advertising Council and the United States Information Service of the Department of State, November 1948), 1, 2. AC archives. The AC holds several examples of cold war campaigns that it waged on behalf of the American Way, both in the United States and abroad.

62. "Nylon Wonderland," *Time*, 24 June 1957, 31. For more on overseas fairs, see "U.S. Packaging Breaks Through the Iron Curtain," 1964 New York World's Fair, Box 4 General Reference, Folder 4, JWT/Duke; "Brussels Fair and Science," *Science News Letter*, 11 January 1958, 26–27; "Our Soft Sell at Brussels," *Reporter*, 29 May 1958, 19–20; "World's Fair—'58: Battle of the 'Best,'" *Newsweek*, 28 April 1958, 41. Haddow, in *Pavilions of Plenty*, asserts that "containing the Soviets required military bases in strategic locations and encouraged trade with all the nations bordering the USSR." Haddow gives the historical development of the international trade fair phenomenon during the cold war and explains how American Way ideology was promoted through elaborate displays of modern comforts and conveniences—most of which were affordable for the average American worker (Haddow, *Pavilions of Plenty*, 1).

63. "Nylon Wonderland," 31.

64. Brooks, "Consumer Markets and Consumer Magazines," 133.

65. William Appleman Williams, "The Large Corporation and American Foreign Policy," in David Horowitz, *Corporations and the Cold War*, 95–99. Eakins concurs with Williams on the fear of a postwar depression as a motivating factor behind the overseas trade solution ("Business Planners," 147–49).

66. Williams, "Large Corporation," 100. According to Eakins, New Deal officials were in favor of overseas expansion as a "solution to overproduction and unemployment at home," agreeing with conservatives on this point. A consensus on this issue had been largely reached among government and business authorities by 1945. Foreign aid in the form of the Marshall Plan was an institutionalization of postwar plans to avoid depression and sustain wartime highs by expanding American commercial interests into foreign markets. Eakins says that the postwar "political crisis was at root an economic crisis," and therefore foreign aid and policy were created from the perspective of sustaining high levels of production, consumption, and employment in the United States. Financial gifts and loans given to foreign countries would need to be spent somewhere, and since the United States was the only major Western country with its full industrial infrastructure intact after the war, it was logical to assume that "those dollars have to be spent in the United States, sooner or later" (Eakins, "Business Planners," 143, 160).

Afterword

1. Robert Higgs, "U.S. Military Spending in the Cold War Era: Opportunity Costs, Foreign Crises, and Domestic Constraints," *Cato Policy Analysis* 114 (30 No-

vember 1988), http://www.cato.org/pubs/pas/pa114.html. Pearson Education's Web site, InfoPlease, provides a table of U.S. military spending (in 2002 dollars). In 1990, military expenditures exceeded $409 billion, declining to the low point of $298.4 billion in 1999. The requested defense budget for 2006 is $419.3 billion. InfoPlease, "U.S. Military Spending, 1946–2004," 11 June 2005, http://www.infoplease.com/ipa/A0904490.html; "Thank '80s Greed for '90s Growth," *Business Week,* 5 April 1999, 96. On defense spending under the 1990s Bush administration, see "White House Shows No Undue Concern for Defense Cuts," *Defense Daily* 163 (29 June 1989, 502). On the military need to outsource due to 1990s budget cuts, see Chris Wood, "The Outsourcing Option: More Attractive Than Ever," *The Public Manager: The New Bureaucrat* 28 (Spring 1999): 43.

2. Joel Andreas, *Addicted to War: Why the U.S. Can't Kick Militarism* (Edinburgh: AK Press, 2003), 38. Andreas says this figure was compiled by the Center for Defense Information (CDI) and is available on their Web site: http://www.cdi.org/issues/milspend.html. The CDI cited its source as the DoD. This particular Web page, however, states that $13.1 trillion was spent by the military between 1948 and 1991. Because of this apparent difference, I will refer to this figure in quotation marks. See also "Pentagon's War Spending Hard to Track," April 13, 2005, http://www.reuters.com/newsArticle.jhtml?type=topNews&storyID=8178749. Apparently, according to Comptroller General David Walker, the DoD actually has no reliable or accurate system for determining how the DoD has spent "tens of millions in war-related emergency funds" from Congress.

3. The "crucible of war" wording was used in the Evans Products ad of 1944 (see fig. 5.2).

4. According to Richard Barnet and John Cavanagh in *Global Dreams: Imperial Corporations and the New World Order* (New York: Touchstone/Simon & Schuster, 1994), "new world order" refers to circumstances that have given rise to and support global corporate reach into virtually every village and neighborhood around the world. Such commercial empires, unlike American corporations of the postwar years, are able to create new commercial and thus social and economic conditions, due to their possession of "earth-spanning technologies" and their ability to manufacture "products that can be produced anywhere and sold everywhere," to expand "credit around the world," and to connect "global channels of communication" (14). A new social and economic order on a global scale, however, as Barnet and Cavanagh argue, is not necessarily to the benefit of those whose lives it penetrates and shapes. Americans, even those of the middle class, are not immune to the pressures of this new world order, which more often than not threatens Americans' job security and standards of living rather than stabilizing them (21, 221, 280).

5. For more on this topic, see Timothy Saasta, *America's Third Deficit: Too Little Investment in People and Infrastructure* (Washington, D.C.: Center for Community Change, 1991), found in Andreas, *Addicted to War,* 68. See also www.communitychange.org. Eric Alterman in *When Presidents Lie: A History of Official Deception and Its Consequences* (New York: Viking/Penguin Group, 2004) stresses how President George W. Bush lied to the public about jobs and the health of the economy (247), painting a rosy picture of progress when the reality for many Americans, even the middle class, was far different. On federal cuts to social services, see the National Governors Association Web site, http://www.nga.org/nga/lobbyIssues/1,1169,C_LOBBY_ISSUE^D_1256,00

.html. Although 1996 marked the historic welfare reform agreement in which Congress agreed to provide the states $2.38 billion each year for the Social Services Block Grant, over the past few years, according to the NGA, this funding has dwindled to $1.7 billion (as of 2002). The unemployment rate for 2001 was recorded at 4.7 percent, in 2002 it climbed to 5.8 percent, and in 2003 it rose again to 6.0 percent. See http://www.census.gov/statab/www/employ.html and the databases on the U.S. Department of Labor, Bureau of Statistics Web site, http://www.bls.gov/data/home .htm. According to the Bureau of Statistics, in 2003 there were 1.3 million more Americans living below the poverty level compared with 2002, raising the poverty rate to 12.5 percent. See http://www.census.gov/Press-Release/www/releases/archives/income _wealth/002484.html.

6. Louis Uchitelle and John Markoff, "Terrorbusters., Inc.: The Rise of the Homeland Security–Industrial Complex," *New York Times,* 17 October 2004, 8. The estimate for 2005 security expenditures had been $47 billion when Uchitelle and Markoff's article was printed. These figures do not include federal spending on the military's budget. Reuters news service reported in April 2005 that Congress had "approved $25 billion in extra defense spending" for that year, but was aiming to approve $81 billion more "outside the normal budget process." See "Pentagon's War Spending Hard to Track."

7. Paul Rutherford, *Weapons of Mass Persuasion: Marketing the War against Iraq* (Toronto: University of Toronto Press, 2004), 185.

8. Uchitelle and Markoff, "Terrorbusters," 8.

9. On the fiscal beneficiaries of 9/11, including the Bush administration, the Pentagon, the CIA, the FBI, and the defense industry, see Nafeez Mosaddeq Ahmed, *The War on Freedom: How and Why America was Attacked September 11, 2001* (Joshua Tree, Calif.: Tree of Life, 2002), 279–82.

10. John Tirman reports that since 9/11 the costs for homeland security in both public and private sectors have "totaled something like a half-trillion dollars," not including U.S. military activity in the Middle East. "Security the Progressive Way," *The Nation,* 11 April 2005, 28.

11. P. W. Singer, *Corporate Warriors: The Rise of the Privatized Military Industry* (Ithaca, N.Y.: Cornell University Press, 2003), 81–82. Singer indicates that nonprofit/nongovernment organizations also engage PMFs.

12. Ibid., 78. According to Singer, 9/11 certainly made the PMF industry healthier. Its stocks "jumped roughly 50 percent in value" when the rest of the U.S. economy took a nosedive (232). PMF Brown & Root "received over $2 billion as part of recurring contracts with the U.S. Army in the Balkans." Their profits were not derived from "the sale of weapons systems . . . but from the provision of military-related systems operators and support" (80). Brown & Root have also attracted U.S. government clients outside the Defense Department, signing a $100 million contract in 2000 to "improve security at U.S. embassies" (147). Halliburton, the company run by Vice President Dick Cheney as CEO from 1995 to 2000, owned Brown & Root, its subsidiary, which it combined with M. W. Kellogg to form KBR (Kellogg, Brown & Root). The end of the war in Iraq promises even greater profits for PMFs and even corporations outside the PMF orbit. Managing and reconstructing Iraq, as well as Afghanistan, which was bombed by the United States in 2002, may cost American taxpayers $87 billion, the amount requested by the Bush administration (Rutherford, *Weapons of Mass Persuasion,* 194).

13. Sheldon Rampton and John Stauber, *Weapons of Mass Deception: The Uses of Propaganda in Bush's War on Iraq* (New York: Jeremy P. Tarcher, Penguin, 2003), 42–43. The largest PR firm in the world, according to Rampton and Stauber, Hill & Knowlton, was behind "a massive PR campaign to persuade Americans" to support a war that would free Kuwait from Iraq. Ironically, it was the Kuwait government-in-exile that paid most of the bill for this campaign. Hill & Knowlton made $10.8 million off the deal (70). "Perception managers" are engaged by the Pentagon to "influence" the "emotions, motives, and objective reasoning" of "foreign audiences." See "Air Force Intelligence and Security Doctrine: Psychological Operations (PSYOP)," Air Force Instruction 10-702, Secretary of the Air Force, 19 July 1994, http://www.fas.org/irp/DoDdir/usaf/10-702.htm, found in Rampton and Stauber, *Weapons of Mass Deception*, 5. Rampton and Stauber's book details the public relations offensive launched in America and abroad prior to the U.S. military's attempt to "liberate" the Iraqi people from their leader and root out terrorists in hiding. See also Danny Schechter, *Embedded: Weapons of Mass Deception: How the Media Failed to Cover the War on Iraq* (Amherst, NY: Prometheus Books, 2003).

14. Rampton and Stauber, *Weapons of Mass Deception*, 49.

15. Ibid., 58. The Bush administration relied on media appearances of high-level staff to flood public perception with the Bush spin on the 9/11 and Iraq "facts." See Rutherford, *Weapons of Mass Persuasion*, 32–33.

16. Rampton and Stauber, 57. Rutherford in *Weapons of Mass Persuasion* covers how the news media was used as a marketing tool by the Bush administration to persuade Americans to accept and support war on Iraq. According to Rutherford, the Undersecretary for Public Diplomacy, Charlotte Beers, has been an advertising executive and brand specialist. Beers was responsible after 9/11 for countering the U.S.'s poor reputation in Arab countries (29–31). See also www.projectcensored.org, organized by a Sonoma State University research group. Project Censored provides public access to the top news stories that were rebuffed by the mainstream media. According to Alterman, the mainstream media often backed up deceitful misinformation that flowed from members of the Bush administration (*When Presidents Lie*, 303–4). Anne E. Kornblut reports that since 2003 "agencies of the federal government have been caught distributing prepackaged television programs that used paid spokesmen acting as newscasters and, in violation of federal law, failed to disclose the administration's role in developing and financing them." Kornblut, "Administration Is Warned about Its 'News' Videos," *New York Times,* 19 February 2005, http://www.nytimes.com/2005/02/19/politics/19gao.html.

17. The national nonprofit group organized for independent, free agent workers, Working Today, posts advertisements in New York City subways with messages that reflect the growing lack of security among middle-class Americans; see for example "Health Insurance vs. Paying Rent. Welcome to Middle-Class Poverty," www.workingtoday.org. For statistics on the rise in numbers of Americans without health care insurance, see http://www.census.gov/apsd/techdoc/cps/cps-main.html. On the rising rate of debt in the United States, especially due to living on credit cards, see: "Why Young Americans are Drowning in Debt," *Christian Science Monitor,* 9 December 2004, http://moneycentral.msn.com/content/CollegeandFamily/Moneyinyour20s/P101676.asp. The Federal Reserve's Web site has a table showing rising revolving and nonrevolving debt among American consumers (see http://www.federalreserve.gov/Releases/),

as does the U.S. Department of the Treasury, Bureau of the Public Debt (see http://www.publicdebt.treas.gov/opd/opd.htm).

18. Uchitelle and Markoff, "Terrorbusters," 8.

19. On the Radiation and Public Health Project, see http://www.radiation.org/index.html. The site lists several books about the health risks of living near a nuclear facility; see especially Ernest Sternglass, Joseph Mangano, William McDonnell, and Jay Gould, *The Enemy Within: The High Cost of Living Near Nuclear Reactors: Breast Cancer, AIDS, Low Birthweights, and Other Radiation-Induced Immune Deficiency Effects* (New York: Four Walls Eight Windows, 1996).

20. Rutherford in *Weapons of Mass Persuasion* describes the war on terror (and the war in Iraq) as a media spectacle, scripted like a marketing strategy that ultimately helped secure the U.S. government's greater latitude of surveillance on its home turf and across the globe as a "free world" policing agent. He writes that this spectacle's power "has become as serious a menace to democracy as the police power. . . . The war on terror . . . created the necessary preconditions to fashion America's own brand of the [Soviet-style] propaganda state" (184). Rutherford also argues that the post-9/11 "terror alert" propaganda and the propaganda used to justify the war provided convenient means to "sell a grand vision, and a moral one at that, of a New World Order" (163). For a critique of the present-day exploitation of fear, see Bob Herbert, "A Radical in the White House," *New York Times,* 18 April 2005, 19; Kathleen Sullivan, "Under a Watchful Eye: Incursions on Personal Privacy," in *The War on Our Freedoms: Civil Liberties in an Age of Terrorism*, edited by Richard C. Leone and Greg Anrig Jr. (New York: BBS Public Affairs, 2003), 128–246; and Susan Hansen, *The USA Patriot Act: The Basics* (n.p.: The Century Foundation, 2004; http://www.homelandsec.org/publications.asp?pubid=191). This Web site offers a free download of the thirty-six-page book.

Some authors and journalists have pointed out that the "war on terrorism" may lead to a more dangerous world. Interestingly, this conclusion was put forward by the Department of Defense (DoD) and published in a February 1, 1998, article: Ivan Eland, "The Terrorist Retaliation U.S. Risks in Attacking Saddam," *Sacramento Bee,* http://www.independent.org/newsroom/article.asp?id=1128. See also Andreas, *Addicted to War,* 32;."Endless Terror and the Infinite Terror War," http://www.publiceye.org/frontpage/911/d-kellner-911-02.html#P128_45146.

On the misleading information about the "facts" behind 9/11 and the consequences for this deceit, see Rampton and Stauber, *Weapons of Mass Deception,* 78–79, 80, 91–95, 105; and David Ray Griffin, *The New Pearl Harbor: Disturbing Questions about the Bush Administration and 9/11* (Northampton, Mass.: Interlink, 2004) and his follow-up book, *The 9/11 Commission Report: Omissions and Distortions* (Northampton, Mass.: Olive Branch Press, Interlink, 2005). For coverage of deception in both George H. W. Bush's and George W. Bush's administrations, see Alterman, *When Presidents Lie.*

21. For more on this issue, see Paul Fussell, *Bad or, the Dumbing of America* (New York: Summit Books, 1991); J. Brauer, "Education Neglect Damages U.S. Competitiveness," *Augusta Chronicle,* 4 April 1992, http://www.aug.edu/~sbajmb/abc008.htm.

SOURCES

Archival Collections

Advertising Council archives. New York Public Library, New York, N.Y. (Hereafter cited as AC archives.) There is also an AC archive in Chicago and at the University of Illinois at Urbana-Champaign.

Bel Geddes, Norman. Industrial Collection. Harry Ransom Humanities Research Center, University of Texas, Austin.

Cooper-Hewitt National Museum of Design. Papers of Donald Deskey, Henry Dreyfuss, Gilbert Rohde, Ladislav Sutnar (including some Knoll papers), and Don Wallance. Smithsonian Institution, New York, N.Y.

Dow Chemical Corporation. Post Street Archives, Midland, Mich.

George Arents Research Library, Special Collections. Egmont Arens, Lurelle Guild, George Nelson, Walter Dorwin Teague, Raymond Spilman, and Russel Wright Papers. Syracuse University, Syracuse, N.Y.

John W. Hartman Center for Sales, Advertising, and Marketing History. Advertising agency collections, including J. Walter Thompson. Duke University, Durham, N.C. (Hereafter cited as JWT/Duke.)

McFadden Publishing Company. *True Story* Collection. New York, N.Y.

National Association of Manufacturers (NAM) Collection, including archival material of the NAM's National Industrial Information Committee (NIIC). Hagley Museum and Library, Wilmington, Delaware. (Hereafter cited as NAM/Hagley.)

National Museum of American History, Archives Center. N. W. Ayer advertising agency and Warshaw Collections. Smithsonian Institution, Washington, D.C.

Saarinen Family. Papers. Cranbrook Archives, Bloomfield Hills, Mich.

Bibliography

Adams, James S. *Working Together for Postwar America.* New York: National Association of Manufacturers, 1943. NAM #1411, Series III, Subject files, NIIC Box 843, Folder: Campaign Promotion 1944. NAM/Hagley.

Adams, Walter. "Mystery Weapon Today—Your Servant Tomorrow." *Better Homes and Gardens,* August 1943, 20–21, 64–67.

"Ad Men's Arsenal." *Business Week,* 11 October 1941, 14.

Advertising: A New Weapon in the World-Wide Fight for Freedom: A Guide for American Business Firms Advertising in Foreign Countries. n.p.: Advertising Council and the United States Information Service of the Department of State, November 1948. AC archives.

Advertising Council, Association of Advertising Agencies, and Association of National Advertisers. *The 1950 Campaign to Explain the American Economic System.* n.p., n.d. "Miracle of America" folder 486A. AC archives.

"Advertising in Wartime." *New Republic,* 21 February 1944, 233–36.

An Advertising Program for the N.A.M. New York: Kenyon & Echhardt, n.d. NAM #1411, NIIC Box 843, Advertising 1943 Folder. NAM/Hagley.

"Advertising Russian Style: Soviets Use Capitalistic Campaign to Help Their Controlled Economy." *Life,* 2 May 1949, 59–60, 62.

"Afterthoughts on Nixon and the Exhibition." *New Republic,* 21 September 1959, 6–7.

Agan, Tessie. *The House: A Text for a College Course on the House.* Chicago: J. B. Lippincott, 1939.

Ahmed, Nafeez Mosaddeq. *The War on Freedom: How and Why America Was Attacked September 11, 2001.* Joshua Tree, Calif.: Tree of Life, 2002.

"Air Force Intelligence and Security Doctrine: Psychological Operations (PSYOP)." *Air Force Instruction* 10–702, Secretary of the Air Force, 19 July 1994. http://www.fas.org/irp/doddir/usaf/10-702.htm.

Albrecht, Donald, ed. *World War II and the American Dream: How Wartime Building Changed a Nation.* Washington, D.C.: National Building Museum; Cambridge, Mass.: MIT Press, 1995.

Alexander, James Rodger. "The Art of Making War: The Political Poster in Global Conflict." In M. Paul Holsinger and Mary Anne Schofield, eds., *Visions of War: World War II in Popular Literature and Culture.* Bowling Green, Ohio: Bowling Green State University Popular Press, 1992.

Alexis, Marcus. "Assessing Fifty Years of African-American Economic Status, 1940–1990." *The American Economic Review* 88, no. 2 (1998): 368–75.

"All Clear." *House Beautiful,* October 1938, 68, 117.

Alterman, Eric. *When Presidents Lie: A History of Official Deception and Its Consequences.* New York: Viking/Penguin Group, 2004.

Altman, Karen E. "Modernity, Gender, and Consumption: Public Discourses on Woman and the Home." Ph.D. diss., University of Iowa, 1987.

"Amazons in the Arsenal." *Nation's Business,* July 1943, 65.

America at War Needs Women at Work: A Plan Book Published by the Information Services of the War Manpower Commission for Use in Recruiting Women in Critical War Areas for War Factories and Necessary Civilian Services. n.p.: War Advertising Council, 1943. JWT/Duke.

"Americans Thinking About Iraq, but Focused on the Economy." Midterm Election Preview, Pew Research Center for the People and the Press, 10 October 2002. http://people-press.org/reports/display.php3?ReportID=162.

Anderson, Karen. "Last Hired, First Fired: Black Women Workers during World War II." *Journal of American History* 69, no. 1 (1982): 82–97.

———. *Wartime Women: Sex Roles, Family Relations, and the Status of Women during World War II.* Westport, Conn.: Greenwood, 1981.

Andreas, Joel. *Addicted to War: Why the U.S. Can't Kick Militarism.* Edinburgh and Oakland, Calif.: AK Press, 2003.

"Another Kind of National Defense." *American Home,* April 1942, 10, 14–17.

"Architects and Defense." *Pencil Points,* October 1941, 657–64.

Arens, Egmont, and Roy Sheldon. *Consumer Engineering: A New Technique for Prosperity.* New York: Harper and Brothers, 1932.

Arnold, Joseph. *The New Deal in the Suburbs: A History of the Greenbelt Program, 1935–1954.* Columbus: Ohio State University Press, 1971.

"Atom Bomb House." *Architects' Journal,* 28 February 1946, 176.

"The Atom: Power by GE." *Newsweek*, 26 October 1953, 82, 85.

Atomic Energy—How?; Atomic Energy—Why?; Atomic Energy Power at Indian Point; Atomic Power and Safety. New York: Consolidated Edison, 1956.

"Atomic Energy Progress." *Scientific American*, March 1955, 50.

"Atomic Miracles We Will See." *Look*, 25 August 1953, 27.

"Atomic Progress: As Bombs Pile Up, Nuclear Energy Finds New Creative Applications." *Life*, 1 January 1951, 22–33.

Atwood, Albert W. "The Miracle of War Production." *National Geographic*, December 1942, 693–715.

Austin, Carl C., Jr. "War as a Proving Ground." *Modern Plastics*, October 1944, n.p. Reprint from Dow Chemical Corporation, Post Street Archives.

Austin, Jean. "Postbaloney." *American Home*, September 1944, 20–21.

"Automatic Housekeeping." *Look*, 14 May 1957, 84–86.

Badger, Anthony J. *The New Deal: The Depression Years, 1933–1940.* New York: Hill & Wang, 1989.

Ballaster, Rose, Margaret Beetham, Elizabeth Frazer, and Sandra Hebron. *Women's Worlds: Ideology, Femininity, and the Woman's Magazine.* London: Macmillan, 1991.

Banner, Lois W. *American Beauty.* New York: Alfred A. Knopf, 1983.

Banta, Martha. *Imaging American Women: Idea and Ideals in Cultural History.* New York: Columbia University Press, 1987.

———. *Taylored Lives: Narrative Productions in the Age of Taylor, Veblen, and Ford.* Chicago: University of Chicago Press, 1993.

Baragar, Arnold E. "Postwar Equipment." *Journal of Home Economics*, January 1946, 11–15.

Baritz, Loren. *The Good Life: The Meaning of Success for the American Middle Class.* 1982. Reprint, New York: Harper & Row, 1990.

Barnet, Richard, and John Cavanagh. *Global Dreams: Imperial Corporations and the New World Order.* New York: Touchstone/Simon & Schuster, 1994.

"Barring Japs in California May Be Boon." *People's Voice*, 21 February 1942, 24.

Barstow, David, and Robin Stein. "Under Bush, a New Age of Prepackaged Television News." 13 March 2005. http://ar.atwola.com/html/93205920/480176268/aoladp?SNM=HIDBFV&width=728&height=90&target=_blank&TZ=300&CT=I.

Batchelor, Ray. *Henry Ford: Mass Production, Modernism, and Design.* Manchester, U.K.: Manchester University Press, 1994.

Baxandall, Rosalyn, and Elizabeth Ewen. *Picture Windows: How the Suburbs Happened.* New York: Basic Books, 2000.

Beaumont, Roger. "Quantum Increase: The Military Industrial Complex in the Second World War." In Benjamin Franklin Cooling, ed., *War, Business, and American Society: Historical Perspective on the Military-Industrial Complex.* Port Washington, N.Y.: Kennikat Press/National University Publications, 1977.

"Beauty—An Aid to Morale!" *Independent Woman*, January 1942, 25.

Becker, Gary S. *The Economics of Discrimination.* Chicago: University of Chicago Press, 1957.

Beebe, Lucius. "Horrors of Progress." *American Mercury*, January 1944, 95–96.

Begg, John M. "The American Idea: Package It for Export." *United States State Department Bulletin*, 12 March 1951, 409–12.

Bel Geddes, Norman. *Magic Motorways*. New York: Random House, 1940.

——. *War Maneuver Models Created for Life Magazine*. New York: Museum of Modern Art, 1944.

Bell, William K. *15 Million Negroes and 15 Billion Dollars*. New York: William K. Bell, 1958.

Bentley, Amy. *Eating for Victory: Food Rationing and the Politics of Domesticity*. Chicago and Urbana: University of Illinois Press, 1998.

Bernstein, Arron. "Are We Better Off Than 4 Years Ago? Overall, Wages Went Up—But Job Losses Have Hit Family Incomes Hard." *Business Week,* 25 October 2004, 99.

Bethune, Mary McLeod. "Along the Battlefronts." *People's Voice,* 14 February 1942, 14.

"'A Better America' Is Banner of Industry's Postwar Program." *Newsweek,* 20 December 1943, 50, 52, 54.

"The Biggest Most Baffled Business." *Business Week,* 10 October 1959, 71–72, 77–78, 83–84, 88, 90.

Bird, William L., Jr. *"Better Living": Advertising, Media, and the New Vocabulary of Business Leadership, 1935–1955*. Evanston, Ill.: Northwestern University Press, 1999.

Bird, William L., Jr., and Harry R. Rubenstein. *Design for Victory: World War II Posters and the American Home Front*. New York: Princeton Architectural Press, 1998.

Birkeland, Gene. "The Organization Mother." *American Mercury,* June 1960, 139–41.

"'Black Light' Examines Kitchen Pots and Pans." *Science Digest,* October 1950, 95.

Blair, Jayson. "Two Utilities Say 9/11 Costs May Raise Rates: U.S. Rejects Requests for Disaster Aid from Con Ed and Verizon." *New York Times,* 28 February 2002, section B, p. 6.

Bletter, Rosemarie Haag. "The Myths of Modernism." In Janet Kardon, ed., *Craft in the Machine Age, 1920–1945*. New York: Harry N. Abrams and the American Craft Museum, 1996.

——. "The World of Tomorrow: The Future with a Past." In *High Styles: Twentieth-Century American Design*. New York: Whitney Museum and Summit Books, 1985.

Bletter, Rosemarie Haag, Robert Rosenblum, Morris Dickstein, Marc H. Miller, Sheldon J. Reaven, Helen A. Harrison, and Ileen Sheppard. *Remembering the Future: The New York World's Fair from 1939 to 1964*. New York: Rizzoli and Queens Museum, 1989.

"Blown-Up House." *Popular Mechanics,* April 1945, 48.

Blum, John Morton. *V Was for Victory: Politics and American Culture during World War II*. New York: Harcourt Brace Jovanovich, 1976.

Bogart, Michele H. *Artists, Advertising, and the Borders of Art*. Chicago: University of Chicago Press, 1995.

Bolin, Brent C. *The Failure of Modern Architecture*. New York: Van Nostrand Reinhold, 1976.

Bosker, Gideon, Michele Mancini, and John Gramstad. *Fabulous Fabrics of the 50s*. San Francisco: Chronicle Books, 1992.

Bowman, Irving H. "An Industrial Approach to Housing." *Architectural Forum,* July 1932, 73–75, 78–79.

Brandes, Stuart D. *Warhogs: A History of War Profits in America*. Lexington: University Press of Kentucky, 1997.

Brauer, J. "Education Neglect Damages U.S. Competitiveness." *Augusta Chronicle,* 4 April 1992. http://www.aug.edu/~sbajmb/abc008.htm.

Braverman, Jordan. *To Hasten the Homecoming: How Americans Fought World War II Through the Media.* Lanham, Md.: Madison Books, 1996.

"Bright Plastics Go to Bat for Metal in the Home." *Popular Mechanics,* June 1942, 16.

Brinkley, Alan. *The End of Reform: New Deal Liberalism in Recession and War.* 1995. Reprint, New York: Vintage Books/Random House, 1996.

Broadhurst, Jean. *Home and Community Hygiene: A Text-Book of Personal and Public Health.* 1918. Reprint, Philadelphia: J. B. Lippincott, 1925.

Brody, David. "The New Deal in World War II." In John Braeman, Robert Bremner, and David Brody, eds., *The New Deal: The National Level,* vol 1. Columbus: Ohio State University Press, 1975.

Bronner, Simon J., ed. *Consuming Visions: Accumulation and Display of Goods in America, 1880–1920.* New York: W. W. Norton; Winterthur, Del.: The Henry Francis du Pont Winterthur Museum, 1989.

Brooks, Dwight Ernest. "Consumer Markets and Consumer Magazines: Black America and the Culture of Consumption, 1920–1960." Ph.D. diss., University of Iowa, 1991.

"Build Frontier Town to House Bomber Builders." *Hotel Monthly,* May 1943, 14–21.

"Building for Defense . . . Headway and Headaches." *Architectural Forum,* April 1941, 10, 12, 14.

"Building for Defense . . . 1,000 Houses a Day at $1,200 Each." *Architectural Forum,* June 1941, 425–29.

"Building for Defense . . . Prefabrication Takes New Shape." *Architectural Forum,* April 1941, 20, 110.

Burch, Philip H., Jr. "The NAM as an Interest Group." *Politics & Society* 4 (Fall 1973): 97–130.

Buszek, Maria-Elena. "War Goddess: The Varga Girls, World War II, and Feminism." *n.paradoxa* 6 (March 1998). http://web.ukonline.co.uk/n.paradoxa/.

"Buy Red or You May Drop Dead." *Life,* 22 June 1962, 27.

A Campaign to Explain the American Economic System. n.p.: Advertising Council, 1948. AC Archives.

Cantelon, Philip L., Richard G. Hewlett, and Robert C. Williams, eds. *The American Atom: A Documentary History of Nuclear Policies from the Discovery of Fission to the Present.* 1984. Reprint, Philadelphia: University of Pennsylvania Press, 1991.

Carlisle, Norman V., and Frank B. Latham. *Miracles Ahead! Better Living in the Postwar World.* New York: Macmillan, 1944.

Catton, Bruce. *The Warlords of Washington.* New York: Harcourt, Brace, 1948.

Cayton, Horace R. "Decline of Racism: Sheer Need of Manpower for Future Wars Will Lessen Race Conflict." *Pittsburgh Courier,* 1 September 1945, 7.

———. "Paging the Liberals." *Pittsburgh Courier,* 8 September 1945, 7.

Céline, Louis-Ferdinand. *Journey to the End of Night.* 1932. Reprint, New York: Penguin, 1966.

Chafe, William. *The Unfinished Journey: America Since World War II.* New York: Oxford University Press, 1986.

Chandler, Alfred D., Jr. *The Visible Hand: The Managerial Revolution in American Business.* Cambridge, Mass.: Harvard University Press/Belknap Press, 1977.

Channing, Helen. "Beauty Up!" *True Story,* July 1942, 97.

Cherne, Leo. "We *Can* Buy Postwar Prosperity." *Science Digest,* February 1945, 1–5.

Churchill, Henry S. "War-Housing Remainders—Post-War Slums." In Paul Zucker, ed., *New Architecture and City Planning: A Symposium.* New York: Philosophical Library, 1944.

"CIO Anti-Discrimination Group Issues Report." *Pittsburgh Courier,* 16 January 1945, 1.

"City of 1960." *Architectural Forum,* July 1937, 57–62.

Clarke, Alison J. *Tupperware: The Promise of Plastic in 1950s America.* Washington, D.C.: Smithsonian Books, 2001.

Cogdell, Christina. *Eugenic Design: Streamlining America in the 1930s.* Philadelphia: University of Pennsylvania Press, 2004.

———. "The Futurama Recontextualized: Norman Bel Geddes's Eugenic 'World of Tomorrow.'" *American Quarterly* 52 (June 2000): 193–245.

———. "Products or Bodies? Streamline Design and Eugenics as Applied Biology." *Design Issues* 19 (Winter 2003): 36–53.

———. "Reconsidering the Streamline Style: Evolutionary Thought, Eugenics, and U.S. Industrial Design, 1925–1940." Ph.D. diss., University of Texas, Austin, 2001.

Cohen, Lizabeth. *A Consumers' Republic: The Politics of Mass Consumption in Postwar America.* New York: Alfred A. Knopf/Borzoi Books, 2003.

Cohen, Stan. *V for Victory: America's Home Front during World War II.* Missoula, Mont.: Pictorial Histories, 1991.

"Cold War Strategy." *Newsweek,* 24 December 1951, 62.

Colean, Miles L. "The Miracle House Myth." *House Beautiful,* December 1944, 78–79, 115–17.

Collins, Robert. "American Corporatism: The Committee for Economic Development, 1942–1964." *Historian* 44 (February 1982): 151–73.

"Command Post . . . for a Housewife." *Sunset,* September 1954, 70.

"Common Cold War." *Newsweek,* 10 November 1947, 47.

"Conference on the Subject: 'What Can Industry Contribute to a Better America After the War.'" NAM #1411, Series III NIIC, Box 843. NAM/Hagley.

"Construction Potentials: Postwar Prospects and Problems, a Basis for Action." *Architectural Record,* December 1943, 1–32.

Consumer Reports. *I'll Buy That! Fifty Small Wonders and Big Deals That Revolutionized the Lives of Consumers.* Mount Vernon, N.Y.: Consumer Reports Books, 1986.

"The Consumer's War." *Fortune,* August 1941, 94–95, 116, 118.

"Control Center: The Kitchen." *New York Times Magazine,* 27 March 1960, 78–79.

"The Convenient Accused." *Pittsburgh Courier,* 9 January 1945, 1.

Cook, Nick. *The Hunt for Zero Point: Inside the Classified World of Antigravity Technology.* New York: Random House/Broadway Books, 2001.

Coontz, Stephanie. *The Way We Never Were: American Families and the Nostalgia Trap.* HarperCollins/Basic Books, 1992.

Corn, David. "Missing WMD Report." *The Nation,* 11 April 2005, 5–6, 7, 10.

Corn, Joseph, ed. *Imagining Tomorrow: History, Technology, and the American Future.* Cambridge, Mass.: MIT Press, 1986.

Corn, Joseph, and Brian Horrigan. *Yesterday's Tomorrows: Past Visions of the American Future.* 1984. Reprint, Washington, D.C.: Smithsonian Institution; Baltimore: Johns Hopkins University Press, 1986.

Cosgrove, Stuart. "The Zoot-Suit and Style Warfare." *History Workshop Journal* 18 (Autumn 1984): 77–91.

Cowan, Ruth Schwartz. *More Work for Mother: The Ironies of Household Technology from the Open Hearth to the Microwave.* New York: HarperCollins/Basic Books, 1983.

Craig, Maxine Leeds. *Ain't I A Beauty Queen? Black Women, Beauty, and the Politics of Race.* New York: Oxford University Press, 2002.

Crawford, Margaret. "Daily Life on the Home Front." In Donald Albrecht, ed., *World War II and the American Dream: How Wartime Building Changed a Nation.* Washington, D.C.: National Building Museum; Cambridge, Mass.: MIT Press, 1995.

Crouch, Christopher. *Modernism in Art, Design & Architecture.* New York: St. Martin's, 1999.

Cusker, Joseph P. "The World of Tomorrow: Science, Culture, and Community at the New York World's Fair." In Helen A. Harrison, ed., *Dawn of a New Day: The New York World's Fair, 1939/40.* New York: New York University Press and the Queens Museum, 1980.

Dailey, Donald. "What Will the Postwar Consumer Want?" *Advertising & Selling,* June 1943, 54, 56.

Danbom, David B. *The Resisted Revolution: Urban America and the Industrialization of Agriculture, 1900–1930.* Ames: Iowa State University Press, 1979.

Davis, Shelby Cullom. "Household Servants Are Gone Forever." *American Magazine,* March 1942, 32–33, 89–92.

Davison, Robert L. "When Science Takes Over the Home." In Paul Zucker, ed., *New Architecture and City Planning: A Symposium.* New York: Philosophical Library, 1944.

Dean, Gordon. "Atomic Miracles We Will See." *Look,* 25 August 1953, 27–30.

"Defense Called Spur to Industrial Design." *New York Times,* 4 October 1941, 28.

"Defense Dept.: Leading Patron of the Sciences." *Business Week,* 12 January 1957, 96–98, 100, 102, 104.

"Defining the American Way of Life Executed in the New American Style." *House Beautiful,* May 1951, 107–35.

de la Peña, Carolyn Thomas. *The Body Electric: How Strange Machines Built the Modern American.* New York: New York University Press, 2003.

"Demand for Better and Cheaper Homes." *Architect & Engineer,* May 1934, 32.

Department of Commerce, Bureau of the Census. *Current Population Reports: Consumer Income.* No. 5, Series P-60. Washington, D.C., 7 February 1949. http://www2.census.gov/prod2/popscan/P60-05.pdf.

"Design for Peace." *Art & Industry,* November 1939, 169–70.

"Design for Socialization." *Business Week,* 23 January 1943, 79.

"The Detergents Strike Back." *Fortune,* June 1956, 102.

Deventer, John. "Jobs in the World of Tomorrow and . . . A Job for the 'World of Tomorrow.'" *Iron Age,* 9 February 1939, n.p.

Dieuaide, Francis R. *Civilian Health in Wartime.* Cambridge, Mass.: Harvard University Press, 1942.

Digest of Findings of Public Opinion Polls on the Subject of Post-war Problems and Planning. New York: Kenyon Research Corporation, 1944. NAM #1411, NIIC, Box 843. NAM/Hagley.

Dikotter, Frank. "Race Culture: Recent Perspectives on the History of Eugenics." *American Historical Review* 103, no. 2 (1998): 467–78.

Dinerstein, Joel. *Swinging the Machine: Modernity, Technology, and African American Culture between the World Wars.* Amherst, Mass.: University of Massachsettes Press, 2003.

"Does Business Have a Program for a Better Postwar America?" NAM #1411, Series III, NIIC Box 848, Oversize Records. NAM/Hagley.

"Domestic Atom Puts on Mufti." *Business Week,* 13 October 1956, 30–31.

Donahue, Mary. "Design and the Industrial Arts in America, 1894–1940: An Inquiry into Fashion Design and Art and Industry." Ph.D. diss., City University of New York, 2001.

"Double Shifts on the Home Front." *Ladies' Home Journal,* April 1941, 108.

Douglas, Mary. *Purity and Danger: An Analysis of Concept of Pollution and Taboo.* 1966. Reprint, London and New York: Routledge Classics, 2002.

"Dream House: Los Angeles Builder Gives Preview of All Things Americans May Someday Have in Their Homes." *Life,* 6 May 1946, 83–85.

Dreyfuss, Henry. *Industrial Design: A Pictorial Accounting, 1929–1957.* New York: Henry Dreyfuss, 1957.

———. *Industrial Design: A Progress Report, 1929–1952.* New York: Henry Dreyfuss, 1952.

———. *A Record of Industrial Designs, 1929 through 1946.* New York: n.p., 1946.

———. *10 Years of Industrial Design, 1929–1939.* New York: Pyson Printers, 1939.

"Dwelling Machines." *Architectural Record,* April 1945, 122.

Eakins, David W. "Business Planners and America's Postwar Expansion." In David Horowitz, ed., *Corporations and the Cold War.* New York: Monthly Review Press/Bertrand Russell Peace Foundation, 1969.

Egan, Timothy. "States, Facing Budget Shortfalls, Cut the Major and the Mundane." *New York Times,* 21 April 2003, A1.

Eidelberg, Martin, ed. *Design, 1935–1965: What Modern Was.* New York: Harry N. Abrams; Montreal: Le Musée des Arts Décoratifs de Montréal, 1991.

Eidinoff, Maxwell Leigh, and Hyman Ruchlis. *Atomics for the Millions.* New York: McGraw-Hill/Whittlesey House, 1947.

"The 8,000 Lb. House." *Architectural Forum,* April 1946, 129, 131, 132–36.

Eland, Ivan. "The Terrorist Retaliation U.S. Risks in Attacking Saddam." *Sacramento Bee,* 1 February 1998, http://www.independent.org/newsroom/article.asp?id=1128.

"Encounter." *Newsweek,* 3 August 1959, 15–20.

Encyclopedia of Advertising. 3 vols. Ed. John McDonough, Karen Egolf, and Jacqueline V. Reid. New York: Taylor & Francis Group/Fitzroy Dearborn, 2003.

"Endless Terror and the Infinite Terror War." http://www.publiceye.org/frontpage/911/d-kellner-911-02.html#P128_45146.

Engelbrecht, H. C., and F. C. Hanighen. *Merchants of Death: A Study of the International Armament Industry.* New York: Dodd, Mead, 1934.

"Equipment for the Modern House." *Architectural Record,* November 1939, 77–81.

"Everything's Under Control." *McCall's,* December 1958, 133.

Ewen, Stuart. *Captains of Consciousness: Advertising and the Social Roots of the Consumer Culture.* New York: McGraw-Hill, 1976.

———. *PR! A Social History of Spin*. New York: HarperCollins/Basic Books, 1996.

Ezekiel, Mordecai. "The Road to Postwar Prosperity." *Science Digest,* September 1943, 37–42.

"The Fabulous Fifteen Years Ahead." *Changing Times,* January 1961, 7–21.

Feagin, Joe R., and Kelly Riddell. "The State, Capitalism, and World War II: The U.S. Case." *Armed Forces & Society* 17, no. 1 (1990): 53–79.

Federal Civil Defense Administration. *Home Protection Exercises: A Family Action Program.* 2nd ed. Washington, D.C.: Government Printing Office, 1956.

———. *This Is Civil Defense*. Washington, D.C.: Government Printing Office, May 1951.

———. *What You Should Know About Radioactive Fallout*. Washington, D.C.: Government Printing Office, 1955.

Fee, Elizabeth, and Steven H. Corey. *Garbage! The History and Politics of Trash in New York City*. New York: New York Public Library, 1994.

Fergusson, W. B. B. "American Advertising at War." *Art & Industry,* December 1943, 173–82.

"Fighting the War in the Kitchen Sink!" *Woman's Home Companion,* November 1943, 121.

"Fighting the War the Axis Way." *Baltimore Afro-American,* 18 April 1942.

Filene, Edward A. *Successful Living in This Machine Age*. New York: Simon & Schuster, 1932.

Finney, Burnham. "The Miracle of American Production." *American Mercury,* September 1943, 279–85.

Fisher, Allan C., Jr. "You and the Obedient Atom." *National Geographic,* September 1958, 303–53.

Fisher, Dorothy Canfield. "From the Lathe to the Hearth." *New York Times Magazine,* 5 December 1943, 16, 46.

Fitzpatrick, Ellen. *Endless Crusade: Women Social Scientists and Progressive Reform*. New York: Oxford University Press, 1990.

Fleischhauer, Carl, and Beverly W. Brannan. *Documenting America, 1935–1943*. Berkeley: University of California Press, 1988.

Flynn, George Q. *The Mess in Washington: Manpower Mobilization in World War II*. Westport, Conn.: Greenwood, 1979.

Folly, Martin. *The United States and World War II: The Awakening Giant*. Edinburgh: Edinburgh University Press, 2002.

Fones-Wolf, Elizabeth. *Selling Free Enterprise: The Business Assault on Labor and Liberalism, 1945–60*. Urbana and Chicago: University of Illinois Press, 1994.

Ford, Daniel. *The Cult of the Atom: The Secret Papers of the Atomic Energy Commission*. New York: Simon & Schuster, 1982.

Forty, Adrian. *Objects of Desire: Design and Society Since 1705*. London: Thames & Hudson, 1986.

"40% of the Nation is Ill-Housed, Federal Health Survey Ups the President's Ratio." *Architectural Forum,* June 1938, 34.

"For us the living . . . better homes." *Time,* 15 September 1941, 31.

Foucault, Michel. *Discipline and Punish: The Birth of the Prison*. Translated by Alan Sheridan. New York: Vintage Books/Random House, 1979.

"Fourteen Million Negro Customers." *Management Review,* June 1947, 336–38.

Fox, Frank. *Madison Avenue Goes to War: The Strange Military Career of American Advertising, 1941–1945.* Provo, Utah: Brigham Young University, 1975.

Frank, Thomas. "Air Travelers Stripped Bare with X-Ray Machine." *USA Today,* 15 May 2005. http://www.usatoday.com/travel/news/2005-05-15-airport-xray-bottomstrip _x.htm.

Fraser, Steve, and Gary Gerstle. *The Rise and Fall of the New Deal Order.* Princeton, N.J.: Princeton University Press, 1989.

Frederick, Christine. *The New Housekeeping: Efficiency Studies in Home Management.* Garden City, N.Y.: Doubleday, 1913.

The Freedom We Defend. n.p.: 1941. New York: NAM, 1943. NAM #1411, Series III, NIIC Box 846. NAM/Hagley.

Freeman, Richard B., R. A. Gordon, Duran Bell, and Robert E. Hall. "Changes in the Labor Market for Black Americans, 1948–1972." *Brookings Papers on Economic Activity,* no. 1 (1973): 67–131.

Friedman, Walter A. *Birth of a Salesman: The Transformation of Selling in America.* Cambridge, Mass.: Harvard University Press, 2004.

"Furniture's War." *Business Week,* 13 June 1942, 62.

Fussell, Paul. *Bad or, the Dumbing of America.* New York: Summit Books, 1991.

———. *Wartime: Understanding and Behavior in the Second World War.* New York: Oxford University Press, 1989.

"The Future of Industrial Design." *Art & Industry,* August 1943, 33–35.

Gammon, Margaret H. "The Consumer Viewpoint: What Women Want in Postwar Merchandise." *Advertising & Selling,* February 1944, 29, 124, 126, 128.

"The Germ's Last Stand?" *Newsweek,* 24 November 1958, 99–100.

Gillies, Mary Davis. *What Women Want in Their Bedrooms of Tomorrow: A Report of the Bedroom of Tomorrow Contest.* New York: McCall Corporation, 1944.

———. *What Women Want in Their Dining Rooms of Tomorrow: A Report of the Dining Room of Tomorrow Contest.* New York: McCall Corporation, 1944.

———. *What Women Want in Their Kitchens of Tomorrow: A Report of the Kitchen of Tomorrow Contest.* New York: McCall Corporation, 1944.

———. *What Women Want in Their Living Rooms of Tomorrow: A Report of the Living Room of Tomorrow Contest.* New York: McCall Corporation, 1944.

"Glamour Goes to War." *Saturday Evening Post,* 29 November 1941, 18–19, 56, 58.

Glimpses into the Wonder World of Tomorrow. Wilmington, Del.: E. I. du Pont de Nemours, 1943.

Goldberg, Hyman. "Push-Button Future." *Cosmopolitan,* January 1958, 66–71.

Gordon, Elizabeth. "Does Design Have a Social Significance?" *House Beautiful,* October 1953, 230–33, 315, 318.

———. "What's Wrong with Plastics?" *House Beautiful,* October 1947, 166.

———. "What the People Say They Want." *House Beautiful,* July 1944, 21–23.

"Gore Says Bush Lied About Iraq to Push for War." *Agence France Presse,* 24 June 2004. http://www.commondreams.org/headlines04/0624-10.htm.

Goslin, Ryllis, and Omar Goslin. *Primer for Americans.* New York: NAM, 1940. NAM #1411, Series III, NIIC Box 846. NAM/Hagley.

"Got Them Ol' Shipyard Closin' Blues." *New Hampshire Gazette,* 20 May 2005, 1.

Gough, Marion. "What Do They Mean When They Say It's Plastic?" *House Beautiful,* September 1947, 142–43, 237–39.

Gould, Stephen Jay. *The Mismeasure of Man.* New York: W. W. Norton, 1981.

Green, Harvey. *The Light of the Home: An Intimate View of the Lives of Women in Victorian America.* New York: Pantheon Books; Rochester, N.Y.: The Margaret Woodbury Strong Museum, 1983.

——. "The Promise and Peril of High Technology." In Janet Kardon, ed., *Craft in the Machine Age, 1920–1945.* New York: Harry N. Abrams and the American Craft Museum, 1996.

Gregory, James. *American Exodus: The Dust Bowl Migration and Okie Culture in California.* New York: Oxford University Press, 1989.

Gregory, Ross. *America 1941: A Nation at the Crossroads.* New York: Macmillan/Free Press, 1989.

——. *Modern America, 1914 to 1945.* New York: Facts on File, 1995.

Griffin, David Ray. *The New Pearl Harbor: Disturbing Questions About the Bush Administration and 9/11.* Northampton, Mass.: Interlink, 2004.

——. *The 9/11 Commission Report: Omissions and Distortions.* Northampton, Mass.: Olive Branch Press/Interlink, 2005.

Griffith, Robert. "Forging America's Postwar Order: Domestic Politics and Political Economy in the Age of Truman." In Michael Lacey, ed., *The Truman Presidency.* 1989. Reprint, Cambridge: Cambridge University Press and Woodrow Wilson International Center for Scholars, 1990.

——. "The Selling of America: The Advertising Council and American Politics, 1942–1960." *Business History Review* 57 (Autumn 1983): 388–412.

Gusterson, Hugh. *People of the Bomb: Portraits of America's Nuclear Complex.* Minneapolis: University of Minnesota Press, 2004.

Haber, Heinz. *The Walt Disney Story of Our Friend the Atom.* New York: Simon & Schuster, 1956.

Haber, Samuel. *Efficiency and Uplift: Scientific Management in the Progressive Era, 1890–1920.* 1964. Reprint, Chicago: University of Chicago Press/Midway Reprint, 1973.

Haddow, Robert H. *Pavilions of Plenty: Exhibiting American Culture Abroad in the 1950s.* Washington, D.C.: Smithsonian Institution Press, 1997.

Hammond, Laurence. "Kitchen Lore Speeds War Production." *Independent Woman,* December 1943, 362.

Hansen, Susan. *The USA Patriot Act: The Basics.* n.p.: The Century Foundation, 2004. http://www.homelandsec.org/publications.asp?pubid=191.

Hardyment, Christina. *From Mangle to Microwave: The Mechanization of Household Work.* Cambridge, Mass.: Polity, 1988.

Harris, Howell John. *The Right to Manage: Industrial Relations Policies of American Business in the 1940s.* Madison: University of Wisconsin Press, 1982.

Harrison, Helen A., ed. *Dawn of a New Day: The New York World's Fair, 1939/40.* New York: New York University Press and the Queens Museum, 1980.

Hart, Sue. "Madison Avenue Goes to War: Patriotism in Advertising during World War II." In M. Paul Holsinger and Marry Anne Schofield, eds., *Visions of War: World War II in Popular Literature and Culture.* Bowling Green, Ohio: Bowling Green State University Popular Press, 1992.

Hartmann, Susan M. *The Home Front and Beyond: American Women in the 1940s.* Boston: Twayne, 1982.

Hasian, Marouf. *The Rhetoric of Eugenics in Anglo-American Thought*. Athens: University of Georgia Press, 1996.

Haskell, Douglas. "Houses Like Fords." *Harper's,* February 1934, 286–98.

Hawkins, Mike. *Social Darwinism in European and American Thought, 1860–1945: Nature as Model and Nature as Threat*. 1997. Reprint, Cambridge: Cambridge University Press, 1998.

Hayden, Dolores. *Building Suburbia: Green Fields and Urban Growth, 1820–2000*. New York: Vintage, 2004.

——. *The Grand Domestic Revolution: A History of Feminist Designs for American Homes, Neighborhoods, and Cities*. Cambridge, Mass.: MIT Press, 1981.

Heide, Robert, and John Gilman. *Home Front America: Popular Culture of the World War II Era*. San Francisco: Chronicle Books, 1995.

Heilbroner, Robert L. *The Future as History*. 1959. Reprint, New York: Harper & Brothers, 1960.

Heimann, Jim, ed. *All-American Ads 40s* and *All-American Ads 50s*. Cologne: Taschen, 2001.

Heiner, Mary Kelly. "Where Research Is Needed." *Journal of Home Economics,* January 1945, 10–12.

Helyar, John. "Permanent Vacation? Fifty and Fired." *Fortune,* 2 May 2005. http://www.fortune.com/fortune/careers/articles/0,15114,1056189,00.html.

Henderson, Leon. "Advertising's Crisis Is Everybody's Crisis." *Advertising & Selling,* December 1941, 16, 92, 94, 96, 100.

Henriksen, Margot A. *Dr. Strangelove's America: Society and Culture in the Atomic Age*. Berkeley: University of California Press, 1997.

Henthorn, Cynthia Lee. "Commercial Fallout: The Image of Progress and the Feminine Consumer from World War II to the Atomic Age." In *The Writing on the Cloud: Conference Proceedings of "The Atomic Age Opens: American Culture Confronts the Atomic Bomb."* Lanham, Md.: University Press of America, 1997.

——. "The Emblematic Kitchen: Household Technology as National Propaganda, U.S.A., 1939–1959." *Journal of Knowledge and Society* 12 (Fall 2000): 153–87.

Henthorn, Thomas C. "A Catholic Dilemma: Urban Flight in Northwest Flint, Michigan." *Michigan Historical Review* 31, no. 2 (Fall 2005): 1–42.

Herbert, Bob. "A Radical in the White House." *New York Times,* 18 April 2005, 19.

Hersh, Seymour M. "The Coming Wars: What the Pentagon Can Now Do in Secret." *The New Yorker,* 31 January 2005. http://www.newyorker.com/printables/fact/050124fa_fact.

Hess, Alan. *Googie: Fifties Coffee Shop Architecture*. San Francisco: Chronicle Books, 1985.

——. *Googie Redux: Ultramodern Roadside Architecture*. San Francisco: Chronicle Books, 2004.

Hewitt, Charles E., Jr. "Housewives and War." *Good Housekeeping,* February 1940, 32–33, 79–80, 82.

Heythum, Antonin. "Industrial Design in Wartime." *Architect & Engineer,* September 1940, 22–26.

Higgins, J. F. "Introducing the Pre-Fabricated House." *House & Garden,* March 1935, 36–37, 76.

Higgs, Robert. "U.S. Military Spending in the Cold War Era: Opportunity Costs, Foreign Crises, and Domestic Constraints." *Cato Policy Analysis* 114 (30 November 1988). http://www.cato.org/pubs/pas/pa114.html.

——. "Wartime Prosperity? A Reassessment of the U.S. Economy in the 1940s." *Journal of Economic History* 52 (March 1992): 41–60.

Higonnet, Margaret Randolph, et al. *Behind the Lines: Gender, and the Two World Wars.* New Haven, Conn.: Yale University Press, 1987.

Hillary, John D. "Cold War on the Common Cold." *Science Digest,* February 1954, 10–14.

Hine, Thomas. *Populuxe.* New York: Alfred A. Knopf, 1986.

Hirose, Arthur P. "Attention Manufacturers! 115 Suggestions for Postwar Product and Home Improvements." *Advertising & Selling,* September 1943, 15–16, 77, 80.

——. "What Postwar Products Do Women Want? A Check-List for Manufacturers of Foods and Cosmetics." *Advertising & Selling,* January 1944, 29–30, 106.

Hitch, Charles J., and Roland N. McKean. *The Economics of Defense in the Nuclear Age.* Cambridge, Mass.: Harvard University Press, 1960.

Hofstadter, Richard. *Social Darwinism in American Thought.* Boston: Beacon, 1966. First published 1944 by University of Pennsylvania Press.

Holden, Thomas S. "New Materials, New Construction Methods, New House Architecture." In Paul Zucker, ed., *New Architecture and City Planning: A Symposium.* New York: Philosophical Library, 1944.

——. "Postwar Realism vs. Romance." *Architectural Record,* April 1943, 60, 84.

"Home Building Goes Indoors." *Architectural Forum,* May 1939, 374–76, supp. 36, 38.

"Home Is a Quonset." *Woman's Home Companion,* December 1946, 64–65.

"Homewood Kitchen at the New York World's Fair." *Good Housekeeping,* July 1939, 138–39.

Honey, Maureen. *Bitter Fruit: African American Women in World War II.* Columbia: University of Missouri Press, 1999.

——. *Creating Rosie the Riveter: Class, Gender and Propaganda during World War II.* Amherst: University of Massachusetts Press, 1984.

——. "The Working-Class Woman and Recruitment Propaganda during World War II: Class Differences in the Portrayal of War Work." *Signs* 8 (Summer 1983): 672–87.

Hopkins, Claude C. *My Life in Advertising & Scientific Advertising, Two Works by Claude C. Hopkins.* 1966. Reprint, Chicago: NTC Business Books, 1998.

Horn, Richard. *Fifties Style.* New York: Friendman/Fairfax, 1993.

Horowitz, Daniel. *The Anxieties of Affluence: Critiques of American Consumer Culture, 1939–1979.* Amherst: University of Massachusetts Press, 2004.

Horowitz, David, ed. *Corporations and the Cold War.* New York: Monthly Review Press/Bertrand Russell Peace Foundation, 1969.

Horrigan, Brian. "The Home of Tomorrow." In Joseph J. Corn, ed., *Imagining Tomorrow: History, Technology, and the American Future.* Cambridge, Mass.: MIT Press, 1986.

Horsfield, Margaret. *Biting the Dust: The Joys of Housework.* New York: St. Martin's, 1998.

Horton, Judith. "Our Kitchen at War." *American Home,* September 1944, 92–93.

Hounshell, David. *From the American System to Mass Production, 1800–1932: The Development of Manufacturing Technology in the United States.* Baltimore: Johns Hopkins University Press, 1984.

"House Beautiful's Ivory Washable House at Rockefeller Home Center, New York." *House Beautiful,* November 1940, 59–62.

"House by Celotex Corporation." *Architectural Forum,* October 1939, 285.

"Houses with All the Comforts of Home." *Good Housekeeping,* September 1935, 84–85, 165.

"A House That Says Made in America." *House Beautiful,* June 1951, 103–4, 106–11, 141–42.

"The House We Live In." *Ebony,* January 1946, 20.

"Housing and Prefabrication: Some Reasons Why the Factory Will Not Soon Supplant the Architect." *Pencil Points,* June 1936, 303–4, 306, 308, 310, 312.

"Housing VI: Solutions." *Fortune,* July 1932, 61, 69, 104–8.

"How Americans Can Earn More, Buy More, Have More." NAM #1411, Series III, NIIC Box 848, Oversize Records, Subject Files, "Advertising," 1944, Ad proofs produced by Kenyon & Eckhardt for the NIIC. NAM/Hagley.

Howard, Vicki. "'At the Curve Exchange': Postwar Beauty Culture and Working Women at Maidenform." In Philip Scranton, ed., *Beauty and Business: Commerce, Gender, and Culture in Modern America.* New York: Routledge, 2001.

How Industry Can Help the Government's Information Program on Woman Power. n.p.: WAC, Office of War Information, and War Manpower Commission, 1944. AC archives.

"How to Build Defense Business." *Business Week,* 10 October 1959, 95–98.

"How to Win the Chore War." *House & Garden,* April 1953, 118–19.

Hoy, Suellen. *Chasing Dirt: The American Pursuit of Cleanliness.* New York: Oxford University Press, 1995.

Huff, Darrell. "Atomic Rays Keep Food Fresh." *Popular Science,* April 1956, 102–5, 248.

Hutchinson, Woods. *Community Hygiene.* Boston: Houghton Mifflin, 1929.

Hyman, Michael R., and Richard Tansey, "Ethical Codes and the Advocacy Advertisements of World War II." *International Journal of Advertising* 12 (1993): 351–66.

"If That Boy Dies, It May Be Your Fault!" *Pittsburgh Courier,* 9 January 1943, 19.

"I'm Fed Up!" *Better Homes and Gardens,* July 1944, 22–23.

"The Impact of Defense on Advertising." *Advertising & Selling,* December 1941, 19–30.

"The Impact of War on Advertising." 32 articles in the series. *Advertising & Selling,* January 1942–July 1944.

"The Industrial Design Consultant." *Art & Industry,* March 1944, 66–79.

"Industrializing Shelter: The Fuller House." *Architectural Record,* May 1946, 118–20, 134.

"Industry Learns from Defense." *Scientific American,* January 1942, 16.

"Industry's Progress Toward Harnessing the Atom." *Newsweek,* 13 April 1953, 88–90.

"Ingenious New World." *Newsweek,* 28 May 1945, 70.

"The Institute Presents the Kitchen and Laundry at the Good Housekeeping–Stran-Steel House, A Century of Progress, Chicago." *Good Housekeeping,* August 1933, 88–89, 124.

"Into the Red Shadowland." *Newsweek,* 27 July 1959, 39–42.

"Introductory Material to Ads Recommended by [Arthur] Kudner." NAM #1411, NIIC Box 843, Advertising 1943 Folder. NAM/Hagley.

"In War, Prepare for Peace." *Business Week,* 9 September 1939, 60.

Issel, William. *Social Change in the United States, 1945–1983.* New York: Schocken Books, 1987.

"Is the 'Whirligig' for You?" *Nation's Business,* April 1947, 49.

It's Time for Total War on Food Waste: How Advertising Can Help the "Food Fights for Freedom" Program during June, July, and August 1944. Washington, D.C.: War Advertising Council and Office of War Information, 1944. AC archives.

Jackson, Kenneth T. *Crabgrass Frontier: The Suburbanization of the United States.* New York: Oxford University Press, 1985.

Jackson, Lesley. *The New Look: Design in the Fifties.* New York: Thames & Hudson; Manchester: Manchester City Art Galleries, 1991.

Jacobs, Meg. "'Democracy's Third Estate:' New Deal Politics and the Construction of a 'Consuming Public.'" *International Labor and Working-Class History* 55 (Spring 1999): 27–51.

———. "'How About Some Meat?' The Office of Price Administration, Consumption Politics, and State Building from the Bottom Up, 1941–1946." *Journal of American History* 84, no. 3 (1997): 910–41.

James, Parker. "Products for Postwar: New and Substitute Materials That Will Be Advertised After the War." *Advertising & Selling,* March 1943, 13–15, 78.

Jeffries, John W. *Wartime America: The World War II Home Front.* Chicago: Ivan R. Dee, 1996.

Jellison, Katherine. *Entitled to Power: Farm Women and Technology, 1913–1963.* Chapel Hill: University of North Carolina Press, 1993.

Johnson, J. Stewart. *American Modern, 1925–1940: Design for a New Age.* New York: Harry N. Abrams and the American Federation of Arts, 2000.

"Join the Millions Cooperating for Victory." *American Home,* May 1942, 6–7.

Jones, David Lloyd. "The U.S. Office of War Information and American Public Opinion during World War II, 1939–1945." Ph.D. diss., State University of New York, Binghamton, 1976.

Kaemffert, Waldemar. "War Brings Peace-Time Gains." *Science Digest,* July 1942, 15–18.

Kahn, Albert. "Producer of Production Lines" and "Architecture for War Production: A Military Aircraft Plant in the East." *Architectural Record,* June 1942, 39–52.

Kaiser, Henry J. "The American Way: Pessimism for Post War Era Assailed." *Vital Speeches of the Day,* 1 December 1942, 118–20.

Kallet, Arthur. "How Good Are Postwar Goods?" *New Republic,* 4 November 1946, 582–84.

Kanigel, Robert. *The One Best Way: Frederick Winslow Taylor and the Enigma of Efficiency.* New York: Viking, 1997.

Kaplan, Wendy. "Building Utopia: Pioneer Modernism on the American West Coast." In Paul Greenhalgh, ed., *Modernism in Design.* London: Reaktion Books, 1990.

———, ed. *Designing Modernity: The Arts of Reform and Persuasion, 1885–1945.* New York: Thames & Hudson; Miami Beach, Fla.: The Wolfsonian, 1995.

Keats, John. *The Crack in the Picture Window.* Boston: Houghton Mifflin, 1959.

Kellogg, Cynthia. "American Home in Moscow." *New York Times Magazine,* 5 July 1959, 24–25.

Kern-Foxworth, Marilyn. *Aunt Jemima, Uncle Ben, and Rastus: Blacks in Advertising, Yesterday, Today, and Tomorrow.* Westport, Conn.: Greenwood, 1994.

Kirkham, Pat. "Beauty and Duty: Keeping Up the (Home) Front." In P. Kirkham and D. Thoms, eds., *War Culture: Social Change and Changing Experience in World War Two Britain.* London: Lawrence & Wishart, 1995.

———. *Charles and Ray Eames: Designers of the Twentieth Century.* Cambridge, Mass.: MIT Press, 1995.

"Kitchen Front." *Time,* 28 August 1944, 84, 86.

"Kitchen Prototype—Designed for Plastics." *Modern Plastics,* June 1945, 97–102.

"Kitchens in Logical Order." *Better Homes and Gardens,* October 1934, 18–19, 100.

"Kitchens of Today, Built for Tomorrow." *House & Garden,* August 1935, 22–23, 72.

"Kitchens of Tomorrow May Look Like This." *Life,* 9 August 1943, 53–54, 56.

Klibansky, Raymond, Erwin Panofsky, and Fritz Saxl. *Saturn and Melancholy: Studies in the History of Natural Philosophy, Religion, and Art.* London: Nelson, 1964.

Koistinen, Paul A. C. *The Military-Industrial Complex: A Historical Perspective.* New York: Praeger, 1980.

——. *Planning for War, Pursuing Peace: The Political Economy of American Warfare, 1920–1939.* Lawrence: University Press of Kansas, 1998.

Koppes, Clayton, and Gregory Black. "Blacks, Loyalty, and Motion-Picture Propaganda in World War II." *Journal of American History* 73 (1986): 383–406.

Kornblut, Anne E. "Administration Is Warned About Its 'News' Videos." *New York Times,* 19 February 2005. http://www.nytimes.com/2005/02/19/politics/19gao .html.

Kraut, Alan. *Silent Travelers: Germs, Genes, and the "Immigrant Menace."* Baltimore: Johns Hopkins University Press, 1994.

"Ku Kluxers Start Riot in Detroit: Heads Are Cracked When Whites Defy President Roosevelt's Housing Order." *Baltimore Afro-American,* 7 March 1942, 2.

Kunstler, James Howard. *The Geography of Nowhere: The Rise and Decline of America's Man-Made Landscape.* New York: Simon & Schuster, 1993.

Laird, Pamela Walker. *Advertising Progress: American Business and the Rise of Consumer Marketing.* Baltimore: Johns Hopkins University Press, 2001.

Laporte, Dominique. *History of Shit.* Trans. Nadia Benabid and Rodolphe el-Khoury. 1978. Reprint, Cambridge, Mass.: MIT Press, 1993.

Larrabee, Eric, and Massimo Vignelli. *Knoll Design.* New York: Harry N. Abrams, 1981.

Lasch, Christopher. *The True and Only Heaven: Progress and Its Critics.* New York: W. W. Norton, 1991.

Lawrence, David. "The Moral Strength of Capitalism." *U.S. News & World Report,* 11 January 1952, 72.

Leach, William. *Land of Desire: Merchants, Power, and the Rise of a New American Culture.* New York: Random House/Vintage Books, 1993.

Lears, Jackson. *Fables of Abundance: A Cultural History of Advertising in America.* New York: HarperCollins/Basic Books, 1994.

Lebergott, Stanley. *Pursuing Happiness: American Consumers in the Twentieth Century.* Princeton, N.J.: Princeton University Press, 1993.

Leff, Mark H. "The Politics of Sacrifice on the American Home Front in World War II." *Journal of American History* 77, no. 4 (1991): 1296–1318.

Leslie, Stuart W. *The Cold War and American Science: The Military-Industrial-Academic Complex at MIT and Stanford.* New York: Columbia University Press, 1993.

"Let's Work for Industrial Peace." NAM #1411, Series III, NIIC Box 862. NAM/Hagley.

Leven, Marice, Harold G. Moulton, and Clark Warburton. *America's Capacity to Consume.* Washington, D.C.: The Brookings Institution, 1934.

"Levitt's Progress." *Fortune,* October 1952, 154, 156, 158, 160, 163, 164, 168.

Lewis, Charles, and John Neville. "Images of Rosie: A Content Analysis of Women Workers in American Magazine Advertising, 1940–1946." *Journalism & Mass Communication Quarterly* 72, no. 1 (1995): 216–27.

Lichtenberg, Bernard. "Business Backs New York World Fair to Meet the New Deal Propaganda." *Public Opinion Quarterly* 2 (April 1938): 314–15.

Lichtenstein, Claude, and Franz Engler, eds. *Streamlined: The Esthetics of Minimized Drag: A Metaphor for Progress.* Baden, Switzerland: Lars Müller, 1995.

Lichtenstein, Nelson. *Labor's War at Home: The CIO in World War II.* New York: Cambridge University Press, 1982.

Lingeman, Richard. *Don't You Know There's a War On? The American Home Front, 1941–1945.* Toronto: Longmans Canada Limited, 1970.

Lippincott, J. Gordon. "As the Crow Flies." *Modern Plastics,* April 1945, 98–99.

Lipsitz, George. *A Rainbow at Midnight: Labor and Culture in the 1940s.* Urbana and Chicago: University of Illinois Press, 1994.

Loader, Jayne. *Public Shelter.* Waxahachie, Tex.: EJL Productions, 1995. CD-ROM.

Loader, Jayne, Pierce Rafferty, and Kevin Rafferty. *The Atomic Café.* n.p.: Archives Project, 1982.

Loewy, Raymond. "Selling Through Design." *Art & Industry,* February 1942, 32–40.

———. "What of the Promised Post-War World." *New York Times Magazine,* 26 September 1943, 14, 27.

Logan, Rayford Whittingham. *The Negro and the Post-War World: A Primer.* Washington, D.C.: The Minorities Publishers, 1945.

Lougee, E. F. "Plastics Post-War." *Art & Industry,* August 1944, 34–40.

Lupton, Ellen. *Mechanical Brides: Women and Machines from Home to Office.* New York: Cooper-Hewitt National Museum of Design and Princeton Architectural Press, 1993.

Lupton, Ellen, and J. Abbott Miller. *The Bathroom, the Kitchen, and the Aesthetics of Waste: A Process of Elimination.* Cambridge, Mass.: MIT List Visual Arts Center, 1992.

Lynd, Robert S., and Helen Merrell Lynd. *Middletown: A Study in Contemporary American Culture.* New York: Harcourt, Brace, 1929.

MacDougall, Robert. "Red, Brown, and Yellow Perils: Images of the American Enemy in the 1940s and 1950s." *Journal of Popular Culture* 32 (Spring 1999): 59–75.

MacKenzie, Donald, and Judy Wajcman, eds. *The Social Shaping of Technology: How the Refrigerator Got Its Hum.* Philadelphia: Milton Keynes/Open University Press, 1985.

"The Magic Kitchen." *American Home,* January 1938, 39, 58.

"Maintenance—The Most Powerful Weapon on the Home Front!" *American Home,* May 1942, 8–9.

"Making Unemployment Work (Sort Of)." *New York Times,* 24 February 2002, section 10, p. 1.

Mannes, Marya. "Our Soft Sell at Brussels." *Reporter,* 29 May 1958, 19–20.

Manring, M. M. *Slave in a Box: The Strange Career of Aunt Jemima.* Charlottesville: University Press of Virginia, 1998.

Marchand, Roland. *Advertising the American Dream: Making Way for Modernity, 1920–1940.* Berkeley: University of California Press, 1985.

———. *Creating the Corporate Soul: The Rise of Public Relations and Corporate Imagery in American Big Business.* Berkeley: University of California Press, 1998.

———. "Suspended in Time: Mom-and-Pop Groceries, Chain Stores, and National Advertising during the World War II Interlude." In Barbara McLean Ward, ed.,

Produce & Conserve, Share & Play Square: The Grocer & The Consumer on the Home-Front Battlefield during World War II. Portsmouth, N.H.: Strawbery Banke Museum; Hanover, N.H.: University Press of New England, 1994.

Marketing in a Defense Economy. New York: J. Walter Thompson, 1951. Box #11, Company Publications 1951–54. JWT/Duke.

Martinson, Tom. *American Dreamscape: The Pursuit of Happiness in Postwar Suburbia.* New York: Carroll & Graf, 2000.

"Mass Layoffs Follow Victory." *Baltimore Afro-American,* 25 August 1945, 2.

May, Elaine Tyler. *Homeward Bound: American Families in the Cold War.* New York: HarperCollins/Basic Books, 1987.

May, Lary, ed. *Recasting America: Culture and Politics in the Age of Cold War.* Chicago: University of Chicago Press, 1989.

"Maymie and the Maid . . . in the Elegant Anderson Kitchen." *Ebony,* 16 November 1946, 16.

Mayo-Smith, Richmond. *Emigration and Immigration: A Study in Social Science.* New York: Scribner's, 1890.

McBroome, Delores Nason. "Catalyst for Change: Wartime Housing and African Americans in California's East Bay." In Sally M. Miller and Daniel A. Cornford, eds., *American Labor in the Era of World War II.* Westport, Conn.: Praeger, 1995.

McCraw, Thomas. *Creating Modern Capitalism: How Entrepreneurs, Companies, and Countries Triumphed in Three Industrial Revolutions.* Cambridge, Mass.: Harvard University Press, 1998.

McCullough, Helen E. "The Kitchen of Tomorrow." *Journal of Home Economics,* January 1945, 8–10.

McFeely, Mary Drake. "The War in the Kitchen." In Barbara McLean Ward, ed., *Produce & Conserve, Share & Play Square: The Grocer & the Consumer on the Home-Front Battlefield during World War II.* Portsmouth, N.H.: Strawbery Banke Museum; Hanover, N.H.: University Press of New England, 1994.

McGinnis, John Vianney. "The Advertising Council and the Cold War." Ph.D. diss., Syracuse University, 1991.

McKenzie, Marjorie. "Pursuit of Democracy." *Pittsburgh Courier,* 8 September 1945, 7.

———. "Supreme Court's Okay of Removal of Japanese Can Affect Negro Rights." *Pittsburgh Courier,* 6 January 1945, 6.

"The Mechanical Wing." *Architectural Forum,* October 1940, 273, supp. 92.

Meikle, Jeffery. *American Plastic: A Cultural History.* New Brunswick, N.J.: Rutgers University Press, 1995.

———. *Twentieth Century Limited: Industrial Design in America, 1925–1939.* Philadelphia: Temple University Press, 1979.

"Microwave Cooking." *Good Housekeeping,* May 1957, 263–64.

Milkman, Ruth. *Gender at Work: The Dynamics of Job Discrimination by Sex during World War II.* Urbana: University of Illinois Press, 1987.

Miller, Arthur C. "Necessity Creates Our Inventions: New Methods and Materials Dictated by Wartime Needs Prove Better Than the Old." *Popular Science,* December 1942, 64–70.

Miller, Sally M., and Cornford, Daniel A., eds. *American Labor in the Era of World War II.* Westport, Conn.: Praeger, 1995.

Mills, C. Wright. *The Power Elite*. 1956. Reprint, New York: Oxford University Press, 1959.

———. *White Collar: The American Middle Classes*. 1953. Reprint, New York: Oxford University Press, 1951.

Moberg, David. "'Ownership' Swindle." *The Nation*, 4 April 2005, 5–8.

Modell, John, Marc Goulden, and Sigurdur Magnusson. "World War II in the Lives of Black Americans: Some Findings and Interpretation." *Journal of American History* 76, no. 3 (1989): 838–48.

Molander, Earl A. "Historical Antecedents of Military-Industrial Criticism." *Military Affairs* 40, no. 2 (1976): 59.

Moore, Michael, director. *Fahrenheit 9/11*. DVD. Culver City, Calif.: Columbia TriStar Home Entertainment, 2004.

Morford, Mark. "Saudi Arabia, Off the Hook: The 9/11 terrorists were mostly Saudi. Suicide bombers in Iraq are Saudi. And we're allies?" 20 May 2005. http://sfgate .com/cgi-bin/article.cgi?f=/gate/archive/2005/05/20/notes052005.DTL.

Moulton, Harold G. "Americans Can Be Eight Times Richer." *American Magazine*, February 1950, 46–47, 76–80.

Mowry, George E. *The Urban Nation*. 1965. Reprint, New York: Hill & Wang, 1968.

Mumford, Lewis. "Mass-Production and the Modern House." *Architectural Record*, January 1930, 13–20.

———. *Technics and Civilization: A History of the Machine and Its Effects upon Civilization*. New York: Harcourt, Brace, 1934.

Myrdal, Gunnar. *An American Dilemma: The Negro Problem and Modern Democracy*. 2 vols. New York: Harper & Row, 1944. Reprint, New Brunswick, N.J.: Transaction, 2002.

"My 30 Day's War." *House Beautiful*, June 1952, 18, 76.

Nadel, Alan. *Containment Culture: American Narratives, Postmodernism, and the Atomic Age*. Durham, N.C.: Duke University Press, 1995.

"National Houses, Inc., Begins Production." *Architectural Record*, July 1936, 71–73.

"National Urban League's 1941 Report Sees Negroes Tensed." *People's Voice*, 4 April 1942, 35.

Nation at War: Shaping Victory on the Home Front. Reprint, n.p.: *Compton's Picture Encyclopedia*, n.d.

"Nation's Health Care Tab Ready to Explode: Cost Projected to Gobble Nearly 20 Percent of Economy." *USA Today*, 24 February 2005, A1.

Nelson, Daniel. *Frederick W. Taylor and the Rise of Scientific Management*. Madison: University of Wisconsin Press, 1980.

Nelson, Donald M. *The Arsenal of Democracy: The Story of American War Production*. New York: Harcourt, Brace, 1946.

Nelson, George, and Henry Wright. *Tomorrow's House*. New York: Simon & Schuster, 1945.

"The Net Gain." *Newsweek*, 17 August 1959, 100.

Neuhart, John, Marilyn Neuhart, and Ralph Caplan. *Connections: The Work of Charles and Ray Eames*. Los Angeles: Frederick S. Wight Art Gallery, University of California, 1976.

"New Demountable Cottages Developed by the Tennessee Valley Authority." *Pencil Points*, June 1941, 397, 400.

"The New Diplomacy." *Time,* 3 August 1959, 11–16.

"News of Planning and Construction." *American Architect,* May 1935, 69.

"New Structural Materials for Your Kitchen." *American Home,* June 1938, 31–32, 54.

"New Trend in Modern Design: Aircraft Idea in Furniture." *Science Illustrated,* June 1948, 98–101.

Nickles, Shelley. "Object Lessons: Household Appliance Design and the American Middle Class, 1920–1960." Ph.D. diss., University of Virginia, 1999.

——. "'Preserving Women': Refrigerator Design as Social Process in the 1930s." *Technology and Culture* 43, no. 4 (2002): 693–727.

NIIC. *A Time for Action: The Job That Industry Must Do Now.* New York: NAM, 1944. NAM #1411, Series III, Box 842. NAM/Hagley.

——. *Vigilance Today for a Free Enterprise Tomorrow.* New York: NAM, 1944. NAM #1411, Series III, Box 846. NAM/Hagley.

"1943—For War Making and Postwar Thinking." *Business Week,* 2 January 1943, 72.

Niska, Vladimir. "Why the Russians Fear 'People's Capitalism.'" *Better Homes and Gardens,* September 1957, 66.

Nixon, Richard M. "Russia as I Saw It." *National Geographic,* December 1959, 715–50.

"Nixon Talks About Russia." *Newsweek,* 27 July 1959, 39–42.

"Noise of Riveting Machines Drowns Out Bells of Christmas as Women War Workers Continue to Produce Fighting Planes." *Pittsburgh Courier,* 2 January 1943, 11.

Nordyke, Lewis. "Atoms in the Home." *New York Times Magazine,* 14 October 1945, 46.

"No Refrigerators, Autos Yet." *Baltimore Afro-American,* 25 August 1945, 4.

Norris, Floyd. "Grasping at the Statistics on the Self-Employed." *New York Times,* 6 December 2003, C1.

"Nylon Wonderland." *Time,* 24 June 1957, 31.

Oakes, Guy. *The Imaginary War: Civil Defense and American Cold War Culture.* New York: Oxford University Press, 1994.

O'Connor, Francis V. "The Usable Future: The Role of Fantasy in the Promotion of a Consumer Society for Art." In Helen A. Harrison, ed., *Dawn of a New Day: The New York World's Fair, 1939/40.* New York: New York University Press and the Queens Museum, 1980.

"Old Newspapers to New Houses." *Architectural Forum,* December 1940, 531–34, supp. 34–36.

Olson, James. *Saving Capitalism: The Reconstruction Finance Corporation and the New Deal, 1933–1940.* Princeton, N.J.: Princeton University Press, 1988.

O'Neil, Martin. "Shabby Showcase: In Red-weary Leipzig, U.S. Auto Show Is Hit of Fair." *Life,* 25 September 1959, 18, 21–24.

O'Neil, Paul. "U.S. Change of Mind." *Life,* 3 March 1958, 91, 92, 94, 96, 98, 100.

O'Neill, William. *A Democracy at War: America's Fight at Home and Abroad in World War II.* New York: Free Press/Macmillan, 1993.

Opler, Daniel J. "For All White Collar Workers: The Possibilities of Radicalism in New York City's Department Store Unions, 1934–1953." Unpublished manuscript in author's possession, 2004.

Ottley, Roi. *New World A-Coming: Inside Black America.* Boston: Houghton Mifflin, 1943.

"Our Kitchen at War." *American Home,* September 1944, 92–93.

Packard, Vance. *The Hidden Persuaders.* New York: Van Rees, 1957.

———. *The Status Seekers.* New York: David McKay, 1959.

Palmer, Gretta. "They Learned About Women." *Reader's Digest,* September 1944, 105–7.

Palmer, Phyllis. *Domesticity and Dirt: Housewives and Domestic Servants in the United States, 1920–1945.* Philadelphia: Temple University Press, 1989.

"Paradise or Doomsday?" *Woman's Home Companion,* May 1948, 32–33, 74–75.

Pattison, Mary. *The Business of Home Management: The Principles of Domestic Engineering.* New York: Robert M. McBride, 1915.

Peacetime Plans of Industrial Companies. n.p.: NAM, April 1943. NAM #1411, Box 860, Series III, Postwar Publications Folder 1942–43. NAM/Hagley.

Pear, Robert. "Governors Want Congress to Ease Welfare Work Rule: Seeking the Change as Shaky Economy Makes Jobs Scarcer." *New York Times,* 24 February 2002, section 1, p. 27.

"Pentagon's War Spending Hard to Track." 13 April 2005. http://www.reuters.com/newsArticle.jhtml?type=topNews&storyID=8178749.

Perlow, Ken. "The Image of Melancholy and the Evolution of the Baroque Idiom." 1995/1997. http://vdgsa.org/hermes/image1.html.

"A Permanent FEPC Needed." *Pittsburgh Courier,* 8 September 1945, 6.

Perry, John. "New Products for Postwar America? The Challenge to Engineers and Business Men." *Harper's,* February 1943, 330–32.

Perry, Steve. "The Bush Administration's Top 40 Lies About War and Terrorism." *Minneapolis City Pages,* 30 July 2003. http://www.commondreams.org/cgi-bin/print.cgi?file=/views03/0730-06.htm.

Pickens, Donald K. *Eugenics and the Progressives.* Nashville, Tenn.: Vanderbilt University Press, 1968.

Pinzon, Charles and Bruce Swain. "The Kid in Upper 4." *Journalism History* 28, no. 3 (2002): 112-20.

"Plastics in Review." *Modern Plastics,* February 1944, 114–15.

"Plywood Prefabrication." *Architectural Record,* February 1937, 42–44.

"Post-War Homes." *Architect & Engineer,* May 1943, 47.

"Post-war Life of Riley?" *Commonweal,* 10 September 1943, 506–8.

"Post-War Promises." *Science News Letter,* 10 July 1943, 26, 28.

Powell, Sr., Rev. A. Clayton. "We Cannot Live in U.S. Concentration Camps." *Baltimore Afro-American,* 29 September 1945, 5.

"Power by GE." *Newsweek,* 26 October 1953, 82, 85.

"The Power of Free Taste." *House Beautiful,* October 1952, 192–96, 198, 258.

A Primer for Postwar Prosperity. New York: J. Walter Thompson, 1945. Box 9, Company Publications 1937–1946. JWT/Duke.

"A Product of General Houses." *Architectural Forum,* July 1932, 65–66, 69, 71–72.

Pulos, Arthur J. *American Design Adventure, 1940–1975.* Cambridge, Mass.: MIT Press, 1988.

Pursell, Carroll. *The Machine in America: A Social History of Technology.* Baltimore: Johns Hopkins University Press, 1995.

"Quonsets Converted to Peace." *Popular Mechanics,* April 1947, 114.

Rabinbach, Anson. *The Human Motor: Energy, Fatigue, and the Origins of Modernity.* New York: HarperCollins/Basic Books, 1990.

"Race Relations in Jersey War Plants: Colored Girl Passing for White, Jewish Girl Who Passes, and Colored Workers Talk for AFRO." *Baltimore Afro-American,* 13 March 1943, 6.

Rampton, Sheldon, and John Stauber. *Weapons of Mass Deception: The Uses of Propaganda in Bush's War on Iraq.* New York: Jeremy P. Tarcher/Penguin, 2003.

Rapaport, Brooke Kamin, and Kevin L. Stayton. *Vital Forms: American Art and Design in the Atomic Age, 1940–1960.* New York: Harry N. Abrams; Brooklyn, N.Y.: The Brooklyn Museum, 2002.

Ratcliff, J. D. "Your Home Tomorrow." *Woman's Home Companion,* July 1943, 34, 54.

Rayack, Elton. "Discrimination and the Occupational Progress of Negroes." *Review of Economic and Statistics* 43, no. 2 (1961): 209–14.

Raymond, Eleanor. "A Model Kitchen: Designed for the Woman Who Does Her Own Work." *House Beautiful,* June 1933, 269–71, 289.

"Reconverting War Research." *Business Week,* 10 January 1948, 56–61.

Redding, J. Saunders. "A Second Look." *Baltimore Afro-American,* 2 February 1946, 4.

"Reds Can't Admit That Communism Is Harder to Sell." *Saturday Evening Post,* 26 July 1952, 10.

"Reducing Breakage in the Navy." *Modern Plastics,* November 1942, 80–81, 122.

Reid, Susan E. "The Khrushchev Kitchen OR Rockets for Housewives: Domesticating the Scientific-Technological Revolution." Unpublished paper delivered at the American Association for the Advancement of Slavic Studies Conference, Pittsburgh, 2002.

Rich, Leo H. "The Public Expects Progress." *Advertising & Selling,* July 1944, 36, 150–52.

Ries, Al, and Jack Trout. *Positioning: The Battle for Your Mind.* New York: McGraw-Hill, 1981. Reprint, New York: Warner Books, 1993.

Riis, Roger William. "Industry's Plan for Prosperity." *Advertising & Selling,* May 1943, 15–16.

"Robots Are a Girl's Best Friend." *House & Garden,* April 1953, 122–23.

Roche, Mary. "Awaiting the New Kitchen." *New York Times Magazine,* 14 October 1945, 34.

Rohde, Gilbert. "Gadgets for 194X." *Architectural Forum,* September 1942, 112–13.

Rollins, Judith. *Between Women: Domestics and Their Employers.* Philadelphia: Temple University Press, 1985.

Rooks, Noliwe M. *Hair Raising: Beauty, Culture, and African American Women.* New Brunswick, N.J.: Rutgers University Press, 1996.

———. *Ladies' Pages: African American Women's Magazines and the Culture That Made Them.* New Brunswick, N.J.: Rutgers University Press, 2004.

Roosevelt, Franklin Delano. "A Changed Moral Climate in America." *Vital Speeches of the Day,* 1 February 1937, 226–28.

———. "Message to Congress: The State of the Union." *Vital Speeches of the Day,* 15 January 1941, 197–200.

———. "Post-War Goals: America's Ability to Produce." *Vital Speeches of the Day,* 15 January 1943, 194–98.

———. "The Preservation of American Independence." *Vital Speeches of the Day,* 15 January 1941, 194, 194–97.

Rosenberg, Emily S. "'Foreign Affairs' After World War II: Connecting Sexual and International Politics." *Diplomatic History* 18 (1994): 59–70.

Ross, Edward Alsworth. *The Old World in the New: The Significance of Past and Present Immigration to the American People.* New York: Century, 1914.

Rupp, Leila J. *Mobilizing Women for War: German and American Propaganda*. Princeton, N.J.: Princeton University Press, 1978.

Rutherford, Paul. *Weapons of Mass Persuasion: Marketing the War Against Iraq*. Toronto: University of Toronto Press, 2004.

Rydell, Robert. *World of Fairs: The Century-of-Progress Expositions*. Chicago: University of Chicago Press, 1993.

Saasta, Timothy. *America's Third Deficit: Too Little Investment in People and Infrastructure*. Washington, D.C.: Center for Community Change, 1991.

Samuel, Lawrence R. *Pledging Allegiance: American Identity and the Bond Drive of World War II*. Washington, D.C.: Smithsonian Institution Press, 1997.

Sasso, John. "Are You Learning the Language of Tomorrow?" *House Beautiful*, March 1943, 21, 75–76.

Schechter, Danny. *Embedded: Weapons of Mass Deception: How the Media Failed to Cover the War on Iraq*. Amherst, N.Y.: Prometheus Books, 2003.

Schuyler, George E. "Views and Reviews." *Pittsburgh Courier*, 25 August 1945, 7; 1 September 1945, 7; and 8 September 1945, 7.

Schwarz, Jordan. *The New Dealers: Power Politics in the Age of Roosevelt*. New York: Alfred A. Knopf, 1993.

"Science Speeds Victory." *Science News Letter*, 23 December 1944, 405.

Scranton, Philip, ed. *Beauty and Business: Commerce, Gender, and Culture in Modern America*. New York: Routledge, 2001.

"Sears Roebuck Boards the Prefabrication Band-Wagon with Plywood Houses." *Architectural Forum*, October 1935, 452.

Second War Congress of American Industry. *Jobs in Peacetime: A Panel Discussion*. New York: NAM, 8 December 1944. Stapled in: "Conference on the Subject: 'What Can Industry Contribute to a Better America After the War.'" NAM #1411, Series III NIIC, Box 843. NAM/Hagley.

Seeley, S. Ward. "Planning Now for the Business of Peace." *Advertising & Selling*, January 1943, 44, 46.

Selden, Steven. *Inheriting Shame: The Story of Eugenics and Racism in America*. New York: Columbia University, Teachers College, 1999.

Seltzer, Mark. *Bodies and Machines*. New York: Routledge, 1992.

Sentman, Mary Alice, and Patrick S. Washburn. "How Excess Profits Tax Brought Ads to Black Newspapers in World War II." *Journalism Quarterly* 64 (1987): 769–74.

Serrin, William. *The Company and the Union: The "Civilized Relationship" of the General Motors Corporation and the United Automobile Workers*. 1970. Reprint, New York: Vintage Books/Random House, 1974.

"Setting Russia Straight on Facts about the U.S." *U.S. News & World Report*, 3 August 1959, 70–72.

Sevareid, Eric. "Super-Dupering the War: A Report on the Battle of the Adjectives." *Saturday Review of Literature*, 12 February 1944, 9–10.

Shanken, Andrew M. "From the Gospel of Efficiency to Modernism: A History of Sweet's Catalogue, 1906–1947." *Design Issues* 21 (Spring 2005): 28–47.

———. "From Total War to Total Living: American Architecture and the Culture of Planning, 1939–194X." Ph.D. diss., Princeton University, 1999.

Sherry, Michael S. *In the Shadow of War: The United States Since the 1930s*. New Haven, Conn.: Yale University Press, 1995.

Silver, Marc, and Martin Melkonian, eds. *Contested Terrain: Power, Politics, and Partici-pation in Suburbia*. Westport, Conn.: Greenwood, 1993.

Simmons, Gordon. "Postwar Daydreams." *Advertising & Selling,* June 1944, 27–28, 48, 150, 152.

Simons, Howard. "Brussels Fair and Science." *Science News Letter,* 11 January 1958, 26–27.

"Simply, Smartly, Adapt Your Home to Wartime Living." *House & Garden,* October 1942, 56–57.

Singer, P. W. *Corporate Warriors: The Rise of the Privatized Military Industry.* Ithaca, N.Y.: Cornell University Press, 2003.

Sivulka, Juliann. *Stronger Than Dirt: A Cultural History of Advertising Personal Hygiene in America, 1875 to 1940.* Amherst, N.Y.: Humanity Books, 2001.

"Six Experts Design Our Ideal House." *House & Garden,* July 1935, 21–23, 64, 66, 69–70, 72.

"Skilled Workers Get Chance, Prove Worth at $1,276,000 Defense Housing Project at Sparrows Point." *Baltimore Afro-American,* 4 April 1942, 20.

Smith, Allen. "Democracy and the Politics of Information: The St. Louis Committee for Nuclear Information." *Gateway Heritage* 17 (Summer 1996): 2–13.

Smith, Elizabeth A. T., ed. *Blueprints for Modern Living: History and Legacy of the Case Study Houses.* Cambridge, Mass.: MIT Press, 1989.

Smith, Geoffrey. "National Security and Personal Isolation: Sex, Gender, and Disease in the Cold-War United States." *International History Review* 14, no. 2 (1992): 221–440.

Smith, H. A. "Don't Promise the Public Too Much—Too Soon." *Advertising & Selling,* June 1944, 28.

Smith, James P., and Finis R. Welch. "Black Economic Progress After Myrdal." *Journal of Economic Literature* 27, no. 2 (1989): 519–64.

Smith, R. Elberton. *Army and Economic Mobilization.* Washington, D.C.: U.S. Department of the Army, 1959.

Smith, Terry. *Making the Modern: Industry, Art, and Design in America.* Chicago: University of Chicago Press, 1993.

Soldiers of Production. NAM #1411, Series III, NIIC Box 846. NAM/Hagley.

Soper, Kerry. "Gunning Down the Criminal Rates: Popularized Eugenic Theory in Chester Gould's Comic Strip, *Dick Tracy,* 1931–1940." Unpublished manuscript, in the author's possession, n.d.

"So You Think He's Ready for the Old Folks' Home!" NAM #1411, Series III, NIIC Box 848, Oversize Records. NAM/Hagley.

"The Standardized House." *Architectural Forum,* September 1938, 188–96.

Steele, Richard W. "Preparing the Public for War: Efforts to Establish a National Propaganda Agency, 1940–1941." *American Historical Review* 75, no. 6 (1970): 1640–53.

Stepan, Nancy Leys. "Race and Gender: The Role of Analogy in Science." In David Theo Goldberg, ed., *Anatomy of Racism.* Minneapolis: University of Minnesota Press, 1990.

Sternberg, B. M. "New Opportunities in Postwar Markets." *Modern Plastics,* April 1945, 103–6.

Sternglass, Ernest, Joseph Mangano, William McDonnell, and Jay Gould. *The Enemy Within: The High Cost of Living Near Nuclear Reactors: Breast Cancer, AIDS, Low*

Birthweights, and Other Radiation-Induced Immune Deficiency Effects. New York: Four Walls Eight Windows, 1996.

Stowell, Kenneth K. "Higher Standards of Living." *Architectural Record,* November 1942, 31.

———. "There's No Place Like Home." *Architectural Record,* December 1943, 41.

Strasser, Susan. *Never Done: A History of American Housework.* New York: Pantheon Books, 1982.

———. *Waste and Want: A Social History of Trash.* New York: Henry Holt, 1999.

Straub, Eleanor. "United States Government Policy Toward Civilian Women during World War II." *Prologue* 5 (Winter 1973): 240–54.

"Streamlined for $9.92!" *American Home,* March 1941, 123.

Stromberg, Roland. "American Business and the Approach of War, 1935–1941." *Journal of Economic History* 13, no. 1 (1953): 58–78.

Stuart, C. W. "New Possibilities of Electric Home Equipment." In Paul Zucker, ed., *New Architecture and City Planning: A Symposium.* New York: Philosophical Library, 1944.

"Suitcase Houses for the Army." *Popular Science,* February 1944, 69.

Sullivan, David J. "The American Negro—An 'Export' Market at Home. *Printer's Ink,* 21 July 1944, 90–94.

———. "Don't Do This—If You Want to Sell Your Products to Negroes!" *Sales Management* 52 (March 1, 1943): 43, 48, 50.

———. "How Negroes Spent Their Incomes, 1920–1943." *Sales Management* 54 (June 15, 1945): 106.

Sullivan, Kathleen. "Under a Watchful Eye: Incursions on Personal Privacy." In Richard C. Leone and Greg Anrig, Jr., eds., *The War on Our Freedoms: Civil Liberties in an Age of Terrorism.* New York: BBS Public Affairs, 2003.

Sundberg, Carl W. "The Realities of the Future." *Modern Plastics,* May 1945, 105–8.

Sunstein, Cass R. *The Second Bill of Rights: FDR's Unfinished Revolution and Why We Need It More Than Ever.* New York: Basic Books, 2004.

Susman, Warren I. *Culture as History: The Transformation of American Society in the Twentieth Century.* New York: Pantheon Books, 1984.

———. "The People's Fair: Cultural Contradictions of a Consumer Society." In Helen A. Harrison, ed., *Dawn of a New Day: The New York World's Fair, 1939/40.* New York: New York University Press and the Queens Museum, 1980.

Sutton-Ramspeck, Beth. *Raising the Dust: The Literary Housekeeping of Mary Ward, Sarah Grand, and Charlotte Perkins Gilman.* Athens: Ohio University Press, 2004.

Sypher, A. H. "Post-War Problem No. 1." *Nation's Business,* May 1943, 21–22, 56–58.

———. "Post-War Problem No. 3." *Nation's Business,* July 1943, 38, 40, 74–75.

Tanner, Laura. "Not Only a New Look But a Look That Stays New." *House Beautiful,* September 1947, 162–63.

Tansey, Richard, Michael R. Hyman, and Gene Brown. "Ethical Judgements About Wartime Ads Depicting Combat." *Journal of Advertising* 21, no. 3 (1992): 57–74.

Taylor, Frederick Winslow. *The Principles of Scientific Management.* 1911. Reprint, Norcross, Ga.: Institute of Industrial Engineers, Engineering and Management Press, 1998.

Taylor, William R., "The Evolution of Public Spaces in New York City: The Commercial Showcase of America." In Simon J. Bronner, ed., *Consuming Visions:*

Accumulation and Display of Goods in America, 1880–1920. Winterthur, Del.: The Henry Francis du Pont Winterthur Museum; New York: W. W. Norton, 1989.

Teague, Walter Dorwin. "Design for Peace." *Studio International,* April 1943, 154–56.

———. "The Growth and Scope of Industrial Design in the U.S." *Journal of the Royal Society of Arts* (July 1959): 640–51.

———. "Industry Plans for the Future." *Advertising & Selling,* February 1943, 109–10, 156, 158–59.

———. "Planning the World of Tomorrow." *Popular Mechanics,* December 1940, 808–10, 158A–59A, 161A, 163A.

———. "A Sane Prediction About the House You'll Live in After the War." *House Beautiful,* August 1943, 48–49, 58, 73, 75.

———. "What of the Post-War World?" *New York Times Magazine,* 26 September 1943, 15, 34.

Tedlow, Richard S. *Keeping the Corporate Image: Public Relations and Business, 1900–1950.* Greenwich, Conn.: JAI Press, 1979.

Telling the Profit Story—In Your Town! New York: NAM, 1948. NAM #1411, Series III, 204/205. NAM/Hagley.

"Thank '80s Greed for '90s Growth." *Business Week,* 5 April 1999, 96.

"That Famous Debate in Close-Up Pictures." *Life,* 3 August 1959, 26–28, 31.

"Their Sheltered Honeymoon." *Life,* 10 August 1959, 51–52.

"They Don't Shirk the *Mean Jobs*—Do You?" *Baltimore Afro-American,* 2 June 1945, 16.

"They Let Us Talk to the Russians." *Ladies' Home Journal,* June 1955, 50–51, 147, 149–54.

"This Kitchen Took Cover." *American Home,* March 1954, 80, 82.

"This New Era of Easy Upkeep." *House Beautiful,* October 1947, 122–24.

"Three Whites Held in No. Philly Riot." *Baltimore Afro-American,* 18 April 1942, 14.

Tirman, John. "Security the Progressive Way." *The Nation,* 11 April 2005, 28.

Tjaarda, John. "Your Home, Your Clothes, Your Car Tomorrow." *American Magazine,* May 1943, 44–45, 115–18.

Tobey, Ronald C. *Technology as Freedom: The New Deal and the Electrical Modernization of the American Home.* Berkeley: University of California Press, 1996.

Tomes, Nancy. *The Gospel of Germs: Men, Women, and the Microbe in American Life.* Cambridge, Mass.: Harvard University Press, 1998.

"Tomorrow's House—and Gadgetry." *Business Week,* 9 March 1946, 18.

Trachtenberg, Alan. *The Incorporation of America: Culture and Society in the Gilded Age.* New York: Hill & Wang, 1982.

"Traveling Salesmen for Two Ways of Life." *New York Times Magazine,* 13 March 1960, 22.

"Trends in Sanitation." *Architectural Record,* November 1939, 66–73.

Trotter, Anne. "Development of the Merchants-of-Death Theory." In Benjamin F. Cooling, ed., *War, Business, and American Society.* Port Washington, N.Y.: National University Publications/Kennikat Press, 1977.

Uchitelle, Louis, and John Markoff. "Terrorbusters., Inc.: The Rise of the Homeland Security–Industrial Complex." *New York Times,* 17 October 2004, 8.

"Uncle Sam's Housekeeping Job." *Journal of Home Economics,* September 1942, 420–24.

"The United States in a New World—III: The Domestic Economy, Appendix, Technology and Postwar Life." *Fortune* supp., December 1942, 18–20.

United States Marine Corps Women's Reserve. N.p., n.d. War Contributions 1941–45, Box 1. JWT/Duke.

"Unit Kitchen." *Business Week,* 10 June 1933, 12–13.

Urbina, Ian. "Bush Budget Would Cut Millions from City's Social Services." *New York Times,* 9 February 2005, B3.

U.S. Congress. *Hearings, 1941, House Select Committee to Investigate the Interstate Migration of Destitute Citizens*. Washington, D.C., 1941.

U.S. Department of Labor, Women's Bureau. *What Job Is Mine on the Victory Line*. Washington, D.C.: Government Printing Office, April 1943.

"U.S. Life Is Different—Sales Figures Prove It." *U.S. News & World Report,* 13 February 1953, 69–70, 72.

"The Vice President in Russia: A Barnstorming Masterpiece." *Life,* 10 August 1959, 22–35.

"Vice President Nixon Opens American Exhibition in Moscow." *United States State Department Bulletin,* 17 August 1959, 227–36.

Vinikas, Vincent. *Soft Soap, Hard Sell: American Hygiene in the Age of Advertisement*. Ames: University of Iowa Press, 1992.

Waddell, Brian. "Economic Mobilization for World War II and the Transformation of the U.S. State." *Politics & Society* 22, no. 2 (1994): 165–94.

Waldron, Webb. "Yankee Kitchens Go on the Production Line." *Better Homes and Gardens,* June 1943, 17, 64–66.

"Wanna Be a Red Cross Nurse? Read This First." *People's Voice,* 4 April 1942, 8.

"War Changes Buying Habits." *Science Digest,* February 1945, 33–36.

Ward, Barbara McLean, ed. *Produce & Conserve, Share & Play Square: The Grocer & the Consumer on the Home-Front Battlefield during World War II*. Portsmouth, N.H.: Strawbery Banke Museum; Hanover, N.H.: University Press of New England, 1994.

Ware, Caroline F. *The Consumer Goes to War: A Guide to Victory on the Home Front*. New York: Funk & Wagnalls, 1942.

War Facts: A Handbook for Speakers on War Production. n.p.: Office of Emergency Management, n.d.

A War Message in Every Ad. n.p.: Magazine Marketing Service and WAC. n.d. AC archives.

"War Race Prejudice Like Blunder at Pearl Harbor." *Baltimore Afro-American,* 11 April 1942, 5.

Warren, H. E. "Take a Kitchen—and Wrap It Well." *Advertising & Selling,* July 1945, 58, 60, 94, 96, 98.

War Theme Digest: A Quick Reference Guide to Home Front Information Campaigns Requiring Advertising Support. 1944. Reprint, n.p.: WAC, 1945. AC archives.

Washburn, Patrick. *A Question of Sedition: The Federal Government's Investigation of the Black Press during World War II*. New York: Oxford University Press, 1986.

"Washing with Sound Waves." *Popular Science,* October 1946, 74.

Weaver, Robert C. "Negro Labor Since 1929." *Journal of Negro History* 35, no. 1 (1950): 20–38.

Weems, Robert E. *Desegregating the Dollar: African American Consumerism in the Twentieth Century*. New York: New York University Press, 1998.

Weibe, Robert H. *The Search for Order, 1877–1920*. New York: Hill & Wang, 1967.

Weinberg, Sydney. "What to Tell America: The Writers' Quarrel in the Office of War Information." *Journal of American History* 60 (June 1968): 73–89.

Weiner, Tim. "Arms Fiascoes Lead to Alarm Inside Pentagon." *New York Times*, 8 June 2005. http://www.nytimes.com/2005/06/08/business/08weapons.html?ex=1118894400&en=79e956c557c5e213&ei=5059&partner=AOL.

Weise, Andrew. "Racial Cleansing in the Suburbs: Suburban Government, Urban Renewal, and Segregation on Long Island." In Marc Silver and Martin Melkonian, eds., *Contested Terrain: Power, Politics, and Participation in Suburbia*. Westport, Conn.: Greenwood, 1993.

Wendt, Gerald. *Science for the World of Tomorrow*. New York: W. W. Norton, 1939.

West, James. *Plainville, U.S.A.* New York: Columbia University Press, 1945.

Westbrook, Robert B. "Fighting for the American Family: Private Interests and Political Obligation in World War II." In Richard Wightman Fox and T. J. Jackson Lears, eds., *The Power of Culture: Critical Essays in American History*. Chicago: University of Chicago Press, 1993.

"What Can We Do Starting Now . . ." Untitled, NIIC typescript, NAM #1411, NIIC Box 843, Advertising 1943 Folder, p. 13. NAM/Hagley.

"What Does Military Design Offer the Architecture of Peace?" *Architectural Record*, January 1939, 50–56.

"What Freedom Means to Us." *Vital Speeches of the Day*, 15 August 1959, 677–82.

"What Happened to the Dreamworld?" *Fortune*, February 1947, 90–93, 214–16.

"What Has Become of Yesterday's Inventions?" *Business Week*, 8 March 1952, 88–89.

"What Is Happening to the Kitchen?" *Good Housekeeping*, January 1933, 84–85.

"What Nixon Learned in Russia." *U.S. News & World Report*, 10 August 1959, 37–39.

"What People Say They Want: *House Beautiful*'s Postwar Primer for Manufacturers." *House Beautiful*, July 1944, 21–23.

"What the Atom Will Do for You." *Changing Times*, August 1957, 43–44.

"What the 'GI' Wants in His Postwar House." *House Beautiful*, August 1944, 31–33.

What the Public Thinks About You. New York: Association of National Advertisers, 1944. NAM #1411, NIIC Box 843, Advertising Subject File. NAM/Hagley.

"What the Russians Will See." *Look*, 21 July 1959, 52–54.

What to Do NOW About Emergency Sanitation at Home: A Family Handbook. Rev. ed. Washington, D.C.: Executive Office of the President, Office of Civil and Defense Mobilization, 1958.

"When Nixon Took on Khrushchev." *U.S. News & World Report*, 3 August 1959, 36–39.

"White House Shows No Undue Concern for Defense Cuts." *Defense Daily* 163, 29 June 1989, 502.

Whitman, Howard. "What We're Afraid Of." *Collier's*, 20 March 1948, 13, 40, 42, 43.

Whitman, Sylvia. *V Is for Victory: The American Home Front during World War II*. Minneapolis: Lerner, 1993.

"Why Negroes Buy Cadillacs." *Ebony*, September 1946, 34.

"Why the Russians Fear 'People's Capitalism.'" *Better Homes and Gardens*, September 1957, 66–67, 176, 178–79, 190.

"Why Young Americans Are Drowning in Debt." *Christian Science Monitor*, 9 December 2004. http://moneycentral.msn.com/content/CollegeandFamily/Moneyinyour20s/P101676.asp.

Wilhelm, Donald. "Business Rushes to Government's Aid in Preparedness Crisis." *Printer's Ink,* 16 August 1940, 11–14.

Williams, William Appleman. "The Large Corporation and American Foreign Policy." In David Horowitz, ed., *Corporations and the Cold War.* New York: Monthly Review Press/Bertrand Russell Peace Foundation, 1969.

"Will Our Military Policy Change?" *Pittsburgh Courier,* 1 June 1945, 6.

Wilson, Kristina, ed. *Livable Modernism: Interior Decorating and Design during the Great Depression.* New Haven, Conn.: Yale University Press, 2004.

Wilson, Richard Guy, Dianne H. Pilgrim, and Dickran Tashjian. *The Machine Age in America, 1918–1941.* New York: Harry N. Abrams; Brooklyn, N.Y.: The Brooklyn Museum, 1986.

Wilson, Robert E. "Atoms in the Homes: How Soon?" *U.S. News & World Report,* 17 December 1954, 116–18.

Winkler, Allan M. *Home Front U.S.A.: America during World War II.* Arlington Heights, Ill.: Harlan Davidson, 1986.

——. *Life Under a Cloud: American Anxiety About the Atom.* New York: Oxford University Press, 1993.

——. *The Politics of Propaganda: The Office of War Information, 1942–1945.* New Haven, Conn.: Yale University Press, 1978.

Women in the War . . . for the Final Push to Victory. n.p.: Office of War Information with U.S. Army, U.S. Navy, U.S. Marine Corps, U.S. Coast Guard, and War Advertising Council, 1944. AC archives.

Wood, Chris. "The Outsourcing Option: More Attractive Than Ever." *The Public Manager: The New Bureaucrat* 28 (Spring 1999): 43.

Wood, Edith Elmer. "Building for Defense . . . Emergency Housing Proposals." *Architectural Forum,* April 1941, 18, 98, 102, 106.

Woodbury, David O. "Your Life Tomorrow." *Collier's,* 8 May 1943, 40.

The Word Is Mightier Than the Sword. n.p.: WAC, n.d. AC archives.

"Worker Loses His Class Identity." *Business Week,* 11 July 1959, 90–92, 96, 98.

"World's Fair—'58: Battle of the 'Best.'" *Newsweek,* 28 April 1958, 41, 43.

Wright, Gwendolyn. *Building the Dream: A Social History of Housing in America.* Cambridge, Mass.: MIT Press, 1981.

Wurts, Richard. *The New York World's Fair 1939/1940.* New York: Dover, 1977.

Wynn, Neil A. *The Afro-American and the Second World War.* 1975. Reprint, New York: Holmes & Meier, 1993.

Yarsley, V. E., and E. G. Couzens. "The Expanding Age of Plastics." *Science Digest,* December 1942, 57–60.

"Yes, Even the Kitchen Sink." *American Home,* March 1945, 142.

Young, James Webb. "How Advertising Can Meet Today's Critical Challenges." *Advertising & Selling,* December 1941, 102, 104, 106, 108.

Young, John Orr. "Stop Shouting 'Free Enterprise' Unless You Give the Term Meaning: A Constructive Suggestion for 'Institutional' Advertisers." *Printer's Ink* (ca. 1940). NAM #1411, Series III, Subject files: NIIC, Box 848, Oversized Records: "Miscellaneous NIIC Material, 1938–1940." NAM/Hagley.

Young, Kenneth. "It Doesn't Look All Plastic, But It Is." *House Beautiful,* October 1947, 140–41.

"Yours to Command." *Time,* 3 August 1959, 38.

Zeman, Zbynek. *Selling the War: Art and Propaganda in World War II*. New York: Exeter Books, 1978.

Zucker, Paul, ed. *New Architecture and City Planning: A Symposium*. New York: Philosophical Library, 1944.

Zunz, Oliver. *Making America Corporate, 1870–1920*. 1992. Reprint, Chicago: University of Chicago Press, 1990.

INDEX

Thanks to Dennis Henthorn and Carol Henthorn for their indefatigable assistance on this index.